STERLING
Test Prep

MCAT®

Physics

Practice Questions

5th edition

www.MasterMCAT.com

5 4 3 2 1

ISBN-13: 978-1-9475562-5-6

Sterling Test Prep products are available at special quantity discounts for sales, promotions, premed counseling offices and other educational purposes.

For more information, contact our Sales Department at:

Sterling Test Prep
6 Liberty Square #11
Boston, MA 02109

info@onlinemcatprep.com

© 2020 Sterling Test Prep

Published by Sterling Test Prep

Congratulations on choosing this book as part of your MCAT preparation!

This book provides over 860 high-yield practice questions that test your knowledge of all physics topics tested on the MCAT. It contains four diagnostic tests to help you identify the topics you are not well prepared for and eleven sections of topical practice questions, so you can selectively work with the topic you want to study and master.

Detailed explanations provide step-by-step solutions for quantitative problems and discuss the foundations and details of important science topics for conceptual questions. By reading these explanations carefully and understanding how they apply to solve the question, you will learn important physical concepts and the relationships between, so you can answer related questions on the MCAT. This will prepare you for the MCAT physics, and you will significantly increase your score.

Scoring well on the MCAT is important for admission into medical school. To achieve a high score, you need to develop skills to properly apply the knowledge you have and quickly choose the correct answer. You must solve numerous practice questions that represent the style and content of MCAT physics questions. Understanding key physical relationships and formulas are more valuable for the test than memorizing terms.

All the questions in this book are prepared by physics instructors with years of experience in applied physics, as well as in academic settings. This team of physics experts analyzed the content of the redesigned MCAT, released by the AAMC, and designed practice questions that will help you build knowledge and develop the skills necessary for your success on the exam. The questions were reviewed for quality and effectiveness by our science editors who possess extensive credentials, are educated in top colleges and universities and have years of teaching and editorial experience.

We wish you great success in your future academic achievements and look forward to being an important part of your successful preparation for the MCAT!

Sterling Test Prep Team

190915gdx

3

Our Commitment to the Environment

Sterling Test Prep is committed to protecting our planet's resources by supporting environmental organizations with proven track records of conservation, ecological research and education and preservation of vital natural resources. A portion of our profits is donated to help these organizations so they can continue their critical missions. These organizations include:

 **Ocean Conservancy**

For over 40 years, Ocean Conservancy has been advocating for a healthy ocean by supporting sustainable solutions based on science and cleanup efforts. Among many environmental achievements, Ocean Conservancy laid the groundwork for an international moratorium on commercial whaling, played an instrumental role in protecting fur seals from overhunting and banning the international trade of sea turtles. The organization created national marine sanctuaries and served as the lead non-governmental organization in the designation of 10 of the 13 marine sanctuaries.

 **RAINFOREST TRUST®**

For 25 years, Rainforest Trust has been saving critical lands for conservation through land purchases and protected area designations. Rainforest Trust has played a central role in the creation of 73 new protected areas in 17 countries, including the Falkland Islands, Costa Rica and Peru. Nearly 8 million acres have been saved thanks to Rainforest Trust's support of in-country partners across Latin America, with over 500,000 acres of critical lands purchased outright for reserves.

 **PACIFIC WHALE FOUNDATION**

Since 1980, Pacific Whale Foundation has been saving whales from extinction and protecting our oceans through science and advocacy. As an international organization, with ongoing research projects in Hawaii, Australia, and Ecuador, PWF is an active participant in global efforts to address threats to whales and other marine life. A pioneer in non-invasive whale research, PWF was an early leader in educating the public, from a scientific perspective, about whales and the need for ocean conservation.

With your purchase, you support environmental causes around the world.

How to Use This Book

To extract the maximum benefit from this book, we recommend that you start by doing the first diagnostic test and use the answer key to identify the topics you need to spend more time on. Spend some time going through the explanations for that diagnostic test. Review all the explanations, not only those that you got right. After this, practice with the topical questions for those topics you identified as your weak areas – take your time and master those questions.

Next, take the second diagnostic test. You should see a dramatic improvement in your performance on the topics that you practiced prior to this. Analyze your performance on the second diagnostic test and find new topics that you can improve on. Work with the corresponding topical practice questions.

Finally, take the third and fourth diagnostic tests. At this point, you should be very strong on all topics. If you still find weaknesses, spend extra time going through the solutions and do more practice. You may also find three additional diagnostic tests on our website.

Ultimately, your goal should be to complete all three diagnostic tests, all topical practice questions and go through all the explanations.

Visit www.MasterMCAT.com for online MCAT® simulated practice tests

Our advanced testing platform allows you to take the tests in the same CBT (computer-based test) format as the AAMC's official MCAT.

- Assess your knowledge of different subjects and topics

- Receive a Scaled Score and Diagnostics Reports with your performance analysis

- Learn important scientific topics and concepts

- Improve your test-taking skills by simulating testing under time constraints

- Comprehensive and cost-effective complete MCAT® science preparation

- Prepare and learn anywhere on your schedule

To access these and other online tests at a special pricing
go to page 407 for access web address

Table of Contents

Test-Taking Strategies For The MCAT **9**

Common Physics Formulas & Conversions **12**

MCAT Physics Diagnostic Tests **23**

Diagnostic Test #1 25

    Answer Key 35

Diagnostic Test #2 37

    Answer Key 47

Diagnostic Test #3 49

    Answer Key 60

Diagnostic Test #4 61

    Answer Key 71

MCAT Physics Topical Practice Questions **73**

Translational Motion 75

    Answer Key 83

Force and Motion 85

    Answer Key 95

Work and Energy of Point Object Systems 97

    Answer Key 105

Periodic Motion 107

    Answer Key 115

Fluids and Gas Phase 117

    Answer Key 126

Electrostatics & Magnetism 127

    Answer Key 137

Circuit Elements 139

    Answer Key 148

Sound 149

    Answer Key 157

Light and Geometrical Optics 159

    Answer Key 167

Thermodynamics 169

    Answer Key 177

Atomic Nucleus and Electronic Structure 179

    Answer Key 188

Table of Contents (*continued*)

MCAT Physics Diagnostic Tests – Detailed Explanations... **189**

    Diagnostic Test #1... 191

    Diagnostic Test #2... 205

    Diagnostic Test #3... 219

    Diagnostic Test #4... 233

Topical Practice Questions – Detailed Explanations... **247**

    Translational Motion.. 249

    Force and Motion.. 263

    Work and Energy of Point Object Systems.. 279

    Periodic Motion.. 295

    Fluids and Gas Phase.. 307

    Electrostatics & Magnetism.. 323

    Circuit Elements... 337

    Sound.. 351

    Light and Geometrical Optics.. 365

    Thermodynamics.. 379

    Atomic Nucleus and Electronic Structure.. 397

We want to hear from you

Your feedback is important to us because we strive to provide the highest quality prep materials. Email us if you have any questions, comments or suggestions, so we can incorporate your feedback into future editions.

Customer Satisfaction Guarantee

If you have any concerns about this book, including printing issues, contact us and we will resolve any issues to your satisfaction.

info@onlinemcatprep.com

We reply to all emails – please check your spam folder

Thank you for choosing our products to achieve your educational goals!

For best results, this book should be supplemented by "MCAT Physics Complete Subject Review"

MCAT Physics Complete Subject Review provides a detailed and thorough review of Physics topics tested on the MCAT. The content covers foundational principles and theories necessary to answer related questions on the test.

· Translational motion
· Force
· Work and energy of point object systems
· Periodic motion
· Fluid statics and dynamics
· Electrostatics
· Circuit elements
· Magnetism
· Sound
· Light and geometrical optics
· Atomic nucleus and electronic structure
· Thermodynamics

Other MCAT products by Sterling Test Prep

MCAT Practice Tests

- **MCAT Physical & Chemical Foundations of Biological Systems + Biological & Biochemical Foundations of Living Systems (8 practice tests)**
- **MCAT Physical & Chemical Foundations of Biological Systems (4 practice tests)**
- **MCAT Biological & Biochemical Foundations of Living Systems (4 practice tests)**

MCAT Practice Questions

- **MCAT Biology & Biochemistry Practice Questions**
- **MCAT General Chemistry Practice Questions**
- **MCAT Organic Chemistry & Biochemistry Practice Questions**

MCAT Content Review

- **Physics Review**
- **General Chemistry Review**
- **Biology and Biochemistry Review**
- **Organic Chemistry and Biochemistry Review**
- **Psychology and Sociology Review**

Test-Taking Strategies for the MCAT

There are strategies, approaches and perspectives that you should learn to apply on the MCAT®. On the test, you need to think and analyze information quickly. This skill cannot be gained from a college course, a review prep course or a textbook. However, you can develop it through repetitive practice and focus.

General Strategies

Intimidation by information. Test developers usually select material for the test that will be completely unknown to most test takers. Don't be overwhelmed, intimidated or discouraged by unfamiliar concepts. While going through a question, try to understand all the relevant material available, while disregarding the distracter information. Being exposed to strange sounding topics and terms that you are not familiar with is normal for this test.

Do not feel disappointed that you're not very familiar with the topic. Most other test takers are not familiar with it either. So, stay calm and work through the questions. Don't turn this into a learning exercise either by trying to memorize the information (in a passage or question) that was not known to you before because your objective on the test is to answer questions by selecting the correct answers.

Find your pace. Everybody reads and processes information at a different rate. You should practice finding your optimal rate, so you can read fast and still comprehend the information. If you have a good pace and don't invest too much time in any one question, you should have enough time to complete each section at a comfortable rate. Avoid two extremes where you either work too slowly, reading every word carefully, or act panicky and rush through the material without understanding.

When you find your pace that allows you to stay focused and calm, you will have enough time for all the questions. It is important to remember, that you are trying to achieve optimal, not maximum, comprehension. If you spend time necessary to achieve a maximum comprehension of a passage or question, you will most likely not have enough time for the whole section.

You should practice MCAT® tests under timed conditions to eventually find your optimal pace. This is why we recommend that you practice the tests from this book on our website (www.MasterMCAT.com/bookowner.htm) where you will get a scaled score and your personalized Diagnostics Report.

Don't be a perfectionist. The test is timed, and you cannot spend too much time on any one question. Get away from thinking that if you spent just one more minute on the question, you'd get it right. You can get sucked into a question that you lose track of time and end up rushing through the rest of the test (which may cause you to miss even more questions).

If you spend your allocated per-question time and are still not sure of the answer, select the best option, note the question number and move on. The test allows you to return to any question and change your answer choice. If you have extra time left after you answered all other questions on that section, return to that question and take a fresh look. Unless you have a sound reason to change your original answer, don't change your answer choice.

You shouldn't go into the MCAT® thinking that you must get every question right. Accept the fact that you will have to guess on some questions (and maybe get them wrong) and still have time for every question. Your goal should be to answer as many questions correctly as you possibly can.

Factually correct, but actually wrong. Often MCAT® questions are written in a way that the incorrect answer choice may be factually correct on its own but doesn't answer the question. When you are reading the answer choices, and one choice jumps out at you because it is factually correct, be careful. Make sure to go back to the question and verify that the answer choice actually answers the question being asked. Some incorrect answer choices will seem to answer the question asked and are even factually correct, but are based on extraneous information within the question stem.

Narrow down your choices. When you find two answer choices that are direct opposites, it is very likely that the correct answer choice is one of the two. You can typically rule out the other two answer choices (unless they are also direct opposites of each other) and narrow down your search for the correct choice that answers the question.

Experiments. If you encounter a passage that describes an experiment, ask some basic questions including: "What is the experiment designed to find out?", "What is the experimental method?", "What are the variables?", "What are the controls?". Understanding this information will help you use the presented information to answer the question associated with the passage.

Multiple experiments. The best way to remember three variations of the same experiment is to focus on the differences between the experiments. What changed between the first and second experiment? What was done differently between the second and the third experiment? This will help you organize the information in your mind.

Passage notes. Pay attention to the notes after a passage. The information provided in those notes is usually necessary to answer some questions associated with that passage. Notes are there for a reason and often contain information necessary to answer at least one of the questions.

Look for units. When solving a problem that you don't know the formula for, try to solve for the units in the answer choices. The units in the answer choices are your clues for understanding the relationship between the question and the correct answer. Review what value is being sought in the question. Sometimes you can eliminate some wrong answers because they contain improper units.

Don't fall for the familiar. When in doubt, it is easy to choose what you are familiar with. If you recognize a term in one of the four answer choices, you may be tempted to pick that choice. However, don't go with familiar answers just because they are familiar. Think through the other answer choices and how they relate to the question before making your selection.

Don't get hung up on the passage. Read through the passage once briefly to understand what items it deals with and take mental notes of some key points. Then look at the questions. You might find that you can answer some questions without using the information in the passage. With other questions, once you know what exactly is being asked, you can read through the passage more effectively looking for a particular answer. This technique will help you save some time that you otherwise would have overinvested in processing the information that had no benefit to you.

Roman numerals. Some questions will present three or four statements and ask which of them are correct. For example:

A. I only
B. III only
C. I and II only
D. I and III only

Notice that statement II doesn't have an answer choice dedicated to it. It is likely that statement II is wrong, and you can eliminate answer choice C. This narrows your search to three choices. However, if you are confident that statement II is part of the answer, you can disregard this strategy.

Extra Tips

• With fact questions that require selecting among numbers, don't go with the smallest or largest number unless you have a reason to believe it is the answer.

• Use the process of elimination for questions that you're not clear about. Try to eliminate the answer choices you know to be wrong before making your selection.

• Don't fall for answers that sound "clever" and don't go with "bizarre" choices. Only choose them if you are confident that the choice is correct.

• None of these strategies will replace the importance of preparation. However, knowing and using them will help you utilize your test time more productively and increase your probability for successful guessing when you simply don't know the answer.

Common Physics Formulas and Conversions

Constants and Conversion Factors

1 unified atomic mass unit	$1\ u = 1.66 \times 10^{-27}\ kg$
	$1\ u = 931\ MeV/c^2$
Proton mass	$m_p = 1.67 \times 10^{-27}\ kg$
Neutron mass	$m_n = 1.67 \times 10^{-27}\ kg$
Electron mass	$m_e = 9.11 \times 10^{-31}\ kg$
Electron charge magnitude	$e = 1.60 \times 10^{-19}\ C$
Avogadro's number	$N_0 = 6.02 \times 10^{23}\ mol^{-1}$
Universal gas constant	$R = 8.31\ J/(mol \cdot K)$
Boltzmann's constant	$k_B = 1.38 \times 10^{-23}\ J/K$
Speed of light	$c = 3.00 \times 10^8\ m/s$
Planck's constant	$h = 6.63 \times 10^{-34}\ J \cdot s$
	$h = 4.14 \times 10^{-15}\ eV \cdot s$
	$hc = 1.99 \times 10^{-25}\ J \cdot m$
	$hc = 1.24 \times 10^3\ eV \cdot nm$
Vacuum permittivity	$\varepsilon_0 = 8.85 \times 10^{-12}\ C^2/N \cdot m^2$
Coulomb's law constant	$k = 1/4\pi\varepsilon_0 = 9.0 \times 10^9\ N \cdot m^2/C^2$
Vacuum permeability	$\mu_0 = 4\pi \times 10^{-7}\ (T \cdot m)/A$
Magnetic constant	$k' = \mu_0/4\pi = 10^{-7}\ (T \cdot m)/A$
Universal gravitational constant	$G = 6.67 \times 10^{-11}\ m^3/kg \cdot s^2$
Acceleration due to gravity at Earth's surface	$g = 9.8\ m/s^2$
1 atmosphere pressure	$1\ atm = 1.0 \times 10^5\ N/m^2$
	$1\ atm = 1.0 \times 10^5\ Pa$
1 electron volt	$1\ eV = 1.60 \times 10^{-19}\ J$
Balmer constant	$B = 3.645 \times 10^{-7}\ m$
Rydberg constant	$R = 1.097 \times 10^7\ m^{-1}$
Stefan constant	$\sigma = 5.67 \times 10^{-8}\ W/m^2K^4$

Units			Prefixes	
Name	**Symbol**	**Factor**	**Prefix**	**Symbol**
meter	m	10^{12}	tera	T
kilogram	kg	10^{9}	giga	G
second	s	10^{6}	mega	M
ampere	A	10^{3}	kilo	k
kelvin	K	10^{-2}	centi	c
mole	mol	10^{-3}	mili	m
hertz	Hz	10^{-6}	micro	μ
newton	N	10^{-9}	nano	n
pascal	Pa	10^{-12}	pico	p
joule	J			
watt	W			
coulomb	C			
volt	V			
ohm	Ω			
henry	H			
farad	F			
tesla	T			
degree Celsius	°C			
electronvolt	eV			

Values of Trigonometric Functions for Common Angles

θ	$\sin\theta$	$\cos\theta$	$\tan\theta$
0°	0	1	0
30°	1/2	$\sqrt{3}/2$	$\sqrt{3}/3$
37°	3/5	4/5	3/4
45°	$\sqrt{2}/2$	$\sqrt{2}/2$	1
53°	4/5	3/5	4/3
60°	$\sqrt{3}/2$	1/2	$\sqrt{3}$
90°	1	0	∞

Newtonian Mechanics

		a = acceleration
	$v = v_0 + a\Delta t$	A = amplitude
	$x = x_0 + v_0\Delta t + \dfrac{1}{2}a\Delta t^2$	E = energy
Translational Motion		
	$v^2 = v_0^2 + 2a\Delta x$	F = force
	$\vec{a} = \dfrac{\sum \vec{F}}{m} = \dfrac{\vec{F}_{net}}{m}$	f = frequency
		h = height
	$\omega = \omega_0 + \alpha t$	I = rotational inertia
	$\theta = \theta_0 + \omega_0 t + \dfrac{1}{2}\alpha t^2$	J = impulse
Rotational Motion		K = kinetic energy
	$\omega^2 = \omega_0^2 + 2\alpha\Delta\theta$	k = spring constant
	$\vec{\alpha} = \dfrac{\sum \vec{\tau}}{I} = \dfrac{\vec{\tau}_{net}}{I}$	ℓ = length
		m = mass
Force of Friction	$\left|\vec{F}_f\right| \leq \mu\left|\vec{F}_n\right|$	N = normal force
Centripetal Acceleration	$a_c = \dfrac{v^2}{r}$	P = power
		p = momentum
Torque	$\tau = r_\perp F = rF\sin\theta$	L = angular momentum
		r = radius of distance
Momentum	$\vec{p} = m\vec{v}$	T = period
Impulse	$\vec{J} = \Delta\vec{p} = \vec{F}\Delta t$	t = time
		U = potential energy
Kinetic Energy	$K = \dfrac{1}{2}mv^2$	v = velocity or speed
		W = work done on a
Potential Energy	$\Delta U_g = mg\Delta y$	system
Work	$\Delta E = W = F_\parallel d = Fd\cos\theta$	x = position
		y = height
Power	$P = \dfrac{\Delta E}{\Delta t} = \dfrac{\Delta W}{\Delta t}$	

Simple Harmonic Motion	$x = A\cos(\omega t) = A\cos(2\pi f t)$	α = angular acceleration
Center of Mass	$x_{cm} = \dfrac{\sum m_i x_i}{\sum m_i}$	μ = coefficient of friction
Angular Momentum	$L = I\omega$	
Angular Impulse	$\Delta L = \tau \Delta t$	θ = angle τ = torque
Angular Kinetic Energy	$K = \dfrac{1}{2}I\omega^2$	ω = angular speed
Work	$W = F\Delta r \, \cos\theta$	
Power	$P = Fv \, \cos\theta$	
Spring Force	$|\vec{F_s}| = k|\vec{x}|$	
Spring Potential Energy	$U_s = \dfrac{1}{2}kx^2$	
Period of Spring Oscillator	$T_s = 2\pi\sqrt{m/k}$	
Period of Simple Pendulum	$T_p = 2\pi\sqrt{\ell/g}$	
Period	$T = \dfrac{2\pi}{\omega} = \dfrac{1}{f}$	
Gravitational Body Force	$|\vec{F_g}| = G\dfrac{m_1 m_2}{r^2}$	
Gravitational Potential Energy of Two Masses	$U_G = -\dfrac{Gm_1 m_2}{r}$	

Electricity and Magnetism

		A = area
Electric Field	$\vec{E} = \dfrac{\vec{F}_E}{q}$	B = magnetic field
		C = capacitance
Electric Field Strength	$\left|\vec{E}\right| = \dfrac{1}{4\pi\varepsilon_0}\dfrac{|q|}{r^2}$	d = distance
		E = electric field
Electric Field Strength	$\left|\vec{E}\right| = \dfrac{|\Delta V|}{|\Delta r|}$	ϵ = emf
		F = force
Electrostatic Force Between Charged Particles	$\left|\vec{F}_E\right| = \dfrac{1}{4\pi\varepsilon_0}\dfrac{|q_1 q_2|}{r^2}$	I = current
		l = length
Electric Potential Energy	$\Delta U_E = q\Delta V$	P = power
		Q = charge
Electrostatic Potential due to a Charge	$V = \dfrac{1}{4\pi\varepsilon_0}\dfrac{q}{r}$	q = point charge
		R = resistance
Capacitor Voltage	$V = \dfrac{Q}{C}$	r = separation
		t = time
Capacitance of Parallel Plate Capacitor	$C = \kappa\varepsilon_0\dfrac{A}{d}$	U = potential energy
		V = electric potential
Electric Field Inside a Parallel Plate Capacitor	$E = \dfrac{Q}{\varepsilon_0 A}$	v = speed
		κ = dielectric constant
Capacitor Potential Energy	$U_C = \tfrac{1}{2}Q\Delta V = \tfrac{1}{2}C(\Delta V)^2$	ρ = resistivity
		θ = angle
Current	$I = \dfrac{\Delta Q}{\Delta t}$	Φ = flux
Resistance	$R = \dfrac{\rho l}{A}$	
Power	$P = I\Delta V$	

Current $\qquad I = \dfrac{\Delta V}{R}$

Resistors in Series $\qquad R_s = \sum_i R_i$

Resistors in Parallel $\qquad \dfrac{1}{R_p} = \sum_i \dfrac{1}{R_i}$

Capacitors in Parallel $\qquad C_p = \sum_i C_i$

Capacitors in Series $\qquad \dfrac{1}{C_s} = \sum_i \dfrac{1}{C_i}$

Magnetic Field Strength
(from a long straight
current-carrying wire) $\qquad B = \dfrac{\mu_0 I}{2\pi r}$

Magnetic Force

$$\vec{F}_M = q\vec{v} \times \vec{B}$$

$$\vec{F}_M = |q\vec{v}||\sin\theta||\vec{B}|$$

$$\vec{F}_M = I\vec{l} \times \vec{B}$$

$$\vec{F}_M = |I\vec{l}||\sin\theta||\vec{B}|$$

Magnetic Flux

$$\Phi_B = \vec{B} \cdot \vec{A}$$

$$\Phi_B = |\vec{B}|\cos\theta|\vec{A}|$$

Electromagnetic Induction

$$\epsilon = \dfrac{-\Delta\Phi_B}{\Delta t}$$

$$\epsilon = Blv$$

Fluid Mechanics and Thermal Physics

Density	$\rho = \dfrac{m}{V}$	A = area
		c = specific heat
Pressure	$P = \dfrac{F}{A}$	d = thickness
		e = emissivity
Absolute Pressure	$P = P_0 + \rho g h$	F = force
Buoyant Force	$F_b = \rho V g$	h = depth
Fluid Continuity Equation	$A_1 v_1 = A_2 v_2$	k = thermal conductivity
		K = kinetic energy
Bernoulli's Equation	$P_1 + \rho g y_1 + \dfrac{1}{2}\rho v_1^2$ $= P_2 + \rho g y_2 + \dfrac{1}{2}\rho v_2^2$	l = length L = latent heat m = mass
Heat Conduction	$\dfrac{Q}{\Delta t} = \dfrac{kA\Delta T}{d}$	n = number of moles n_c = efficiency N = number of molecules
Thermal Radiation	$P = e\sigma A(T^4 - T_C^4)$	P = pressure or power
Ideal Gas Law	$PV = nRT = Nk_BT$	Q = energy transferred to a system by heating
Average Energy	$K = \dfrac{3}{2}k_BT$	T = temperature t = time
Work	$W = -P\Delta V$	E = internal energy
Conservation of Energy	$\Delta E = Q + W$	V = volume v = speed
Linear Expansion	$\Delta l = \alpha l_o \Delta T$	W = work done on a system
Heat Engine Efficiency	$n_c = |W/Q_H|$	
		y = height
Carnot Heat Engine Efficiency	$n_c = \dfrac{T_H - T_C}{T_H}$	σ = Stefan constant α = coefficient of linear expansion
Energy of Temperature Change	$Q = mc\Delta T$	ρ = density
Energy of Phase Change	$Q = mL$	

Optics

Wavelength to Frequency	$\lambda = \dfrac{v}{f}$	d = separation
		f = frequency or focal length
Index of Refraction	$n = \dfrac{c}{v}$	h = height
		L = distance
Snell's Law	$n_1 \sin \theta_1 = n_2 \sin \theta_2$	M = magnification
		m = an integer
Thin Lens Equation	$\dfrac{1}{s_i} + \dfrac{1}{s_0} = \dfrac{1}{f}$	n = index of refraction
		R = radius of curvature
Magnification Equation	$\|M\| = \left\|\dfrac{h_i}{h_o}\right\| = \left\|\dfrac{s_i}{s_o}\right\|$	s = distance
		v = speed
Double Slit Diffraction	$d \sin \theta = m\lambda$	x = position
	$\Delta L = m\lambda$	λ = wavelength
		θ = angle
Critical Angle	$\sin \theta_c = \dfrac{n_2}{n_1}$	
Focal Length of Spherical Mirror	$f = \dfrac{R}{2}$	

Acoustics

Standing Wave/ Open Pipe Harmonics	$\lambda = \dfrac{2L}{n}$	f = frequency
		L = length
Closed Pipe Harmonics	$\lambda = \dfrac{4L}{n}$	m = mass
		M = molecular mass
Harmonic Frequencies	$f_n = nf_1$	
		n = harmonic number
Speed of Sound in Ideal Gas	$v_{sound} = \sqrt{\dfrac{yRT}{M}}$	R = gas constant
		T = tension
Speed of Wave Through Wire	$v = \sqrt{\dfrac{T}{m/L}}$	v = velocity
		y = adiabatic constant
Doppler Effect (Approaching Stationary Observer)	$f_{observed} = (\dfrac{v}{v - v_{source}})f_{source}$	λ = wavelength
Doppler Effect (Receding Stationary Observer)	$f_{observed} = (\dfrac{v}{v + v_{source}})f_{source}$	
Doppler Effect (Observer Moving towards Source)	$f_{observed} = (1 + \dfrac{v_{observer}}{v})f_{source}$	
Doppler Effect (Observer Moving away from Source)	$f_{observed} = (1 - \dfrac{v_{observer}}{v})f_{source}$	

Modern Physics

Photon Energy	$E = hf$	$B = $ Balmer constant
		$c = $ speed of light
Photoelectric Electron Energy	$K_{max} = hf - \phi$	$E = $ energy
		$f = $ frequency
Electron Wavelength	$\lambda = \dfrac{h}{p}$	$K = $ kinetic energy
		$m = $ mass
Energy Mass Relationship	$E = mc^2$	$p = $ momentum
Rydberg Formula	$\dfrac{1}{\lambda} = R\left(\dfrac{1}{n_f^2} - \dfrac{1}{n_i^2}\right)$	$R = $ Rydberg constant
		$v = $ velocity
Balmer Formula	$\lambda = B\left(\dfrac{n^2}{n^2 - 2^2}\right)$	$\lambda = $ wavelength
		$\phi = $ work function
Lorentz Factor	$\gamma = \dfrac{1}{\sqrt{1 - \dfrac{v^2}{c^2}}}$	$\gamma = $ Lorentz factor

Geometry and Trigonometry

Rectangle	$A = bh$	$A = area$
		$C = circumference$
Triangle	$A = \frac{1}{2}bh$	$V = volume$
		$S = surface\ area$
Circle	$A = \pi r^2$	$b = base$
	$C = 2\pi r$	$h = height$
Rectangular Solid	$V = lwh$	$l = length$
		$w = width$
Cylinder	$V = \pi r^2 l$	$r = radius$
	$S = 2\pi rl + 2\pi r^2$	$\theta = angle$
Sphere	$V = \frac{4}{3}\pi r^3$	
	$S = 4\pi r^2$	
Right Triangle	$a^2 + b^2 = c^2$	
	$\sin\theta = \frac{a}{c}$	
	$\cos\theta = \frac{b}{c}$	
	$\tan\theta = \frac{a}{b}$	

MCAT Physics

Diagnostic Tests

These Diagnostic Tests should be used to assess your level of proficiency on each topic and NOT to mimic the actual test. Use your test results and identify your areas of strength and weakness to adjust your study plan where necessary and enhance your fundamental knowledge.

These are NOT simulated practice tests and are used for self-evaluation and studying.

Diagnostic Test #1

Answer Sheet

#	Answer:				Mark for review	#	Answer:				Mark for review
1:	A	B	C	D	___	31:	A	B	C	D	___
2:	A	B	C	D	___	32:	A	B	C	D	___
3:	A	B	C	D	___	33:	A	B	C	D	___
4:	A	B	C	D	___	34:	A	B	C	D	___
5:	A	B	C	D	___	35:	A	B	C	D	___
6:	A	B	C	D	___	36:	A	B	C	D	___
7:	A	B	C	D	___	37:	A	B	C	D	___
8:	A	B	C	D	___	38:	A	B	C	D	___
9:	A	B	C	D	___	39:	A	B	C	D	___
10:	A	B	C	D	___	40:	A	B	C	D	___
11:	A	B	C	D	___	41:	A	B	C	D	___
12:	A	B	C	D	___	42:	A	B	C	D	___
13:	A	B	C	D	___	43:	A	B	C	D	___
14:	A	B	C	D	___	44:	A	B	C	D	___
15:	A	B	C	D	___	45:	A	B	C	D	___
16:	A	B	C	D	___	46:	A	B	C	D	___
17:	A	B	C	D	___	47:	A	B	C	D	___
18:	A	B	C	D	___	48:	A	B	C	D	___
19:	A	B	C	D	___	49:	A	B	C	D	___
20:	A	B	C	D	___	50:	A	B	C	D	___
21:	A	B	C	D	___	51:	A	B	C	D	___
22:	A	B	C	D	___	52:	A	B	C	D	___
23:	A	B	C	D	___	53:	A	B	C	D	___
24:	A	B	C	D	___	54:	A	B	C	D	___
25:	A	B	C	D	___	55:	A	B	C	D	___
26:	A	B	C	D	___						
27:	A	B	C	D	___						
28:	A	B	C	D	___						
29:	A	B	C	D	___						
30:	A	B	C	D	___						

This Diagnostic Test is designed for you to assess your proficiency on each topic and NOT to mimic the actual test. Use your test results and identify areas of your strength and weakness to adjust your study plan and enhance your fundamental knowledge.

The length of the Diagnostic Tests is proven to be optimal for a single study session.

1. The slope of a tangent line at a given time value on a position vs. time graph indicates:

A. instantaneous acceleration

B. change in acceleration

C. instantaneous velocity

D. average velocity

2. Which statement must be true for an object moving with constant nonzero velocity?

A. The net force on the object is zero

B. The net force on the object is positive

C. A constant force is being applied to the object in the direction opposite of motion

D. A constant force is being applied to the object in the direction of motion

3. A solid cylindrical bar conducts heat at a rate of 30 W from a hot to a cold reservoir under steady-state conditions. What is the rate at which it conducts heat between these reservoirs if both the diameter and length of the bar are doubled? Assume heat transfer is lengthwise and sides of the bar are perfectly insulated.

A. 30 W   **B.** 60 W   **C.** 15 W   **D.** 120 W

4. An ideal, massless spring with a spring constant of 3 N/m has a 0.9 kg mass attached to one end, and the other end is attached to a beam. If the system is initially at equilibrium and the mass is then down 18 cm below the equilibrium length and released, what is the magnitude of the net force on the mass just after its release? (Use the acceleration due to gravity is $g = 10$ m/s^2)

A. 0.54 N   **B.** 0.75 N   **C.** 6 N   **D.** 0.35 N

5. A 30.0 N block is attached to the free end of an anchored spring and is allowed to slide back and forth on a frictionless table. Determine the frequency of motion if the spring constant $k = 40.0$ N/m. (Use the acceleration due to gravity $g = 9.8$ m/s^2)

A. 0.30 Hz   **B.** 0.58 Hz   **C.** 2.3 Hz   **D.** 3.6 Hz

6. A piano is tuned so that the frequency of the third harmonic of one string is 786.3 Hz. If the fundamental frequency of another string is 785.8 Hz, then what is the beat frequency between the notes?

A. 0 Hz   **B.** 1 Hz   **C.** 0.5 Hz   **D.** 786.3 Hz

7. A 600 N weight sits on the small piston of a hydraulic machine. The small piston has an area of 5 cm^2. If the large piston has an area of 50 cm^2, how much force can the large piston support?

A. 200 N   **B.** 300 N   **C.** 3,000 N   **D.** 6,000 N

8. A cube with 0.1 m sides is constructed of six insulated metal plates. Plates I and IV are opposite to each other and are maintained at 500 V. Plates II and V are opposite to each other and are maintained at 0 V. Plates III and VI are opposite to each other and are maintained at –500 V. What is the change in potential energy, if an electron is transferred from plate I to plate III? (Use the charge of $e = 1.6 \times 10^{-19}$ C)

    A. -3.2×10^{-14} J   **B.** -1.6×10^{-15} J   **C.** 3.2×10^{-12} J   **D.** 1.6×10^{-16} J

9. What quantity does the slope of this graph represent if the graph shows the power dissipated in a resistor as a function of the resistance?

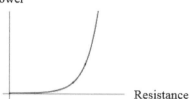

    A. Maximum power transferred across the resistor
    B. Square of the current across resistor
    C. Current across the resistor
    D. Potential difference across the resistor

10. What color light allows the investigator to see with the greatest resolution in a light microscope?

    A. Red light because it is refracted less than other colors by the objective lens
    B. Blue light because it has a shorter wavelength
    C. Violet light because it has a longer wavelength
    D. Blue light because it is brighter

11. A blue laser beam is incident on a metallic surface, causing electrons to be ejected from the metal. What is the effect on the rate of ejected electrons if the frequency of the laser beam is increased, while the intensity of the beam is held fixed?

    A. Remains the same, but the maximum kinetic energy decreases
    B. Decreases and the maximum kinetic energy decreases
    C. Decreases, but the maximum kinetic energy remains the same
    D. Decreases, but the maximum kinetic energy increases

12. A car and a truck are initially alongside each other at time $t = 0$. Their motions along a straight road are represented by the velocity vs. time graph. At time T, which statement is true for the vehicles?

    A. The car traveled farther than the truck
    B. The truck traveled farther than the car
    C. They traveled the same distance
    D. The truck had a greater acceleration than the car

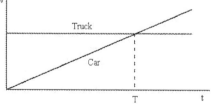

13. A 1,500 kg car moving at 45 km/h locks its brakes and skids 30 m. How far does the same car skid if it is traveling at 150 km/h?

    A. 230 m   **B.** 160 m   **C.** 445 m   **D.** 333 m

14. How does the frequency of vibration relate to the time it takes to complete one cycle?

    A. Inversely with the time   **C.** Directly with the time
    B. Inversely with the amplitude   **D.** Directly with the amplitude

15. A mosquito produces 1.5×10^{-11} W of sound energy. How many mosquitoes are needed to power a 30 W bulb if the sound energy could be used for this purpose?

    A. 6×10^{11} **B.** 2×10^{12} **C.** 2×10^{11} **D.** 6×10^{12}

16. How many grams of ethanol should be added to 5 grams of chloroform for the resulting mixture to have a specific gravity of 1.2? (Use the specific gravity of ethanol = 0.8, the specific gravity of chloroform = 1.5 and the conversion factor of 1 mL = 1 g)

    A. 1.5 g   **B.** 2.6 g   **C.** 2.0 g   **D.** 1.0 g

17. What is the unit of the product of amps × volts?

    A. Watt   **B.** Amp   **C.** Joule   **D.** Ohm

18. Which statement is correct about the equivalent resistance when four unequal resistors are connected in parallel?

    A. It is the average of the largest and smallest resistance
    B. It is less than the smallest resistance
    C. It is more than the largest resistance
    D. It is the average of the four resistances

19. What is the distance between a lens and a screen so that when the screen and the converging lens of focal length *f* are arranged, an image of the Moon falls on the screen? Assume that the Moon is infinity ∞ away from the lens.

    A. *f*/2   **B.** *2f*   **C.** *f*   **D.** infinity

20. What is the nuclear particle which is described by the symbol $_{1}^{1}H$?

    A. positron   **B.** β particle   **C.** γ particle   **D.** proton

21. With all other factors equal, the most likely situation in which a person burns her mouth is with food that has:

 A. specific heat is not applicable   **C.** higher specific heat
 B. requires more information   **D.** lower specific heat

22. Why does it take more force to start moving a heavy bookcase across the carpet than to keep it moving?

 A. For objects in motion, kinetic friction is a force in the same direction as the motion
 B. The coefficient of static friction is greater than the forces of movement
 C. The coefficient of static friction is greater than the coefficient of kinetic friction
 D. The coefficient of kinetic friction is greater than the coefficient of static friction

23. What is the wavelength of the standing wave when a 12 m string, fixed at both ends, is resonating at a frequency that produces 4 nodes?

 A. 6 m   **B.** 8 m   **C.** 4 m   **D.** 24 m

24. A silver necklace that has a mass of 60 grams and a volume of 5.7 cm^3 is lowered into a container of water and is tied to a string connected to a force meter. What is the reading on the force meter? (Use the density of water = 1 g/cm^3 and the acceleration due to gravity g = 9.8 m/s^2)

 A. 0.53 N   **B.** 0.22 N   **C.** 0.62 N   **D.** 0.38 N

25. A charged particle is traveling in a circular path of radius r in a uniform magnetic field. The plane of the circular path is perpendicular to the magnetic field. What is the radius of the circular path if the particle travels twice as fast?

 A. $\sqrt{2}r$ **B.** $r/2$ **C.** $4r$ **D.** $2r$

26. In which direction is the magnetic field if a positive charge is moving to the right and experiences a vertical (upward) magnetic force?

 A. Out of the page   **C.** To the left
 B. Into the page   **D.** To the right

27. Which statement is true for the angle of incidence?

 A. It may be greater than or less than, but never equal to, the angle of reflection
 B. It is always greater than the angle of reflection
 C. It must equal the angle of reflection
 D. It is always less than the angle of reflection

28. ^{14}C is generated in the atmosphere by the nuclear reaction: $^{14}_{7}$N $+ \, ^{1}_{0}$n $\rightarrow \, ^{14}_{6}$C $+$ __?

What species is not shown?

A. neutron   **B.** positron   **C.** α particle   **D.** proton

29. The graph shows the position of an object as a function of time. At which moment in time is the speed of the object equal to zero?

    A. A
    B. B
    C. C
    D. D

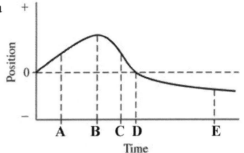

30. Michelle takes off down a 50 m high, 10° slope on her jet-powered skis. The skis have a thrust of 260 N. The combined mass of the skis and Michelle is 50 kg. Michelle's speed at the bottom of the slope is 40 m/s. Assuming the mass of the fuel is negligible, what is the coefficient of kinetic friction of her skis on the snow? (Use the acceleration due to gravity $g = 9.8$ m/s^2)

A. 0.23   **B.** 0.53   **C.** 0.68   **D.** 0.42

31. A hockey puck slides on a surface of frictionless ice. If the mass of the puck is 300 grams, and it moves in a straight line with a constant velocity of 5 m/s, what is the net force acting on the puck?

A. 0 N   **B.** 1 N   **C.** 30 N   **D.** 750 N

32. A 4 kg mass is affixed to the end of a vertical spring with a spring constant of 10 N/m. When the mass comes to rest, how much has the spring stretched?

A. 1 m   **B.** 4 m   **C.** 5 m   **D.** 0.1 m

33. In music, the 3rd harmonic corresponds to which overtone?

A. 1st   **B.** 2nd   **C.** 3rd   **D.** 4th

34. Two identical blocks of steel, one at 20 °C and the other at 30 °C, are placed into contact. Suppose the cooler block cools to 15 °C and the warmer block warms to 35 °C. This violates the:

    I. First law of thermodynamics
    II. Second law of thermodynamics
    III. Third law of thermodynamics

    A. I only   **B.** II only   **C.** III only   **D.** I and II only

35. What is the orientation and magnification of the image of a light bulb if the light bulb is placed 2 m in front of a mirror and the image is 6 m behind the mirror?

A. Upright and × 3
B. Inverted and × 3

C. Upright and × 0.5
D. Inverted and × 1.5

36. A series circuit has a 50 Hz AC source, a 0.4 H inductor, a 50 µF capacitor and a 30 Ω resistor. If the rms current in the circuit is 1.8 A, what is the voltage of the source?

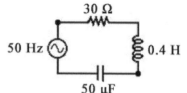

A. 142 V **B.** 124 V **C.** 75.5 V **D.** 96.7 V

37. A fixed distance separates two particles of like charge and equal mass. What is the effect on the repulsive force between the particles if the mass of one particle is doubled?

A. Doubles
B. Quadruples

C. Increases by ½
D. Remains the same

38. A water tank is filled to a depth of 6 m, and the bottom of the tank is 22 m above ground. A water-filled hose that is 2 cm in diameter extends from the bottom of the tank to the ground, but no water is flowing in the hose. What is the gauge water pressure at ground level in the hose? (Use the density of water $\rho = 1,000$ kg/m^3 and the acceleration due to gravity $g = 9.8$ m/s^2)

A. 2.7×10^5 N/m^2
B. 5.3×10^4 N/m^2

C. 8.7 N/m^2
D. Requires the cross-sectional area of the tank

39. The tension in each of two strings is adjusted so that both vibrate at exactly 822 Hz. The tension in one string is then increased slightly. Five beats per second are then heard when both strings vibrate. What is a new frequency of the string that was tightened?

A. 824 Hz **B.** 816 Hz **C.** 827 Hz **D.** 818 Hz

40. When a light ray traveling in glass strikes an air boundary, which type of phase change occurs in the reflected ray?

A. 45° phase change
B. 180° phase change

C. –45° phase change
D. No phase change

41. A stone of mass m is dropped from a height h toward the ground. Ignoring air resistance, which statement is true about the stone as it hits the ground?

A. Its KE is proportional to h
B. Its KE is proportional to h^2

C. Its speed is proportional to h
D. Its speed is inversely proportional to h^2

42. The image shows three beams of radiation passing between two electrically-charged plates. Which of the beams is due to a high-energy electron?

    I. a
    II. b
    III. c

A. I only   **B.** II only   **C.** III only   **D.** I and II only

43. A 40 kg runner is running around a track. The curved portions of the track are arcs of a circle that has a radius of 16 m. The runner is running at a constant speed of 4 m/s. What is the net force on the runner on the curved portion of the track?

A. 150 N   **B.** 5 N   **C.** 40 N   **D.** 100 N

44. If an object is accelerating, which values must change?

    I. Speed   II. Velocity   III. Direction

A. I only   **B.** II only   **C.** III only   **D.** I and II only

45. A 1,140 g empty iron kettle is on a hot stove. How much heat must it absorb to raise its temperature from 18 °C to 90 °C? (Use the specific heat for iron = 113 cal/kg·°C and the conversion of 1 cal = 4.186 J)

A. 8,230 J   **B.** 20,340 J   **C.** 38,825 J   **D.** 41,650 J

46. A 1.2 kg bowling ball is dropped from a height of 6 m. During its fall, it is constantly acted upon by air resistance, with a force of 3.4 N. Accounting for air resistance, what is the speed of the bowling ball as it hits the ground? (Use acceleration due to gravity $g = 10$ m/s^2)

A. 9.2 m/s   **B.** 10.6 m/s   **C.** 11.3 m/s   **D.** 13.4 m/s

47. Sound intensity is defined as:

    A. power per unit time
    B. power passing through a unit of area per unit time
    C. energy passing through a unit of volume per unit time
    D. energy passing through a unit of area per unit time

48. A kilowatt-hour is a unit of:

    A. work   **B.** current   **C.** power   **D.** charge

49. The index of refraction of the core of a piece of fiber optic cable is 1.6. If the index of the surrounding cladding is 1.3, what is the critical angle for total internal reflection of a light ray in the core, incident on the core-cladding interface?

    A. 82°   **B.** 40°   **C.** 34°   **D.** 54°

50. For constant linear acceleration, the velocity vs. time graph is a:

    A. sloped line   **B.** curve   **C.** horizontal line   **D.** cubic graph

51. How much heat is needed to melt a 70 kg sample of ice that is at 0 °C? (Use latent heat of fusion for water L_f = 334,000 J/kg and heat of vaporization for water $L_v = 2.3 \times 10^6$ J/kg)

    A. 1.3×10^5 kJ   **B.** 5.7×10^4 kJ   **C.** 4.0×10^6 kJ   **D.** 2.3×10^4 kJ

52. As a water wave passes, a floating leaf oscillates up and down completely for two cycles in 1 s. What is the wave's speed, if the wave's wavelength is 12 m?

    A. 1 m/s   **B.** 10 m/s   **C.** 24 m/s   **D.** 6 m/s

53. When a dam began to leak, Mike placed his finger in the hole to stop the flow. The dam is 20 m high and 100 km long and sits on top of a lake which is another 980 m deep, 100 km wide, and 100 km long. The hole that Mike blocked is a square 0.01 m by 0.01 m located 1 m below the surface of the water. Assuming that the viscosity of the water is negligible, what force does Mike have to exert to prevent water from leaking? (Use atmospheric pressure $P_{atm} = 10^5$ Pa, the density of water $\rho = 10^3$ kg/m³ and the acceleration due to gravity $g = 10$ m/s²)

    A. 10 N   **B.** 1 N   **C.** 1,000 N   **D.** 0.1 N

54. For a graph of potential vs. power, what does the slope represent for a DC circuit?

    A. 1 / resistance   **C.** 1 / current

    B. current   **D.** resistance

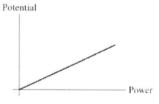

55. What is the amount of energy required to ionize a hydrogen atom from the ground state? (Use Rydberg formula where $E_0 = -13.6$ eV)

    A. 4.1 eV   **B.** 9.8 eV   **C.** 13.6 eV   **D.** 22.3 eV

> Check your answers using the answer key. Then, go to the explanations section and review the explanations in detail, paying particular attention to questions you didn't answer correctly or marked for review. Note the topic that those questions belong to.
>
> We recommend that you do this BEFORE taking the next Diagnostic Test.

Diagnostic test #1

1	C	Translational motion
2	A	Force & motion
3	B	Thermodynamics
4	A	Work & energy of point object systems
5	B	Periodic motion
6	C	Sound
7	D	Fluids & gas phase
8	D	Electrostatics & magnetism
9	B	Circuit elements
10	B	Light & geometrical optics
11	D	Atomic nucleus & electronic structure
12	B	Translational motion
13	D	Work & energy of point object systems
14	A	Periodic motion
15	B	Sound
16	C	Fluids & gas phase
17	A	Electrostatics & magnetism
18	B	Circuit elements
19	C	Light & geometrical optics
20	D	Atomic nucleus & electronic structure
21	C	Thermodynamics
22	C	Force & motion
23	B	Sound
24	A	Fluids & gas phase
25	D	Electrostatics & magnetism
26	B	Circuit elements
27	C	Light & geometrical optics
28	D	Atomic nucleus & electronic structure
29	B	Translational motion
30	D	Force & motion

31	A	Force & motion
32	B	Work & energy of point object systems
33	B	Periodic motion
34	B	Thermodynamics
35	A	Light & geometrical optics
36	B	Circuit elements
37	D	Electrostatics & magnetism
38	A	Fluids & gas phase
39	C	Sound
40	D	Periodic motion
41	A	Work & energy of point object systems
42	A	Atomic nucleus & electronic structure
43	C	Force & motion
44	B	Translational motion
45	C	Thermodynamics
46	A	Work & energy of point object systems
47	D	Sound
48	A	Electrostatics & magnetism
49	D	Light & geometrical optics
50	A	Translational motion
51	D	Thermodynamics
52	C	Periodic motion
53	B	Fluids & solids
54	C	Circuit elements
55	C	Atomic nucleus & electronic structure

Diagnostic Test #2

Answer Sheet

#	Answer:				Mark for review	#	Answer:				Mark for review
1:	A	B	C	D	___	31:	A	B	C	D	___
2:	A	B	C	D	___	32:	A	B	C	D	___
3:	A	B	C	D	___	33:	A	B	C	D	___
4:	A	B	C	D	___	34:	A	B	C	D	___
5:	A	B	C	D	___	35:	A	B	C	D	___
6:	A	B	C	D	___	36:	A	B	C	D	___
7:	A	B	C	D	___	37:	A	B	C	D	___
8:	A	B	C	D	___	38:	A	B	C	D	___
9:	A	B	C	D	___	39:	A	B	C	D	___
10:	A	B	C	D	___	40:	A	B	C	D	___
11:	A	B	C	D	___	41:	A	B	C	D	___
12:	A	B	C	D	___	42:	A	B	C	D	___
13:	A	B	C	D	___	43:	A	B	C	D	___
14:	A	B	C	D	___	44:	A	B	C	D	___
15:	A	B	C	D	___	45:	A	B	C	D	___
16:	A	B	C	D	___	46:	A	B	C	D	___
17:	A	B	C	D	___	47:	A	B	C	D	___
18:	A	B	C	D	___	48:	A	B	C	D	___
19:	A	B	C	D	___	49:	A	B	C	D	___
20:	A	B	C	D	___	50:	A	B	C	D	___
21:	A	B	C	D	___	51:	A	B	C	D	___
22:	A	B	C	D	___	52:	A	B	C	D	___
23:	A	B	C	D	___	53:	A	B	C	D	___
24:	A	B	C	D	___	54:	A	B	C	D	___
25:	A	B	C	D	___	55:	A	B	C	D	___
26:	A	B	C	D	___						
27:	A	B	C	D	___						
28:	A	B	C	D	___						
29:	A	B	C	D	___						
30:	A	B	C	D	___						

This Diagnostic Test is designed for you to assess your proficiency on each topic and NOT to mimic the actual test. Use your test results and identify areas of your strength and weakness to adjust your study plan and enhance your fundamental knowledge.

The length of the Diagnostic Tests is proven to be optimal for a single study session.

1. When an object moves with constant acceleration, can it's velocity change direction?

   A. Yes, a car that starts from rest, speeds up, slows to a stop, and then backs up is an example

   B. No, because it is always slowing down

   C. No, because it is always speeding up

   D. Yes, a Frisbee thrown straight up is an example

2. An auto mechanic needs to remove a tight-fitting pin of material X from a hole in a block made of material Y. The mechanic heats both the pin and the block to the same high temperature and removes the pin easily. What statement relates the coefficient of thermal expansion of material X to that of material Y?

   A. Material Y has a negative coefficient of expansion, and material X has a positive coefficient of expansion

   B. Material Y has the same coefficient of expansion as material X

   C. The situation is not possible; heating material Y shrinks the hole in the material as the material expands with increasing temperature

   D. Material Y has a greater coefficient of expansion than material X

3. What is the primary heat transfer mechanism by which the sun warms the Earth?

     I. Convection   II. Radiation   III. Conduction

   A. I only   **B.** II only   **C.** III only   **D.** I and II only

4. What is the power output necessary for a 54 kg person to run at constant velocity up a 10 m hillside in 4 s, if the hillside is inclined at 30° above the horizontal? (Use the acceleration due to gravity $g = 9.8$ m/s^2 and the conversion of 1 hp = 745 W)

   A. 1.92 hp   **B.** 1.12 hp   **C.** 0.89 hp   **D.** 3.94 hp

5. Some of a wave's energy dissipates as heat. In time, this reduces the wave's:

   A. amplitude   **B.** frequency   **C.** speed   **D.** wavelength

6. A piano tuned with the frequency of the third harmonic of the C_3 string is 783 Hz. What is the frequency of the C_3 fundamental?

   A. 473 Hz   **B.** 261 Hz   **C.** 387 Hz   **D.** 185 Hz

7. What is the density of an object if it weighs 7.86 N when it is in air and 6.92 N when it is immersed in water? (Use the acceleration due to gravity $g = 9.8$ m/s^2 and the density of water $\rho = 1,000$ kg/m^3)

   A. 6,042 kg/m^3 **B.** 7,286 kg/m^3 **C.** 8,333 kg/m^3 **D.** 9,240 kg/m^3

8. A water fountain pump recirculates water from a pool and pumps it up to a trough, where it flows along the trough and passes through a hole in the bottom of it. As the water falls back into the pool, it turns a water wheel. What aspect of this water fountain is analogous to an electric potential within an electric circuit?

A. Height of water

C. Flow velocity

B. Volume flow rate

D. Mass of water

9. If a sheet of copper is quickly passed through a strong permanent magnet with the plane of the sheet perpendicular to the magnetic field, which statement is true?

A. There is no movement because there is no magnetic force

B. The force experienced by the sheet of copper is due mainly to lead impurities in the copper, since copper is not magnetic

C. There is a magnetic force opposing the motion of the sheet

D. There is a magnetic force assisting the motion of the sheet

10. A light ray in water passes into the air where the angle of incidence in the water is 42°. What is the angle of refraction in the air? (Use the index of refraction of air n = 1 and the index of refraction of water = 1.33)

A. 63°   **B.** 18°   **C.** 46°   **D.** 74°

11. ^{3}Hydrogen can be used as a chemical tracer. What is the half-life of the radionuclide if 3,200 μg decays to 800 μg after 24.6 years?

A. 6.1 years   **B.** 12.3 years   **C.** 24.6 years   **D.** 49.2 years

12. An object with a mass of 60 kg moves across a level surface with a constant speed of 13.5 m/s. If there is a frictional force, and the coefficient of kinetic friction is 0.8, which must be true about the forces acting on the object?

A. There must be an unbalanced amount of vertical force acting on the object allowing it to move

B. No forces are doing work on the object

C. There must be some other horizontal force acting on the object

D. The force exerted on the object by kinetic friction is negligible

13. The total mechanical energy of a system is:

A. either all kinetic energy or all potential energy, at any one instant

B. constant if there are only conservative forces acting

C. found through the product of potential energy and kinetic energy

D. equally divided between kinetic energy and potential energy in every instance

14. A 340 nm thick oil film floats on the surface of the water. The surface of the oil is illuminated from above at normal incidence with white light. What are the two wavelengths of light that are in the 400 nm to 800 nm wavelength band, which are most strongly reflected? (Use the index of refraction for oil n = 1.5 and the index of refraction for water n = 1.33)

    A. 420 nm and 750 nm   **C.** 410 nm and 760 nm
    B. 406 nm and 706 nm   **D.** 408 nm and 680 nm

15. A 1 m string is fixed at both ends and plucked. What is the wavelength corresponding to the fourth harmonic if the speed of the waves on this string is 4.2×10^4 m/s?

    A. 1 m   **B.** 0.5 m   **C.** 4/3 m   **D.** 3/2 m

16. A ball is projected upward at time $t = 0$ s from a point on a roof 50 m above the ground. The ball rises, then falls and strikes the ground. The initial velocity of the ball is 24 m/s. Consider all quantities as positive in the upward direction. At time $t = 3.8$ s, the acceleration of the ball is:

    A. 10 m/s²   **B.** –5 m/s²   **C.** –10 m/s²   **D.** 24 m/s²

17. A distance of 15 cm separates two point charges of +18 μC and –6 μC. What is the electric field E midway between the two charges? (Coulomb's constant $k = 9 \times 10^9$ N·m²·C⁻²)

    A. 28.8×10^6 N/C toward the positive charge
    B. 28.8×10^6 N/C toward the negative charge
    C. 38.4×10^6 N/C toward the positive charge
    D. 38.4×10^6 N/C toward the negative charge

18. When the current through a resistor is increased by a factor of 4, by what factor does the power dissipated by the resistor change?

    A. Increases by 16   **B.** Increases by 4   **C.** Decreases by 4   **D.** Decreases by 16

19. The image of an object placed outside the focal point of a concave mirror is:

    A. virtual and inverted   **C.** real and inverted
    B. virtual and upright   **D.** real and upright

20. What is the term for the amount of radiation that produces 2.1×10^9 units of charge in 1 cm³ of air?

    A. gray   **B.** rad   **C.** curie   **D.** roentgen

21. A 500 g empty iron pot is put on a stove. How much heat must it absorb to raise its temperature from 20 °C to 70 °C? (Use the specific heat c of iron = 92 cal/kg·°C and the conversion of 1 cal = 4.186 J)

    A. 8,110 J   **B.** 9,628 J   **C.** 20,100 J   **D.** 12,500 J

22. In a binary star system, two stars revolve about their combined center of mass and are attracted to each other by the force of gravity. The force of gravity between the stars (masses M_1 and M_2) is F. If the mass of one of the stars is decreased by a factor of 2, how would this affect the force between them?

    A. Remains the same   **C.** Decreases by a factor of 4
    B. Increases by a factor of 2   **D.** Decreases by a factor of 2

23. In motion pictures, when a character falls off a cliff, he screams. If portrayed correctly, from the vantage point of an observer at the top of the cliff, the pitch of the scream the observer hears is:

    A. higher than the actual pitch and increasing as he falls
    B. lower than the actual pitch and decreasing as he falls
    C. higher than the actual pitch and constant
    D. lower than the actual pitch and increasing as he falls

24. As a cubical block of marble is lowered at a steady rate into the ocean by a crane, the top and bottom faces are kept horizontal. Which graph depicts the total pressure (P) on the bottom of the block as a function of time (t) as the block just enters the water at $t = 0$ s?

A.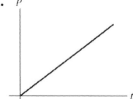

C.

B.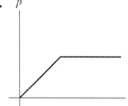

D.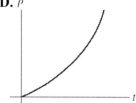

25. Two parallel metal plates separated by a distance of 0.03 m are charged to create a uniform electric field (4×10^4 N/C) between them, which points down. How does the force exerted on an α particle between the plates compare with the force exerted on a proton between the plates? (Use the acceleration due to gravity $g = 10$ m/s^2 and the charge on a proton $= 1.6 \times 10^{-19}$ C)

    A. Twice as large and in the same direction
    B. Four times as large and in the same direction
    C. The same magnitude, but in the opposite direction
    D. The same magnitude and in the same direction

26. How much current flows through a 57 m length of copper wire with a radius of 5.7 mm if it is connected to a source supplying 70 V? (Use resistivity of copper = 1.68×10^{-8} Ω·m)

    A. 180 nA   **B.** 3,600 A   **C.** 7,447 A   **D.** 3.7×10^8 A

27. Which statement about images is correct?

    A. A real image is always upright
    B. A virtual image cannot be photographed
    C. A virtual image cannot be seen by the unaided eye
    D. A virtual image cannot be formed on a screen

28. When a β^+ particle is emitted from an unstable nucleus, the atomic number of the nucleus:

    A. decreases by 2   **B.** increases by 2   **C.** decreases by 1   **D.** increases by 1

29. Describe the forces on a system which consists of a bicycle and a rider as the rider pedals at a constant speed in a straight line? (Ignore friction in the bearings of the bicycle)

    A. The force of air resistance is greater than the force of friction between the tires and the road
    B. The force of air resistance is less than the force of friction between the tires and the road
    C. The force of the rider's foot on the pedals is greater than the force of air resistance
    D. All external forces are balanced

30. A suitcase of mass 80 kg is pushed in a straight line across a horizontal floor at a constant speed of 3 m/s. What is the net force on the suitcase? (Use the coefficient of kinetic friction $\mu_k = 0.3$)

    A. 0 N   **B.** 240 N   **C.** 800 N   **D.** 27 N

31. Two astronauts conducted an experiment where a 3,500 kg spacecraft was connected with an orbiting rocket. The rocket thrusters were fired to provide 900 N for 8 s. What was the mass of the rocket, if the change in velocity of the spacecraft and rocket was 0.9 m/s?

    A. 3,100 kg   **B.** 4,500 kg   **C.** 10,820 kg   **D.** 2,430 kg

32. A motor is connected to a power supply that supplies 5 A of current with a 25 V potential difference. The motor has a 30% efficiency rating and is used to lift a 50 kg box. How far does the motor lift the box in 60 s? (Use acceleration due to gravity $g = 10$ m/s²)

    A. 4.5 m   **B.** 7.4 m   **C.** 1.8 m   **D.** 18 m

33. If the height that a pendulum reaches is doubled, what happens to its velocity as it passes its equilibrium position?

    A. Remains the same   **C.** Increases by a factor of 2
    B. Increases by a factor of 4   **D.** Increases by a factor of $\sqrt{2}$

34. Two metal rods are made of the same material and have the same cross-sectional area. The two rods differ only in their lengths of L and $3L$. The two rods are heated from the same initial temperature to the same final temperature. The short rod expands its length by an amount of ΔL. What is the amount by which the length of the long rod increases?

A. $\sqrt{3}\Delta L$ **B.** $3\Delta L$ **C.** ΔL **D.** $3/2\Delta L$

35. If n_1 is the index of refraction for the incident medium, and n_2 is the index of the refracting medium, what conditions are necessary for the critical angle to exist?

A. $n_1 = n_2$ **B.** $n_1 < n_2$ **C.** $n_1 < 2n_2$ **D.** $n_1 > n_2$

36. Which graph is representative for a semiconductor material? R = resistivity, T = temperature.

A.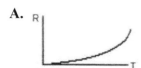

C.

B.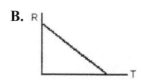

D.

37. A volt is a unit of electrical:

A. resistance   **B.** current   **C.** potential difference   **D.** charge

38. A spherical inflated balloon is submerged in a swimming pool. How is the buoyant force affected if the balloon is inflated to double its radius?

A. 8 times larger   **B.** 2 times larger   **C.** 4 times larger   **D.** 2 times smaller

39. An atom of He is twice as massive as a molecule of H. How much faster is the speed of sound in H compared to the speed of sound in He?

A. 4 times faster   **B.** 8 times faster   **C.** 1.41 times faster   **D.** 2 times faster

40. If the energy that starts a vibration increases, this increases the:

A. number of cycles/sec   **B.** wavelength   **C.** frequency   **D.** amplitude

41. The potential energy of a box on a shelf, relative to the floor, is a measure of the:

    I. work done putting the box on the shelf from the floor
    II. energy the box has because of its position above the floor
    III. weight of the box × the distance above the floor

A. I only   **B.** II only   **C.** III only   **D.** I, II and III

42. The Bohr model of the hydrogen atom was not able to explain:

    A. why some emission lines were brighter than other emission lines
    B. the wavelengths of the emission lines in the ultraviolet range
    C. the observation that the atom does not lose energy to radiation as the electron orbits
    D. the Bohr model explained the exact characteristics of a hydrogen atom

43. A massless string connects a 10 kg block to a 70 kg mass, which hangs over the edge of the table. Ignoring friction, what is the acceleration of the 10 kg block when the other block is released? (Use the acceleration due to gravity $g = 10$ m/s^2)

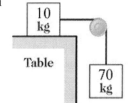

    A. 5.5 m/s^2 **B.** 10.5 m/s^2 **C.** 8.8 m/s^2 **D.** 7.3 m/s^2

44. An object with an initial velocity of 4 m/s moves along the *x*-axis with constant acceleration. How far did it travel in 2 s, if its final velocity is 16 m/s?

    A. 9 m   **B.** 20 m   **C.** 32 m   **D.** 26 m

45. When grinding a culinary knife, the 70 g of metal becomes heated to 450 °C. What is the minimum amount of 25 °C water is needed if the water is to remain liquid and not rise above 100 °C when the hot knife is cooled in it? (Use the specific heat of the knife = 0.11 cal/g·°C and the specific heat of water = 1 cal/g·°C)

    A. 36 g   **B.** 28 g   **C.** 47 g   **D.** 18 g

46. A horizontal spring-mass system oscillates on a frictionless table. If the ratio of the mass to the spring constant is 0.031 kg·m/N, and the maximum speed of the mass is 30 m/s, what is the maximum extension of the spring?

    A. 0.67 m   **B.** 460 cm   **C.** 5.3 m   **D.** 2.6 cm

47. A guitar is louder than a harp because it has:

    I. lower pitch   II. sounding board   III. thicker strings

    A. I only   **B.** II only   **C.** III only   **D.** I and II only

48. The H nucleus, which has a charge of e^+, is situated to the left of a C nucleus, which has a charge of 6 e^+. Which is true regarding the direction and magnitude of the electrical force experienced by the H nucleus?

    A. To the right and equal to the force exerted on the C nucleus
    B. To the left and less than the force exerted on the C nucleus
    C. To the right and greater than the force exerted on the C nucleus
    D. To the left and equal to the force exerted on the C nucleus

49. An object is viewed at various distances using a concave mirror with a focal length of 10 m. Where is the image relative to the mirror when the object is 20 m away from the mirror?

    A. 20 m behind   **B.** 20 m in front   **C.** 10 m behind   **D.** 10 m in front

50. How fast an object moves, with reference to direction, is a property of motion known as:

    A. velocity   **B.** acceleration   **C.** momentum   **D.** speed

51. It is necessary to determine the specific heat of a 185 g object. It is determined experimentally that it takes 14 J to raise the temperature 10° C. What is the specific heat of the object?

    A. 343 J/kg·K   **B.** 1.6 J/kg·K   **C.** 25.9 J/kg·K   **D.** 7.6 J/kg·K

52. By what factor does the time required to complete one full cycle increase for a simple pendulum when the length is tripled?

    A. 1/3   **B.** 3   **C.** $\sqrt{3}$ **D.** 9

53. A water tank is 30 m above ground and is filled to a depth of 15 m. What is the gauge pressure at ground level in a 3 cm diameter hose? (Use the acceleration due to gravity $g = 9.8$ m/s^2 and the density of water $\rho = 1{,}000$ kg/m^3)

    A. 7.2×10^3 N/m^2 **C.** 1.4×10^4 N/m^2
    B. 6.1×10^1 N/m^2 **D.** 4.4×10^5 N/m^2

54. Consider two copper wires of equal length. How do the resistances of these two wires compare if one wire has twice the cross-sectional area?

    A. The thicker wire has one-half the resistance of the thinner wire
    B. The thicker wire has four times the resistance of the thinner wire
    C. The thicker wire has twice the resistance of the thinner wire
    D. The thicker wire has eight times the resistance of the thinner wire

55. For a given value of the principal quantum number n, what are the allowable orbital angular momentum quantum numbers?

    A. $\ell = 1, 2, 3, \ldots, n$ **C.** $\ell = 0, 1, 2, \ldots, n$
    B. $\ell = 0, 1, 2, \ldots, (n-1)$ **D.** $\ell = 1, 2, 3, \ldots, (n-1)$

Check your answers using the answer key. Then, go to the explanations section and review the explanations in detail, paying particular attention to questions you didn't answer correctly or marked for review. Note the topic that those questions belong to.

We recommend that you do this BEFORE taking the next Diagnostic Test.

Diagnostic test #2

1	D	Translational motion
2	D	Thermodynamics
3	B	Thermodynamics
4	C	Work & energy of point object systems
5	A	Periodic motion
6	B	Sound
7	C	Fluids & gas phase
8	A	Electrostatics & magnetism
9	C	Circuit elements
10	A	Light & geometrical optics
11	B	Atomic nucleus & electronic structure
12	C	Force & motion
13	B	Work & energy of point object systems
14	D	Periodic motion
15	B	Sound
16	C	Translational motion
17	D	Electrostatics & magnetism
18	A	Circuit element
19	C	Light & geometrical optics
20	D	Atomic nucleus & electronic structure
21	B	Thermodynamics
22	D	Force & motion
23	B	Sound
24	C	Fluids & gas phase
25	A	Electrostatics & magnetism
26	C	Circuit elements
27	D	Light & geometrical optics
28	C	Atomic nucleus & electronic structure
29	D	Translational motion
30	A	Force & motion
31	B	Force & motion
32	A	Work & energy of point object systems
33	D	Periodic motion
34	B	Thermodynamics
35	D	Light & geometrical optics
36	B	Circuit elements
37	C	Electrostatics & magnetism
38	A	Fluids & gas phase
39	C	Sound
40	D	Periodic motion
41	D	Work & energy of point object systems
42	A	Atomic nucleus & electronic structure
43	C	Force & motion
44	B	Translational motion
45	A	Thermodynamics
46	C	Work & energy of point object systems
47	B	Sound
48	D	Electrostatics & magnetism
49	B	Light & geometrical optics
50	A	Translational motion
51	D	Thermodynamics
52	C	Periodic motion
53	D	Fluids & gas phase
54	A	Circuit element
55	B	Atomic nucleus & electronic structure

Diagnostic Test #3

Answer Sheet

#	Answer:				Mark for review	#	Answer:				Mark for review
1:	A	B	C	D	___	31:	A	B	C	D	___
2:	A	B	C	D	___	32:	A	B	C	D	___
3:	A	B	C	D	___	33:	A	B	C	D	___
4:	A	B	C	D	___	34:	A	B	C	D	___
5:	A	B	C	D	___	35:	A	B	C	D	___
6:	A	B	C	D	___	36:	A	B	C	D	___
7:	A	B	C	D	___	37:	A	B	C	D	___
8:	A	B	C	D	___	38:	A	B	C	D	___
9:	A	B	C	D	___	39:	A	B	C	D	___
10:	A	B	C	D	___	40:	A	B	C	D	___
11:	A	B	C	D	___	41:	A	B	C	D	___
12:	A	B	C	D	___	42:	A	B	C	D	___
13:	A	B	C	D	___	43:	A	B	C	D	___
14:	A	B	C	D	___	44:	A	B	C	D	___
15:	A	B	C	D	___	45:	A	B	C	D	___
16:	A	B	C	D	___	46:	A	B	C	D	___
17:	A	B	C	D	___	47:	A	B	C	D	___
18:	A	B	C	D	___	48:	A	B	C	D	___
19:	A	B	C	D	___	49:	A	B	C	D	___
20:	A	B	C	D	___	50:	A	B	C	D	___
21:	A	B	C	D	___	51:	A	B	C	D	___
22:	A	B	C	D	___	52:	A	B	C	D	___
23:	A	B	C	D	___	53:	A	B	C	D	___
24:	A	B	C	D	___	54:	A	B	C	D	___
25:	A	B	C	D	___	55:	A	B	C	D	___
26:	A	B	C	D	___						
27:	A	B	C	D	___						
28:	A	B	C	D	___						
29:	A	B	C	D	___						
30:	A	B	C	D	___						

This Diagnostic Test is designed for you to assess your proficiency on each topic and NOT to mimic the actual test. Use your test results and identify areas of your strength and weakness to adjust your study plan and enhance your fundamental knowledge.

The length of the Diagnostic Tests is proven to be optimal for a single study session.

1. An object is at height h above the surface of the Earth, where h is much smaller than the radius of the Earth. It takes t seconds to fall to the ground. Ignoring air resistance, at what height would this object need to be released to take $2t$ s to fall?

    A. $4h$ **B.** $4gh$ **C.** $2h$ **D.** $2gh$

2. Two 1 kg blocks are connected by rope 1. Rope 2 hangs beneath the block B. Each rope has a mass of 350 g. The entire assembly is accelerated upward at 5.5 m/s² by force F. What is the tension at the bottom end of rope 1? (Use the acceleration due to gravity $g = 9.8$ m/s²)

    A. 7.9 N   **B.** 31.5 N   **C.** 23 N   **D.** 20.6 N

3. A fluid in an insulated, flexible bottle is heated by a high-resistance wire and expands. If 9 kJ of heat is applied to the system and the system does 5 kJ of work, how much does the internal energy change?

    A. –4 kJ   **B.** 32 kJ   **C.** 4 kJ   **D.** 12 kJ

4. One end of a spring, with a spring constant 50 N/m, is fixed at point A, while the other end is connected to a 5 kg mass. The fixed end and the mass sit on a horizontal frictionless surface so that the mass and the spring rotate about point A. The mass moves in a circle with $r = 4$ m and the force on the mass is 20 N. How long does it take for the mass to make one complete revolution around point A?

    A. 5.7 s   **B.** 6.3 s   **C.** 4.4 s   **D.** 3.2 s

5. All of the following are true statements, EXCEPT:

    A. Waves transport energy and matter from one region to another
    B. The speed of a wave and the speed of the vibrating particles of the wave are not the same entities
    C. A wave that is being reflected at the same frequency as it is being produced is referred to as a standing wave
    D. For a transverse wave, the motion of the particles is perpendicular to the velocity vector of the wave

6. What are the wavelengths of the three lowest tones produced by an open pipe of length L?

    A. $2L, L, 2L/3$ **B.** $4L, 4L/3, 4L/5$ **C.** $4L, 2L, L$ **D.** $2L, L, L/2$

7. A 10 N falling object encounters 4 N of air resistance. What is the magnitude of the net force on the object?

    A. 0 N   **B.** 4 N   **C.** 6 N   **D.** 10 N

8. A circular loop of wire is positioned in a region of a changing magnetic field; the direction of the field remains constant, but the magnitude is fluctuating. What must the orientation of the loop's area vector be in relation to the magnetic field direction to create the maximum induced emf?

    A. An angle of 45° to the magnetic field
    B. An angle of −45° to the magnetic field
    C. An angle of 90° to the magnetic field
    D. Parallel to the magnetic field

9. A charged, parallel-plate capacitor has an electric field E_0 between its plates. The bare nuclei of ^{1}H and ^{3}H, both at rest, are placed between the plates. Ignoring the force of gravity, how does the force, F_1, of the light ^{1}H nucleus compare with the force, F_3, of the heavy ^{3}H nucleus?

    A. $F_3 = 3F_1$ **B.** $F_3 = \sqrt{2}F_1$ **C.** $F_3 = F_1$ **D.** $F_3 = (1/3)F_1$

10. Which statement about thin, single lenses is correct?

    A. A diverging lens can only sometimes produce a virtual, erect image
    B. A diverging lens always produces a virtual, erect image
    C. A converging lens always produces a real, inverted image
    D. A diverging lens always produces a real, inverted image

11. During β^+ decay:

    A. a proton is transformed to a neutron   **C.** a neutron is transformed to a positron
    B. an electron is released from its orbit   **D.** a neutron is transformed to a proton

12. Which of the following expressions could represent velocity?

    A. 7 m/s   **B.** 7 m/s North   **C.** 7 m   **D.** 7 m North

13. A child, while pulling a box from the ground up to his tree house with a rope, does 400 J of work. What is the mass of the box if the tree house is 4 m above the ground? (Use the acceleration due to gravity $g = 9.8$ m/s^2)

    A. 13.2 kg   **B.** 6.6 kg   **C.** 5.2 kg   **D.** 10.2 kg

14. What is the frequency of the wave shown in the figure?

    A. 0.5 Hz   **B.** 1 Hz   **C.** 2 Hz   **D.** 4 Hz

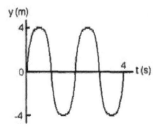

15. Some wavefronts are emitted by a source S. This diagram illustrates why:

   A. beats are heard
   B. sonar works
   C. a sound appears louder as the observer moves closer to the source
   D. the siren on a fire engine truck changes its pitch as it passes the observer

16. A plastic container in the shape of a cube with 0.2 m sides is suspended in a vacuum. The container is filled to 3 atm with 10 g of N_2 gas. What is the force that the N_2 gas exerts on one face of the cube? (Use the ideal gas constant $R = 0.0821$ L atm/K mol and the conversion of 1 atm $= 1.01 \times 10^5$ Pa)

   A. 2.1×10^3 N   **C.** 1.2×10^4 N
   B. 5.6×10^4 N   **D.** 4.2×10^4 N

17. What is the maximum magnetic field for a wave if an electromagnetic wave is traveling in a vacuum that has a maximum electric field of 1,200 V/m? (Use the speed of light c in a vacuum $= 3 \times 10^8$ m/s)

   A. 4×10^{-6} T   **C.** 3.3×10^{-4} T
   B. 2×10^{-5} T   **D.** 8×10^{-6} T

18. An alternating voltage, oscillating at 60 Hz, has a maximum value of 200 V during each cycle. What would be the reading if an RMS (root mean square) voltmeter is connected to the circuit?

   A. 142 V   **B.** 100 V   **C.** 35 V   **D.** 284 V

19. Where is the resulting image if a candle 21 cm tall is placed 4 m away from a diverging lens with a focal length of 3 m?

   A. 12/7 m from the lens on the opposite side from the object
   B. 12 m from the lens on the opposite side from the object
   C. 12/7 m from the lens on the same side as the object
   D. 12 m from the lens on the same side as the object

20. An energy level diagram of a certain atom is shown below whereby the energy difference between levels 1 and 2 is twice the energy difference between levels 2 and 3. A wavelength λ is emitted when an electron makes a transition from level 3 to 2. What possible radiation λ might be produced by other transitions between the three energy levels?

   A. 2λ only   **B.** both 2λ and 3λ **C.** $\frac{1}{2}\lambda$ only   **D.** both $\frac{1}{2}\lambda$ and $\lambda/3$

21. A person running in place on an exercise machine for 10 min expends 19 kcal. Another person exercises by repeatedly lifting two 3 kg weights a distance of 50 cm. How many repetitions of this exercise are equivalent to 10 minutes of running in place? Assume that the person uses negligible energy in letting down the weights after each lift. (Use the acceleration due to gravity $g = 9.8$ m/s^2 and 1 kcal = 1,000 cal and 1 cal = 4.186 J)

    A. 2,705 repetitions   **C.** 1,360 repetitions
    B. 1,800 repetitions   **D.** 3,940 repetitions

22. An 18 kg block is on a ramp that is inclined at 20° above the horizontal and is connected by a string to a 21 kg mass that hangs over the edge of the ramp. Ignoring frictional forces, what is the acceleration of the 21 kg block? (Use the acceleration due to gravity $g = 9.8$ m/s^2)

    A. 3.2 m/s^2 **B.** 2.6 m/s^2 **C.** 3.7 m/s^2 **D.** 5.3 m/s^2

23. A transverse wave in a string, with a wavelength of 8 m, is traveling at 4 m/s. At $t = 0$, a point on the string has a displacement of $+x$, where x is the amplitude of the wave. At what value of t is the same point on the string at a displacement of $-x$?

    A. 1 s   **B.** 2 s   **C.** ¼ s   **D.** ½ s

24. If the amount of fluid flowing through a tube remains constant, by what factor does the speed of the fluid change when the radius of the tube decreases from 16 cm to 4 cm?

    A. Increases by √2   **C.** Decreases by 16
    B. Increases by 16   **D.** Decreases by 4

25. Two identically-charged balls are a certain distance apart as shown in the vector diagram.

If the charge of the ball on the left is doubled (represented by ++), which diagram represents the forces now acting on the two balls?

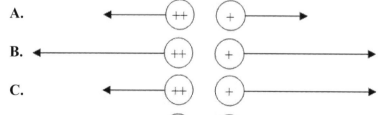

26. Which of the following quantities is equivalent to 1 Ω?

 A. 1 V·A **B.** 1 V/A **C.** 1 J/s **D.** 1 W/A

27. Which statement is true if the magnification of a mirror or lens is negative?

 A. Object is closer to the mirror or lens than to the image
 B. Image is inverted
 C. Image is erect and smaller than the object
 D. Image is smaller than the object

28. The masses of all isotopes are based on a comparison to the mass of which isotope?

 A. ^{232}Uranium **B.** ^{13}Carbon **C.** ^{12}Carbon **D.** ^{1}Hydrogen

29. Ignoring air resistance, a 30 kg and a 60 kg rock are thrown upward with the same initial speed (v_i). If the 30 kg rock reaches a maximum height h, what maximum height does the 60 kg ball reach?

 A. $2h$ **B.** h **C.** $h / 2$ **D.** $h / 4$

30. A hockey puck is set in motion across a frozen pond. Ignoring the friction of ice and air resistance, what is the force required to keep the puck sliding at constant velocity?

 A. mass of the puck × 9.8 m/s^2 **C.** weight of the puck
 B. weight of the puck / mass of the puck   **D.** 0 N

31. A 0.24 kg piece of clay is thrown at a wall with an initial velocity of 16 m/s. What is the average force experienced by the clay if it stops after 91 milliseconds?

 A. 84 N **B.** 32 N **C.** 24 N **D.** 42 N

32. A car drives 5 km North, then 7.3 km East, then 3.4 km Northeast, all at a constant speed. What was the magnitude of the average frictional force on the car if it performed 2.6 × 10^6 J of work during this trip?

 A. 1.7×10^2 N **B.** 4.2×10^2 N **C.** 7×10^1 N **D.** 5.7×10^2 N

33. A redshift for light indicates that the light source moves:

 I. at right angles to the observer
 II. towards the observer
 III. away from the observer

 A. I only **B.** II only **C.** III only **D.** I and II only

34. An object having an emissivity 0.867 radiates heat at a rate of 15 W when it is at a temperature T. If its temperature is doubled, what is the rate at which it radiates heat?

A. 30 W   **B.** 60 W   **C.** 80 W   **D.** 240 W

35. A lens of focal length 50 mm is used as a magnifier to view a 6.4 mm object that is positioned at the focal point of the lens. The user of the magnifier has a near point at 25 cm. What is the angular magnification of the magnifier?

A. 5   **B.** 6.9   **C.** 5.8   **D.** 8.1

36. In Experiment 1, a magnet was moved toward the end of a solenoid, and a voltage was induced between the two ends of the solenoid wire. In Experiment 2, a higher voltage was observed. What might have changed between the two experiments?

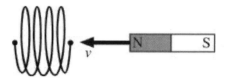

I. A stronger magnet replaced the bar magnet
II. The solenoid was replaced by one with more loops but the same length
III. The speed of the magnet increased

A. I only   **B.** II only   **C.** III only   **D.** I, II and III

37. An ampere is a unit of electrical:

I. pressure   II. resistance   III. current

A. I only   **B.** II only   **C.** III only   **D.** I and II only

38. In the equation PV = NkT, the k is known as:

A. Planck's constant
B. Boltzmann's constant
C. Avogadro's number
D. The spring (compressibility) constant

39. A 0.2 m long string vibrates in the n = 5 harmonic. What is the distance between a node and an adjacent antinode? (Use the speed of sound in air v = 340 m/s)

A. 30 mm   **B.** 60 mm   **C.** 7.5 mm   **D.** 20 mm

40. The graph shows position *x* as a function of time *t* for a system undergoing simple harmonic motion. Which graph represents the velocity of this system as a function of time?

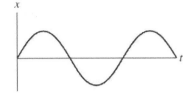

A.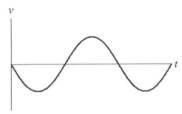

C.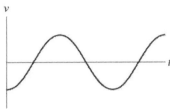

B.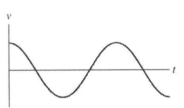

D.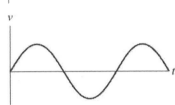

41. What is the potential energy with respect to the ground for a 2 kg mass that is held 4 m above the ground? (Use the acceleration due to gravity $g = 9.8$ m/s^2)

   A. 20 J   **B.** 40 J   **C.** 60 J   **D.** 80 J

42. Why do heavy nuclei contain more neutrons than protons?

   A. Neutrons are heavier than protons
   B. Neutrons and heavy nuclei are not radioactive
   C. Neutrons reduce the electric repulsion of the protons
   D. Neutrons are lighter than protons

43. A 1,400 kg car pulls a 400 kg trailer along level ground. The car accelerates at 1.5 m/s^2. Ignoring friction, what is the force exerted by the car on the trailer?

   A. 480 N   **B.** 510 N   **C.** 600 N   **D.** 680 N

44. A box is being dragged to the right at a constant velocity along a level floor by a string which is horizontal with tension *T*. The magnitude of the frictional force is *F*, the gravitational force is *G*, and the normal force is *N*. Which relationship is true?

   A. $T + F = G + N$ **B.** $T = F$ **C.** $T + F = G - N$ **D.** $T < F$

45. A gas is confined to a rigid container that cannot expand as heat energy is added to it. This process is referred to as:

   A. isokinetic   **B.** isentropic   **C.** isothermal   **D.** isometric

46. Which of the following expressions is equal to a watt?

A. $kg \cdot m^2/s^3$ **B.** $kg^2 \cdot m^2 \cdot s^2$ **C.** $kg \cdot m/s^3$ **D.** $kg \cdot m/s$

47. An organ pipe is a cylindrical tube that opens at both ends whereby the air column vibrates from air flowing through the lower portion of the pipe. On an 8 °C day, the speed of sound is 3% slower than on a 20 °C day. How is the *f* affected?

A. Remains the same   **C.** Decreases by 9%
B. Increases by $\sqrt{3}$%   **D.** Decreases by 3%

48. Three particles travel through a region of space where the magnetic field is pointing out of the page. What are the signs of the charges of these three particles?

A. 1 is negative, 2 is positive, and 3 is neutral
B. 1 is negative, 2 is neutral, and 3 is positive
C. 1 is positive, 2 is neutral, and 3 is negative
D. 1 is neutral, 2 is positive, and 3 is negative

49. Which form of electromagnetic radiation has the lowest frequency?

A. X-rays   **B.** γ rays   **C.** Radio waves   **D.** Microwaves

50. Ignoring air resistance, a purple marble is thrown upwards from a cliff with an initial speed of v_0. A grey marble is thrown downwards with the same initial speed. When the marbles reach the ground, the:

A. two marbles travel at speed proportional to their mass
B. two marbles have the same speed
C. grey marble moves faster than the purple marble
D. purple marble moves faster than the grey marble

51. How much heat is required to raise the temperature of a 300 g lead ball from 20 °C to 30 °C? The specific heat of lead is 128 J/kg·K.

A. 224 J   **B.** 168 J   **C.** 576 J   **D.** 384 J

52. What is the speed of transverse waves on a steel cable that lifts a 2,500 kg mass where the cable has a mass per unit length of 0.65 kg/m? (Use acceleration due to gravity $g = 9.8$ m/s²)

A. 410 m/s   **B.** 920 m/s   **C.** 668 m/s   **D.** 194 m/s

53. A viscous oil flows through a narrow pipe at a constant velocity. By what factor does the flow rate increase if the diameter of the pipe is doubled?

    A. 4   **B.** $\sqrt{2}$ **C.** 6   **D.** 8

54. Magnetic field lines about a current-carrying wire:

    I. extend radially from the wire
    II. circle the wire in closed loops
    III. circle the wire in a spiral

    A. I only   **B.** II only   **C.** III only   **D.** I and II only

55. Which forces hold the protons in a nucleus together?

    A. dipole–dipole   **C.** nuclear
    B. gravitational   **D.** electrostatic attraction

Check your answers using the answer key. Then, go to the explanations section and review the explanations in detail, paying particular attention to questions you didn't answer correctly or marked for review. Note the topic that those questions belong to.

We recommend that you do this BEFORE taking the next Diagnostic Test.

Diagnostic test #3

1	A	Translational Motion	31	D	Force
2	D	Force & motion	32	A	Work & energy of point object systems
3	C	Thermodynamics	33	C	Periodic motion
4	B	Work & energy of point object systems	34	D	Thermodynamics
5	A	Periodic motion	35	A	Light & geometrical optics
6	A	Sound	36	D	Electric circuits
7	C	Force & motion	37	C	Electrostatics & magnetism
8	D	Electrostatics & magnetism	38	B	Fluids & gas phase
9	C	Electric circuits	39	D	Sound
10	B	Light & geometrical optics	40	B	Periodic motion
11	A	Atomic nucleus & electronic structure	41	D	Work & energy of point object systems
12	B	Translational Motion	42	C	Atomic nucleus & electronic structure
13	D	Work & energy of point object systems	43	C	Force & motion
14	A	Periodic motion	44	B	Translational Motion
15	D	Sound	45	D	Thermodynamics
16	C	Fluids & gas phase	46	A	Work & energy of point object systems
17	A	Electrostatics & magnetism	47	D	Sound
18	A	Electric circuits	48	B	Electrostatics & magnetism
19	C	Light & geometrical optics	49	C	Light & geometrical optics
20	D	Atomic nucleus & electronic structure	50	B	Translational Motion
21	A	Thermodynamics	51	D	Thermodynamics
22	C	Force & motion	52	D	Periodic motion
23	A	Sound	53	A	Fluids & gas phase
24	B	Fluids & gas phase	54	B	Electric circuits
25	B	Electrostatics & magnetism	55	C	Atomic nucleus & electronic structure
26	B	Electric circuits			
27	B	Light & geometrical optics			
28	C	Atomic nucleus & electronic structure			
29	B	Translational Motion			
30	D	Force & motion			

Diagnostic Test #4

Answer Sheet

#	Answer:				Mark for review	#	Answer:				Mark for review
1:	A	B	C	D	___	31:	A	B	C	D	___
2:	A	B	C	D	___	32:	A	B	C	D	___
3:	A	B	C	D	___	33:	A	B	C	D	___
4:	A	B	C	D	___	34:	A	B	C	D	___
5:	A	B	C	D	___	35:	A	B	C	D	___
6:	A	B	C	D	___	36:	A	B	C	D	___
7:	A	B	C	D	___	37:	A	B	C	D	___
8:	A	B	C	D	___	38:	A	B	C	D	___
9:	A	B	C	D	___	39:	A	B	C	D	___
10:	A	B	C	D	___	40:	A	B	C	D	___
11:	A	B	C	D	___	41:	A	B	C	D	___
12:	A	B	C	D	___	42:	A	B	C	D	___
13:	A	B	C	D	___	43:	A	B	C	D	___
14:	A	B	C	D	___	44:	A	B	C	D	___
15:	A	B	C	D	___	45:	A	B	C	D	___
16:	A	B	C	D	___	46:	A	B	C	D	___
17:	A	B	C	D	___	47:	A	B	C	D	___
18:	A	B	C	D	___	48:	A	B	C	D	___
19:	A	B	C	D	___	49:	A	B	C	D	___
20:	A	B	C	D	___	50:	A	B	C	D	___
21:	A	B	C	D	___	51:	A	B	C	D	___
22:	A	B	C	D	___	52:	A	B	C	D	___
23:	A	B	C	D	___	53:	A	B	C	D	___
24:	A	B	C	D	___	54:	A	B	C	D	___
25:	A	B	C	D	___	55:	A	B	C	D	___
26:	A	B	C	D	___						
27:	A	B	C	D	___						
28:	A	B	C	D	___						
29:	A	B	C	D	___						
30:	A	B	C	D	___						

This Diagnostic Test is designed for you to assess your proficiency on each topic and NOT to mimic the actual test. Use your test results and identify areas of your strength and weakness to adjust your study plan and enhance your fundamental knowledge.

The length of the Diagnostic Tests is proven to be optimal for a single study session.

1. How far will an object have traveled after 3 s if it starts from rest and undergoes uniform acceleration given that it reaches 5 m/s after 1 s?

    A. 5 m   **B.** 10 m   **C.** 18 m   **D.** 22.5 m

2. A block is at rest on the surface of an inclined plane as the angle of elevation is gradually increased. Which statement is true about the normal force exerted by the plane on the block?

  A. It decreases as the angle of elevation increases
  B. It is inversely dependent on the coefficient of static friction between the block and plane
  C. It increases as the angle of elevation increases
  D. It is independent of the total amount of forces acting upon it

3. An aluminum rod 10 cm long and a steel rod 80 cm long are joined end-to-end. Both rods are at a temperature of 15 °C and have the same diameter. What is the increase in the length of the joined rod when the temperature is raised to 90 °C? (Use the coefficient of linear expansion α for aluminum $= 2.4 \times 10^{-5}$ K^{-1} and α for steel $= 1.2 \times 10^{-5}$ K^{-1})

    A. 0.7 mm   **B.** 1.1 mm   **C.** 0.9 mm   **D.** 0.8 mm

4. Which quantity is conserved when a falling object strikes the ground?

        I. Momentum of the object   II. KE of the object   III. Total energy

    A. I only   **B.** III only   **C.** I and III only   **D.** II and III only

5. If the frequency of the motion of a simple harmonic oscillator is doubled, by what factor does the maximum speed of the oscillator change?

    A. ½   **B.** $\sqrt{2}$ **C.** 4   **D.** 2

6. A standing wave of the third overtone is induced in a 1.2 m pipe that is open at one end and closed at the other. What is the number of antinodes in the standing wave? (Use the speed of sound $= 340$ m/s)

    A. 3   **B.** 4   **C.** 5   **D.** 6

7. A wire circle and solid circle of the same diameter are resting on the surface of the water. Which one can have the larger maximum mass without sinking?

  A. The solid circle, by a factor of 2   **C.** The wire circle, by a factor of 2
  B. The solid circle, by a factor of 4   **D.** They have the same maximum mass

8. Which statement applies to the 120 V circuit shown?

    A. 120 J of energy is given to each Coulomb of charge making up the current in the circuit

    B. 120 J of energy is equally shared among all Coulombs in the circuit at any instant

    C. 120 C of charge flow through the lamp every second

    D. 120 C of energy is converted to heat and light in the circuit every second

9. How many electrons pass a given point in a minute for a wire that has a current of 6 mA? (Use the charge of an electron = 1.602×10^{-19} C)

    A. 5.3×10^{14} electrons   **C.** 2.3×10^{18} electrons

    B. 5.4×10^{-15} electrons   **D.** 3.7×10^{12} electrons

10. How does an image appear if an object is placed in front of a convex mirror at a distance larger than twice the magnitude of the focal length of the mirror?

    A. upright and smaller   **C.** inverted and smaller

    B. inverted and larger   **D.** inverted and the same size

11. According to the de Broglie hypothesis, the idea of matter waves describes the wave-like behavior of:

    I. Positively-charged stationary particles

    II. Negatively-charged stationary particles

    III. Particles that are moving

    A. I only   **B.** II only   **C.** III only   **D.** I and II

12. Block I and block II slide on a frictionless level surface in one dimension and stick together when they make contact. Block II is also connected to a massless, ideal spring that extends horizontally and is connected to a wall. Initially, block II is at rest, and block I approaches from the right. The two blocks move before oscillating. Take the system to be the two blocks and the spring. Which statement is true?

    I. Momentum is conserved

    II. The sum of the spring PE and KE is conserved

    III. KE is conserved

    A. I only   **B.** II only   **C.** I and II only   **D.** II and III only

---

13. Ignoring air resistance, when a pebble is thrown straight upward with an initial speed v, it reaches a maximum height h. At what speed should the pebble be thrown upward vertically for it to go twice as high?

    A. $16v$ **B.** $8v$ **C.** $4v$ **D.** $\sqrt{2}v$

14. If the mass and the length of a simple pendulum are doubled, the period:

    A. increases by a factor of 4   **C.** remains the same
    B. increases by a factor of $\sqrt{2}$ **D.** increases by a factor of 2

15. Which type of organ pipe can produce only odd harmonics?

    I. open   II. long   III. closed

    A. I only   **B.** II only   **C.** III only   **D.** II and III only

16. Determine the speed at which water exits a tank through a very small hole in the bottom of the tank that is 20 cm in diameter and filled with water to a height of 50 cm. (Use the acceleration due to gravity $g = 9.8$ m/s^2)

    A. 3.1 m/s   **B.** 17.8 m/s   **C.** 31.2 m/s   **D.** 21.6 m/s

17. While being pulled apart, the plates of a parallel-plate capacitor are maintained with constant voltage by a battery. What happens to the strength of the electric field between the plates during this process?

    A. Remains constant   **C.** Increases by the $\sqrt{}$voltage
    B. Decreases   **D.** Increases by the (distance)^2

18. An electron and a deuteron (^{2}H nucleus) are placed in an electric field (E_0) between the plates of a charged parallel-plate capacitor. Ignoring the force of gravity, how does the magnitude of the force on an electron F_{elec} compare with the force on the deuteron F_d? (Use the mass of proton $m_{proton} \approx 1,850 \times m_{electron}$)

    A. $F_{elec} = \frac{1}{2}F_d$ **B.** $F_{elec} = 1,850\ F_d$ **C.** $F_{elec} = F_d$ **D.** $F_{elec} = 3,700\ F_d$

19. A 1.8×10^{14} Hz electromagnetic wave propagates in CCl$_4$ with a speed of 2.43×10^8 m/s. The wave then leaves the CCl$_4$ and enters a vacuum. What is the wavelength of the wave in the vacuum? (Use the speed of light in a vacuum $c = 3 \times 10^8$ m/s)

    A. 2,260 nm   **B.** 1,280 nm   **C.** 1,040 nm   **D.** 1,667 nm

20. How much energy does a photon of wavelength 580 nm have? (Use Planck's constant $h = 6.626 \times 10^{-34}$ J·s and the speed of light $c = 3 \times 10^8$ m/s)

    A. 6.4×10^{-32} J   **B.** 8.8 eV   **C.** 3.4×10^{-19} J   **D.** 1.3×10^{-19} eV

21. At constant pressure and temperature, Graham's Law states that the diffusion rate for a gas molecule is:

    A. inversely proportional to √mass   **C.** proportional to the log of the mass

    B. inversely proportional to mass   **D.** proportional to the mass

22. A skier falls while skiing, and one ski, with weight *w*, loosens and slides down an icy slope which makes an angle *θ* with the horizontal. Ignoring friction, what is the force that pushes the ski down the hill?

    A. $w^2 \cos \theta$ **B.** $w \sin \theta$ **C.** w **D.** $w \cos \theta$

23. By what factor does the velocity of sound in a gas change when the absolute temperature of that gas is doubled?

    A. It increases by 4   **B.** It increases by √2   **C.** It remains the same   **D.** It increases by 2

24. A pipe with a circular cross-section has water flowing within it from the point I to point II. The radius of the pipe at point I is 12 cm, while the radius at point II is 6 cm. If at the end of point I the flow rate is 0.09 m³/s, what is the flow rate at the end of point II?

    A. 0.6 m³/s   **B.** 0.09 m³/s   **C.** 0.15 m³/s   **D.** 1.2 m³/s

25. What is the path for an electron moving on the page toward the right when subjected to a magnetic field pointing out of the page?

    A. Curves upward (path X)
    B. Continues straight ahead (path Y)
    C. Curves downward (path Z)
    D. Decelerates

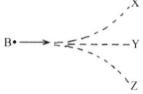

26. A positively-charged particle is traveling on a path parallel to a straight wire that contains a current. Which change increases the magnetic field at a point along the particle's path?

    A. Increasing the speed of the particle
    B. Increasing the distance of the particle from the wire
    C. Decreasing the distance of the particle from the wire
    D. Decreasing the current in the wire

27. If parallel light rays were incident on a lens of power 4 D, which statement is true for the rays on the other side of the lens?

    A. The rays diverge as if from a point 4 m behind the lens
    B. The rays diverge as if from a point ¼ m in front of the lens
    C. The rays converge with a focal length of ¼ m
    D. The rays converge with a focal length of 4 m

28. The α particle has twice the electric charge of the β particle but deflects less than the β in a magnetic field because it:

   A. is smaller   **B.** has less inertia   **C.** moves slower   **D.** has more inertia

29. Which statement explains why a sponge ball of the same size as a marble ball takes a longer time to reach the ground?

   A. Air resistance is more significant for the sponge ball than for the marble
   B. There is a stronger gravitational force between the marble ball and the ground
   C. The force of gravity only acts on the marble ball
   D. The force of gravity on the sponge ball is less than that on the marble ball

30. A vehicle is driving in reverse at 6 m/s. After 10 s of uniform acceleration, the vehicle is going forward at 12 m/s. What is the acceleration?

   A. 1.8 m/s^2 **B.** 2.5 m/s^2 **C.** 3 m/s^2 **D.** 4.5 m/s^2

31. What happens to the atomic mass number of a nucleus when a β^- particle is emitted from an unstable nucleus?

   A. Decreases by 2   **C.** Decreases by 1
   B. Remains the same   **D.** Increases by 1

32. The brakes of a car are applied abruptly whereby the car skids a certain distance on a straight, level road. If the car had been traveling twice as fast, what is the distance that the car would have skidded, under the same conditions?

   A. $\sqrt{2}$ times farther   **B.** Half as far   **C.** 4 times farther   **D.** Twice as far

33. A pair of narrow slits, separated by 1.8 mm, is illuminated by a monochromatic light source. Light waves arrive at the two slits in phase. A fringe pattern is observed on a screen 4.8 m from the slits. There are 5 bright fringes per cm on the screen. What is the λ of the monochromatic light?

   A. 750 nm   **B.** 600 nm   **C.** 650 nm   **D.** 700 nm

34. A 0.4 kg ice cube at 0 °C has sufficient heat added to it to cause total melting, and the resulting water is heated to 60 °C. How much heat is added? (Use the latent heat of fusion for water L_f = 334,000 J/kg, the latent heat of vaporization for water L_v = 2.256 × 10^6 J/kg and the specific heat c = 4.186 × 10^3 J/kg·°C)

   A. 56 kJ   **B.** 84 kJ   **C.** 470 kJ   **D.** 234 kJ

35. A concave spherical mirror has a focal length of 20 cm. Where, relative to the mirror, is the image located if an object is placed 10 cm in front of the mirror?

    A. 7.5 cm in front   **C.** 20 cm in front

    B. 7.5 cm behind   **D.** 20 cm behind

36. For a DC circuit, what physical quantity does the slope of the graph represent?

    A. potential   **C.** 1 / resistance

    B. 1 / potential   **D.** resistance

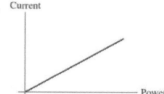

37. Two identical metal balls, each with a radius of 0.15 m, are located 4 m apart, are neutral and have an electrical potential of zero. Electrons are transferred as an isolated system from ball I to II. After the transfer, ball I has acquired a potential of 8,000 V and ball II a potential of –8,000 V. How much work is required to transfer 10^{-10} C from ball I to ball II?

    A. -1.6×10^{-6} J   **B.** -4.7×10^{-7} J   **C.** 7.1×10^{-5} J   **D.** 3.3×10^{-6} J

38. Which answer best describes what happens to a spherical lead ball with a density of 11.3 g/cm^3 when it is placed in a tub of mercury with a density of 13.6 g/cm^3?

    A. It sinks slowly to the bottom of the mercury

    B. It floats with about 17% of its volume above the surface of the mercury

    C. It floats with its top exactly even with the surface of the mercury

    D. It floats with about 83% of its volume above the surface of the mercury

39. An ambulance is moving directly towards a police station at 50 m/s. The ambulance emits a siren at 420 Hz. What is the frequency of the signal heard by police at the station? (Use the speed of sound v_s = 350 m/s)

    A. 280 Hz   **B.** 330 Hz   **C.** 420 Hz   **D.** 490 Hz

40. A simple pendulum has a period of 3 s on Earth. If it is taken to the Moon, where the acceleration due to gravity is 1/6 of that on Earth, what is its period on the Moon?

    A. 0.5 s   **B.** 3.7 s   **C.** 7.3 s   **D.** 5 s

41. An ideal, massless spring with a spring constant of 3 N/m has a resting length 0.25 m. The spring is hanging from the ceiling when a 1.2 kg block is added to the bottom end of the spring. What is the length of the spring at static equilibrium? (Use the acceleration due to gravity g = 10 m/s^2)

    A. 2.35 m   **B.** 1.45 m   **C.** 4.96 m   **D.** 4.25 m

42. A boy jumps with a velocity of 20 m/s at an angle of 25° above the horizontal. What is the horizontal component of the boy's velocity?

    A. 8.7 m/s   **B.** 14.6 m/s   **C.** 18.1 m/s   **D.** 14.9 m/s

43. Which of the following is true about the force due to friction when a block is sliding down the surface of an inclined plane while the elevation angle is gradually decreased?

    A. Increases and the weight of the block remains constant
    B. Increases and the weight of the block increases
    C. Increases and the weight of the block decreases
    D. Decreases and the weight of the block remains constant

44. The average velocity of an object is equal to the instantaneous velocity only when the velocity is:

    I. increasing at a constant rate
    II. constant
    III. decreasing at a constant rate

    A. I only   **B.** II only   **C.** III only   **D.** I and II only

45. A sphere of surface area 1.25 m^2 and emissivity 1 is at a temperature of 100 °C. What is the rate at which it radiates heat into space? (Use the Stefan-Boltzmann constant $\sigma = 5.67 \times 10^{-8}$ W/m^{2}K^4)

    A. 1.4 kW   **B.** 7.6 kW   **C.** 27.3 kW   **D.** 0.63 kW

46. Power is:

    I. the rate at which work is done
    II. work per unit of time
    III. the rate at which energy is expended

    A. I only   **B.** II only   **C.** III only   **D.** I, II and III

47. Which of the following increases when a sound becomes louder?

    A. Amplitude   **B.** Period   **C.** Frequency   **D.** Wavelength

48. A given distance separates two particles of like charge. What is the resulting force between the particles if the charge on each particle and the distance between the two particles are doubled?

    A. 4 × original   **B.** 2 × original   **C.** equal to the original   **D.** √2 × original

49. If an object is placed inside the focal point of a diverging lens, the image is:

   A. virtual, inverted and enlarged
   B. real, upright and enlarged

   C. real, inverted and enlarged
   D. virtual, upright and reduced

50. The velocity vs. time graph plots the velocities of projectiles A and B along the same straight path. Which projectile reverses direction?

   A. Projectile A
   B. Projectile B

   C. Cannot be determined
   D. Both projectiles

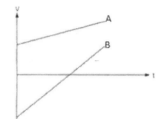

51. Which is an example of a reversible process?

   A. Hooke's cycle
   B. Carnot cycle

   C. Swinn cycle
   D. Boltzmann's cycle

52. In which medium do sound waves travel the fastest?

   A. Cool air   **B.** Warm air   **C.** A vacuum   **D.** Icy cold air

53. The Bernoulli Equation is described by: $P_1 + \frac{1}{2}\rho v_1^2 + \rho g h_1 = P_2 + \frac{1}{2}\rho v_2^2 + \rho g h_2$. What is the origin of the relation within this expression?

   A. the conservation of energy for a moving fluid
   B. the continuity principle for moving particles
   C. the conservation of linear momentum across an uneven surface
   D. Newton's Third Law that relates equal action and reaction

54. How do the resistances of two copper wires compare where one has twice the length and twice the cross-sectional area?

   A. The longer wire has one fourth the resistance of the shorter wire
   B. The shorter wire has $\sqrt{2}$ times the resistance of the longer wire
   C. The shorter wire has twice the resistance of the longer wire
   D. Both wires have the same resistance

55. Which type of emission from the reactant nucleus causes the transformation:

   $$^{15}_{8}\text{O} \rightarrow {}^{15}_{7}\text{N}?$$

   A. Neutron emission
   B. Alpha particle

   C. Positron emission
   D. Proton emission

Diagnostic test #4

1	D	Translational motion	31	B	Atomic nucleus & electronic structure
2	A	Force & motion	32	C	Work & energy of point object systems
3	C	Thermodynamics	33	A	Periodic motion
4	B	Work & energy of point object systems	34	D	Thermodynamics
5	D	Periodic motion	35	D	Light & geometrical optics
6	B	Sound	36	B	Circuit elements
7	C	Fluids & gas phase	37	A	Electrostatics & magnetism
8	A	Electrostatics & magnetism	38	B	Fluids & gas phase
9	C	Circuit elements	39	D	Sound
10	A	Light & geometrical optics	40	C	Periodic motion
11	C	Atomic nucleus & electronic structure	41	D	Work & energy of point object systems
12	B	Work & energy of point object systems	42	C	Equilibrium & momentum
13	D	Work & energy of point object systems	43	A	Force & motion
14	B	Periodic motion	44	B	Translational motion
15	C	Sound	45	A	Thermodynamics
16	A	Fluids & gas phase	46	D	Work & energy of point object systems
17	B	Electrostatics & magnetism	47	A	Sound
18	C	Circuit elements	48	C	Electrostatics & magnetism
19	D	Light & geometrical optics	49	D	Light & geometrical optics
20	C	Atomic nucleus & electronic structure	50	B	Translational motion
21	A	Thermodynamics	51	B	Thermodynamics
22	B	Force & motion	52	B	Periodic motion
23	B	Sound	53	A	Fluids & gas phase
24	B	Fluids & gas phase	54	D	Circuit elements
25	A	Electrostatics & magnetism	55	C	Atomic nucleus & electronic structure
26	C	Circuit elements			
27	C	Light & geometrical optics			
28	D	Atomic nucleus & electronic structure			
29	A	Translational motion			
30	A	Translational motion			

MCAT Physics

Topical
Practice Questions

Translational Motion

1. Starting from rest, how long does it take for a sports car to reach 60 mi/h if it has an average acceleration of 13.1 mi/h·s?

    A. 6.6 s   **B.** 3.1 s   **C.** 4.5 s   **D.** 4.6 s

2. A cannonball is fired with an initial speed of 20 m/s at a 30° angle with the horizontal. Ignoring air resistance, how long does it take the cannonball to reach the top of its trajectory? (Use the acceleration due to gravity $g = 10$ m/s^2)

    A. 0.5 s   **B.** 1 s   **C.** 1.5 s   **D.** 2 s

3. Darlene starts her car from rest and accelerates at a constant 2.5 m/s^2 for 9 s to get to her cruising speed. She then drives for 15 minutes at constant speed. She arrives at her destination, which is a straight-line distance of 31.5 km away, exactly 1.25 hours later. What is her average velocity during the interval of 1.25 hours?

    A. 3 m/s   **B.** 7 m/s   **C.** 18 m/s   **D.** 22.5 m/s

4. Which of the following cannot be negative?

    A. Instantaneous speed   **C.** Acceleration of gravity
    B. Instantaneous acceleration   **D.** Displacement

5. How far does a car travel while accelerating from 5 m/s to 21 m/s at a rate of 3 m/s^2?

    A. 15 m   **B.** 21 m   **C.** 69 m   **D.** 105 m

6. Acceleration is sometimes expressed in multiples of g, where g is the acceleration due to gravity. How many g are experienced, on average, by the driver in a car crash if the car's velocity changes from 30 m/s to 0 m/s in 0.15 s? (Use acceleration due to gravity $g = 9.8$ m/s^2)

    A. 22 g **B.** 28 g **C.** 20 g **D.** 14 g

7. Ignoring air resistance, how many forces are acting on a bullet fired horizontally after it leaves the rifle?

    A. Two (one from the gunpowder explosion and one from gravity)
    B. One (from the motion of the bullet)
    C. One (from the gunpowder explosion)
    D. One (from the pull of gravity)

8. Suppose that a car traveling to the East begins to slow down as it approaches a traffic light. Which of the following statements about its acceleration is correct?

    A. The acceleration is towards the East
    B. The acceleration is towards the West
    C. Since the car is slowing, its acceleration is positive
    D. The acceleration is zero

9. On a planet where the acceleration due to gravity is 20 m/s^2, a freely falling object increases its speed each second by about:

    A. 20 m/s   **B.** 10 m/s   **C.** 30 m/s   **D.** 40 m/s

10. What is a car's acceleration if it accelerates uniformly in one direction from 15 m/s to 40 m/s in 10 s?

    A. 1.75 m/s^2 **B.** 2.5 m/s^2 **C.** 3.5 m/s^2 **D.** 7.6 m/s^2

11. If the fastest a person can drive is 65 mi/h, what is the longest time she can stop for lunch if she wants to travel 540 mi in 9.8 h?

    A. 1 h   **B.** 2.4 h   **C.** 1.5 h   **D.** 2 h

12. What is a racecar's average velocity if it completes one lap around a 500 m track in 10 s?

    A. 10 m/s   **B.** 0 m/s   **C.** 5 m/s   **D.** 20 m/s

13. What is a ball's net displacement after 5 s if it is initially rolling up a slight incline at 0.2 m/s and decelerates uniformly at 0.05 m/s^2?

    A. 0.38 m   **B.** 0.6 m   **C.** 0.9 m   **D.** 1.2 m

14. What does the slope of a line connecting two points on a velocity vs. time graph represent?

    A. Change in acceleration   **C.** Average acceleration
    B. Instantaneous acceleration   **D.** Instantaneous velocity

15. An airplane needs to reach a speed of 210.0 km/h to take off. On a 1,800.0 m runway, what is the minimum acceleration necessary for the plane to reach this speed, assuming acceleration is constant?

    A. 0.78 m/s^2 **B.** 0.95 m/s^2 **C.** 1.47 m/s^2 **D.** 1.1 m/s^2

16. A test rocket is fired straight up from rest with a net acceleration of 22 m/s². What maximum elevation does the rocket reach if the motor turns off after 4 s, but the rocket continues to coast upward? (Use the acceleration due to gravity $g = 10$ m/s²)

    A. 408 m   **B.** 320 m   **C.** 357 m   **D.** 563 m

17. Without any reference to direction, how fast an object moves refers to its:

    A. speed   **B.** impulse   **C.** momentum   **D.** velocity

18. Ignoring air resistance, a 10 kg rock and a 20 kg rock are dropped at the same time. If the 10 kg rock falls with acceleration a, what is the acceleration of the 20 kg rock?

    A. $a / 2$ **B.** a **C.** $2a$ **D.** $4a$

19. As an object falls freely, its magnitude of:

    I. velocity increases   II. acceleration increases   III. displacement increases

    A. I only   **B.** I and II only   **C.** II and III only   **D.** I and III only

20. A man stands in an elevator that is ascending at a constant velocity. What forces are being exerted on the man, and which direction does the net force point?

    A. Gravity pointing downward, normal force from the floor pointing upward, and tension force from the elevator cable pointing upward; net force points upward
    B. Gravity pointing downward and the normal force from the floor pointing upward; net force points upward
    C. Gravity pointing downward and normal force from the floor pointing upward; net force is 0
    D. Gravity pointing downward; net force is 0

21. A football kicker is attempting a field goal from 44 m away, and the ball just clears the lower bar with a time of flight of 2.9 s. What was the initial speed of the ball if the angle of the kick was 45° with the horizontal?

    A. 37 m/s   **B.** 2.5 m/s   **C.** 18.3 m/s   **D.** 21.4 m/s

22. Ignoring air resistance, if a rock, starting at rest, is dropped from a cliff and strikes the ground with an impact velocity of 14 m/s, from what height was it dropped? (Use acceleration due to gravity $g = 10$ m/s²)

    A. 10 m   **B.** 30 m   **C.** 45 m   **D.** 70 m

23. An SUV is traveling at 20 m/s. Then Joseph steps on the accelerator pedal, accelerating at a constant 1.4 m/s² for 7 s. How far does he travel during these 7 s?

    A. 205 m   **B.** 174 m   **C.** 143 m   **D.** 158 m

24. Which of the following is NOT a scalar?

  A. temperature   **B.** distance   **C.** mass   **D.** force

25. Two identical balls (A and B) fall from rest from different heights to the ground. Ignoring air resistance, what is the ratio of the heights from which A and B fall if ball B takes twice as long as ball A to reach the ground?

  A. $1 : \sqrt{2}$ **B.** $1 : 4$ **C.** $1 : 2$ **D.** $1 : 8$

26. How far does a car travel in 10 s when it accelerates uniformly in one direction from 5 m/s to 30 m/s?

  A. 175 m   **B.** 25 m   **C.** 250 m   **D.** 650 m

27. Which graph represents an acceleration of zero?

  A. I only   **C.** I and II only
  B. II only   **D.** II and III only

28. Doubling the distance between an orbiting satellite and the Earth results in what change in the gravitational attraction between the two?

  A. Twice as much   **C.** One half as much
  B. Four times as much   **D.** One fourth as much

29. An object is moving in a straight line. Consider its motion during some interval of time: under what conditions is it possible for the instantaneous velocity of the object at some point during the interval to be equal to the average velocity over the interval?

    I. When velocity is constant during the interval
    II. When velocity is increasing at a constant rate during the interval
    III. When velocity is increasing at an irregular rate during the interval

  A. II only   **C.** II and III only
  B. I and III only   **D.** I, II and III

30. A freely falling object on Earth, 10 s after starting from rest, has a speed of about: (Use the acceleration due to gravity $g = 10$ m/s^2)

  A. 10 m/s   **B.** 20 m/s   **C.** 100 m/s   **D.** 150 m/s

31. A truck travels a certain distance at a constant velocity v for time t. If the truck travels three times as fast, covering the same distance, then by what factor does the time of travel in relation to t change?

    A. Increases by 3   **B.** Decreases by 3   **C.** Decreases by $\sqrt{3}$ **D.** Increases by 9

32. Assuming equal rates of acceleration, how much farther would Steve travel if he braked from 59 mi/h to rest than from 29 mi/h to rest?

    A. 2 times farther   **C.** 4 times farther

    B. 16 times farther   **D.** 3.2 times farther

33. What is the average speed of a racehorse if the horse does one lap around a 400 m track in 20 s?

    A. 0 m/s   **B.** 7.5 m/s   **C.** 15 m/s   **D.** 20 m/s

34. What was a car's initial velocity if the car is traveling up a slight slope while decelerating at 0.1 m/s^2 and comes to a stop after 5 s?

    A. 0.5 m/s   **B.** 0.25 m/s   **C.** 2 m/s   **D.** 1.5 m/s

35. Average velocity equals the average of an object's initial and final velocity when acceleration is:

    A. constantly decreasing   **C.** constant

    B. constantly increasing   **D.** equal to zero

36. Ignoring air resistance, compared to a rock dropped from the same point, how much earlier does a thrown rock strike the ground if it is thrown downward with an initial velocity of 10 m/s from the top of a 300 m building? (Use acceleration due to gravity $g = 9.8$ m/s^2)

    A. 0.75 s   **B.** 0.33 s   **C.** 0.66 s   **D.** 0.95 s

37. With all other factors equal, what happens to the acceleration if the unbalanced force on an object of a given mass is doubled?

    A. Increased by one-fourth   **C.** Increased fourfold

    B. Increased by one-half   **D.** Doubled

38. How fast an object is changing speed or direction of travel is a property of motion known as:

    A. velocity   **B.** acceleration   **C.** speed   **D.** flow

39. Which statement concerning a car's acceleration must be correct if a car traveling to the North (+*y* direction) begins to slow down as it approaches a stop sign?

A. Acceleration is positive

B. Acceleration is zero

C. Acceleration is negative

D. Acceleration decreases in magnitude as the car slows

40. For the velocity vs. time graph of a basketball player traveling up and down the court in a straight-line path, what is the total distance run by the player in the 10 s?

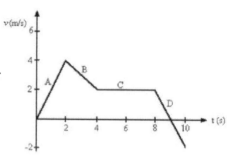

A. 20 m

C. 14 m

B. 22 m

D. 18 m

41. At the same time that a bullet is dropped into a river from a high bridge, another bullet is fired from a gun, straight down towards the water. Ignoring air resistance, the acceleration just before striking the water:

A. is greater for the dropped bullet

B. is greater for the fired bullet

C. is the same for each bullet

D. depends on how high the bullets started

42. Sarah starts her car from rest and accelerates at a constant 2.5 m/s² for 9 s to get to her cruising speed. What was her final velocity?

A. 22.5 m/s **B.** 12.3 m/s **C.** 4.6 m/s **D.** 8.5 m/s

43. A bat hits a baseball, and the baseball's direction is completely reversed, and its speed is doubled. If the actual time of contact with the bat is 0.45 s, what is the ratio of the acceleration to the original velocity?

A. $-2.5 \text{ s}^{-1} : 1$ **B.** $-0.15 \text{ s}^{-1} : 1$ **C.** $-9.8 \text{ s}^{-1} : 1$ **D.** $-6.7 \text{ s}^{-1} : 1$

44. A 2 kg weight is thrown vertically upward from the surface of the Moon at a speed of 3.2 m/s, and it returns to its starting point in 4 s. What is the magnitude of acceleration due to gravity on the Moon?

A. 0.8 m/s² **B.** 1.6 m/s² **C.** 3.7 m/s² **D.** 8.4 m/s²

45. What is the change in velocity for a bird that is cruising at 1.5 m/s and then accelerates at a constant 0.3 m/s² for 3 s?

A. 0.9 m/s **B.** 0.6 m/s **C.** 1.6 m/s **D.** 0.3 m/s

46. All of the following are vectors, except:

A. velocity **B.** displacement **C.** acceleration **D.** mass

Questions **47-49** are based on the following:

A toy rocket is launched vertically from ground level where $y = 0$ m, at time $t = 0$ s. The rocket engine provides constant upward acceleration during the burn phase. At the instant of engine burnout, the rocket has risen to 64 m and acquired a velocity of 60 m/s. The rocket continues to rise in unpowered flight, reaches the maximum height and then falls back to the ground. (Use the acceleration due to gravity $g = 9.8$ m/s^2)

47. What is the maximum height reached by the rocket?

   A. 274 m   **B.** 248 m   **C.** 223 m   **D.** 120 m

48. What is the upward acceleration of the rocket during the burn phase?

   A. 9.9 m/s^2 **B.** 4.8 m/s^2 **C.** 28 m/s^2 **D.** 11.8 m/s^2

49. What is the time interval during which the rocket engine provides upward acceleration?

   A. 1.5 s   **B.** 1.9 s   **C.** 2.3 s   **D.** 2.1 s

50. A car accelerates uniformly from rest along a straight track that has markers spaced at equal distances along it. As it passes Marker 2, the car reaches a speed of 140 km/h. Where on the track is the car when it is traveling at 70 km/h?

   A. Close to Marker 2   **C.** Before Marker 1
   B. Between Marker 1 and Marker 2   **D.** Close to the starting point

51. What are the two measurements necessary for calculating average speed?

   A. Distance and time   **C.** Velocity and time
   B. Distance and acceleration   **D.** Velocity and acceleration

52. A pedestrian traveling at speed v covers a distance x during a time interval t. If a bicycle travels at speed $3v$, how much time does it take the bicycle to travel the same distance?

   A. $t / 3$ **B.** $t - 3$ **C.** $t + 3^2$ **D.** $3t$

53. Ignoring air resistance, how much time passes before a ball strikes the ground if it is thrown straight upward with a velocity of 39 m/s? (Use acceleration due to gravity $g = 9.8$ m/s^2)

    A. 2.2 s   **B.** 8 s   **C.** 12 s   **D.** 4 s

54. A particle travels to the right along a horizontal axis with a constantly decreasing speed. Which one of the following describes the direction of the particle's acceleration?

    A. ↑   **B.** ↓   **C.** →   **D.** ←

55. Larry is carrying a 25-kg package at a constant velocity of 1.8 m/s across a room for 12 s. What is the work done by Larry on the package during the 12 s? (Use acceleration due to gravity $g = 10$ m/s^2)

    A. 0 J   **B.** 280 J   **C.** 860 J   **D.** 2,200 J

56. What does the slope of a tangent line at a time on a velocity vs. time graph represent?

    A. Instantaneous acceleration   **C.** Instantaneous velocity
    B. Average acceleration   **D.** Position

57. A car is traveling North at 17.7 m/s. After 12 s, its velocity is 14.1 m/s in the same direction. What is the magnitude and direction of the car's average acceleration?

    A. 0.3 m/s^2, North   **C.** 0.3 m/s^2, South
    B. 2.7 m/s^2, North   **D.** 3.6 m/s^2, South

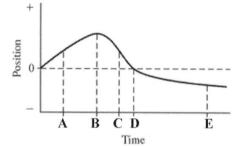

58. The graph below shows the position of an object as a function of time. The letters A –E represent particular moments in time. At which moment in time is the speed of the object the highest?

    A. A   **B.** B   **C.** C   **D.** D

59. At speed less than terminal velocity, what is happening to the speed of an object falling toward the surface of the Earth?

    A. Decreasing at a decreasing rate   **C.** Decreasing
    B. Increasing at a decreasing rate   **D.** Constant

60. How far does a car travel if it starts from rest and accelerates at a constant 2 m/s^2 for 10 s, then travels with the constant speed it has achieved for another 10 s and finally slows to a stop with a constant deceleration of magnitude 2 m/s^2?

    A. 150 m   **B.** 200 m   **C.** 350 m   **D.** 400 m

Translational Motion

1: D	11: C	21: D	31: B	41: C	51: A
2: B	12: B	22: A	32: C	42: A	52: A
3: B	13: A	23: B	33: D	43: D	53: B
4: A	14: C	24: D	34: A	44: B	54: D
5: C	15: B	25: B	35: C	45: A	55: A
6: C	16: D	26: A	36: D	46: D	56: A
7: D	17: A	27: C	37: D	47: B	57: C
8: B	18: B	28: D	38: B	48: C	58: C
9: A	19: D	29: D	39: C	49: D	59: B
10: B	20: C	30: C	40: A	50: C	60: D

Force and Motion

1. A boy attaches a weight to a string, which he swings counter-clockwise in a horizontal circle. Which path does the weight follow when the string breaks at point P?

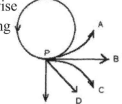

   A. path A   **C.** path C

   B. path B   **D.** path D

2. A garment bag hangs from a clothesline. The tension in the clothesline is 10 N on the right side of the garment bag and 10 N on the left side of the garment bag. The clothesline makes an angle of 60° from vertical. What is the mass of the garment bag? (Use the acceleration due to gravity g = 10.0 m/s^2)

   A. 0.5 kg   **B.** 8 kg   **C.** 4 kg   **D.** 1 kg

3. A sheet of paper can be withdrawn from under a milk carton without toppling the carton if the paper is jerked away quickly. This demonstrates:

   A. the inertia of the milk carton

   B. that gravity tends to hold the milk carton secure

   C. there is an action-reaction pair of forces

   D. that the milk carton has no acceleration

4. A car of mass *m* is going up a shallow slope with an angle *θ* to the horizontal when the driver suddenly applies the brakes. The car skids as it comes to a stop. The coefficient of static friction between the tires and the road is *μ*$_s$, and the coefficient of kinetic friction is *μ*$_k$. Which expression represents the normal force on the car?

   A. *mg* tan *θ*   **B.** *mg* sin *θ*   **C.** *mg* cos *θ*   **D.** *mg*

5. A 27 kg object is accelerated at a rate of 1.7 m/s^2. How much force does the object experience?

   A. 62 N   **B.** 46 N   **C.** 7 N   **D.** 18 N

6. How are two identical masses moving if they are attached by a light string that passes over a small pulley? Assume that the table and the pulley are frictionless.

   A. With an acceleration equal to *g*

   B. With an acceleration greater than *g*

   C. At a constant speed

   D. With an acceleration less than *g*

7. An object is moving to the right in a straight line. The net force acting on the object is also directed to the right, but the magnitude of the force is decreasing with time. What happens to the object?

    A. Continues to move to the right with its speed increasing with time

    B. Continues to move to the right with a constant speed

    C. Continues to move to the right with its speed decreasing with time

    D. Continues to move to the right, slowing quickly to a stop

8. A crate is sliding down an inclined ramp at a constant speed of 0.55 m/s. Where does the vector sum of all the forces acting on this crate point?

    A. Perpendicular to the ramp   **C.** Vertically upward

    B. Vertically downward   **D.** None of the above

9. Consider an inclined plane that makes an angle θ with the horizontal. What is the relationship between the length of the ramp L and the vertical height of the ramp h?

    A. $h = L \sin \theta$ **B.** $h = L \tan \theta$ **C.** $L = h \sin \theta$ **D.** $h = L \cos \theta$

10. What is the force exerted by the table on a 2 kg book resting on it? (Use the acceleration due to gravity $g = 10$ m/s^2)

    A. 100 N   **B.** 20 N   **C.** 10 N   **D.** 0 N

11. Sean is pulling his son in a toy wagon. His son and the wagon together are 60 kg. For 3 s Sean exerts a force which uniformly accelerates the wagon from 1.5 m/s to 3.5 m/s. What is the acceleration of the wagon with his son?

    A. 0.67 m/s^2 **B.** 0.84 m/s^2 **C.** 1.66 m/s^2 **D.** 15.32 m/s^2

12. When an object moves in uniform circular motion, the direction of its acceleration is:

    A. directed away from the center of its circular path

    B. dependent on its speed

    C. directed toward the center of its circular path

    D. in the same direction as its velocity vector

13. What happens to a moving object in the absence of an external force?

    A. Gradually accelerates until it reaches its terminal velocity, at which point it continues at a constant velocity

    B. Moves with constant velocity

    C. Stops immediately

    D. Slows and eventually stops

14. A force of 1 N causes a 1 kg mass to have an acceleration of 1 m/s². From this information, a force of 9 N applied to a 9 kg mass would have what magnitude of acceleration?

    A. 18 m/s²   **B.** 9 m/s²   **C.** 1 m/s²   **D.** 3 m/s²

15. Which of the following statements is true about an object in two-dimensional projectile motion with no air resistance?

    A. The acceleration of the object is zero at its highest point
    B. The horizontal acceleration is always zero, and the vertical acceleration is always a nonzero constant downward
    C. The velocity is always in the same direction as the acceleration
    D. The acceleration of the object is $+g$ when the object is rising and $-g$ when it is falling

16. A can of paint with a mass of 10 kg hangs from a rope. If the can is to be pulled up to a rooftop with a constant velocity of 0.5 m/s, what must the tension on the rope be? (Use the acceleration due to gravity $g = 10$ m/s²)

    A. 100 N   **B.** 40 N   **C.** 0 N   **D.** 120 N

17. What is the magnitude of the force exerted on a 1,000 kg object that accelerates at 2 m/s²?

    A. 500 N   **B.** 1,000 N   **C.** 1,200 N   **D.** 2,000 N

18. A 1,300 kg car is driven at a constant speed of 4 m/s and turns to the right on a curve on the road, which has an effective radius of 4 m. What is the acceleration of the car?

    A. 0 m/s²   **B.** 3 m/s²   **C.** 4 m/s²   **D.** 9.8 m/s²

19. A block of mass m is resting on a 20° slope. The block has coefficients of friction $\mu_s = 0.55$ and $\mu_k = 0.45$ with the surface. Block m is connected via a massless string over a massless, frictionless pulley to a hanging 2 kg block. What is the minimum mass of block m so that it does not slip? (Use the acceleration due to gravity $g = 9.8$ m/s²)

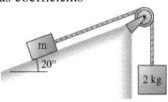

    A. 2.3 kg   **B.** 1.3 kg   **C.** 3.7 kg   **D.** 4.1 kg

20. As shown in the figure to the right, two identical masses, attached by a light cord passing over a massless, frictionless pulley on an Atwood's machine, are hanging at different heights. If the two masses are suddenly released, then the:

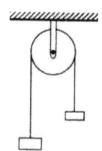

    A. lower mass moves down   **C.** higher mass moves down
    B. masses remain stationary   **D.** motion is unpredictable

21. When Victoria jumps up in the air, which of the following statements is the most accurate?

    A. The ground cannot exert the upward force necessary to lift her into the air, because the ground is stationary. Rather, Victoria is propelled into the air by the internal force of her muscles acting on her body

    B. When Victoria pushes down on the Earth with force greater than her weight, the Earth pushes back with the same magnitude force and propels her into the air

    C. Victoria is propelled up by the upward force exerted by the ground, but this force cannot be greater than her weight

    D. The Earth exerts an upward force on Victoria that is stronger than the downward force she exerts on the Earth; therefore Victoria is able to spring up

22. If a feather is pounded with a hammer, which experiences a greater force?

    A. The magnitude of the force is always the same on both

    B. If the feather moves, then it felt the greater force

    C. Depends on the force with which the hammer strikes the feather

    D. Always the hammer

23. A block is moving down a slope of a frictionless inclined plane. Compared to the weight of the block, what is the force parallel to the surface of the plane experienced by the block?

    A. Greater   **B.** Unrelated   **C.** Less than   **D.** Equal

24. A package falls off a truck that is moving at 30 m/s. Ignoring air resistance, the horizontal speed of the package just before it hits the ground is:

    A. 0 m/s   **B.** 30 m/s   **C.** $\sqrt{60}$ m/s   **D.** $\sqrt{30}$ m/s

25. A carousel with the radius r is turning counterclockwise at a frequency f. How does the velocity of a seat on the carousel change when f is doubled?

    A. Increases by a factor of $2r$ **C.** Remains unchanged

    B. Increases by a factor of r **D.** Doubles

26. What is the mass of a car if it takes 4,500 N to accelerate it at a rate of 5 m/s^2?

    A. 900 kg   **B.** 1,320 kg   **C.** 620 kg   **D.** 460 kg

27. Steve is standing facing forward in a moving bus. What force causes Steve to suddenly move forward when the bus comes to an abrupt stop?

    A. Force due to the air pressure inside the previously moving bus

    B. Force due to kinetic friction between Steve and the floor of the bus

    C. Force due to stored kinetic energy

    D. No forces were responsible for Steve's movement

28. A plastic ball in a liquid is acted upon by its weight and a buoyant force. The weight of the ball is 4.4 N. The buoyant force of 8.4 N acts vertically upward. An external force acting on the ball maintains it in a state of rest. What is the magnitude and direction of the external force?

    A. 4 N, upward   **C.** 4.4 N, upward
    B. 8.4 N, downward   **D.** 4 N, downward

29. A passenger on a train traveling in the forward direction notices that a piece of luggage starts to slide directly toward the front of the train. From this, it can be concluded that the train is:

    A. slowing down   **C.** moving at a constant velocity forward
    B. speeding up   **D.** changing direction

30. An object has a mass of 36 kg and weighs 360 N at the surface of the Earth. If this object is transported to an altitude that is twice the Earth's radius, what is the object's mass and weight, respectively?

    A. 9 kg and 90 N   **C.** 4 kg and 90 N
    B. 36 kg and 90 N   **D.** 36 kg and 40 N

31. A truck is moving at constant velocity. Inside the storage compartment, a rock is dropped from the midpoint of the ceiling and strikes the floor below. The rock hits the floor:

    A. just behind the midpoint of the ceiling
    B. exactly halfway between the midpoint and the front of the truck
    C. exactly below the midpoint of the ceiling
    D. just ahead of the midpoint of the ceiling

32. Jason takes off across level water on his jet-powered skis. The combined mass of Jason and his skis is 75 kg (the mass of the fuel is negligible). The skis have a thrust of 200 N and a coefficient of kinetic friction on the water of 0.1. If the skis run out of fuel after only 67 s, how far has Jason traveled before he stops?

    A. 10,331 m   **B.** 3,793 m   **C.** 8,224 m   **D.** 7,642 m

33. A 200 g hockey puck is launched up a metal ramp that is inclined at a 30° angle. The puck's initial speed is 63 m/s. What vertical height does the puck reach above its starting point? (Use the acceleration due to gravity $g = 9.8$ m/s^2, the coefficient of static friction μ_s = 0.40 and the kinetic friction μ_k = 0.30 between the hockey puck and the metal ramp)

    A. 66 m   **B.** 200 m   **C.** 170 m   **D.** 130 m

34. When a 4 kg mass and a 10 kg mass are pushed from rest with equal force:

    A. 4 kg mass accelerates 2.5 times faster than the 10 kg mass

    B. 10 kg mass accelerates 10 times faster than the 4 kg mass

    C. 4 kg mass accelerates at the same rate as the 10 kg mass

    D. 10 kg mass accelerates 2.5 times faster than the 4 kg mass

35. An object at rest on an inclined plane starts to slide when the incline is increased to 17°. What is the coefficient of static friction between the object and the plane? (Use the acceleration due to gravity $g = 9.8$ m/s^2)

    A. 0.37   **B.** 0.43   **C.** 0.24   **D.** 0.31

36. Which of the following statements must be true when a 20-ton truck collides with a 1,500 lb car?

    A. During the collision, the force on the truck is equal to the force on the car

    B. The truck did not slow down during the collision, but the car did

    C. During the collision, the force on the truck is greater than the force on the car

    D. During the collision, the force on the truck is smaller than the force on the car

37. A block is on a frictionless table on Earth. The block accelerates at 3 m/s^2 when a 20 N horizontal force is applied to it. The block and table are then transported to the Moon. What is the weight of the block on the Moon? (Use the acceleration due to gravity at the surface of the Moon = 1.62 m/s^2)

    A. 5.8 N   **B.** 14.2 N   **C.** 8.5 N   **D.** 11 N

38. Two forces of equal magnitude are acting on an object as shown. If the magnitude of each force is 2.3 N and the angle between them is 40°, which third force causes the object to be in equilibrium?

    A. 4.3 N pointing to the right   **C.** 3.5 N pointing to the right

    B. 2.2 N pointing to the right   **D.** 6.6 N pointing to the right

39. Car A starts from rest and accelerates uniformly for time t to travel a distance of d. Car B, which has four times the mass of car A, starts from rest and also accelerates uniformly. If the magnitudes of the forces accelerating car A and car B are the same, how long does it take car B to travel the same distance d?

    A. t **B.** $2t$ **C.** $t/2$ **D.** $16t$

40. A 1,100 kg vehicle is traveling at 27 m/s when it starts to decelerate. What is the average braking force acting on the vehicle, if after 578 m it comes to a complete stop?

    A. –440 N   **B.** –740 N   **C.** –690 N   **D.** –540 N

41. An ornament of mass *M* is suspended by a string from the ceiling inside an elevator. What is the tension in the string holding the ornament when the elevator is traveling upward at a constant speed?

    A. Equal to *Mg*   **C.** Greater than *Mg*
    B. Less than *Mg*   **D.** Equal to *M* / *g*

42. An object that weighs 75 N is pulled on a horizontal surface by a force of 50 N to the right. The friction force on this object is 30 N to the left. What is the acceleration of the object? (Use the acceleration due to gravity $g = 9.8$ m/s^2)

    A. 0.46 m/s^2 **B.** 1.7 m/s^2 **C.** 2.6 m/s^2 **D.** 10.3 m/s^2

43. While flying horizontally in an airplane, a string attached from the overhead luggage compartment hangs at rest 15° away from the vertical toward the front of the plane. From this observation, it can be concluded that the airplane is:

    A. accelerating forward   **C.** accelerating upward at 15° from horizontal
    B. accelerating backward   **D.** moving backward

44. An object slides down an inclined ramp with a constant speed. If the ramp's incline angle is θ, what is the coefficient of kinetic friction (μ_k) between the object and the ramp?

    A. $\mu_k = 1$ **C.** $\mu_k = \sin\theta / \cos\theta$
    B. $\mu_k = \cos\theta / \sin\theta$ **D.** $\mu_k = \sin\theta$

45. What are the readings on the spring scales when a 17 kg fish is weighed with two spring scales if each scale has negligible weight?

    A. The top scale reads 17 kg, and the bottom scale reads 0 kg
    B. Each scale reads greater than 0 kg and less than 17 kg, but the sum of
        the scales is 17 kg
    C. The bottom scale reads 17 kg, and the top scale reads 0 kg
    D. The sum of the two scales is 34 kg

46. What is the acceleration of a 105 kg tiger that accelerates uniformly from rest to 20 m/s in 10 s?

    A. 4.7 m/s^2 **B.** 1.5 m/s^2 **C.** 2 m/s^2 **D.** 3.4 m/s^2

47. Yana tries to pull an object by tugging on a rope attached to the object with a force of F. If the object does not move, what does this imply?

    A. The object has reached its natural state of rest and can no longer be set into motion
    B. The rope is not transmitting the force to the object
    C. No other forces are acting on the object
    D. There are one or more other forces that act on the object with a sum of $-F$

48. If a force F is exerted on an object, the force which the object exerts back:

    A. equals $-F$ **C.** depends on if the object is moving
    B. depends on the density of the object   **D.** depends on if the object is stationary

49. Two forces acting on an object have magnitudes $F_1 = -6.6$ N and $F_2 = 2.2$ N. Which third force causes the object to be in equilibrium?

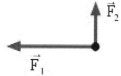

    A. 4.4 N at 162° counterclockwise from F_1
    B. 4.4 N at 108° counterclockwise from F_1
    C. 7 N at 162° counterclockwise from F_1
    D. 7 N at 108° counterclockwise from F_1

50. Sarah and her father Bob (who weighs four times as much) are standing on identical skateboards (with frictionless ball bearings), both initially at rest. For a short time, Bob pushes Sarah on the skateboard. When Bob stops pushing:

    A. Sarah and Bob move away from each other, and Sarah's speed is four times that of Bob's
    B. Sarah and Bob move away from each other, and Sarah's speed is one-fourth of Bob's
    C. Sarah and Bob move away from each other with equal speeds
    D. Sarah moves away from Bob, and Bob is stationary

51. Considering the effects of friction, which statement best describes the motion of an object along a surface?

    A. Less force is required to start than to keep the object in motion at a constant velocity
    B. The same force is required to start as to keep the object in motion at a constant velocity
    C. More force is required to start than to keep the object in motion at a constant velocity
    D. Once the object is set in motion, no force is required to keep it in motion at constant velocity

52. An object maintains its state of motion because it has:

    A. mass   **B.** acceleration   **C.** speed   **D.** weight

53. Joe and Bill are playing tug-of-war. Joe is pulling with a force of 200 N, while Bill is simply holding onto the rope. What is the tension of the rope if neither person is moving?

    A. 75 N   **B.** 0 N   **C.** 100 N   **D.** 200 N

54. A 4 kg wooden block A slides on a frictionless table pulled by a hanging 5 kg block B via a massless string and pulley system as shown. What is the acceleration of block A as it slides? (Use acceleration due to gravity $g = 9.8$ m/s²)

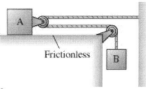

Frictionless

    A. 2.8 m/s²   **B.** 1.6 m/s²   **C.** 4.1 m/s²   **D.** 4.9 m/s²

55. Which of the following best describes the direction in which the force of kinetic friction acts relative to the interface between the interacting bodies?

    A. Parallel to the interface and in the same direction as the relative velocity
    B. Parallel to the interface and in the opposite direction of the relative velocity
    C. Perpendicular to the interface and in the same direction as the relative velocity
    D. Perpendicular to the interface and in the opposite direction of the relative velocity

56. A person who normally weighs 600 N is standing on a scale in an elevator. The elevator is initially moving upwards at a constant speed of 8 m/s and starts to slow down at a rate of 6 m/s². What is the reading of the person's weight on the scale in the elevator during the slowdown? (Use the acceleration due to gravity $g = 9.8$ m/s²)

    A. 600 N   **B.** 588 N   **C.** 98 N   **D.** 233 N

57. How large is the force of friction impeding the motion of a bureau when the 120 N bureau is being pulled across the sidewalk at a constant speed by a force of 30 N?

    A. 0 N   **B.** 30 N   **C.** 120 N   **D.** 3 N

58. What is the acceleration of a 40 kg crate that is being pulled along a frictionless surface by a force of 140 N that makes an angle of 30° with the surface?

    A. 1.5 m/s²   **B.** 2 m/s²   **C.** 2.5 m/s²   **D.** 3 m/s²

59. A force is a vector quantity because it has both:

    I. action and reaction counterparts
    II. mass and acceleration
    III. magnitude and direction

    A. I only   **B.** II only   **C.** III only   **D.** I and II only

Questions **60-61** are based on the following:

Alice pulls her daughter on a sled by a rope on level snow. Alice is 70 kg and her daughter is 20 kg. The sled has a mass of 10 kg, which slides along the snow with a coefficient of kinetic friction of 0.09. The tension in the rope is 30 N, making an angle of 30° with the ground. They are moving at a constant 2.5 m/s for 4 s. (Use acceleration due to gravity $g = 10$ m/s^2)

60. What is the work done by the force of gravity on the sled?

    A. −3,000 J   **B.** 0 J   **C.** 1,000 J   **D.** 3,000 J

61. What is the work done by the rope on the sled?

    A. 260 J   **B.** 130 J   **C.** 65 J   **D.** 520 J

Force & Motion

1: B	11: A	21: B	31: C	41: A	51: C
2: D	12: C	22: A	32: A	42: C	52: A
3: A	13: B	23: C	33: D	43: B	53: D
4: C	14: C	24: B	34: A	44: C	54: C
5: B	15: B	25: D	35: D	45: D	55: B
6: D	16: A	26: A	36: A	46: C	56: D
7: A	17: D	27: D	37: D	47: D	57: B
8: D	18: C	28: D	38: A	48: A	58: D
9: A	19: A	29: A	39: B	49: C	59: C
10: B	20: B	30: D	40: C	50: A	60: B
					61: A

Work and Energy of Point Object Systems

1. Consider the following ways that a girl might throw a stone from a bridge. The speed of the stone as it leaves her hand is the same in each of the three cases.

> I. Thrown straight up
> II. Thrown straight down
> III. Thrown straight out horizontally

Ignoring air resistance, in which case is the vertical speed of the stone the greatest when it hits the water below?

   A. I only   **B.** II only   **C.** III only   **D.** I and II only

2. A package is being pulled along the ground by a 5 N force *F* directed 45º above the horizontal. Approximately how much work is done by the force when it pulls the package 10 m?

   A. 14 J   **B.** 35 J   **C.** 70 J   **D.** 46 J

3. Which quantity has the greatest influence on the amount of kinetic energy that a large truck has while moving down the highway?

   A. Velocity   **B.** Mass   **C.** Density   **D.** Direction

4. No work is done by gravity on a bowling ball that rolls along the floor of a bowling alley because:

   A. no potential energy is being converted to kinetic energy
   B. the force on the ball is at a right angle to the ball's motion
   C. its velocity is constant
   D. the total force on the ball is zero

5. A 5 kg toy car is moving along the level ground. At a given time, it is traveling at a speed of 2 m/s and accelerating at 3 m/s². What is the cart's kinetic energy at this time?

   A. 20 J   **B.** 8 J   **C.** 10 J   **D.** 4 J

6. A tree house is 8 m above the ground. If Peter does 360 J of work while pulling a box from the ground up to his tree house with a rope, what is the mass of a box? (Use acceleration due to gravity $g = 10$ m/s²)

   A. 4.5 kg   **B.** 3.5 kg   **C.** 5.8 kg   **D.** 2.5 kg

7. For an ideal elastic spring, what does the slope of the curve represent for a displacement (*x*) vs. applied force (*F*) graph?

   A. The acceleration of gravity   **C.** The spring constant
   B. The square root of the spring constant   **D.** The reciprocal of the spring constant

8. A spring with a spring constant of 22 N/m is stretched from equilibrium to 3 m. How much work is done in the process?

A. 33 J   **B.** 66 J   **C.** 99 J   **D.** 198 J

9. A baseball is thrown straight up. Compare the sign of the work done by gravity while the ball goes up with the sign of the work done by gravity while it goes down:

A. negative on the way up and positive on the way down
B. negative on the way up and negative on the way down
C. positive on the way up and positive on the way down
D. positive on the way up and negative on the way down

10. Let A_1 represent the magnitude of the work done by gravity as mass A's gravitational energy increases by 400 J. Let B_1 represent the total amount of work necessary to increase mass B's kinetic energy by 400 J. How do A_1 and B_1 compare?

A. $A_1 > B_1$ **C.** $A_1 < B_1$
B. $A_1 = B_1$ **D.** $A_1 = 400 B_1$

11. According to the definition of work, pushing on a rock accomplishes no work unless there is:

A. an applied force equal to the rock's weight
B. movement perpendicular to the force
C. an applied force greater than the rock's weight
D. movement parallel to the force

12. A job is done slowly, while an identical job is done quickly. Both jobs require the same amount of work, but different amounts of:

    I. energy   II. power   III. torque

A. I only   **B.** II only   **C.** I and II only   **D.** I and III only

13. On a force (*F*) vs. distance (*d*) graph, what represents the work done by the force *F*?

A. The area under the curve   **C.** The slope of the curve
B. A line connecting two points on the curve   **D.** The length of the curve

14. A 3 kg cat leaps from a tree to the ground, which is a distance of 4 m. What is its kinetic energy just before the cat reaches the ground? (Use acceleration due to gravity $g = 10$ m/s^2)

A. 0 J   **B.** 9 J   **C.** 120 J   **D.** 60 J

15. A book is resting on a plank of wood. Jackie pushes the plank and accelerates it in such a way that the book is stationary with respect to the plank. The work done by static friction is:

A. zero   **B.** positive   **C.** negative   **D.** parallel to the surface

16. 350 J of work is required to drive a stake into the ground fully. If the average resistive force on the stake by the ground is 900 N, how long is the stake?

    A. 2.3 m   **B.** 0.23 m   **C.** 3 m   **D.** 0.39 m

17. A lightweight object and a very heavy object are sliding with equal speeds along a level, frictionless surface. They both slide up the same frictionless hill with no air resistance. Which object rises to a greater height?

    A. They both slide to the same height
    B. The heavy object, because it has more kinetic energy to carry it up the hill
    C. The heavy object, because it has greater potential energy
    D. The lightweight object, because it has more kinetic energy to carry it up the hill

18. If Investigator II does 3 times the work of Investigator I in one third the time, the power output of Investigator II is:

    A. 9 times greater   **C.** 1/3 times greater
    B. 3 times greater   **D.** the same

19. A diver who weighs 450 N steps off a diving board that is 9 m above the water. What is the kinetic energy when the diver strikes the water?

    A. 160 J   **B.** 540 J   **C.** 45 J   **D.** 4,050 J

20. A vertical, hanging spring stretches by 23 cm when a 160 N object is attached. What is the weight of a hanging plant that stretches the spring by 34 cm?

    A. 237 N   **B.** 167 N   **C.** 158 N   **D.** 309 N

21. A mule pulls with a horizontal force F on a covered wagon of mass M. The mule and covered wagon are traveling at a constant speed v on level ground. How much work is done by the mule on the covered wagon during time Δt? (Use acceleration due to gravity $g = 10$ m/s^2)

    A. $-Fv\Delta t$ **B.** $Fv\Delta t$ **C.** 0 J   **D.** $-F\sqrt{v}\Delta t$

22. Jane pulls on the strap of a sled at an angle of 32° above the horizontal. If 540 J of work is done by the strap while moving the sled a horizontal distance of 18 m, what is the tension in the strap?

    A. 86 N   **B.** 112 N   **C.** 24 N   **D.** 35 N

23. A vertical spring stretches 6 cm from equilibrium when a 120 g mass is attached to the bottom. If an additional 120 g mass is added to the spring, how does the potential energy of the spring change?

    A. the same   **B.** 4 times greater   **C.** 2 times greater   **D.** $\sqrt{2}$ times greater

24. A Ferrari, Maserati and Lamborghini are moving at the same speed and each driver slams on his brakes and brings the car to a stop. The most massive is the Ferrari, and the least massive is the Lamborghini. If the tires of all three cars have identical coefficients of friction with the road surface, which car experiences the greatest amount of work done by friction?

A. Maserati   **C.** Ferrari
B. Lamborghini   **D.** The amount is the same

25. A hammer does the work of driving a nail into a wooden board. Compared to the moment before the hammer strikes the nail after it impacts the nail, the hammer's mechanical energy is:

A. the same
B. less, because work has been done on the hammer
C. greater, because the hammer has done work
D. less, because the hammer has done work

26. A 1,500 kg car is traveling at 25 m/s on a level road and the driver slams on the brakes. The skid marks are 10 m long. What is the work done by the road on the car?

A. -4.7×10^5 J   **B.** 0 J   **C.** 2×10^5 J   **D.** 3.5×10^5 J

27. A 1,000 kg car is traveling at 4.72 m/s. If a 2,000 kg truck has 20 times the kinetic energy of the car, how fast is the truck traveling?

A. 23.6 m/s   **B.** 47.2 m/s   **C.** 94.4 m/s   **D.** 14.9 m/s

28. A 1,500 kg car is traveling at 25 m/s on a level road and the driver slams on the brakes. The skid marks are 30 m long. What forces are acting on the car while it is coming to a stop?

A. Gravity down, normal force up, and a frictional force forwards
B. Gravity down, normal force up, and the engine force forwards
C. Gravity down, normal force up, and a frictional force backward
D. Gravity down, normal force forward, and the engine force backward

29. A 6,000 N piano is being raised via a pulley. For every 1 m that the rope is pulled down, the piano rises 0.15 m. In this pulley system, what is the force needed to lift the piano?

A. 60 N   **B.** 900 N   **C.** 600 N   **D.** 300 N

30. What does the area under the curve on a force vs. position graph represent?

A. Kinetic energy   **B.** Momentum   **C.** Work   **D.** Displacement

31. What is the form in which most energy comes to and leaves the Earth?

A. Kinetic   **B.** Radiant   **C.** Chemical   **D.** Light

32. A driver abruptly slams on the brakes in her car, and the car skids a certain distance on a straight level road. If she had been traveling twice as fast, what distance would the car have skid, under the same conditions?

    A. 1.4 times farther   **B.** ½ as far   **C.** 4 times farther   **D.** 2 times farther

33. A crane hoists an object weighing 2,000 N to the top of a building. The crane raises the object straight upward at a constant rate. Ignoring the forces of friction, at what rate is energy consumed by the electric motor of the crane if it takes 60 s to lift the mass 320 m?

    A. 2.5 kW   **B.** 6.9 kW   **C.** 3.50 kW   **D.** 10.7 kW

34. A barbell with a mass of 25 kg is raised 3.0 m in 3.0 s before it reaches constant velocity. What is the net power expended by all forces in raising the barbell? (Use acceleration due to gravity $g = 9.8$ m/s^2 and the acceleration of the barbell is constant)

    A. 17 W   **B.** 34 W   **C.** 67 W   **D.** 98 W

35. Susan carried a 6.5 kg bag of groceries 1.4 m above the ground at a constant velocity for 2.4 m across the kitchen. How much work did Susan do on the bag in the process? (Use the acceleration due to gravity $g = 10$ m/s^2)

    A. 52 J   **B.** 0 J   **C.** 164 J   **D.** 138 J

36. A 1,000 kg car experiences a net force of 9,600 N while decelerating from 30 m/s to 22 m/s. How far does it travel while slowing down?

    A. 17 m   **B.** 22 m   **C.** 12 m   **D.** 34 m

37. What is the power output in relation to the work W if a person exerts 100 J in 50 s?

    A. ¼ W   **B.** ½ W   **C.** 2 W   **D.** 4 W

38. If a ball is released from a cliff ledge 58 m above the ground, how fast is the ball traveling when it reaches the ground? (Use the acceleration due to gravity $g = 10$ m/s^2)

    A. 68 m/s   **B.** 16 m/s   **C.** 44 m/s   **D.** 34 m/s

39. A stone is held at a height h above the ground. A second stone with four times the mass is held at the same height. What is the gravitational potential energy of the second stone compared to that of the first stone?

    A. Four times as much   **C.** One-fourth as much
    B. The same   **D.** One-half as much

40. A 1.3 kg coconut falls off a coconut tree, landing on the ground 600 cm below. How much work is done on the coconut by the gravitational force? (Use the acceleration due to gravity $g = 10$ m/s^2)

    A. 6 J   **B.** 78 J   **C.** 168 J   **D.** 340 J

41. The potential energy of a pair of interacting objects is related to their:

A. relative position   **C.** acceleration

B. momentum   **D.** kinetic energy

42. A spring has a spring constant of 65 N/m. One end of the spring is fixed at point P, while the other end is connected to a 7 kg mass *m*. The fixed end and the mass sit on a horizontal, frictionless surface so that the mass and the spring can rotate about P. The mass moves in a circle of radius $r = 4$ m, and the centripetal force of the mass is 15 N. What is the potential energy stored in the spring?

A. 1.7 J   **B.** 2.8 J   **C.** 3.7 J   **D.** 7.5 J

43. If electricity costs 8.16 cents/kW·h, how much would it cost you to run a 120 W stereo system 3.5 hours per day for 5 weeks?

A. $1.11   **B.** $1.46   **C.** $1.20   **D.** $0.34

44. A boy does 120 J of work to pull his sister back on a swing that has a 5.1 m chain until the swing makes an angle of 32° with the vertical. What is the mass of his sister? (Use the acceleration due to gravity $g = 9.8$ m/s²)

A. 18 kg   **B.** 15.8 kg   **C.** 13.6 kg   **D.** 11.8 kg

45. What is the value of the spring constant if 111 J of work are needed to stretch a spring from 1.4 m to 2.9 m if the spring's equilibrium position is at 0.0 m?

A. 58 N/m   **B.** 53 N/m   **C.** 67 N/m   **D.** 34 N/m

46. The metric unit of a joule (J) is a unit of:

      I. potential energy   II. kinetic energy   III. work

A. I only   **B.** II only   **C.** III only   **D.** I, II and III

47. A horizontal spring-mass system oscillates on a frictionless table. Find the maximum extension of the spring if the ratio of the mass to the spring constant is 0.038 kg·m/N, and the maximum speed of the mass is 18 m/s?

A. 3.5 m   **B.** 0.67 m   **C.** 3.4 cm   **D.** 67 cm

48. A truck weighs twice as much as a car and is moving at twice the speed of the car. Which statement is true about the truck's kinetic energy compared to that of the car?

A. The truck has 8 times the KE   **C.** The truck has $\sqrt{2}$ times the KE

B. The truck has twice the KE   **D.** The truck has 4 times the KE

49. When a car brakes to a stop, it's kinetic energy is transformed into:

    A. energy of rest   **C.** heat

    B. energy of momentum   **D.** stopping energy

50. A 30 kg block hangs from a spring with a spring constant of 900 N/m. How far does the spring stretch from its equilibrium position? (Use acceleration due to gravity $g = 10$ m/s^2)

    A. 12 cm   **B.** 33 cm   **C.** 50 cm   **D.** 0.5 cm

51. What is the kinetic energy of a 0.33 kg baseball thrown at a velocity of 40 m/s?

    A. 426 J   **B.** 574 J   **C.** 318 J   **D.** 264 J

52. An object is acted upon by a force as represented by the force vs. position graph below. What is the work done as the object moves from 0 m to 4 m?

    A. 10 J   **C.** 20 J

    B. 50 J   **D.** 30 J

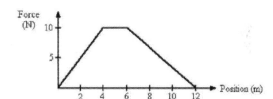

53. James and Bob throw identical balls vertically upward. James throws his ball with an initial speed twice that of Bob's. Assuming no air resistance, what is the maximum height of James's ball compared with that of Bob's ball?

    A. Equal   **C.** Four times

    B. Eight times   **D.** Two times

54. The graphs show the magnitude of the force (*F*) exerted by a spring as a function of the distance (*x*) the spring has been stretched. Which of the graphs shows a spring that obeys Hooke's Law?

A.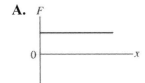

C.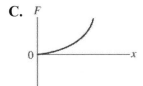

B.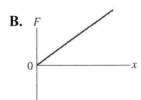

D.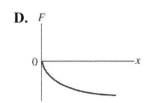

---

55. If a rocket travels through the air, it loses some of its kinetic energy due to air resistance. Some of this transferred energy:

    A. decreases the temperature of the air around the rocket
    B. is found in increased KE of the rocket
    C. is found in increased KE of the air molecules
    D. decreases the temperature of the rocket

56. A car moves four times as fast as an identical car. Compared to the slower car, the faster car has how much more kinetic energy?

    A. 4 times   **B.** 8 times   **C.** $\sqrt{2}$ times   **D.** 16 times

57. A massless, ideal spring with spring constant k is connected to a wall on one end and a massless plate on the other end. A mass m is sitting on a frictionless floor. The mass m is slid against the plate and pushed back a distance x. After release, it achieves a maximum speed v_1. In a second experiment, the same mass is pushed back a distance $4x$. After its release, it reaches a maximum speed v_2. How does v_2 compare with v_1?

    A. $v_2 = v_1$ **B.** $v_2 = 2v_1$ **C.** $v_2 = 4v_1$ **D.** $v_2 = 16v_1$

58. A N·m/s is a unit of:

    I. work   II. force   III. power

    A. I only   **B.** II only   **C.** III only   **D.** I and II only

59. For the work-energy theorem, which statement is accurate regarding the net work done?

    A. The net work done plus the initial KE is the final KE
    B. Final KE plus the net work done is the initial KE
    C. The net work done minus the final KE is the initial KE
    D. The net work done is equal to the initial KE plus the final KE

60. A 1,320 kg car climbs a 5° slope at a constant velocity of 70 km/h. Ignoring air resistance, at what rate must the engine deliver energy to drive the car? (Use the acceleration due to gravity $g = 9.8$ m/s^2)

    A. 45.1 kW   **B.** 12.7 kW   **C.** 6.3 kW   **D.** 22.6 kW

Work & Energy of Point Object Systems

1: D	11: D	21: B	31: B	41: A	51: D
2: B	12: B	22: D	32: C	42: A	52: C
3: A	13: A	23: B	33: D	43: C	53: C
4: B	14: C	24: C	34: A	44: B	54: B
5: C	15: B	25: D	35: B	45: D	55: C
6: A	16: D	26: A	36: B	46: D	56: D
7: D	17: A	27: D	37: C	47: A	57: C
8: C	18: A	28: C	38: D	48: A	58: C
9: A	19: D	29: B	39: A	49: C	59: A
10: B	20: A	30: C	40: B	50: B	60: D

Periodic Motion

1. A simple harmonic oscillator oscillates with frequency f when its amplitude is A. What is the new frequency if the amplitude is doubled to 2A?

   A. $f / 2$ **B.** f **C.** $4f$ **D.** $2f$

2. Springs A and B are attached in series with the free end of spring B attached to a wall. The free end of spring A is pulled, and both springs expand from their equilibrium lengths. The length of spring A increases by L_A, and the length of spring B increases by L_B. What is the expression for the spring constant k_B of spring B?

   A. L_B/k_A **B.** $k_A{}^2$ **C.** $k_A L_B$ **D.** $(k_A L_A) / L_B$

3. Particles of a material that move back and forth in the same direction the wave is moving are in what type of wave?

   A. Standing   **B.** Torsional   **C.** Transverse   **D.** Longitudinal

4. If a wave has a wavelength of 25 cm and a frequency of 1.68 kHz, what is its speed?

   A. 44 m/s   **B.** 160 m/s   **C.** 420 m/s   **D.** 314 m/s

5. The total stored energy in a system undergoing simple harmonic motion (SHM) is proportional to the:

   A. (amplitude)^2 **B.** wavelength   **C.** (spring constant)^2 **D.** amplitude

6. An 11 kg mass m is attached to a spring and allowed to hang in the Earth's gravitational field. The spring stretches 3 cm before reaching its equilibrium position. If the spring were allowed to oscillate, what would be its frequency? (Use the acceleration due to gravity $g = 9.8$ m/s^2)

   A. 0.7 Hz   **B.** 1.8 Hz   **C.** 4.1 Hz   **D.** 2.9 Hz

7. The time required for one cycle of any repeating event is the:

   A. amplitude   **B.** frequency   **C.** period   **D.** rotation

8. A pendulum of length L is suspended from the ceiling of an elevator. When the elevator is at rest, the period of the pendulum is T. How does T change when the elevator moves upward with a constant velocity?

   A. Decreases only if the upward acceleration is less than ½g
   B. Decreases
   C. Increases
   D. Remains the same

9. What is the period of a transverse wave with a frequency of 100 Hz?

   A. 0.01 s   **B.** 0.05 s   **C.** 0.2 s   **D.** 20 s

10. Two radio antennae are located on a seacoast 10 km apart on a North-South axis. The antennas broadcast identical in-phase AM radio waves at a frequency of 4.7 MHz. 200 km offshore, a steamship travels North at 15 km/h passing East of the antennae with a radio tuned to the broadcast frequency. From the moment of the maximum reception of the radio signal on the ship, what is the time interval until the next occurrence of maximum reception? (Use the speed of radio waves equals the speed of light $c = 3 \times 10^8$ m/s and the path difference = 1 λ)

   A. 7.7 min   **B.** 5.1 min   **C.** 3.8 min   **D.** 8.9 min

11. A 2.31 kg rope is stretched between supports 10.4 m apart. If one end of the rope is tweaked, how long will it take for the resulting disturbance to reach the other end? Assume that the tension in the rope is 74.4 N.

   A. 0.33 s   **B.** 0.74 s   **C.** 0.65 s   **D.** 0.57 s

12. Simple pendulum A swings back and forth at twice the frequency of simple pendulum B. Which statement is correct?

   A. Pendulum A is ¼ as long as B   **C.** Pendulum A is ½ as long as B
   B. Pendulum A is twice as massive as B   **D.** Pendulum B is twice as massive as A

13. A weight attached to the free end of an anchored spring is allowed to slide back and forth in simple harmonic motion on a frictionless table. How many times greater is the spring's restoring force at $x = 5$ cm compared to $x = 1$ cm (measured from equilibrium)?

   A. 2.5   **B.** 5   **C.** 7.5   **D.** 15

14. A massless, ideal spring projects horizontally from a wall and is connected to a 1 kg mass. The mass is oscillating in one dimension, such that it moves 0.5 m from one end of its oscillation to the other. It undergoes 10 complete oscillations in 60 s. What is the period of the oscillation?

   A. 9 s   **B.** 3 s   **C.** 6 s   **D.** 12 s

15. The total mechanical energy of a simple harmonic oscillating system is:

   A. a nonzero constant
   B. maximum when it reaches the maximum displacement
   C. zero when it reaches the maximum displacement
   D. zero as it passes the equilibrium point

16. What is the frequency of the oscillations when a vibrating spring moves from its position of maximum elongation to its position of maximum compression in 1 s?

    A. 0.75 Hz   **B.** 0.5 Hz   **C.** 1 Hz   **D.** 2.5 Hz

17. Which of the following is not a transverse wave?

    I. Radio   II. Light   III. Sound

    A. I only   **B.** II only   **C.** III only   **D.** I and II only

18. If a wave has a speed of 362 m/s and a period of 4 ms, its wavelength is closest to:

    A. 8.6 m   **B.** 1.5 m   **C.** 0.86 m   **D.** 15 m

19. Simple harmonic motion is characterized by:

    A. acceleration that is proportional to the negative displacement
    B. acceleration that is proportional to the velocity
    C. constant positive acceleration
    D. acceleration that is inversely proportional to the negative displacement

20. If the frequency of a harmonic oscillator doubles, by what factor does the maximum value of acceleration change?

    A. $2/\pi$ **B.** $\sqrt{2}$ **C.** 2   **D.** 4

21. An object that hangs from the ceiling of a stationary elevator by an ideal spring oscillates with a period T. If the elevator were to accelerate upwards with an acceleration of 2g, what is the period of oscillation of the object?

    A. T/2   **B.** T   **C.** 2T   **D.** 4T

22. Which of the following changes made to a transverse wave must increase wavelength?

    A. An increase in frequency and a decrease in speed
    B. The wavelength is only affected by a change in amplitude
    C. A decrease in frequency and an increase in speed
    D. A decrease in frequency and a decrease in speed

23. If a wave travels 30 m in 1 s, making 60 vibrations per second, what are its frequency and speed, respectively?

    A. 30 Hz and 60 m/s   **C.** 30 Hz and 30 m/s
    B. 60 Hz and 30 m/s   **D.** 60 Hz and 15 m/s

24. Transverse waves propagate at 40 m/s in a string that is subjected to a tension of 60 N. If the string is 16 m long, what is its mass?

A. 0.6 kg **B.** 0.9 kg **C.** 0.2 kg **D.** 9 kg

25. Doubling only the amplitude of a vibrating mass-on-spring system, changes the system frequency by what factor?

A. Increases by 3 **B.** Increases by 2 **C.** Increases by 5 **D.** Remains the same

26. A leaky faucet drips 60 times in 40 s. What is the frequency of the dripping?

A. 0.75 Hz **B.** 0.67 Hz **C.** 1.5 Hz **D.** 12 Hz

27. Particles of a material that move up and down perpendicular to the direction that the wave is moving are in what type of wave?

A. Torsional **B.** Mechanical **C.** Longitudinal **D.** Transverse

28. The figure shows a graph of the velocity *v* as a function of time *t* for a system undergoing simple harmonic motion. Which one of the following graphs represents the acceleration of this system as a function of time?

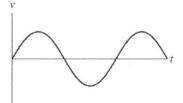

A. *a*

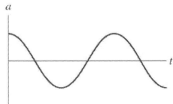

C. *a*

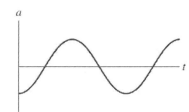

B. *a*

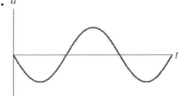

D. *a*

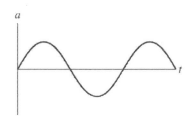

29. When compared, a transverse wave and a longitudinal wave are found to have amplitudes of equal magnitude. Which statement is true about their speeds?

A. The waves have the same speeds
B. The transverse wave has exactly twice the speed of the longitudinal wave
C. The speeds of the two waves are unrelated to their amplitudes
D. The longitudinal wave has a slower speed

30. What is the frequency when a weight on the end of a spring bobs up and down and completes one cycle every 2 s?

   A. 0.5 Hz   **B.** 1 Hz   **C.** 2 Hz   **D.** 2.5 Hz

31. The velocity of a given longitudinal sound wave in an ideal gas is $v = 340$ m/s at constant pressure and constant volume. Assuming an ideal gas, what is the wavelength for a 2,100 Hz sound wave?

   A. 0.08 m   **B.** 0.16 m   **C.** 1.6 m   **D.** 7.3 m

32. When the mass of a simple pendulum is quadrupled, how does the time t required for one complete oscillation change?

   A. Decreases to ¼t **B.** Decreases to ¾t **C.** Increases to $4t$ **D.** Remains the same

33. An object undergoing simple harmonic motion has an amplitude of 2.5 m. If the maximum velocity of the object is 15 m/s, what is the object's angular frequency (ω)?

   A. 6.0 rad/s   **B.** 3.6 rad/s   **C.** 37.5 rad/s   **D.** 8.8 rad/s

34. Unpolarized light is incident upon two polarization filters that do not have their transmission axes aligned. If 14% of the light passes through, what is the measure of the angle between the transmission axes of the filters?

   A. 73°   **B.** 81°   **C.** 43°   **D.** 58°

35. A mass on a spring undergoes simple harmonic motion. Which of the statements is true when the mass is at its maximum distance from the equilibrium position?

   A. KE is nonzero   **C.** Speed is zero
   B. Acceleration is at a minimum   **D.** Speed is maximum

36. What is the frequency if the speed of a sound wave is 240 m/s and its wavelength is 10 cm?

   A. 2.4 Hz   **B.** 24 Hz   **C.** 240 Hz   **D.** 2,400 Hz

37. Unlike a transverse wave, a longitudinal wave has no:

   A. wavelength   **B.** crests or troughs   **C.** amplitude   **D.** frequency

38. The density of aluminum is 2,700 kg/m³. If transverse waves propagate at 36 m/s in a 9.2 mm diameter aluminum wire, what is the tension in the wire?

   A. 43 N   **B.** 68 N   **C.** 233 N   **D.** 350 N

39. When a wave obliquely crosses a boundary into another medium, it is:

   A. always slowed down   **B.** reflected   **C.** diffracted   **D.** refracted

40. A floating leaf oscillates up and down two complete cycles each second as a water wave passes by. What is the wave's frequency?

A. 0.5 Hz   **B.** 1 Hz   **C.** 2 Hz   **D.** 3 Hz

41. A higher pitch for a sound wave means the wave has a greater:

A. frequency   **B.** wavelength   **C.** amplitude   **D.** period

42. An object is attached to a vertical spring and bobs up and down between points A and B. Where is the object located when its kinetic energy is at a maximum?

A. One-fourth of the way between A and B   **C.** Midway between A and B

B. One-third of the way between A and B   **D.** At either A or B

43. A pendulum consists of a 0.5 kg mass attached to the end of a 1 m rod of negligible mass. What is the magnitude of the torque τ about the pivot when the rod makes an angle θ of 60º with the vertical? (Use acceleration due to gravity $g = 10$ m/s^2)

A. 2.7 N·m   **B.** 4.4 N·m   **C.** 5.2 N·m   **D.** 10.6 N·m

44. The Doppler effect is characteristic of:

       I. light waves   II. sound waves   III. water waves

A. I only   **B.** II only   **C.** III only   **D.** I, II and III

45. A crane lifts a 2,500 kg cement block using a steel cable which has a mass per unit length of 0.65 kg/m. What is the speed of the transverse waves on this cable? (Use acceleration due to gravity $g = 10$ m/s^2)

A. 196 m/s   **B.** 1,162 m/s   **C.** 322 m/s   **D.** 558 m/s

46. A simple pendulum consists of a mass M attached to a weightless string of length L. Which statement about the frequency f is accurate for this system when it experiences small oscillations?

A. The f is directly proportional to the period

B. The f is independent of the mass M

C. The f is inversely proportional to the amplitude

D. The f is independent of the length L

47. A child on a swing set swings back and forth. If the length of the supporting cables for the swing is 3.3 m, what is the period of oscillation? (Use acceleration due to gravity $g = 10$ m/s^2)

A. 3.6 s   **B.** 5.9 s   **C.** 4.3 s   **D.** 2.7 s

48. A massless, ideal spring projects horizontally from a wall and is connected to a 0.3 kg mass. The mass is oscillating in one dimension, such that it moves 0.4 m from one end of its oscillation to the other. It undergoes 15 complete oscillations in 60 s. How does the frequency change if the spring constant is increased by a factor of 2?

A. Increases by 200%   **C.** Increases by 41%

B. Decreases by 59%   **D.** Decreases by 41%

49. A ball swinging at the end of a massless string undergoes simple harmonic motion. At what point(s) is the instantaneous acceleration of the ball the greatest?

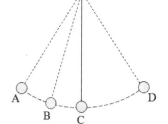

A. A   **C.** C

B. B   **D.** A and D

50. A simple pendulum, consisting of a 2 kg weight connected to a 10 m massless rod, is brought to an angle of 90° from the vertical, and then released. What is the speed of the weight at its lowest point? (Use the acceleration due to gravity $g = 10$ m/s^2)

A. 14 m/s   **B.** 10 m/s   **C.** 20 m/s   **D.** 25 m/s

51. A sound source of high pitch emits a wave with a high:

    I. frequency   II. amplitude   III. speed

A. I only   **B.** II only   **C.** III only   **D.** I, II and III

52. Find the wavelength of a train whistle that is heard by a fixed observer as the train moves toward him with a velocity of 50 m/s. Wind blows at 5 m/s from the observer to the train. The whistle has a natural frequency of 500 Hz. (Use the v of sound = 340 m/s)

A. 0.75 m   **B.** 0.43 m   **C.** 0.58 m   **D.** 7.5 m

53. Considering a vibrating mass on a spring, what effect on the system's mechanical energy is caused by doubling of the amplitude only?

A. Increases by a factor of two   **C.** Increases by a factor of three

B. Increases by a factor of four   **D.** Produces no change

54. Which of the following is an accurate statement?

A. Tensile stress is measured in N·m

B. Stress is a measure of external forces on a body

C. The ratio stress/strain is called the elastic modulus

D. Tensile strain is measured in meters

55. The efficient transfer of energy taking place at a natural frequency occurs in a phenomenon called:

A. reverberation   **C.** beats

B. the Doppler effect   **D.** resonance

56. A simple pendulum and a mass oscillating on an ideal spring both have period T in an elevator at rest. If the elevator now accelerates downward uniformly at 2 m/s², what is true about the periods of these two systems?

A. The period of the pendulum increases, but the period of the spring remains the same

B. The period of the pendulum increases and the period of the spring decreases

C. The period of the pendulum decreases, but the period of the spring remains the same

D. The periods of the pendulum and the spring both increase

57. All of the following is true of a pendulum that has swung to the top of its arc and has not yet reversed its direction, EXCEPT:

A. The PE of the pendulum is at a maximum

B. The acceleration of the pendulum equals zero

C. The KE of the pendulum equals zero

D. The velocity of the pendulum equals zero

58. The Doppler effect occurs when a source of sound moves:

I. toward the observer

II. away from the observer

III. with the observer

A. I only   **B.** II only   **C.** III only   **D.** I and II only

59. Consider the wave shown in the figure. The amplitude is:

A. 1 m

B. 2 m

C. 4 m

D. 8 m

60. Increasing the mass *m* of a mass-and-spring system causes what kind of change on the resonant frequency *f* of the system?

A. The *f* decreases

B. There is no change in the *f*

C. The *f* decreases only if the ratio *k* / *m* is < 1

D. The *f* increases

Periodic Motion

1: B	11: D	21: B	31: B	41: A	51: A
2: D	12: A	22: C	32: D	42: C	52: C
3: D	13: B	23: B	33: A	43: B	53: B
4: C	14: C	24: A	34: D	44: D	54: C
5: A	15: A	25: D	35: C	45: A	55: D
6: D	16: B	26: C	36: D	46: B	56: A
7: C	17: C	27: D	37: B	47: A	57: B
8: D	18: B	28: B	38: C	48: C	58: D
9: A	19: A	29: C	39: D	49: D	59: C
10: B	20: D	30: A	40: C	50: A	60: A

Fluids and Gas Phase

Questions **1-3** are based on the following:

A container has a vertical tube with an inner radius of 20 mm that is connected to the container at its side. An unknown liquid reaches level A in the container and level B in the tube. Level A is 5 cm higher than level B. The liquid supports a 20 cm high column of oil between levels B and C that has a density of 850 kg/m³. (Use acceleration due to gravity $g = 9.8$ m/s²)

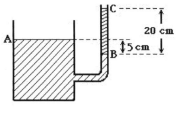

1. What is the density of the unknown liquid?

   A. 2,800 kg/m³   **B.** 2,100 kg/m³   **C.** 3,400 kg/m³   **D.** 3,850 kg/m³

2. The gauge pressure at level B is closest to:

   A. 1,250 Pa   **B.** 1,830 Pa   **C.** 340 Pa   **D.** 1,666 Pa

3. What is the mass of the oil?

   A. 210 g   **B.** 453 g   **C.** 620 g   **D.** 847 g

4. A cubical block of stone is lowered at a steady rate into the ocean by a crane, always keeping the top and bottom faces horizontal. Which of the following graphs best describes the gauge pressure P on the bottom of this block as a function of time *t* if the block just enters the water at time $t = 0$ s?

A. 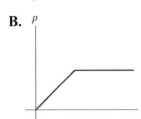   **C.**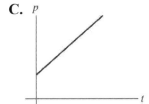

B. 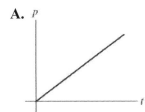   **D.**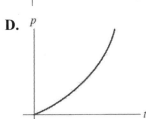

5. Consider a very small hole in the bottom of a tank that is 19 cm in diameter and is filled with water to a height of 80 cm. What is the speed at which the water exits the tank through the hole? (Use acceleration due to gravity $g = 9.8$ m/s²)

   A. 8.6 m/s   **B.** 12 m/s   **C.** 14.8 m/s   **D.** 4 m/s

6. An ideal gas at standard temperature and pressure is compressed until its volume is half the initial volume, and then it is allowed to expand until its pressure is half the initial pressure. This is achieved while holding the temperature constant. If the initial internal energy of the gas is U, the final internal energy of the gas is:

A. U/2   **B.** U/3   **C.** U   **D.** 2U

7. Ice has a lower density than water because ice:

A. molecules vibrate at lower rates than water molecules
B. is made of open-structured, hexagonal crystals
C. is denser and therefore sinks when in liquid water
D. molecules are more compact in the solid state

8. An object is sinking in a fluid. What is the weight of the fluid displaced by the sinking object when the object is completely submerged?

A. Dependent on the viscosity of the liquid   **C.** Less than the weight of the object
B. Equal to the weight of the object   **D.** Zero

9. A submarine in neutral buoyancy is 100 m below the surface of the water. For the submarine to surface, how much air pressure must be supplied to remove water from the ballast tanks? (Use the acceleration due to gravity $g = 9.8$ m/s^2 and the density of water $\rho = 10^3$ kg/m^3)

A. 9.8×10^5 N/m^2 **C.** 7.6×10^5 N/m^2
B. 4.7×10^5 N/m^2 **D.** 5.6×10^5 N/m^2

10. When atmospheric pressure increases, what happens to the absolute pressure at the bottom of a pool?

A. It does not change   **C.** It increases by the same amount
B. It increases by double the amount   **D.** It increases by half the amount

11. When soup gets cold, it often tastes greasy because oil spreads out on the surface of the soup, instead of staying in small globules. This is explained in terms of the:

A. increase in the surface tension of water with a decreasing temperature
B. Archimedes' principle
C. decrease in the surface tension of water with a decreasing temperature
D. Joule-Thomson effect

12. A particular grade of motor oil, which has a viscosity of 0.3 N·s/m^2, is flowing through a 1 m long tube with a radius of 3.2 mm. What is the average speed of the oil, if the drop in pressure over the length of the tube is 225 kPa?

A. 0.82 m/s   **B.** 0.96 m/s   **C.** 1.2 m/s   **D.** 1.4 m/s

13. An object whose weight is 60 N is floating at the surface of a container of water. How much of the object's volume is submerged? (Use acceleration due to gravity $g = 10$ m/s^2)

    A. 0.006 m^3 **B.** 0.06 m^3 **C.** 0.6 m^3 **D.** 6%

14. What is the volume flow rate of a fluid, if it flows at 2.5 m/s through a pipe of diameter 3 cm?

    A. 0.9 m^3/s   **C.** 5.7×10^{-4} m^3/s

    B. 1.8×10^{-3} m^3/s   **D.** 5.7×10^{-3} m^3/s

15. What is the specific gravity of a cork that floats with three-quarters of its volume in and one-quarter of its volume out of the water?

    A. 0.25   **B.** 0.5   **C.** 0.75   **D.** 2

16. What volume does 600 g of cottonseed oil occupy, if the density of cottonseed oil is 0.93 g/cm^3?

    A. 255 cm^3 **B.** 360 cm^3 **C.** 470 cm^3 **D.** 645 cm^3

17. The kinetic theory of a monatomic gas suggests the average kinetic energy per molecule is:

    A. 1/3 k_BT   **B.** 2 k_BT   **C.** 3/2 k_BT   **D.** 2/3 k_BT

18. An object is weighed in air, and it is also weighed while totally submerged in water. If it weighs 150 N less when submerged, find the volume of the object. (Use the acceleration due to gravity $g = 10$ m/s^2 and the density of water $\rho = 1,000$ kg/m^3)

    A. 0.0015 m^3 **B.** 0.015 m^3 **C.** 0.15 m^3 **D.** 1 m^3

19. When a container of water is placed on a laboratory scale, the scale reads 140 g. Now a 30 g piece of copper is suspended from a thread and lowered into the water without making contact with the bottom of the container. What does the scale read? (Use the acceleration due to gravity $g = 9.8$ m/s^2, density of water $\rho = 1$ g/cm^3 and density of copper $\rho = 8.9$ g/cm^3)

    A. 122 g   **B.** 168 g   **C.** 143 g   **D.** 110 g

20. An ideal, incompressible fluid flows through a 6 cm diameter pipe at 1 m/s. There is a 3 cm decrease in diameter within the pipe. What is the speed of the fluid in this constriction?

    A. 3 m/s   **B.** 1.5 m/s   **C.** 8 m/s   **D.** 4 m/s

21. Two blocks are submerged in a fluid. Block A has dimensions 2 cm high × 3 cm wide × 4 cm long and Block B is 2 cm × 3 cm × 8 cm. Both blocks are submerged with their large faces pointing up and down (i.e., the blocks are horizontal), and they are submerged to the same depth. Compared to the fluid pressure on the bottom of Block A, the bottom of Block B experiences:

    A. equal fluid pressure
          C. exactly double the fluid pressure
    B. greater fluid pressure
          D. less fluid pressure

22. A piece of thread of diameter d is in the shape of a rectangle (length l, width w) and is lying on the surface of the water in a beaker. If A is the surface tension of the water, what is the maximum weight that the thread can have without sinking?

    A. $Ad(l + w) / \pi$
      B. $A(l + w)$
      C. $4A(l + w)$
      D. $A(l + w) / 2$

23. What is the difference between the pressure inside and outside a tire called?

    A. Absolute pressure
          C. Atmospheric pressure
    B. Fluid pressure
          D. Gauge pressure

24. Which of the following is NOT a unit of pressure?

    A. atm
      B. $N \cdot m^2$
      C. inches of mercury
      D. Pascal

25. Which of the following is a dimensionless number?

       I. Reynolds number
          II. specific gravity
          III. shear stress

    A. I only
      B. II only
      C. III only
      D. I and II only

26. Water flows out of a large reservoir through a 5 cm diameter pipe. The pipe connects to a 3 cm diameter pipe that is open to the atmosphere, as shown.

What is the speed of the water in the 5 cm pipe? Treat the water as an ideal incompressible fluid. (Use the acceleration due to gravity g = 9.8 m/s^2)

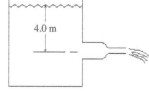
4.0 m

    A. 2.6 m/s
      B. 3.2 m/s
      C. 4.8 m/s
      D. 8.9 m/s

27. If the pressure acting on an ideal gas at constant temperature is tripled, what is the resulting volume of the ideal gas?

    A. Increased by a factor of two
          C. Reduced to one-third
    B. Remains the same
          D. Increased by a factor of three

28. A circular plate with an area of 1 m² covers a drain-hole at the bottom of a tank of water that is 1 m deep. Approximately how much force is required to lift the cover if it weighs 1,500 N? (Use the acceleration due to gravity $g = 10$ m/s²)

A. 4,250 N **B.** 9,550 N **C.** 16,000 N **D.** 11,500 N

29. A bowling ball that weighs 80 N is dropped into a swimming pool filled with water. If the buoyant force on the bowling ball is 20 N when the ball is 1 m below the surface (and sinking), what is the normal force exerted by the bottom of the pool on the ball when it comes to rest there, 4 m below the surface?

A. 0 N **B.** 60 N **C.** 50 N **D.** 70 N

30. A block of an unknown material is floating in a fluid, half-submerged. If the specific gravity of the fluid is 1.6, what is the block's density? (Use specific gravity = $\rho_{fluid} / \rho_{water}$ and the density of water $\rho = 1,000$ kg/m³)

A. 350 kg/m³ **B.** 800 kg/m³ **C.** 900 kg/m³ **D.** 1,250 kg/m³

31. A solid sphere of mass 9.2 kg, made of metal whose density is 3,650 kg/m³, hangs by a cord. When the sphere is immersed in a liquid of unknown density, the tension in the cord is 42 N. What is the density of the liquid? (Use acceleration due to gravity $g = 9.8$ m/s²)

A. 1,612 kg/m³ **B.** 1,468 kg/m³ **C.** 1,950 kg/m³ **D.** 1,742 kg/m³

32. In a closed container of fluid, object A is submerged at 6 m from the bottom, and object B is submerged at 12 m from the bottom. Compared to object A, object B experiences:

A. less fluid pressure **C.** equal fluid pressure
B. double the fluid pressure **D.** triple the fluid pressure

33. Ideal, incompressible water flows at 14 m/s in a horizontal pipe with a pressure of 3.5 × 10⁴ Pa. If the pipe widens to twice its original radius, what is the pressure in the wider section? (Use density of water $\rho = 1,000$ kg/m³)

A. 7.6×10^4 Pa **B.** 12.7×10^4 Pa **C.** 2×10^5 Pa **D.** 11.1×10^3 Pa

34. Two kilometers above the surface of the Earth, the atmospheric pressure is:

A. unrelated to the atmospheric pressure at the surface
B. twice the atmospheric pressure at the surface
C. triple the atmospheric pressure at the surface
D. less than the atmospheric pressure at the surface

35. An 80 kg man would weigh 784 N if there were no atmosphere. By how much does the buoyancy due to air reduce the man's weight? (Use the density of the man = 1 g/cm³, the density of the air = 1.2×10^{-3} g/cm³, m = 80 kg and the acceleration due to gravity g = 9.8 m/s²)

    A. 0.58 N   **B.** 0.32 N   **C.** 0.94 N   **D.** 2.8 N

36. Diffusion is described by which law?

    A. Dulong's   **B.** Faraday's   **C.** Kepler's   **D.** Graham's

37. An object has a volume of 4.2 m³ and weighs 41,800 N. What is its apparent weight in water? (Use acceleration due to gravity g = 9.8 m/s² and density of water ρ = 1,000 kg/m³)

    A. 1,140 N   **B.** 230 N   **C.** 800 N   **D.** 640 N

38. A pump uses a piston 12 cm in diameter that moves 3 cm/s. What is the fluid velocity in a tube that is 2 mm in diameter?

    A. 218 cm/s   **B.** 88 cm/s   **C.** 136 cm/s   **D.** 108 m/s

39. What is its specific gravity of an object floating with one-tenth of its volume out of the water?

    A. 0.3   **B.** 0.9   **C.** 1.3   **D.** 2.1

40. If each of the factors listed below was changed by 15%, which would have the greatest effect on the flow rate?

    A. Fluid density   **C.** Radius of the pipe
    B. Pressure difference   **D.** Fluid viscosity

41. A 680 g steel hammer (m_h) is tied to a string that is hung from a force meter. A 5 kg container of water (m_w) sits on a scale. The hammer is lowered completely into the water but above the bottom. What does the force meter read? (Use the density of steel ρ = 7.9 g/cm³, density of water ρ = 1 g/cm³ and acceleration due to gravity g = 10 m/s²)

    A. 5.9 N   **B.** 8.4 N   **C.** 10.7 N   **D.** 5.2 N

42. An external pressure applied to an enclosed fluid that is transmitted unchanged to every point within the fluid is known as:

    A. Torricelli's law   **C.** Archimedes' principle
    B. Bernoulli's principle   **D.** Pascal's principle

43. A submarine rests on the bottom of the sea. What is the normal force exerted upon the submarine by the sea floor equal to?

   A. weight of the submarine
   B. weight of the submarine minus the weight of the displaced water
   C. buoyant force minus the atmospheric pressure acting on the submarine
   D. weight of the submarine plus the weight of the displaced water

44. Consider a brick that is totally immersed in water, with the long edge of the brick vertical. Which statement describes the pressure on the brick?

   A. Greatest on the sides of the brick   **C.** Smallest on the sides with largest area
   B. Greatest on the top of the brick   **D.** Greatest on the bottom of the brick

45. Water is flowing in a drainage channel of a rectangular cross-section. The width of the channel is 14 m, the depth of water is 7 m, and the speed of the flow is 3 m/s. What is the mass flow rate of the water? (Use the density of water $\rho = 1{,}000 \ \text{kg/m}^3$)

   A. $2.9 \times 10^5 \ \text{kg/s}$ **C.** $6.2 \times 10^5 \ \text{kg/s}$
   B. $4.8 \times 10^4 \ \text{kg/s}$ **D.** $9.3 \times 10^4 \ \text{kg/s}$

46. What is the magnitude of the buoyant force if a 3 kg object floats motionlessly in a fluid of specific gravity 0.8? (Use the acceleration due to gravity $g = 10 \ \text{m/s}^2$)

   A. 15 N   **B.** 7.5 N   **C.** 30 N   **D.** 45 N

47. What is the pressure 6 m below the surface of the ocean? (Use density of water $\rho = 10^3$ kg/m^3, atmospheric pressure $P_{atm} = 1.01 \times 10^5$ Pa and acceleration due to gravity $g = 10 \ \text{m/s}^2$)

   A. $1.6 \times 10^5 \ \text{Pa}$ **B.** $0.8 \times 10^5 \ \text{Pa}$ **C.** $2.7 \times 10^4 \ \text{Pa}$ **D.** $3.3 \times 10^4 \ \text{Pa}$

48. Density is:

   A. inversely proportional to both mass and volume
   B. proportional to mass and inversely proportional to the volume
   C. inversely proportional to mass and proportional to the volume
   D. proportional to both mass and volume

49. Which of the following would be expected to have the smallest bulk modulus?

   A. Solid plutonium   **C.** Helium vapor
   B. Liquid water   **D.** Liquid mercury

50. A 14,000 N car is raised using a hydraulic lift. The lift consists of a U-tube with arms of unequal areas, initially at the same level. The lift is filled with oil with a density of 750 kg/m^3 with tight-fitting pistons at each end. The narrower arm has a radius of 6 cm, while the wider arm of the U-tube has a radius of 16 cm. The car rests on the piston on the wider arm of the U-tube. What is the force that must be applied to the smaller piston to lift the car after it has been raised 1.5 m? (Ignore the weight of the pistons and use the acceleration due to gravity $g = 9.8$ m/s^2)

    A. 4,568 N   **B.** 3,832 N   **C.** 2,094 N   **D.** 1,379 N

51. A polar bear of mass 240 kg stands on a floating ice 100 cm thick. What is the minimum area of the ice that will just support the bear? (Use the specific gravity of ice = 0.98 and the specific gravity of saltwater = 1.03)

    A. 2.6 m^2 **B.** 4.9 m^2 **C.** 4.8 m^2 **D.** 11.2 m^2

52. If atmospheric pressure increases by an amount ΔP, which of the following statements about the pressure in a large pond is true?

    A. The gauge pressure increases by ΔP
    B. The absolute pressure increases by ΔP
    C. The absolute pressure increases, but by an amount less than ΔP
    D. The absolute pressure does not change

53. A cubical box with 25 cm sides is immersed in a fluid. The pressure at the top surface of the box is 108 kPa, and the pressure on the bottom surface is 114 kPa. What is the density of the fluid? (Use the acceleration due to gravity $g = 9.8$ m/s^2)

    A. 980 kg/m^3 **B.** 1,736 kg/m^3 **C.** 2,452 kg/m^3 **D.** 2,794 kg/m^3

54. Fluid is flowing through a 19 cm long tube with a radius of 2.1 mm at an average speed of 1.8 m/s. What is the viscosity of the fluid, if the drop in pressure is 970 Pa?

    A. 0.036 N·s/m^2 **B.** 0.013 N·s/m^2 **C.** 0.0044 N·s/m^2 **D.** 0.0016 N·s/m^2

55. The pressure differential across the cross-section of a condor's wing due to the difference in air flow is explained by:

    A. Torricelli's law   **C.** Bernoulli's equation
    B. Poiseuille's law   **D.** Newton's First Law

56. An air bubble underwater has the same pressure as the water. As the air bubble rises toward the surface (with its temperature remaining constant), the volume of the air bubble:

    A. increases   **B.** decreases   **C.** remains constant   **D.** depends on the rate it rises

57. At a depth of about 1,060 m in the ocean, the pressure has increased by 110 atmospheres (to about 10^7 N/m^2). By how much has 1 m^3 of water been compressed by this pressure? (Use the bulk modulus B of water = 2.3×10^9 N/m^2)

    A. 2.7×10^{-3} m^3 **C.** 5.2×10^{-3} m^3

    B. 4.3×10^{-3} m^3 **D.** 7.6×10^{-2} m^3

58. The hydraulic lift is a practical application of:

    A. Huygens' principle   **C.** Fermat's principle

    B. Pascal's principle   **D.** Kepler's law

59. What is the gauge pressure in the water at the deepest point of the Pacific Ocean which is 11,030 m? (Use the density of seawater $\rho = 1,025$ kg/m^3 and the acceleration due to gravity $g = 9.8$ m/s^2)

    A. 1.1×10^8 Pa   **C.** 4.2×10^7 Pa

    B. 3.1×10^8 Pa   **D.** 7.6×10^7 Pa

60. A man is breathing through a snorkel while swimming in the ocean. When his chest is about 1 meter underwater, he has a difficult time breathing. What is the net pressure that his lungs must expand against for him to breathe? (Use the atmospheric pressure $P_{atm} = 1.01 \times 10^5$ Pa, the density of water $\rho = 10^3$ kg/m^3, the density of air $\rho = 1.2$ kg/m^3 and the acceleration due to gravity $g = 9.8$ m/s^2)

    A. 3.2×10^5 Pa   **C.** 4.1×10^5 Pa

    B. 1.1×10^5 Pa   **D.** 1×10^4 Pa

Fluids & Gas Phase

1: C	11: A	21: A	31: C	41: A	51: C
2: D	12: B	22: C	32: A	42: D	52: B
3: A	13: A	23: D	33: B	43: B	53: C
4: A	14: B	24: B	34: D	44: D	54: D
5: D	15: C	25: D	35: C	45: A	55: C
6: C	16: D	26: B	36: D	46: C	56: A
7: B	17: C	27: C	37: D	47: A	57: B
8: C	18: B	28: D	38: D	48: B	58: B
9: A	19: C	29: B	39: B	49: C	59: A
10: C	20: D	30: B	40: C	50: C	60: D

Electrostatics and Magnetism

1. How many excess electrons are present for an object that has a charge of -1 Coulomb? (Use Coulomb's constant $k = 9 \times 10^9$ N·m^2/C^2 and charge of an electron $e = -1.6 \times 10^{-19}$ C)

    A. 3.1×10^{19} electrons   **C.** 6.3×10^{18} electrons

    B. 6.3×10^{19} electrons   **D.** 1.6×10^{19} electrons

2. A flat disk 1 m in diameter is oriented so that the area vector of the disk makes an angle of $\pi/6$ radians with a uniform electric field. What is the electric flux through the surface if the field strength is 740 N/C?

    A. 196π N·m^2/C   **C.** 644π N·m^2/C

    B. $250/\pi$ N·m^2/C   **D.** 160π N·m^2/C

3. A positive charge $Q = 1.3 \times 10^{-9}$ C is located along the *x*-axis at $x = -10^{-3}$ m and a negative charge of the same magnitude is located at the origin. What is the magnitude and direction of the electric field at the point along the *x*-axis where $x = 10^{-3}$ m? (Use Coulomb's constant $k = 9 \times 10^9$ N·m^2/C^2 and to the right as the positive direction)

    A. 8.8×10^6 N/C to the left   **C.** 5.5×10^7 N/C to the right

    B. 3.25×10^7 N/C to the right   **D.** 2.75×10^6 N/C to the right

4. Two charges $Q_1 = 2.4 \times 10^{-10}$ C and $Q_2 = 9.2 \times 10^{-10}$ C are near each other, and charge Q_1 exerts a force F_1 on Q_2. How does F_1 change if the distance between Q_1 and Q_2 is increased by a factor of 4?

    A. Decreases by a factor of 4   **C.** Decreases by a factor of 16

    B. Increases by a factor of 16   **D.** Increases by a factor of 4

5. A proton is located at ($x = 1$ nm, $y = 0$ nm) and an electron is located at ($x = 0$ nm, $y = 4$ nm). Find the attractive Coulomb force between them. (Use Coulomb's constant $k = 9 \times 10^9$ N·m^2/C^2 and the charge of an electron $e = -1.6 \times 10^{-19}$ C)

    A. 5.3×10^8 N   **C.** 9.3×10^4 N

    B. 1.4×10^{-11} N   **D.** 2.6×10^{-18} N

6. Which form of electromagnetic radiation has photons with the highest energy?

    A. Gamma rays   **C.** Microwaves

    B. Visible light   **D.** Ultraviolet radiation

7. A 54,000 kg asteroid carrying a negative charge of 15 µC is 180 m from another 51,000 kg asteroid carrying a negative charge of 11 µC. What is the net force the asteroids exert upon each other? (Use the gravitational constant $G = 6.673 \times 10^{-11}$ N·m^2/kg^2 and Coulomb's constant $k = 9 \times 10^9$ N·m^2/C^2)

    A. 400,000 N   **B.** 5,700 N   **C.** -4.0×10^{-5} N   **D.** 4.0×10^{-5} N

8. Two small beads are 30 cm apart with no other charges or fields present. Bead A has 20 µC of charge and bead B has 5 µC. Which of the following statements is true about the electric forces on these beads?

    A. The force on A is 120 times the force on B
    B. The force on A is exactly equal to the force on B
    C. The force on B is 4 times the force on A
    D. The force on A is 20 times the force on B

Questions **9-10** are based on the following:

Two parallel metal plates separated by 0.01 m are charged to create a uniform electric field of 3.5×10^4 N/C between them, which points down. A small, stationary 0.008 kg plastic ball m is located between the plates and has a small charge Q on it. The only forces acting on it are the force of gravity and the electric field. (Use Coulomb's constant $k = 9 \times 10^9$ N·m^2/C^2, the charge of an electron $= -1.6 \times 10^{-19}$ C, the charge of a proton $= 1.6 \times 10^{-19}$ C, the mass of a proton $= 1.67 \times 10^{-27}$ kg, the mass of an electron $= 9.11 \times 10^{-31}$ kg and the acceleration due to gravity $g = 9.8$ m/s^2)

9. What is the charge on the ball?

    A. -250 C   **B.** 250 C   **C.** 3.8×10^{-6} C   **D.** -2.2×10^{-6} C

10. How would the acceleration of an electron between the plates compare to the acceleration of a proton between the plates?

    A. One thousand eight hundred thirty times as large, and in the opposite direction
    B. The square root times as large, and in the opposite direction
    C. Twice as large, and in the opposite direction
    D. The same magnitude, but in the opposite direction

11. A positive charge $Q = 2.3 \times 10^{-11}$ C is 10^{-2} m away from a negative charge of equal magnitude. Point P is located equidistant between them. What is the magnitude of the electric field at point P? (Use Coulomb's constant $k = 9 \times 10^9$ N·m^2/C^2)

    A. 9.0×10^3 N/C   **B.** 4.5×10^3 N/C   **C.** 3.0×10^4 N/C   **D.** 1.7×10^4 N/C

12. A point charge $Q = -10$ μC. What is the number of excess electrons on charge Q? (Use the charge of an electron $e = -1.6 \times 10^{-19}$ C)

    A. 6.3×10^{13} electrons   **C.** 9.0×10^{13} electrons

    B. 1.6×10^{13} electrons   **D.** 8.5×10^{13} electrons

13. A distance of 3 m separates an electron and a proton. What happens to the magnitude of the force on the proton if the electron is moved 1.5 m closer to the proton?

    A. It increases to twice its original value

    B. It decreases to one-fourth its original value

    C. It increases to four times its original value

    D. It decreases to one-half its original value

14. How will the magnitude of the electrostatic force between two objects be affected, if the distance between them and both of their charges are doubled?

    A. It will increase by a factor of 4   **C.** It will decrease by a factor of 2

    B. It will increase by a factor of 2   **D.** It will be unchanged

15. Which statement is true for an H nucleus, which has a charge $+e$ that is situated to the left of a C nucleus, which has a charge $+6e$?

    A. The electrical force experienced by the H nucleus is to the right, and the magnitude is equal to the force exerted on the C nucleus

    B. The electrical force experienced by the H nucleus is to the right, and the magnitude is less than the force exerted on the C nucleus

    C. The electrical force experienced by the H nucleus is to the left, and the magnitude is greater than the force exerted on the C nucleus

    D. The electrical force experienced by the H nucleus is to the left, and the magnitude is equal to the force exerted on the C nucleus

16. Two oppositely charged particles are slowly separated from each other. What happens to the force as the particles are slowly moved apart?

    A. attractive and decreasing   **C.** attractive and increasing

    B. repulsive and decreasing   **D.** repulsive and increasing

17. Electrons move in an electrical circuit:

    A. because the wires are so thin

    B. by interacting with an established electric field

    C. by colliding with each other

    D. by being repelled by protons

18. If the number of turns on the secondary coil of a transformer is less than those on the primary, the result is a:

   A. 240 V transformer   **C.** step-up transformer

   B. 110 V transformer   **D.** step-down transformer

19. Two charges $Q_1 = 3 \times 10^{-8}$ C and $Q_2 = 9 \times 10^{-8}$ C are near each other, and charge Q_1 exerts a force F_1 on Q_2. What is F_2, the force that charge Q_2 exerts on charge Q_1?

   A. $F_1 / 3$ **B.** F_1 **C.** $3F_1$ **D.** $2F_1$

20. Two electrons are passing 30 mm apart. What is the electric repulsive force that they exert on each other? (Use Coulomb's constant $k = 9 \times 10^9$ N·m²/C² and the charge of an electron $= -1.6 \times 10^{-19}$ C)

   A. 1.3×10^{-25} N   **C.** 2.56×10^{-25} N

   B. 3.4×10^{-27} N   **D.** 3.4×10^{10} N

21. A light bulb is connected in a circuit and has a wire leading to it in a loop. What happens when a strong magnet is quickly passed through the loop?

   A. The brightness of the light bulb dims or gets brighter due to an induced emf produced by the magnet

   B. The light bulb's brightness remains the same although current decreases

   C. The light bulb gets brighter because more energy is being added to the system by the magnet inside the coil

   D. The light bulb gets brighter because there is an induced emf that drives more current through the light bulb

22. Suppose a van de Graaff generator builds a negative static charge, and a grounded conductor is placed near enough to it so that an 8 μC of negative charge arcs to the conductor. What is the number of electrons that are transferred? (Use the charge of an electron $e = -1.6 \times 10^{-19}$ C)

   A. 1.8×10^{14} electrons   **C.** 5×10^{13} electrons

   B. 48 electrons   **D.** 74 electrons

23. Which statement must be true if two objects are electrically attracted to each other?

   A. One of the objects could be electrically neutral

   B. One object must be negatively charged, and the other must be positively charged

   C. At least one of the objects must be positively charged

   D. At least one of the objects must be negatively charged

24. An amp is a unit of electrical:

A. capacity   **B.** current   **C.** potential difference   **D.** charge

25. A loop of wire is rotated about a diameter (which is perpendicular to a given magnetic field). In one revolution, the induced current in the loop reverses direction how many times?

A. 2   **B.** 1   **C.** 0   **D.** 4

26. Two charges ($Q_1 = 2.3 \times 10^{-8}$ C and $Q_2 = 2.5 \times 10^{-9}$ C) are a distance 0.1 m apart. How much energy is required to bring them to a distance 0.01 m apart? (Use Coulomb's constant $k = 9 \times 10^9$ N·m^2/C^2)

A. 2.2×10^{-4} J   **C.** 1.7×10^{-5} J
B. 8.9×10^{-5} J   **D.** 4.7×10^{-5} J

27. A solid aluminum cube rests on a wooden table in a region where a uniform external electric field is directed straight upward. What can be concluded regarding the charge on the top surface of the cube?

A. The top surface is neutral
B. The top surface is charged negatively
C. The top surface is charged positively
D. The top surface's charge cannot be determined without further information

28. A point charge of $+Q$ is placed at the center of an equilateral triangle, as shown. When a second charge of $+Q$ is placed at one of the triangle's vertices, an electrostatic force of 5 N acts on it. What is the magnitude of the force that acts on the center charge when a third charge of $+Q$ is placed at one of the other vertices?

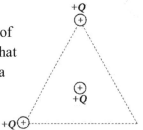

A. 0 N   **B.** 4 N   **C.** 5 N   **D.** 8 N

29. In the figure below, the charge in the middle is fixed and $Q = -7.5$ nC. For what fixed, positive charge q_1 will non-stationary, negative charge q_2 be in static equilibrium?

A. 53 nC   **B.** 7.5 nC   **C.** 15 nC **D.** 30 nC

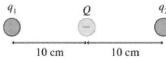

30. Which form of electromagnetic radiation has the highest frequency?

A. Gamma radiation   **C.** Visible light
B. Ultraviolet radiation   **D.** Radio waves

31. All of the following affect the electrostatic field strength at a point at a distance from a source charge, EXCEPT:

    A. the sign of the source charge
    B. the distance from the source charge
    C. the magnitude of the source charge
    D. the nature of the medium surrounding the source charge

32. A charged particle is observed traveling in a circular path in a uniform magnetic field. If the particle had been traveling twice as fast, the radius of the circular path would be:

    A. three times the original radius   **C.** one-half of the original radius
    B. twice the original radius   **D.** four times the original radius

33. Two charges separated by 1 m exert a 1 N force on each other. If the magnitude of each charge is doubled, the force on each charge is:

    A. 1 N   **B.** 2 N   **C.** 4 N   **D.** 6 N

34. In a water solution of NaCl, the NaCl dissociates into ions surrounded by water molecules. Consider a water molecule near a Na^+ ion. What tends to be the orientation of the water molecule?

    A. The hydrogen atoms are nearer the Na^+ ion because of their positive charge
    B. The hydrogen atoms are nearer the Na^+ ion because of their negative charge
    C. The oxygen atom is nearer the Na^+ ion because of the oxygen's positive charge
    D. The oxygen atom is nearer the Na^+ ion because of the oxygen's negative charge

35. A metal sphere is insulated electrically and is given a charge. If 30 electrons are added to the sphere in giving a charge, how many Coulombs are added to the sphere? (Use Coulomb's constant $k = 9 \times 10^9$ N·m²/C² and the charge of an electron $e = -1.6 \times 10^{-19}$ C)

    A. −2.4 C   **B.** −30 C   **C.** -4.8×10^{-18} C   **D.** -4.8×10^{-16} C

36. What happens to the cyclotron frequency of a charged particle if its speed doubles?

    A. It remains the same   **C.** It doubles
    B. It is ½ as large   **D.** It is √2 times as large

37. A positive test charge q is released near a positive fixed charge Q. As q moves away from Q, it experiences:

    A. increasing acceleration   **C.** constant velocity
    B. decreasing acceleration   **D.** decreasing velocity

38. If a value has SI units kg m^2/s^2/C, this value can be:

    A. electric potential difference

    B. resistance

    C. electric field strength

    D. Newton's forces

39. A Coulomb is a unit of electrical:

    A. capacity   **B.** resistance   **C.** charge   **D.** potential difference

40. To say that electric charge is conserved means that no case has ever been found where:

    A. charge has been created or destroyed

    B. the total charge on an object has increased

    C. the net negative charge on an object is unbalanced by a positive charge on another object

    D. the total charge on an object has changed by a significant amount

41. Two charges $Q_1 = 1.7 \times 10^{-10}$ C and $Q_2 = 6.8 \times 10^{-10}$ C are near each other. How would F change if the charges were both doubled, but the distance between them remained the same?

    A. F increases by a factor of 2   **C.** F decreases by a factor of $\sqrt{2}$

    B. F increases by a factor of 4   **D.** F decreases by a factor of 4

42. Two like charges of the same magnitude are 10 mm apart. If the force of repulsion they exert upon each other is 4 N, what is the magnitude of each charge? (Use Coulomb's constant $k = 9 \times 10^9$ N·m^2/C^2)

    A. 6×10^{-5} C   **C.** 2×10^{-7} C

    B. 6×10^5 C   **D.** 1.5×10^{-7} C

43. A circular loop of wire is rotated about an axis whose direction at constant angular speed can be varied. In a region where a uniform magnetic field points straight down, what orientation of the axis of the rotation guarantees that the emf will be zero (regardless of how the axis is aligned to the loop)?

    A. It must be vertical

    B. It must make an angle of 45° to the direction South

    C. It could have any horizontal orientation

    D. It must make an angle of 45° to the vertical

44. Two identical small charged spheres are a certain distance apart, and each initially experiences an electrostatic force of magnitude F due to the other. With time, charge gradually diminishes on both spheres. What is the magnitude of the electrostatic force when each of the spheres has lost half its initial charge?

    A. $1/16\ F$ **B.** $1/8\ F$ **C.** $1/4\ F$ **D.** $2\ F$

45. A proton, moving in a uniform magnetic field, moves in a circle perpendicular to the field lines and takes time T for each circle. If the proton's speed tripled, what would now be its time to go around each circle?

    A. T/3   **B.** T   **C.** 6T   **D.** 3T

46. As measurements of the electrostatic field strength are taken at points that progressively approach a negatively-charged particle, the field vectors will point:

    A. away from the particle and have a constant magnitude
    B. away from the particle and have progressively decreasing the magnitude
    C. towards the particle and have progressively increasing the magnitude
    D. towards the particle and have progressively decreasing the magnitude

47. Every proton in the universe is surrounded by its own:

    I. electric field   II. gravitational field   III. magnetic field

    A. I only   **B.** II only   **C.** III only   **D.** I, II and III

48. A charge $Q = 3.1 \times 10^{-5}$ C is fixed in space while another charge $q = -10^{-6}$ C is 6 m away. Charge q is slowly moved 4 m in a straight line directly toward the charge Q. How much work is required to move charge q? (Use Coulomb's constant $k = 9 \times 10^9$ N·m^2/C^2)

    A. −0.09 J   **B.** −0.03 J   **C.** 0.16 J   **D.** 0.08 J

49. A point charge $Q = -600$ nC. What is the number of excess electrons in charge Q? (Use the charge of an electron $e = -1.6 \times 10^{-19}$ C)

    A. 5.6×10^{12} electrons   **C.** 2.8×10^{11} electrons
    B. 2.1×10^{10} electrons   **D.** 3.8×10^{12} electrons

50. In electricity, what quantity is analogous to the acceleration of gravity, g (i.e., a force per unit mass)?

    A. Electric charge   **C.** Electric field
    B. Electric current   **D.** Electromagnetic force

51. Which type of electromagnetic (EM) wave travels through space the slowest?

    A. Visible light   **C.** Gamma rays

    B. Ultraviolet light   **D.** All EM waves travel at the same speed

52. As a proton moves in the direction of the electric field lines, it is moving from:

    A. high potential to low potential and losing electric potential energy

    B. high potential to low potential and gaining electric potential energy

    C. low potential to high potential and gaining electric potential energy

    D. low potential to high potential and retaining electric potential energy

53. Which of the following requires a measure of time?

    A. Joule   **B.** Watt   **C.** Volt   **D.** Coulomb

54. If an object is characterized as electrically polarized:

    A. its internal electric field is zero

    B. it is a strong insulator

    C. it is electrically charged

    D. its charges have been rearranged

55. Two positive charges Q_1 and $Q_2 = 3.4 \times 10^{-10}$ C are located 10^{-3} m away from each other, and point P is exactly between them. What is the magnitude of the electric field at point P?

    A. 0 N/C   **C.** 6.8×10^{-7} N/C

    B. 10^{-10} N/C   **D.** 1.7×10^{-5} N/C

56. Two equally-charged spheres of mass 1 g are placed 2 cm apart. When released, they begin to accelerate at 440 m/s^2. What is the magnitude of the charge on each sphere? (Use Coulomb's constant $k = 9 \times 10^9$ N·m^2/C^2)

    A. 80 nC   **B.** 65 nC   **C.** 140 nC   **D.** 100 nC

57. Which of the following is an accurate statement?

    A. A conductor cannot carry a net charge

    B. The electric field at the surface of a conductor is not necessarily parallel to the surface

    C. If a solid metal sphere carries a net charge, the charge distributes uniformly throughout

    D. If a solid metal sphere carries a net charge, the charge will move to the sphere surface

58. Two equal and opposite charges a certain distance apart are called an electric 'dipole.' A positive test charge $+q$ is placed as shown, equidistant from the two charges.

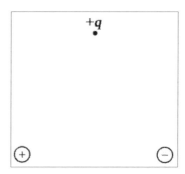

Which diagram below gives the direction of the net force on the test charge?

   A. ←   **B.** →   **C.** ↑   **D.** ↓

59. A charged particle moves and experiences no magnetic force. What can be concluded?

   A. Either no magnetic field exists, or the particle is moving parallel to the field
   B. No magnetic field exists in that region of space
   C. The particle is moving at right angles to a magnetic field
   D. The particle is moving parallel to a magnetic field

60. Find the magnitude of the electrostatic force between a +3 C point charge and a −12 C point charge if they are separated by 50 cm of space. (Use Coulomb's constant $k = 9 \times 10^9$ N·m^2/C^2)

   A. 9.2×10^{12} N   **C.** 7.7×10^{12} N
   B. 1.3×10^{12} N   **D.** 4.8×10^{12} N

Electrostatics & Magnetism

1: C	11: D	21: A	31: A	41: B	51: D
2: D	12: A	22: C	32: B	42: C	52: A
3: A	13: C	23: A	33: C	43: A	53: B
4: C	14: D	24: B	34: D	44: C	54: D
5: B	15: D	25: A	35: C	45: B	55: A
6: A	16: A	26: D	36: A	46: C	56: C
7: D	17: B	27: C	37: B	47: D	57: D
8: B	18: D	28: C	38: A	48: A	58: B
9: D	19: B	29: D	39: C	49: D	59: A
10: A	20: C	30: A	40: A	50: C	60: B

Circuit Elements

1. What is the new resistance of wire if the length of a certain wire is doubled and its radius is also doubled?

    A. It is √2 times as large   **C.** It stays the same

    B. It is ½ as large   **D.** It is 2 times as large

2. A 6 Ω resistor is connected across the terminals of a 12 V battery. If 0.6 A of current flows, what is the internal resistance of the battery?

    A. 2 Ω   **B.** 26 Ω   **C.** 20 Ω   **D.** 14 Ω

3. Three 8 V batteries are connected in series to power light bulbs A and B. The resistance of light bulb A is 60 Ω and the resistance of light bulb B is 30 Ω. How does the current through light bulb A compare with the current through light bulb B?

    A. The current through light bulb A is less

    B. The current through light bulb A is greater

    C. The current through light bulb A is the same

    D. The current through light bulb A is exactly doubled that through light bulb B

4. A sphere with radius 2 mm carries a 1 μC charge. What is the potential difference, $V_B - V_A$, between point B 3.5 m from the center of the sphere and point A 8 m from the center of the sphere? (Use Coulomb's constant $k = 9 \times 10^9$ N·m^2/C^2)

    A. −485 V   **B.** 1,140 V   **C.** −140 V   **D.** 1,446 V

5. Which of the following effect (s) capacitance of capacitors?

       I. material between the conductors

       II. distance between the conductors

       III. geometry of the conductors

    A. I only   **B.** II only   **C.** III only   **D.** I, II and III

6. A proton with an initial speed of 1.5×10^5 m/s falls through a potential difference of 100 volts, gaining speed. What is the speed reached? (Use the mass of a proton = 1.67×10^{-27} kg and the charge of a proton = 1.6×10^{-19} C)

    A. 2×10^5 m/s   **B.** 4×10^5 m/s   **C.** 8.6×10^5 m/s   **D.** 7.6×10^5 m/s

7. The current flowing through a circuit of constant resistance is doubled. What is the effect on the power dissipated by that circuit?

    A. Decreases to one-half its original value   **C.** Quadruples its original value

    B. Decreases to one-fourth its original value   **D.** Doubles its original value

8. A positively-charged particle is at rest in an unknown medium. What is the magnitude of the magnetic field generated by this particle?

   A. Constant everywhere and dependent only on the mass of the medium
   B. Less at points near to the particle compared to a distant point
   C. Greater at points near to the particle compared to a distant point
   D. Equal to zero

9. The heating element of a toaster is a long wire of some metal, often a metal alloy, which heats up when a 120 V potential difference is applied across it. Consider a 300 W toaster connected to a wall outlet. Which statement would result in an increase in the rate by which heat is produced?

   A. Use a longer wire   **C.** Use a thicker and longer wire
   B. Use a thicker wire   **D.** Use a thinner and longer wire

10. A 4 μC point charge and an 8 μC point charge are initially infinitely far apart. How much work is required to bring the 4 μC point charge to ($x = 2$ mm, $y = 0$ mm), and the 8 μC point charge to ($x = -2$ mm, $y = 0$ mm)? (Use Coulomb's constant $k = 9 \times 10^9$ N·m^2/C^2)

   A. 32.6 J   **B.** 9.8 J   **C.** 72 J   **D.** 81 J

11. What current flows when a 400 Ω resistor is connected across a 220 V circuit?

   A. 0.55 A   **B.** 1.8 A   **C.** 5.5 A   **D.** 0.18 A

12. Which statement is accurate for when different resistors are connected in parallel across an ideal battery?

   A. Power dissipated in each is the same
   B. Potential difference across each is the same
   C. Current flowing in each is the same
   D. Their equivalent resistance is equal to the average of the individual resistances

13. An electron was accelerated from rest through a potential difference of 990 V. What is its speed? (Use the mass of an electron = 9.11×10^{-31} kg, the mass of a proton = 1.67×10^{-27} kg and the charge of a proton = 1.6×10^{-19} C)

   A. 0.8×10^7 m/s   **B.** 3.7×10^7 m/s   **C.** 7.4×10^7 m/s   **D.** 1.9×10^7 m/s

14. A circular conducting loop with a radius of 0.5 m and a small gap filled with a 12 Ω resistor is oriented in the *xy*-plane. If a magnetic field of 1 T, making an angle of 30° with the *z*-axis, increases to 12 T, in 5 s, what is the magnitude of the current flowing in the conductor?

   A. 0.33 A   **B.** 0.13 A   **C.** 0.88 A   **D.** 1.5 A

15. For an electric motor with a resistance of 35 Ω that draws 10 A of current, what is the voltage drop?

   A. 3.5 V   **B.** 25 V   **C.** 350 V   **D.** 3,500 V

16. A charged parallel-plate capacitor has an electric field E_0 between its plates. The bare nuclei of a stationary ^{1}H and ^{4}He are between the plates. Ignoring the force of gravity, how does the magnitude of the acceleration of the hydrogen nucleus a_H compare with the magnitude of the acceleration of the helium nucleus a_{He}? (Use mass of an electron = 9×10^{-31} kg, mass of a proton = 1.67×10^{-27} kg, mass of a neutron = 1.67×10^{-27} kg and charge of a proton = 1.6×10^{-19} C)

   A. $a_H = 2a_{He}$ **B.** $a_H = 4a_{He}$ **C.** $a_H = \frac{1}{4}a_{He}$ **D.** $a_H = a_{He}$

17. Identical light bulbs are attached to identical batteries in three different ways (A, B, or C), as shown in the figure. What is the ranking (from lowest to highest) of the total power produced by the battery?

   A. C, B, A   **C.** A, C, B

   B. B, A, C   **D.** A, B, C

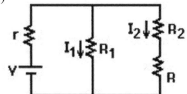

18. A parallel-plate capacitor consists of two parallel, square plates that have dimensions 1 cm by 1 cm. If the plates are separated by 1 mm, and the space between them is filled with Teflon, what is the capacitance? (Use the dielectric constant k for Teflon = 2.1 and the electric permittivity $\varepsilon_0 = 8.854 \times 10^{-12}$ F/m)

   A. 0.83 pF   **B.** 2.2 pF   **C.** 0.46 pF   **D.** 1.9 pF

19. The resistor R has a variable resistance. Which statement is true when R is decreased? (Neglect the very small internal resistance r of the battery)

   A. I_1 decreases, I_2 increases

   B. I_1 increases, I_2 remains the same

   C. I_1 remains the same, I_2 increases

   D. I_1 remains the same, I_2 decreases

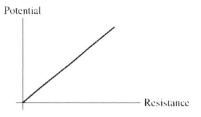

20. What physical quantity does the slope of the graph represent?

   A. 1 / Current   **C.** Current

   B. Voltage   **D.** Resistivity

21. An alternating current is supplied to an electronic component with a rating that it be used only for voltages below 12 V. What is the highest V_{rms} that can be supplied to this component while staying below the voltage limit?

    A. 6 V   **B.** $6\sqrt{2}$ V   **C.** $3\sqrt{2}$ V   **D.** $12\sqrt{2}$ V

22. A generator produces alternating current electricity with a frequency of 40 cycles per second. What is the maximum potential difference created by the generator, if the RMS voltage is 150 V?

    A. 54 V   **B.** 91 V   **C.** 212 V   **D.** 141 V

23. Kirchhoff's junction rule is a statement of:

    A. Law of conservation of energy   **C.** Law of conservation of momentum
    B. Law of conservation of angular momentum   **D.** Law of conservation of charge

24. Four identical capacitors are connected in parallel to a battery. If a total charge of Q flows from the battery, how much charge does each capacitor carry?

    A. $Q/4$ **B.** Q **C.** $4Q$ **D.** $16Q$

25. Which statement is correct for two conductors that are joined by a long copper wire?

    A. The electric field at the surface of each conductor is the same
    B. Each conductor must be at the same potential
    C. Each conductor must have the same resistivity
    D. A free charge must be present on either conductor

26. Electromagnetic induction occurs in a coil when there is a change in the:

    A. coil's charge   **C.** magnetic field intensity in the coil
    B. current in the coil   **D.** electric field intensity in the coil

27. When unequal resistors are connected in series across an ideal battery, the:

    A. current flowing in each is the same
    B. equivalent resistance of the circuit is less than that of the greatest resistor
    C. power dissipated in each turn is the same
    D. potential difference across each is the same

28. Electric current flows only from the point of:

    A. equal potential
    B. high pressure to the point of lower pressure
    C. low pressure to the point of higher pressure
    D. high potential to the point of lower potential

29. Consider the group of charges in this figure. All three charges have $Q = 3.8$ nC. What is their electric potential energy?

(Use Coulomb's constant $k = 9.0 \times 10^9 \, \text{N·m}^2/\text{C}^2$)

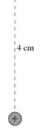

    A. 1.9×10^{-6} J   **C.** 8.8×10^{-6} J
    B. 1.0×10^{-5} J   **D.** 9.7×10^{-6} J

30. A positively-charged and negatively-charged particle are traveling on the same path perpendicular to a constant magnetic field. How do the forces experienced by the two particles differ, if the magnitudes of the charges are equal?

    A. Differ in direction, but not in magnitude
    B. Differ in magnitude, but not in direction
    C. No difference in magnitude or direction
    D. Differ in both magnitude and direction

31. An electron moves in a direction opposite to an electric field. The potential energy of the system:

    A. decreases, and the electron moves toward a region of lower potential
    B. increases, and the electron moves toward a region of higher potential
    C. decreases, and the electron moves toward a region of higher potential
    D. remains constant, and the electron moves toward a region of higher potential

32. What is the name of a device that transforms electrical energy into mechanical energy?

    A. Magnet   **C.** Turbine
    B. Transformer   **D.** Motor

33. A hydrogen atom consists of a proton and an electron. If the orbital radius of the electron increases, the absolute magnitude of the potential energy of the electron:

    A. remains the same   **C.** increases
    B. decreases   **D.** depends on the potential of the electron

34. Copper wire A has a length L and a radius r. Copper wire B has a length $2L$ and a radius $2r$. Which of the following is true regarding the resistances across the ends of the wires?

    A. The resistance of wire A is one-half that of wire B

    B. The resistance of wire A is four times higher than that of wire B

    C. The resistance of wire A is twice as high as that of wire B

    D. The resistance of wire A is equal to that of wire B

35. When a negative charge is free, it tries to move:

    A. toward infinity

    B. away from infinity

    C. from high potential to low potential

    D. from low potential to high potential

36. Four 6 V batteries (in a linear sequence of A → B → C → D) are connected in series to power lights A and B. The resistance of light A is 50 Ω and the resistance of light B is 25 Ω. What is the potential difference at a point between battery C and battery D? (Assume that the potential at the start of the sequence is zero)

    A. 4 volts   **B.** 12 volts   **C.** 18 volts   **D.** 26 volts

37. By what factor does the dielectric constant change when a material is introduced between the plates of a parallel-plate capacitor if the capacitance increases by a factor of 4?

    A. ½   **B.** 4   **C.** 0.4   **D.** ¼

38. Two isolated copper plates, each of area 0.4 m², carry opposite charges of magnitude 6.8×10^{-10} C. They are placed opposite each other in parallel alignment. What is the potential difference between the plates when their spacing is 4 cm? (Use the dielectric constant $k = 1$ in air and the electric permittivity $\varepsilon_0 = 8.854 \times 10^{-12}$ F/m)

    A. 1.4 V   **B.** 4.1 V   **C.** 7.7 V   **D.** 3.2 V

39. The force on an electron moving in a magnetic field is largest when its direction is:

    A. perpendicular to the magnetic field direction

    B. at an angle greater than 90° to the magnetic field direction

    C. at an angle less than 90° to the magnetic field direction

    D. exactly opposite to the magnetic field direction

40. What is the quantity that is calculated in units of A·s?

    A. Passivity   **B.** Capacitance   **C.** Potential   **D.** Charge

41. A proton with a speed of 1.7×10^5 m/s falls through a potential difference V and thereby increases its speed to 3.2×10^5 m/s. Through what potential difference did the proton fall? (Use the mass of a proton $= 1.67 \times 10^{-27}$ kg and the charge of a proton $= 1.6 \times 10^{-19}$ C)

A. 880 V

B. 1,020 V

C. 384 V

D. 430 V

42. Three capacitors are connected to a battery as shown. The capacitances are: $C_1 = 2C_2$ and $C_1 = 3C_3$. Which of the three capacitors stores the smallest amount of charge?

A. C_1

B. C_1 or C_3

C. C_2

D. The amount of charge is the same in all three capacitors

43. Two isolated copper plates, each of area 0.6 m^2, carry opposite charges of magnitude 7.08×10^{-10} C. They are placed opposite each other in parallel alignment, with a spacing of 2 mm. What will be the potential difference between the plates when their spacing is increased to 6 cm? (Use the dielectric constant $k = 1$ in air and electric permittivity $\varepsilon_0 = 8.854 \times 10^{-12}$ F/m)

A. 8.0 V   **B.** 3.1 V   **C.** 4.3 V   **D.** 7.2 V

44. Electric current can only flow:

A. in a region of negligible resistance

B. through a potential difference

C. in a perfect conductor

D. in the absence of resistance

45. The metal detectors used to screen passengers at airports operate via:

A. Newton's Laws   **B.** Bragg's Law   **C.** Faraday's Law   **D.** Ohm's Law

46. A 7 µC negative charge is attracted to a large, well-anchored, positive charge. How much kinetic energy does the negatively-charged object gain if the potential difference through which it moves is 3.5 mV?

A. 24.5 nJ   **B.** 6.7 µJ   **C.** 36.7 µJ   **D.** 0.5 kJ

47. A wire of resistivity ρ is replaced in a circuit by a wire of the same material but four times as long. If the total resistance remains the same, the diameter of the new wire must be:

A. one-fourth the original diameter

B. two times the original diameter

C. the same as the original diameter

D. one-half the original diameter

48. The addition of resistors in series to a resistor in an existing circuit, while voltage remains constant, would result in [   ] in the original resistor.

A. an increase in current

B. a decrease in resistance

C. an increase in resistance

D. a decrease in current

49. In an experiment, a battery is connected to a variable resistor R, where resistance can be adjusted by turning a knob. The potential difference across the resistor and the current through it are recorded for different settings of the resistor knob. The battery is an ideal potential source in series with an internal resistor. The emf of the potential source is 9 V, and the internal resistance is 0.1 Ω. What is the current if the variable resistor is set at 0.5 Ω?

A. 15 A   B. 0.9 A   C. 4.5 A   D. 45 A

50. Two parallel plates that are initially uncharged are separated by 1.6 mm. What charge must be transferred from one plate to the other if 10 kJ of energy is to be stored in the plates? The area of each plate is 24 mm². (Use the dielectric constant $k = 1$ in air and the electric permittivity $\varepsilon_0 = 8.854 \times 10^{-12}$ F/m)

A. 78 μC   B. 15 mC   C. 52 μC   D. 29 μC

51. When a proton is moving in the direction of the electric field, the potential energy of the system [   ] and it moves toward [   ] electric potential. (Use the dielectric constant $k = 1$ in air and the electric permittivity $\varepsilon_0 = 8.854 \times 10^{-12}$ F/m)

A. increases ... increasing

B. decreases ... decreasing

C. increases ... decreasing

D. decreases ... increasing

52. Each plate of a parallel-plate air capacitor has an area of 0.004 m², and the separation of the plates is 0.02 mm. An electric field of 8.6×10^6 V/m is present between the plates. What is the energy density between the plates? (Use the electric permittivity $\varepsilon_0 = 8.854 \times 10^{-12}$ F/m)

A. 100 J/m³   B. 400 J/m³   C. 220 J/m³   D. 330 J/m³

53. What is the quantity that is calculated with units of kg·m²/(s·C²)?

A. Resistance   B. Capacitance   C. Potential   D. Resistivity

54. At a constant voltage, an increase in the resistance of a circuit results in:

A. no change in I or V

B. an increase in I

C. a decrease in I

D. constant power

55. A charge $+Q$ is located at one of the corners of a square. The absolute potential at the center of a square is 3 V. If a second charge $-Q$ is placed at one of the other three corners, what is the absolute potential at the square's center?

    A. –6 V   **B.** 12 V   **C.** 6 V   **D.** 0 V

56. A uniform electric field has a strength of 6 N/C. What is the electric energy density of the field? (Use the electric permittivity $\varepsilon_0 = 8.854 \times 10^{-12}$ F/m)

    A. 1.5×10^{12} J/m^3 **B.** 1.6×10^{-10} J/m^3 **C.** 2.3×10^{12} J/m^3 **D.** 2.7×10^{-11} J/m^3

57. Which change to a circuit element will always increase the current?

    A. Increased voltage and decreased resistance
    B. Decreased voltage and increased resistance
    C. Increased voltage and increased resistance
    D. Only a decrease in resistance, the voltage does not affect current

58. Three capacitors are arranged as shown. C_1 has a capacitance of 9 pF, C_2 has a capacitance of 18 pF, and C_3 has a capacitance of 24 pF. What is the voltage drop across the entire system if the voltage drop across C_2 is 240 V?

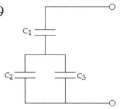

    A. 430 V   **B.** 870 V   **C.** 1,200 V   **D.** 1,350 V

59. Doubling the capacitance of a capacitor that is holding a constant charge causes the energy stored in that capacitor to:

    A. decrease to one-half   **C.** quadruple
    B. decrease to one-fourth   **D.** double

60. When three resistors are added in series to a resistor in a circuit, the original resistor's voltage [   ] and its current [   ].

    A. decreases ... increases   **C.** decrease ... decreases
    B. increases ... increases   **D.** decreases ... remains the same

Circuit Elements

1: B	11: A	21: B	31: C	41: C	51: B
2: D	12: B	22: C	32: D	42: D	52: D
3: C	13: D	23: D	33: B	43: A	53: A
4: D	14: B	24: A	34: C	44: B	54: C
5: D	15: C	25: B	35: D	45: C	55: D
6: A	16: A	26: C	36: C	46: A	56: B
7: C	17: B	27: A	37: B	47: B	57: A
8: D	18: D	28: D	38: C	48: D	58: D
9: B	19: C	29: B	39: A	49: A	59: A
10: C	20: C	30: A	40: D	50: C	60: C

Sound

1. A 20 decibel (dB) noise is heard from a cricket 30 m away. How loud would it sound if the cricket were 3 m away?

   A. 30 dB   **B.** 40 dB   **C.** $20 \times \sqrt{2}$ dB   **D.** 80 dB

2. A thunderclap occurs at a distance of 6 km from a stationary person. How soon does the person hear it? (Use the speed of sound in air $v = 340$ m/s)

   A. 18 s   **B.** 30 s   **C.** 48 s   **D.** 56 s

3. Enrico Caruso, a famous opera singer, is said to have made a crystal chandelier shatter with his voice. This is a demonstration of:

   A. ideal frequency   **C.** a standing wave
   B. resonance   **D.** sound refraction

4. A taut 2 m string is fixed at both ends and plucked. What is the wavelength corresponding to the third harmonic?

   A. 2/3 m   **B.** 1 m   **C.** 4/3 m   **D.** 3 m

5. High-pitched sound has a high:

      I. number of partial tones   II. frequency   III. speed

   A. I only   **B.** II only   **C.** III only   **D.** I and II only

6. A light ray in air strikes a medium whose index of refraction is 1.5. If the angle of incidence is 60°, which of the following expressions gives the angle of refraction? (Use $n_{air} = 1$)

   A. $\sin^{-1}(0.67 \sin 60°)$ **C.** $\sin^{-1}(1.5 \sin 30°)$
   B. $\sin^{-1}(1.5 \cos 60°)$ **D.** $\sin^{-1}(0.67 \sin 30°)$

7. A string, 2 m in length, is fixed at both ends and tightened until the wave speed is 92 m/s. What is the frequency of the standing wave shown?

   A. 46 Hz   **B.** 33 Hz   **C.** 240 Hz   **D.** 138 Hz

8. A 0.6 m uniform bar of metal, with a diameter of 2 cm, has a mass of 2.5 kg. A 1.5 MHz longitudinal wave is propagated along the length of the bar. A wave compression traverses the length of the bar in 0.14 ms. What is the wavelength of the longitudinal wave in the metal?

   A. 2.9 mm   **B.** 1.8 mm   **C.** 3.2 mm   **D.** 4.6 mm

Questions **9-12** are based on the following:

The velocity of a wave on a wire or string is not dependent (to a close approximation) on frequency or amplitude and is given by $v^2 = T / \rho_L$. T is the tension in the wire. The linear mass density ρ_L (rho) is the mass per unit length of wire. Therefore, ρ_L is the product of the mass density and the cross-sectional area (A).

A sine wave is traveling to the right with frequency 250 Hz. Wire A is composed of steel and has a circular cross-section diameter of 0.6 mm, and a tension of 2,000 N. Wire B is under the same tension and is made of the same material as wire A, but has a circular cross-section diameter of 0.3 mm. Wire C has the same tension as wire A and is made of a composite material. (Use the density of steel wire $\rho = 7$ g/cm^3 and the density of the composite material $\rho = 3$ g/cm^3)

9. By how much does the tension need to be increased to increase the wave velocity on a wire by 30%?

    A. 37%   **B.** 60%   **C.** 69%   **D.** 81%

10. What is the linear mass density of wire B compared to wire A?

    A. $\sqrt{2}$ times   **B.** 2 times   **C.** 1/8   **D.** 1/4

11. What must the diameter of wire C be to have the same wave velocity as wire A?

    A. 0.41 mm   **B.** 0.92 mm   **C.** 0.83 mm   **D.** 3.2 mm

12. How does the cross-sectional area change if the diameter increases by a factor of 4?

    A. Increases by a factor of 16   **C.** Increases by a factor of 2
    B. Increases by a factor of 4   **D.** Decreases by a factor of 4

13. A bird, emitting sounds with a frequency of 60 kHz, is moving at a speed of 10 m/s toward a stationary observer. What is the frequency of the sound waves detected by the observer? (Use the speed of sound in air $v = 340$ m/s)

    A. 55 kHz   **B.** 62 kHz   **C.** 68 kHz   **D.** 76 kHz

14. What is observed for a frequency heard by a stationary person when a sound source is approaching?

    A. Equal to zero   **C.** Higher than the source
    B. The same as the source   **D.** Lower than the source

15. Which of the following is a false statement?

   A. The transverse waves on a vibrating string are different from sound waves
   B. Sound travels much slower than light
   C. Sound waves are longitudinal pressure waves
   D. Sound can travel through a vacuum

16. Which of the following is a real-life example of the Doppler effect?

   A. Changing pitch of the siren as an ambulance passes by the observer
   B. Radio signal transmission
   C. Sound becomes quieter as the observer moves away from the source
   D. Human hearing is most acute at 2,500 Hz

17. Two sound waves have the same frequency and amplitudes of 0.4 Pa and 0.6 Pa, respectively. When they arrive at point X, what is the range of possible amplitudes for sound at point X?

   A. 0 – 0.4 Pa   **B.** 0.4 – 0.6 Pa   **C.** 0.2 – 1.0 Pa   **D.** 0.4 – 0.8 Pa

18. The intensity of the waves from a point source at a distance d from the source is I. What is the intensity at a distance $2d$ from the source?

   A. I/2   **B.** I/4   **C.** 4I   **D.** 2I

19. Sound would be expected to travel most slowly in a medium that exhibited:

   A. low resistance to compression and high density
   B. high resistance to compression and low density
   C. low resistance to compression and low density
   D. high resistance to compression and high density

20. Which is true for a resonating pipe that is open at both ends?

   A. Displacement node at one end and a displacement antinode at the other end
   B. Displacement antinodes at each end
   C. Displacement nodes at each end
   D. Displacement node at one end and a one-fourth antinode at the other end

21. In a pipe of length L that is open at both ends, the lowest tone to resonate is 200 Hz. Which of the following frequencies does not resonate in this pipe?

   A. 400 Hz   **B.** 600 Hz   **C.** 500 Hz   **D.** 800 Hz

22. In general, a sound is conducted fastest through:

   A. vacuum   **B.** gases   **C.** liquids   **D.** solids

23. If an electric charge is shaken up and down:

    A. electron excitation occurs   **C.** sound is emitted

    B. a magnetic field is created   **D.** its charge changes

24. What is the wavelength of a sound wave of frequency 620 Hz in steel, given that the speed of sound in steel is 5,000 m/s?

    A. 1.8 m   **B.** 6.2 m   **C.** 8.1 m   **D.** 2.6 m

25. If the sound from a constant sound source is radiating equally in all directions, as the distance doubles, by what amount is the intensity of the sound reduced?

    A. ¼   **B.** 1/16   **C.** $1/\sqrt{2}$ **D.** ½

26. Why does the intensity of waves from a sound source decrease with the square of the distance from the source?

    A. The medium through which the waves travel absorbs the energy of the waves

    B. The waves speed up as they travel away from the source

    C. The waves lose energy as they travel

    D. The waves spread out as they travel

Questions **27-30** are based on the following:

Steven is preparing a mailing tube that is 1.5 m long and 4 cm in diameter. The tube is open at one end and sealed at the other. Before he inserted his documents, the mailing tube fell to the floor and produced a note. (Use the speed of sound in air $v = 340$ m/s)

27. What is the wavelength of the fundamental?

    A. 0.04 m   **B.** 6 m   **C.** 0.75 m   **D.** 1.5 m

28. If the tube was filled with helium, in which sound travels at 960 m/s, what would be the frequency of the fundamental?

    A. 160 Hz   **B.** 320 Hz   **C.** 80 Hz   **D.** 640 Hz

29. What is the wavelength of the fifth harmonic?

    A. 3.2 m   **B.** 1.2 m   **C.** 2.4 m   **D.** 1.5 m

30. What is the frequency of the note that Steven heard?

    A. 57 Hz   **B.** 85 Hz   **C.** 30 Hz   **D.** 120 Hz

31. A 4 g string, 0.34 m long, is under tension. The string vibrates in the third harmonic. What is the wavelength of the standing wave in the string? (Use the speed of sound in air v = 344 m/s)

    A. 0.56 m   **B.** 0.33 m   **C.** 0.23 m   **D.** 0.61 m

32. Two pure tones are sounded together, and a particular beat frequency is heard. What happens to the beat frequency if the frequency of one of the tones is increased?

    A. Increases   **C.** Remains the same

    B. Decreases   **D.** Either increase or decrease

33. Consider a closed pipe of length L. What are the wavelengths of the three lowest tones produced by this pipe?

    A. $4L$, $4/3L$, $4/5L$ **C.** $2L$, L, $\frac{1}{2}L$

    B. $2L$, L, $2/3L$ **D.** $4L$, $2L$, L

34. Mary hears the barely perceptible buzz of a mosquito one meter away from her ear in a quiet room. How much energy does a mosquito produce in 200 s? (Note: an almost inaudible sound has a threshold value of 9.8×10^{-12} W/m²)

    A. 6.1×10^{-8} J   **C.** 6.4×10^{-10} J

    B. 1.3×10^{-8} J   **D.** 2.5×10^{-8} J

35. How long does it take for a light wave to travel 1 km through the water with a refractive index of 1.33? (Use the speed of light $c = 3 \times 10^8$ m/s)

    A. 4.4×10^{-6} s   **C.** 2.8×10^{-9} s

    B. 4.4×10^{-9} s   **D.** 2.8×10^{-12} s

36. In designing a music hall, an acoustical engineer deals mainly with:

    A. wave interference   **C.** forced vibrations

    B. resonance   **D.** modulation

37. Which curve in the figure represents the variation of wave speed (v) as a function of tension (T) for transverse waves on a stretched string?

    A. A

    B. B

    C. C

    D. D

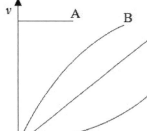

38. A string, 4 meters in length, is fixed at both ends and tightened until the wave speed is 20 m/s. What is the frequency of the standing wave shown?

A. 13 Hz   **B.** 8.1 Hz   **C.** 5.4 Hz   **D.** 15.4 Hz

39. Compared to the velocity of a 600 Hz sound, the velocity of a 300 Hz sound through air is:

A. one-half as great   **B.** the same   **C.** twice as great   **D.** four times as great

40. Consider a string having a linear mass density of 0.40 g/m stretched to a length of 0.50 m by tension of 75 N, vibrating at the 6th harmonic. It excites an open pipe into the second overtone. What is the length of the pipe?

A. 0.25 m   **B.** 0.1 m   **C.** 0.20 m   **D.** 0.6 m

41. A string of length L is under tension, and the speed of a wave in the string is v. What is the speed of a wave in a string of the same mass under the same tension but twice as long?

A. $v\sqrt{2}$ **B.** $2v$ **C.** $v/2$ **D.** $v/\sqrt{2}$

42. If a guitar string has a fundamental frequency of 500 Hz, which one of the following frequencies can set the string into resonant vibration?

A. 450 Hz   **B.** 760 Hz   **C.** 1,500 Hz   **D.** 2,250 Hz

43. When a light wave is passing from a medium with a lower refractive index to a medium with a higher refractive index, some of the incident light is refracted, while some are reflected. What is the angle of refraction?

A. Greater than the angle of incidence and less than the angle of reflection
B. Less than the angle of incidence and greater than the angle of reflection
C. Greater than the angles of incidence and reflection
D. Less than the angles of incidence and reflection

44. The speed of a sound wave in air depends on:

   I. the air temperature   II. it's wavelength   III. it's frequency

A. I only   **B.** II only   **C.** III only   **D.** I and II only

45. Which of the following statements is false?

A. The speed of a wave and the speed of the vibrating particles that constitute the wave are different entities
B. Waves transport energy and matter from one region to another
C. In a transverse wave, the particle motion is perpendicular to the velocity vector of the wave
D. Not all waves are mechanical in nature

46. A 2.5 g string, 0.75 m long, is under tension. The string produces a 700 Hz tone when it vibrates in the third harmonic. What is the wavelength of the tone in the air? (Use the speed of sound in air $v = 344$ m/s)

    A. 0.65 m   **B.** 0.57 m   **C.** 0.33 m   **D.** 0.5 m

47. Suppose that a source of sound is emitting waves uniformly in all directions. If an observer moves to a point twice as far away from the source, what is the frequency of the sound?

    A. $\sqrt{2}$ as large   **B.** Twice as large   **C.** Unchanged   **D.** Half as large

48. A 2.5 kg rope is stretched between supports 8 m apart. If one end of the rope is tweaked, how long will it take for the resulting disturbance to reach the other end? Assume that the tension in the rope is 40 N.

    A. 0.71 s   **B.** 0.62 s   **C.** 0.58 s   **D.** 0.47 s

49. An office machine is making a rattling sound with an intensity of 10^{-5} W/m^2 when perceived by an office worker that is sitting 3 m away. What is the sound level in decibels for the sound of the machine? (Use the threshold of hearing $I_0 = 10^{-12}$ W/m^2)

    A. 10 dB   **B.** 35 dB   **C.** 70 dB   **D.** 95 dB

50. A taut 1 m string is plucked. Point B is midway between both ends, and a finger is placed on point B such that a waveform exists with a node at B. What is the lowest frequency that can be heard? (Use the speed of waves on the string $v = 3.8 \times 10^4$ m/s)

    A. 4.8×10^5 Hz   **B.** 3.8×10^4 Hz   **C.** 9.7×10^3 Hz   **D.** 7.4×10^3 Hz

51. For a light wave traveling in a vacuum, which of the following properties is true?

    A. Increased f results in increased amplitude
    B. Increased f results in decreased speed
    C. Increased f results in an increased wavelength
    D. Increased f results in a decreased wavelength

52. Which wave is a different classification than the others (i.e., does not belong to the same grouping)?

    A. Pressure wave   **B.** Radio wave   **C.** Ultrasonic wave   **D.** Infrasonic wave

53. Two speakers are placed 2 m apart, and both produce a sound wave (in phase) with wavelength 0.8 m. A microphone is placed an equal distance from both speakers to determine the intensity of the sound at various points. What point is precisely halfway between the two speakers? (Use the speed of sound $v = 340$ m/s)

    A. Both an antinode and a node   **C.** A node
    B. Neither an antinode nor a node   **D.** An antinode

---

54. The siren of an ambulance blares at 1,200 Hz when the ambulance is stationary. What frequency does a stationary observer hear after this ambulance passes her while traveling at 30 m/s? (Use the speed of sound $v = 342$ m/s)

    A. 1,240 Hz   **B.** 1,128 Hz   **C.** 1,103 Hz   **D.** 1,427 Hz

55. Compared to the wavelength of a 600 Hz sound, the wavelength of a 300 Hz sound in air is:

    A. one-half as long   **C.** one-fourth as long
    B. the same   **D.** twice as long

56. An organ pipe that is open at both ends is tuned to a given frequency. A second pipe with both ends open resonates with twice this frequency. What is the ratio of the length of the first pipe to the second pipe?

    A. 0.5   **B.** 1   **C.** 2   **D.** 2.5

57. The frequency of the third harmonic of the C_4 string of a piano is 783.7 Hz. The fundamental frequency of the G_5 string is 782.4 Hz. When the key for C_4 is held down so that the string can vibrate, and the G_5 key is stricken loudly, the third harmonic of the C_4 string is excited. Then, when striking the G_5 key again more softly, the volume of the two strings are matched. What phenomenon is demonstrated when the G_5 string is used to excite the vibration of the C_4 string?

    A. Resonance   **C.** Beats
    B. Dispersion   **D.** Interference

58. Crests of an ocean wave pass a pier every 10 s. If the waves are moving at 4.5 m/s, what is the wavelength of the ocean waves?

    A. 38 m   **B.** 16 m   **C.** 45 m   **D.** 25 m

59. Which statement explains why sound travels faster in water than in air?

    A. Sound shifts to increased frequency
    B. Sound shifts to decreased density
    C. Density of water increases more quickly than its resistance to compression
    D. Density of water increases more slowly than its resistance to compression

60. When visible light is incident upon clear glass, the electrons in the atoms in the glass:

    I. convert the light energy into internal energy
    II. resonate
    III. vibrate

    A. I only   **B.** II only   **C.** III only   **D.** I and II only

Sound

1: B	11: B	21: C	31: C	41: A	51: D
2: A	12: A	22: D	32: D	42: C	52: B
3: B	13: B	23: B	33: A	43: D	53: D
4: C	14: C	24: C	34: D	44: A	54: C
5: B	15: D	25: A	35: A	45: B	55: D
6: A	16: A	26: D	36: A	46: D	56: C
7: D	17: C	27: B	37: B	47: C	57: A
8: A	18: B	28: A	38: D	48: A	58: C
9: C	19: A	29: B	39: B	49: C	59: D
10: D	20: B	30: A	40: C	50: B	60: C

Light and Geometrical Optics

1. What is the minimum thickness of a soap film that reflects a given wavelength of light?

  A. ¼ the wavelength   **C.** One wavelength
  B. ½ the wavelength   **D.** Two wavelengths

2. As the angle of an incident ray of light increases, the angle of the reflected ray:

  A. increases   **C.** stays the same
  B. decreases   **D.** increases or decreases

3. At what distance from a concave spherical mirror (with a focal length of 100 cm) must a woman stand to see an upright image of herself that is twice her actual height?

  A. 100 cm   **B.** 50 cm   **C.** 300 cm   **D.** 25 cm

4. If a person's eyeball is too long from front to back, what is the name of the condition that the person likely suffers?

  A. Hyperopia   **C.** Presbyopia
  B. Astigmatism   **D.** Myopia

5. According to the relationship between frequency and energy of light ($E = hf$), which color of light has more energy?

  A. Red   **B.** Yellow   **C.** Blue   **D.** Orange

6. A candle 18 cm tall sits 4 m away from a diverging lens with a focal length of 3 m. What is the size of the image?

  A. 6.3 cm   **B.** 7.7 cm   **C.** 2.9 cm   **D.** 13.5 cm

Questions **7-8** are based on the following:

A tank holds a layer of oil 1.58 m thick that floats on a layer of syrup that is 0.66 m thick. Both liquids are clear and do not intermix. A ray, which originates at the bottom of the tank on a vertical axis (see figure), crosses the oil-syrup interface at a point 0.9 m to the right of the vertical axis. The ray continues and arrives at the oil-air interface, 2 m from the axis and at the critical angle. (Use the refractive index $n = 1$ for air)

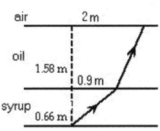

7. The index of refraction of the oil is closest to:

  A. 1.39   **B.** 1.56   **C.** 1.75   **D.** 1.82

---

8. What is the index of refraction of the syrup?

   A. 1.53   **B.** 1.46   **C.** 1.17   **D.** 1.24

9. Which of the following cannot be explained with the wave theory of light?

   A. Photoelectric effect   **C.** Polarization
   B. Interference   **D.** Diffusion

10. The use of wavefronts and rays to describe optical phenomena is known as:

   A. dispersive optics   **C.** wave optics
   B. reflector optics   **D.** geometrical optics

11. In the investigation of a new type of optical fiber (index of refraction $n = 1.26$), a laser beam is incident on the flat end of a straight fiber in air, as shown in the figure below. What is the maximum angle of incidence (θ_1) if the beam is not to escape from the fiber?

   A. 36°   **B.** 43°   **C.** 58°   **D.** 50°

12. An object is placed at a distance of 0.5 m from a converging lens with a power of 10 diopters. At what distance from the lens does the image appear?

   A. 0.13 m   **B.** 0.47 m   **C.** 0.7 m   **D.** 1.5 m

13. A virtual image is:

   I. produced by light rays

   II. the brain's interpretations of light rays

   III. found only on a concave mirror

   A. I only   **B.** II only   **C.** III only   **D.** I and II only

14. If Karen stands in front of a convex mirror, at the same distance from it as its radius of curvature:

   A. Karen does not see her image because it's focused at a different distance
   B. Karen sees her image, and she appears the same size
   C. Karen does not see her image, and she is not within its range
   D. Karen sees her image, and she appears smaller

15. An object is viewed at various distances using a mirror with a focal length of 10 m. If the object is 20 m away from the mirror, what best characterizes the image?

   A. Inverted and real   **C.** Upright and real
   B. Inverted and virtual   **D.** Upright and virtual

16. If an object is placed at a position beyond *2f* of the focal point of a converging lens, the image is:

    A. real, upright and enlarged   **C.** virtual, upright and reduced

    B. real, inverted and reduced   **D.** real, inverted and enlarged

17. Which form of electromagnetic radiation has photons with the lowest energy?

    A. X-rays   **B.** Ultraviolet radiation   **C.** Radio waves   **D.** Microwaves

18. If the index of refraction of diamond is 2.43, a given wavelength of light travels:

    A. 2.43 times faster in diamond than it does in air

    B. 2.43 times faster in a vacuum than it does in diamond

    C. 2.43 times faster in diamond than it does in a vacuum

    D. 2.43 times faster in a vacuum than it does in air

19. An object is placed 15 cm to the left of a double-convex lens of focal length 20 cm. Where is the image of this object located?

    A. 15 cm to the left of the lens   **C.** 60 cm to the right of the lens

    B. 30 cm to the left of the lens   **D.** 60 cm to the left of the lens

20. A sheet of red paper appears black when it is illuminated with:

    A. orange light   **B.** cyan light   **C.** red light   **D.** yellow light

21. Where is an object if the image produced by a lens appears very close to its focal point?

    A. Near the center of curvature of the lens   **C.** Near the lens

    B. Far from the lens   **D.** Near the focal point

22. A light with the frequency 4.9×10^{14} Hz is produced by a source located 6 m from a converging lens with a focal length of 3 m. For a different frequency of light, the focal length of the lens is different than 3 m. This phenomenon is called:

    A. Dispersion   **B.** Incidence   **C.** Interference   **D.** Refraction

23. If an image appears at the same distance from a mirror as the object, the size of the image is:

    A. exactly quadruple the size of the object   **C.** the same size as the object

    B. exactly ¼ the size of the object   **D.** exactly twice the size of the object

24. When viewed straight down (90° to the surface), an incident light ray moving from water to air is refracted:

    A. 37° away from the normal   **C.** 28° toward the normal

    B. 37° toward the normal   **D.** 0°

25. Suppose that a beachgoer uses two lenses from a pair of disassembled polarized sunglasses and places one on top of the other. What would he observe if he rotates one lens 90° with respect to the normal position of the other lens and looks directly at the sun overhead?

    A. Light with an intensity reduced to about 50% of what it would be with one lens
    B. Light with an intensity that is the same of what it would be with one lens
    C. Complete darkness, since no light would be transmitted
    D. Light with an intensity reduced to about 25% of what it would be with one lens

26. A glass plate with an index of refraction of 1.45 is immersed in a liquid. The liquid is an oil with an index of refraction of 1.35. The surface of the glass is inclined at an angle of 54° with the vertical. A horizontal ray in the glass is incident on the interface of glass and liquid. The incident horizontal ray refracts at the interface. The angle that the refracted ray in the oil makes with the horizontal is closest to:

    A. 8.3°   **B.** 14°   **C.** 6°   **D.** 12°

27. Two plane mirrors make an angle of 30°. A light ray enters the system and is reflected once off each mirror. Through what angle is the ray turned?

    A. 60°   **B.** 90°   **C.** 120°   **D.** 160°

28. Which of the following statements about light is TRUE?

    A. A packet of light energy is known as a photon
    B. Color can be used to determine the approximate energy of visible light
    C. Light travels through space at a speed of 3.0×10^8 m/s
    D. All of the above

29. The angle of incidence:

    A. may be greater than, less than, or equal to the angle of refraction
    B. is always less than the angle of refraction
    C. must equal the angle of refraction
    D. is always greater than the angle of refraction

30. A 5-foot-tall woman stands next to a plane mirror on a wall. As she walks away from the mirror, her image:

    A. is always a real image, no matter how far she is from the mirror.
    B. remains 5 feet tall.
    C. has a height less than 5 feet.
    D. may or may not get smaller, depending on where she is positioned.

31. If a spherical concave mirror has a radius of curvature R, its focal length is:

    A. 2R   **B.** R   **C.** R/2   **D.** R/4

32. Let n_1 be the index of refraction of the incident medium and let n_2 be the index of refraction of the refracting medium. Which of the following must be true if the angle that the refracted ray makes with the boundary (not with the normal) is less than the angle that the incident ray makes with the boundary?

A. $n_1 < n_2$ **B.** $n_1 > n_2$ **C.** $n_1 < 1$ **D.** $n_2 < 1$

33. If a person's eyeball is too short from front to back, the person is likely to suffer from:

A. nearsightedness **B.** farsightedness **C.** presbyopia **D.** astigmatism

34. The shimmering that is observed over a hot surface is:

A. changing refraction from the mixing of warm and cool air
B. a mirage
C. heat rays
D. reflections from evaporating water vapor

35. When two parallel white rays pass through the outer edges of a converging glass lens, chromatic aberrations cause colors to appear on the screen in what order, from the top down?

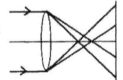

A. Blue, blue, red, red
B. Red, blue, blue, red
C. Blue, red, red, blue
D. Red, red, blue, blue

36. Two thin converging lenses are near each other so that the lens on the left has a focal length of 2 m and the one on the right has a focal length of 4 m. What is the focal length of the combination?

A. 1/4 m **B.** 4/3 m **C.** 3/4 m **D.** 4 m

37. A cylindrical tank is 50 ft deep, 37.5 ft in diameter, and filled to the top with water. A flashlight shines into the tank from above. What is the minimum angle θ that its beam can make with the water surface if the beam is to illuminate part of the bottom? (Use the index of refraction $n = 1.33$ for water)

A. 25° **B.** 31° **C.** 37° **D.** 53°

38. Which color of the visible spectrum has the shortest wavelength (400 nm)?

A. Violet **B.** Green **C.** Orange **D.** Blue

39. An object is placed at a distance d in front of a plane mirror. The size of the image is:

A. dependent on where the observer is positioned when looking at the image
B. twice the size of the object
C. half the size of the object
D. the same as the object, independent of the position of the observer or distance d

40. If a single lens forms a virtual image of an object, then the:

    I. image must be upright

    II. lens must be a converging lens

    III. lens could be either diverging or converging

  A. I only   **B.** I and III only   **C.** III only   **D.** I and II only

41. When neon light passes through a prism, what is observed?

  A. White light   **C.** The same neon light

  B. Bright spots or lines   **D.** Continuous spectrum

42. The law of reflection holds for:

    I. plane mirrors   II. curved mirrors   III. spherical mirrors

  A. I only   **B.** II only   **C.** III only   **D.** I, II and III

43. The image formed by a single concave lens:

  A. can be real or virtual but is always real when the object is placed at the focal point

  B. can be real or virtual, depending on the object's distance compared to the focal length

  C. is always virtual

  D. is always real

44. A lens forms a virtual image of an object. Which of the following must be true of the image?

  A. It is inverted   **C.** It is larger than the object and upright

  B. It is upright   **D.** It is smaller than the object and inverted

45. Light with the lowest frequency (longest wavelength) detected by your eyes is perceived as:

  A. red   **B.** green   **C.** yellow   **D.** orange

46. A 0.1 m tall candle is observed through a converging lens that is 3 m away and has a focal length of 6 m. The resulting image is:

  A. 3 m from the lens on the opposite side of the object

  B. 6 m from the lens on the opposite side of the object

  C. 3 m from the lens on the same side as the object

  D. 6 m from the lens on the same side as the object

47. Which statement about thin lenses is correct when considering only a single lens?

  A. A diverging lens always produces a virtual, erect image

  B. A diverging lens always produces a real, erect image

  C. A diverging lens always produces a virtual, inverted image

  D. A diverging lens always produces a real, inverted image

48. A double-concave lens has equal radii of curvature of 15 cm. An object placed 14 cm from the lens forms a virtual image 5 cm from the lens. What is the index of refraction of the lens material?

    A. 0.8   **B.** 1.4   **C.** 2   **D.** 2.6

49. The magnification m for an object reflected from a mirror is the ratio of what characteristic of the image to the object?

    A. Center of curvature   **B.** Distance   **C.** Orientation   **D.** Angular size

50. Suppose Mike places his face in front of a concave mirror. Which of the following statements is correct?

    A. Mike's image is diminished in size
    B. Mike's image is always inverted
    C. No matter where Mike places himself, a virtual image is formed
    D. If Mike positions himself between the center of curvature and the focal point of the mirror, he will not be able to see his image

51. Single-concave spherical mirrors produce images that:

    A. are always smaller than the actual object
    B. are always the same size as the actual object
    C. are always larger than the actual object
    D. could be smaller than, larger than, or the same size as the actual object, depending on the placement of the object

52. When two converging lenses of equal focal lengths are used together, the effective combined focal length is less than the focal length of either one of the individual lens. The combined power of the two lenses used together is:

    A. greater than the power of either individual lens
    B. the same as the power of either individual lens
    C. less than the power of either individual lens
    D. greater than the sum of the powers of both individual lens

53. The index of refraction is based on the ratio of the speed of light in:

    A. water to the speed of light in the transparent material
    B. a vacuum to the speed of light in the transparent material
    C. two different transparent materials
    D. air to the speed of light in the transparent material

54. An object is located 2.2 m in front of a plane mirror. The image formed by the mirror appears:

A. 4.4 m behind the mirror's surface   **C.** 4.4 m in front of the mirror's surface
B. 2.2 m in front of the mirror's surface   **D.** 2.2 m behind the mirror's surface

55. An upright object is 40 cm from a concave mirror with a radius of 50 cm. The image is:

A. virtual and inverted   **C.** real and inverted
B. virtual and upright   **D.** real and upright

56. In the figure, a ray in glass arrives at the glass-water interface at an angle of 48° with the normal. The refracted ray makes an angle of 68° with the normal. If another ray in the glass makes an angle of 29° with the normal, what is the angle of refraction in the water? (Use the index of refraction of water $n = 1.33$)

A. 29°   **C.** 31°
B. 37°   **D.** 46°

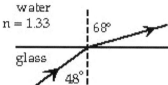

57. In a compound microscope:

A. the image of the objective serves as the object for the eyepiece
B. magnification is provided by the objective and not by the eyepiece. The eyepiece merely
   increases the brightness of the image viewed
C. magnification is provided by the objective and not by the eyepiece. The eyepiece
   merely increases the resolution of the image viewed
D. both the objective and the eyepiece form real images

58. Except for air, the refractive index of all transparent materials is:

A. equal to 1   **C.** less than 1
B. less than or equal to 1   **D.** greater than 1

59. The radius of curvature of the curved side of a plano-convex lens made of glass is 33 cm. What is the focal length of the lens? (Use the index of refraction for glass $n = 1.64$)

A. −28 cm   **B.** 28 cm   **C.** 38 cm   **D.** 52 cm

60. The part of the electromagnetic spectrum most absorbed by water is:

A. lower frequencies in the visible   **C.** infrared
B. higher frequencies in the visible   **D.** ultraviolet

Light & Geometrical Optics

1: A	11: D	21: B	31: C	41: B	51: D
2: A	12: A	22: A	32: B	42: D	52: A
3: B	13: D	23: C	33: B	43: C	53: B
4: D	14: D	24: D	34: A	44: B	54: D
5: C	15: A	25: C	35: C	45: A	55: C
6: B	16: B	26: C	36: B	46: D	56: B
7: C	17: C	27: A	37: C	47: A	57: A
8: D	18: B	28: D	38: A	48: C	58: D
9: A	19: D	29: A	39: D	49: B	59: D
10: D	20: B	30: B	40: B	50: D	60: C

Thermodynamics

1. Compared to the initial value, what is the resulting pressure for an ideal gas that is compressed isothermally to one-third of its initial volume?

    A. Equal   **C.** Larger, but less than three times larger
    B. Three times larger   **D.** More than three times larger

2. A uniform hole in a brass plate has a diameter of 1.2 cm at 25 °C. What is the diameter of the hole when the plate is heated to 225 °C? (Use the coefficient of linear thermal expansion for brass $= 19 \times 10^{-6}$ K^{-1})

    A. 2.2 cm   **B.** 2.8 cm   **C.** 1.2 cm   **D.** 1.6 cm

3. A student heats 90 g of water using 50 W of power, with 100% efficiency. How long does it take to raise the temperature of the water from 10 °C to 30 °C? (Use the specific heat of water $c = 4.186$ J/g·°C)

    A. 232 s   **B.** 81 s   **C.** 59 s   **D.** 151 s

4. A runner generates 1,260 W of thermal energy. If her heat is to be dissipated only by evaporation, how much water does she shed in 15 minutes of running? (Use the latent heat of vaporization of water $L_v = 22.6 \times 10^5$ J/kg)

    A. 500 g   **B.** 35 g   **C.** 350 g   **D.** 50 g

5. Phase changes occur as temperature:

      I. decreases   II. increases   III. remains the same

    A. I only   **B.** II only   **C.** III only   **D.** I and II only

6. How much heat is needed to melt a 55 kg sample of ice that is at 0 °C? (Use the latent heat of fusion for water $L_f = 334$ kJ/kg and the latent heat of vaporization $L_v = 2,257$ kJ/kg)

    A. 0 kJ   **C.** 3×10^5 kJ
    B. 1.8×10^4 kJ   **D.** 4.6×10^6 kJ

7. Metals are both good heat conductors and good electrical conductors because of the:

    A. relatively high densities of metals
    B. high elasticity of metals
    C. ductility of metals
    D. looseness of outer electrons in metal atoms

8. Solar houses are designed to retain the heat absorbed during the day so that the stored heat can be released during the night. A botanist produces steam at 100 °C during the day, and then allows the steam to cool to 0 °C and freeze during the night. How many kilograms of water are needed to store 200 kJ of energy for this process? (Use the latent heat of vaporization of water $L_v = 22.6 \times 10^5$ J/kg, the latent heat of fusion of water $L_f = 33.5 \times 10^4$ J/kg, and the specific heat capacity of water $c = 4{,}186$ J/kg·K)

   A. 0.066 kg   **B.** 0.103 kg   **C.** 0.482 kg   **D.** 1.18 kg

9. The heat required to change a substance from the solid to the liquid state is referred to as the heat of:

   A. condensation   **B.** freezing   **C.** fusion   **D.** vaporization

10. A rigid container holds 0.2 kg of hydrogen gas. How much heat is needed to change the temperature of the gas from 250 K to 280 K? (Use specific heat of hydrogen gas = 14.3 J/g·K)

   A. 46 kJ   **B.** 72 kJ   **C.** 56 kJ   **D.** 86 kJ

11. An aluminum electric tea kettle with a mass of 500 g is heated with a 500 W heating coil. How many minutes are required to heat 1 kg of water from 18 °C to 98 °C in the tea kettle? (Use the specific heat of aluminum = 900 J/kg·K and specific heat of water = 4,186 J/kg·K)

   A. 16 min   **B.** 12 min   **C.** 8 min   **D.** 4 min

12. Heat is added at a constant rate to a pure substance in a closed container. The temperature of the substance as a function of time is shown in the graph. If $L_f =$ latent heat of fusion and $L_v =$ latent heat of vaporization, what is the value of the ratio L_v / L_f for this substance?

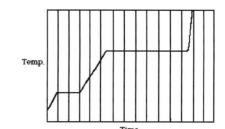

   A. 3.5   **B.** 7.2   **C.** 4.5   **D.** 5.0

13. The moderate temperatures of islands throughout the world have much to do with water's:

   A. high evaporation rate   **C.** vast supply of thermal energy
   B. high specific heat capacity   **D.** poor conductivity

14. A 4.5 g lead BB moving at 46 m/s penetrates a wood block and comes to rest inside the block. If the BB absorbs half of the kinetic energy, what is the change in the temperature of the BB? (Use the specific heat of lead = 128 J/kg·K)

   A. 2.8 K   **B.** 3.6 K   **C.** 1.6 K   **D.** 4.1 K

15. The heat required to change a substance from the liquid to the vapor state is referred to as the heat of:

   A. melting   **B.** condensation   **C.** vaporization   **D.** fusion

16. A Carnot engine operating between a reservoir of liquid mercury at its melting point and a colder reservoir extracts 18 J of heat from the mercury and does 5 J of work during each cycle. What is the temperature of the colder reservoir? (Use melting temperature of mercury = 233 K)

    A. 168 K   **B.** 66 K   **C.** 57 K   **D.** 82 K

17. A 920 g empty iron pan is put on a stove. How much heat in joules must the iron pan absorb to raise its temperature from 18 °C to 96 °C? (Use the specific heat for iron = 113 cal/kg·°C and the conversion of 1 cal = 4.186 J)

    A. 50,180 J   **B.** 81,010 J   **C.** 63,420 J   **D.** 33,940 J

18. When a solid melts, what change occurs in the substance?

    A. Heat energy dissipates   **C.** Temperature increases
    B. Heat energy enters   **D.** Temperature decreases

19. Which of the following is an accurate statement about the work done for a cyclic process carried out in a gas? (Use P for pressure and V for volume on the graph)

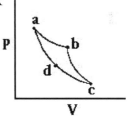

    A. It is equal to the area under *ab* minus the area under *dc*
    B. It is equal to the area under the curve *adc*
    C. It is equal to the area enclosed by the cyclic process
    D. It equals zero

20. Substance A has a higher specific heat than substance B. With all other factors equal, which substance requires more energy to be heated to the same temperature?

    A. Substance A   **C.** Both require the same amount of heat
    B. Substance B   **D.** Depends on the density of each substance

21. A 6.5 g meteor hits the Earth at a speed of 300 m/s. If the meteor's kinetic energy is entirely converted to heat, by how much does its temperature rise? (Use the specific heat of the meteor = 120 cal/kg·°C and the conversion of 1 cal = 4.186 J)

    A. 134 °C   **B.** 68 °C   **C.** 120 °C   **D.** 90 °C

22. When a liquid freezes, what change occurs in the substance?

    A. Heat energy dissipates   **C.** Temperature increases
    B. Heat energy enters   **D.** Temperature decreases

23. A monatomic ideal gas (C_v = 3/2 R) undergoes an isothermal expansion at 300 K, as the volume increases from 0.05 m³ to 0.2 m³. The final pressure is 130 kPa. What is the heat transfer of the gas? (Use the ideal gas constant R = 8.314 J/mol·K)

    A. −14 kJ   **B.** 36 kJ   **C.** 14 kJ   **D.** −21 kJ

24. What is the maximum temperature rise expected for 1 kg of water falling from a waterfall with a vertical drop of 30 m? (Use the acceleration due to gravity $g = 9.8$ m/s^2 and the specific heat of water = 4,186 J/kg·K)

    A. 0.1 °C   **B.** 0.06 °C   **C.** 0.15 °C   **D.** 0.07 °C

25. When 0.75 kg of water at 0 °C freezes, what is the change in entropy of the water? (Use the latent heat of fusion of water $L_f = 33,400$ J/kg)

    A. –92 J/K   **B.** –18 J/K   **C.** 44 J/K   **D.** 80 J/K

26. When a bimetallic bar made of a copper and iron strip is heated, the copper part of the bar bends toward the iron strip. The reason for this is:

    A. copper expands more than iron   **C.** iron gets hotter before copper
    B. iron expands more than copper   **D.** copper gets hotter before iron

27. In a flask, 110 g of water is heated using 60 W of power, with perfect efficiency. How long does it take to raise the temperature of the water from 20 °C to 30 °C? (Use the specific heat of water $c = 4,186$ J/kg·K)

    A. 132 s   **B.** 57 s   **C.** 9.6 s   **D.** 77 s

28. When a liquid evaporates, what change occurs in the substance?

    A. Heat energy dissipates   **C.** Temperature increases
    B. Heat energy enters   **D.** Temperature decreases

29. A flask of liquid nitrogen is at a temperature of –243 °C. If the nitrogen is heated until the average energy of the particles is doubled, what is the new temperature?

    A. 356 °C   **B.** –356 °C   **C.** –213 °C   **D.** 134 °C

30. If a researcher is attempting to determine how much the temperature of a particular piece of material would rise when a known amount of heat is added to it, knowing which of the following quantities would be most helpful?

    A. Density   **C.** Initial temperature
    B. Coefficient of linear expansion   **D.** Specific heat

31. A substance has a density of 1,800 kg/m^3 in the liquid state. At atmospheric pressure, the substance has a boiling point of 170 °C. The vapor has a density of 6 kg/m^3 at the boiling point at atmospheric pressure. What is the change in the internal energy of 1 kg of the substance, as it vaporizes at atmospheric pressure? (Use the heat of vaporization $L_v = 1.7 \times 10^5$ J/kg)

    A. 180 kJ   **B.** 170 kJ   **C.** 6 kJ   **D.** 12 kJ

32. If an aluminum rod that is at 5 °C is heated until it has twice the thermal energy, its temperature is:

    A. 10 °C   **B.** 56 °C   **C.** 278 °C   **D.** 283 °C

33. A thermally isolated system is made up of a hot piece of aluminum and a cold piece of copper, with the aluminum and the copper in thermal contact. The specific heat capacity of aluminum is more than double that of copper. Which object experiences the greater temperature change during the time the system takes to reach thermal equilibrium?

    A. Both experience the same magnitude of temperature change   **C.** The copper
    B. The mass of each is required   **D.** The aluminum

34. In liquid water of a given temperature, the water molecules are moving randomly at different speeds. Electrostatic forces of cohesion tend to hold them together. However, occasionally one molecule gains enough energy through multiple collisions to pull away from the others and escape from the liquid. Which of the following is an illustration of this phenomenon?

    A. When a large steel suspension bridge is built, gaps are left between the girders
    B. When a body gets too warm, it produces sweat to cool itself down
    C. Increasing the atmospheric pressure over a liquid causes the boiling temperature to decrease
    D. If snow begins to fall when Mary is skiing, she feels colder than before it started to snow

35. A 2,200 kg sample of water at 0 °C is cooled to –30 °C, and freezes in the process. Approximately how much heat is liberated during this process? (Use heat of fusion for water L_f = 334 kJ/kg, heat of vaporization L_v = 2,257 kJ/kg and specific heat for ice = 2,050 J/kg·K)

    A. 328,600 kJ   **B.** 190,040 kJ   **C.** 637,200 kJ   **D.** 870,100 kJ

36. Object 1 has three times the specific heat capacity and four times the mass of Object 2. The same amount of heat is transferred to the two objects. If the temperature of Object 1 changes by an amount of ΔT, what is the change in temperature of Object 2?

    A. 12ΔT   **B.** 3ΔT   **C.** ΔT   **D.** (3/4)ΔT

37. The process whereby heat flows using molecular collisions is known as:

    A. radiation   **B.** inversion   **C.** conduction   **D.** convection

38. The graph shows a PV diagram for 5.1 g of oxygen gas in a sealed container. The temperature of T_1 is 20 °C. What are the values for temperatures of T_3 and T_4, respectively? (Use the gas constant R= 8.314 J/mol·K)

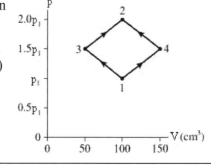

    A. –53 °C and 387 °C   **C.** 210 °C and 640 °C
    B. –14 °C and 34 °C   **D.** 12 °C and 58 °C

39. On a cold day, a piece of steel feels much colder to the touch than a piece of plastic. This is due to the difference in which one of the following physical properties of these materials?

    A. Emissivity   **B.** Thermal conductivity   **C.** Density   **D.** Specific heat

40. What is the term for a process when a gas is allowed to expand as heat is added to it at constant pressure?

    A. Isochoric   **B.** Isobaric   **C.** Adiabatic   **D.** Isothermal

41. A Carnot engine is used as an air conditioner to cool a house in the summer. The air conditioner removes 20 kJ of heat per second from the house, and maintains the inside temperature at 293 K, while the outside temperature is 307 K. What is the power required for the air conditioner?

    A. 2.3 kW   **B.** 3.22 kW   **C.** 1.6 kW   **D.** 0.96 kW

42. Heat energy is measured in units of:

    I. Joules   II. calories   III. work

    A. I only   **B.** II only   **C.** I and II only   **D.** III only

43. The process in which heat flows by the mass movement of molecules from one place to another is known as:

    I. conduction   II. convection   III. radiation

    A. I only   **B.** II only   **C.** III only   **D.** I and II only

44. The process whereby heat flows in the absence of any medium is known as:

    A. radiation   **C.** conduction
    B. inversion   **D.** convection

45. The figure shows 0.008 mol of gas that undergoes the process $1 \rightarrow 2 \rightarrow 3$. What is the volume of V_3?

(Use the ideal gas constant R = 8.314 J/mol·K and the conversion of 1 atm = 101,325 Pa)

    A. 435 cm^3 **C.** 656 cm^3
    B. 568 cm^3 **D.** 800 cm^3

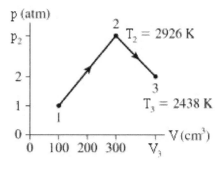

46. When a gas expands adiabatically:

    A. it does no work   **C.** the internal (thermal) energy of the gas decreases
    B. work is done on the gas   **D.** the internal (thermal) energy of the gas increases

---

47. Why is it that when a swimmer gets out of a swimming pool and stands in a breeze dripping wet, he feels much colder compared to when he dries off?

    A. This is a physiological effect resulting from the skin's sensory nerves
    B. To evaporate a gram of water from his skin requires heat and most of this heat flows out of his body
    C. The moisture on his skin has good thermal conductivity
    D. Water has a relatively small specific heat

48. Which method of heat flow requires the movement of energy through solid matter to a new location?

    I. Conduction   II. Convection   III. Radiation

    A. I only   **B.** II only   **C.** III only   **D.** I and II only

49. An ideal gas is compressed via an isobaric process to one-third of its initial volume. Compared to the initial pressure, the resulting pressure is:

    A. more than three times greater   **C.** three times greater
    B. nine times greater   **D.** the same

50. Which of the following would be the best radiator of thermal energy?

    A. A metallic surface   **B.** A black surface   **C.** A white surface   **D.** A shiny surface

51. A brass rod is 59.1 cm long, and an aluminum rod is 39.3 cm long when both rods are at an initial temperature of 0 °C. The rods are placed with a distance of 1.1 cm between them. The distance between the far ends of the rods is maintained at 99.5 cm. The temperature is raised until the two rods are barely in contact.

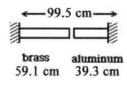

In the figure, what is the temperature at which contact of the rods barely occurs? (Use a coefficient of linear expansion of brass $= 2 \times 10^{-5} \text{ K}^{-1}$ and the coefficient of linear expansion of aluminum $= 2.4 \times 10^{-5} \text{ K}^{-1}$)

    A. 424 °C   **B.** 588 °C   **C.** 518 °C   **D.** 363 °C

52. At room temperature, a person loses energy to the surroundings at the rate of 60 W. If an equivalent food intake compensates this energy loss, how many kilocalories does he need to consume every 24 hours? (Use conversion of 1 cal = 4.186 J)

    A. 1,240 kcal   **B.** 1,660 kcal   **C.** 600 kcal   **D.** 880 kcal

53. By what primary heat transfer mechanism does one end of an iron bar become hot when the other end is placed in a flame?

    A. Convection   **B.** Forced convection   **C.** Radiation   **D.** Conduction

Questions **54-55** are based on the following:

Two experiments are performed to determine the calorimetric properties of an alcohol which has a melting point of –10 °C. In the first trial, a 220 g cube of frozen alcohol, at the melting point, is added to 350 g of water at 26 °C in a Styrofoam container. When thermal equilibrium is reached, the alcohol-water solution is at a temperature of 5 °C. In the second trial, an identical cube of alcohol is added to 400 g of water at 30 °C, and the temperature at thermal equilibrium is 10 °C. (Use the specific heat of water = 4,190 J/kg·K and assume no heat exchange between the Styrofoam container and the surroundings).

54. What is the specific heat capacity of the alcohol?

   A. 2,150 J/kg·K   **B.** 2,475 J/kg·K   **C.** 1,175 J/kg·K   **D.** 1,820 J/kg·K

55. What is the heat of fusion of the alcohol?

   A. 7.2×10^3 J/kg   **B.** 1.9×10^5 J/kg   **C.** 5.2×10^4 J/kg   **D.** 10.3×10^4 J/kg

56. The silver coating on the glass surface of a Thermos bottle reduces the energy that is transferred by:

      I. conduction   II. convection   III. radiation

   A. I only   **B.** II only   **C.** III only   **D.** I and II only

57. A person consumes a snack containing 16 kcal. What is the power this food produces if it is to be expended during exercise in 5 hours? (Use the conversion 1 cal = 4.186 J)

   A. 0.6 W   **B.** 3.7 W   **C.** 9.7 W   **D.** 96.3 W

58. If 50 kcal of heat is added to 5 kg of water, what is the resulting temperature change? (Use the specific heat of water = 1 kcal/kg·°C)

   A. 10 °C   **B.** 20 °C   **C.** 5 °C   **D.** 40 °C

59. How much heat is needed to melt a 30 kg sample of ice that is at 0 °C? (Use latent heat of fusion for water L_f = 334 kJ/kg and latent heat of vaporization for water L_v = 2,257 kJ/kg)

   A. 0 kJ   **B.** 5.6×10^4 kJ   **C.** 1×10^4 kJ   **D.** 2.4×10^6 kJ

60. A 6 kg aluminum rod is originally at 12 °C. If 160 kJ of heat is added to the rod, what is its final temperature? (Use the specific heat capacity of aluminum = 910 J/kg·K)

   A. 32 °C   **B.** 41 °C   **C.** 54 °C   **D.** 23 °C

Thermodynamics

1: B	13: B	25: A	37: C	49: D
2: C	14: D	26: A	38: A	50: B
3: D	15: C	27: D	39: B	51: C
4: A	16: A	28: B	40: B	52: A
5: C	17: D	29: C	41: D	53: D
6: B	18: B	30: D	42: C	54: B
7: D	19: C	31: B	43: B	55: D
8: A	20: A	32: D	44: A	56: C
9: C	21: D	33: B	45: D	57: B
10: D	22: A	34: B	46: C	58: A
11: B	23: B	35: D	47: B	59: C
12: A	24: D	36: A	48: A	60: B

Atomic Nucleus and Electronic Structure

1. Which statement(s) about alpha particles is/are FALSE?

      I. They are a harmless form of radiation
      II. They have low penetrating power
      III. They have high ionization power

  A. I only   **B.** II only   **C.** III only   **D.** I and II only

2. What is the term for nuclear radiation that is identical to an electron?

  A. Positron   **C.** Beta minus particle
  B. Gamma ray   **D.** Alpha particle

3. Protons are being accelerated in a particle accelerator. When the speed of the protons is doubled, by what factor does their de Broglie wavelength change? Note: consider this situation non-relativistic.

  A. Increases by $\sqrt{2}$ **C.** Increases by 2
  B. Decreases by $\sqrt{2}$ **D.** Decreases by 2

4. The Bohr model of the atom was able to explain the Balmer series because:

  A. electrons were allowed to exist only in specific orbits and nowhere else
  B. differences between the energy levels of the orbits matched the differences between the energy levels of the line spectra
  C. smaller orbits require electrons to have more negative energy to match the angular momentum
  D. differences between the energy levels of the orbits were exactly half the differences between the energy levels of the line spectra

5. Radioactivity is the tendency for an element to:

  A. become ionized easily   **C.** emit radiation
  B. be dangerous to living things   **D.** emit protons

6. Which is the missing species in the nuclear equation: $^{100}_{44}\text{Ru} + ^{0}_{-1}\text{e}^- \rightarrow$ ___?

  A. $^{100}_{45}\text{Ru}$ **B.** $^{100}_{43}\text{Ru}$ **C.** $^{101}_{44}\text{Ru}$ **D.** $^{100}_{43}\text{Tc}$

7. The term nucleon refers to:

  A. the nucleus of a specific isotope
  B. both protons and neutrons
  C. positrons that are emitted from an atom that undergoes nuclear decay
  D. electrons that are emitted from a nucleus in a nuclear reaction

8. An isolated ^{9}Be atom spontaneously decays into two alpha particles. What can be concluded about the mass of the ^{9}Be atom?

    A. The mass is less than twice the mass of the ^{4}He atom, but not equal to the mass of ^{4}He

    B. No conclusions can be made about the mass

    C. The mass is exactly twice the mass of the ^{4}He atom

    D. The mass is greater than twice the mass of the ^{4}He atom

9. Which of the following isotopes contains the most neutrons?

    A. $^{178}_{84}$Po   **B.** $^{178}_{87}$Fr   **C.** $^{181}_{86}$Rn   **D.** $^{170}_{83}$Bi

10. Which of the following correctly balances this nuclear fission reaction?

$$^1_0n + {}^{235}_{92}U \rightarrow {}^{131}_{53}I + \underline{\quad} + 3\,{}^1_0n$$

    A. $^{102}_{39}$Y   **B.** $^{102}_{36}$Kr   **C.** $^{104}_{39}$Y   **D.** $^{105}_{36}$Kr   **E.** $^{131}_{54}$I

11. What is the frequency of the light emitted by atomic hydrogen according to the Balmer formula where n = 12? (Use the Balmer series constant $B = 3.6 \times 10^{-7}$ m and the speed of light $c = 3 \times 10^8$ m/s)

    A. 5.3×10^6 Hz   **B.** 8.1×10^{14} Hz   **C.** 5.9×10^{13} Hz   **D.** 1.2×10^{11} Hz

12. Gamma rays require the heaviest shielding of all the common types of nuclear radiation because gamma rays have the:

    A. heaviest particles   **C.** most intense color

    B. lowest energy   **D.** highest energy

13. In making a transition from state n = 1 to state n = 2, the hydrogen atom must [ ] a photon of [ ]. (Use Planck's constant $h = 4.14 \times 10^{-15}$ eV·s, the speed of light $c = 3 \times 10^8$ m/s and the Rydberg constant $R = 1.097 \times 10^7 \, \text{m}^{-1}$)

    A. absorb … 10.2 Ev   **C.** emit … 8.6 eV

    B. absorb … 8.6 eV   **D.** emit … 10.2 eV

14. Rubidium $^{87}_{37}$Rb is a naturally-occurring nuclide which undergoes β^- decay. What is the resultant nuclide from this decay?

    A. $^{86}_{36}$Rb   **B.** $^{87}_{38}$Kr   **C.** $^{87}_{38}$Sr   **D.** $^{87}_{36}$Kr

15. Which of the following statements best describes the role of neutrons in the nucleus?

    A. The neutrons stabilize the nucleus by attracting protons

    B. The neutrons stabilize the nucleus by balancing charge

    C. The neutrons stabilize the nucleus by attracting other nucleons

    D. The neutrons stabilize the nucleus by repelling other nucleons

16. A Geiger–Muller counter detects radioactivity by:

    A. ionizing argon gas in a chamber which produces an electrical signal

    B. analyzing the mass and velocity of each particle

    C. developing film which is exposed by radioactive particles

    D. slowing the neutrons using a moderator and then counting the secondary charges produced

17. What percentage of the radionuclides in a given sample remains after three half-lives?

    A. 25%   **B.** 12.5%   **C.** 6.25%   **D.** 33.3%

18. The Lyman series is formed by electron transitions in hydrogen that:

    A. begin on the n = 2 shell   **C.** begin on the n = 1 shell

    B. end on the n = 2 shell   **D.** end on the n = 1 shell

19. Most of the volume of an atom is occupied by:

    A. neutrons   **B.** space   **C.** electrons   **D.** protons

20. Alpha and beta minus particles are deflected in opposite directions in a magnetic field because:

        I. they have opposite charges

        II. alpha particles contain nucleons, and beta minus particles do not

        III. they spin in opposite directions

    A. I only   **B.** II only   **C.** III only   **D.** I and II only

21. The conversion of mass to energy is measurable only in:

    A. chemiluminescent transformations   **C.** endothermic reactions

    B. spontaneous chemical reactions   **D.** nuclear reactions

22. What is the term given to the amount of a radioactive substance that undergoes 3.7×10^{10} disintegrations per second?

    A. Rem   **B.** Rad   **C.** Curie   **D.** Roentgen

23. An isolated ^{235}U atom spontaneously undergoes fission into two approximately equal-sized fragments. What is missing from the product side of the reaction:

$$^{235}\text{U} \rightarrow {}^{141}\text{Ba} + {}^{92}\text{Kr} + \underline{\quad}?$$

A. A neutron   **C.** Two protons and two neutrons
B. Two neutrons   **D.** Two protons and a neutron

24. How many protons and neutrons are in $^{34}_{16}$S?

A. 18 neutrons and 34 protons   **C.** 16 protons and 34 neutrons
B. 16 neutrons and 18 protons   **D.** 16 protons and 18 neutrons

25. The radioactive isotope Z has a half-life of 12 hours. What is the fraction of the original amount remaining after 2 days?

A. 1/16   **B.** 1/8   **C.** 1/4   **D.** 1/2

26. Which of the following nuclear equations correctly describes alpha emission?

A. $^{238}_{92}\text{U} \rightarrow {}^{242}_{94}\text{Pu} + {}^{4}_{2}\text{He}$ **C.** $^{238}_{92}\text{U} \rightarrow {}^{234}_{90}\text{Th} + {}^{4}_{2}\text{He}$

B. $^{238}_{92}\text{U} \rightarrow {}^{4}_{2}\text{He}$ **D.** $^{238}_{92}\text{U} \rightarrow {}^{235}_{90}\text{Th} + {}^{4}_{2}\text{He}$

27. A hydrogen atom makes a downward transition from the $n = 20$ state to the $n = 5$ state. Find the wavelength of the emitted photon. (Use Planck's constant $h = 4.14 \times 10^{-15}$ eV·s, the speed of light $c = 3 \times 10^{8}$ m/s and the Rydberg constant $R = 1.097 \times 10^{7}\,\text{m}^{-1}$)

A. 1.93 µm   **B.** 2.82 µm   **C.** 1.54 µm   **D.** 2.43 µm

28. A nuclear equation is balanced when the:

A. same elements are found on both sides of the equation
B. sums of the atomic numbers of the particles and atoms are the same on both sides of the equation
C. sum of the mass numbers of the particles and the sum of atoms are the same on both sides of the equation
D. sum of the mass numbers and the sum of the atomic numbers of the particles and atoms are the same on both sides of the equation

29. A blackbody is an ideal system that:

A. absorbs 50% of the light incident upon it and emits 50% of the radiation it generates
B. absorbs 0% of the light incident upon it and emits 100% of the radiation it generates
C. absorbs 100% of the light incident upon it and emits 100% of the radiation it generates
D. emits 100% of the light it generates and absorbs 50% of the radiation incident upon it

30. Recent nuclear bomb tests have created an extra-high level of atmospheric ^{14}C. When future archaeologists date samples, without knowing of these nuclear tests, will the dates they calculate be correct?

    A. Correct, because biological materials do not gather ^{14}C from bomb tests

    B. Correct, since the ^{14}C decays within the atmosphere at the natural rate

    C. Incorrect, they would appear too old

    D. Incorrect, they would appear too young

31. When an isotope releases gamma radiation, the atomic number:

    A. and the mass number remain the same

    B. and the mass number decrease by one

    C. and the mass number increase by one

    D. remains the same and the mass number increases by one

32. If ^{14}Carbon is a beta emitter, what is the likely product of radioactive decay?

    A. ^{22}Silicon   **B.** ^{13}Boron   **C.** ^{14}Nitrogen   **D.** ^{12}Carbon

33. In a nuclear equation, the:

        I. sum of the mass numbers on both sides must be equal

        II. sum of the atomic numbers on both sides must be equal

        III. daughter nuclide appears on the right side of the arrow

    A. I only   **B.** II only   **C.** III only   **D.** I, II and III

34. What is the term for the number that characterizes an element and indicates the number of protons found in the nucleus of the atom?

    A. Mass number   **C.** Atomic mass

    B. Atomic number   **D.** Neutron number

35. Hydrogen atoms can emit four spectral lines with visible colors from red to violet. These four visible lines emitted by hydrogen atoms are produced by electrons that:

    A. end in the ground state   **C.** end in the n = 2 level

    B. end in the n = 3 level   **D.** start in the ground state

36. The electron was discovered through experiments with:

    A. quarks   **B.** foil   **C.** light   **D.** electricity

Questions **37-39** are based on the following:

The image shows a beam of radiation passing between two electrically-charged plates.

I. a

II. b

III. c

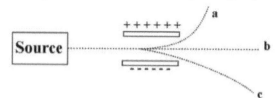

37. Which of the beams is due to an energetic light wave?

A. I only   **B.** II only   **C.** III only   **D.** I and II only

38. Which of the beams is/are composed of particles?

A. I only   **B.** II only   **C.** I, II and III   **D.** I and III only

39. Which of the beams is due to a positively-charged helium nucleus?

A. I only   **B.** II only   **C.** III only   **D.** I, II and III

40. Lithium atoms can absorb photons transitioning from the ground state (at –5.37 eV) to an excited state with one electron removed from the atom, which corresponds to the zero energy state. What is the wavelength of light associated with this transition? (Use Planck's constant $h = 4.14 \times 10^{-15}$ eV·s and the speed of light $c = 3 \times 10^8$ m/s)

A. 6.6×10^{-6} m   **C.** 3.6×10^6 m

B. 2.3×10^{-7} m   **D.** 4.2×10^5 m

41. All of the elements with atomic numbers of 84 and higher are radioactive because:

A. strong attractions between their nucleons make them unstable

B. their atomic numbers are larger than their mass numbers

C. strong repulsions between their electrons make them unstable

D. strong repulsions between their protons make their nuclei unstable

42. Which of the following statements about β particles is FALSE?

A. They have a smaller mass than α particles

B. They have high energy and a charge

C. They are created when neutrons become protons and vice versa

D. They are a harmless form of radioactivity

43. The material used in nuclear bombs is ^{239}Pu, with a half-life of about 20,000 years. What is the approximate amount of time that must elapse for a buried stockpile of this substance to decay to 3% of its original ^{239}Pu mass?

    A. 0.8 thousand years   **C.** 90 thousand years

    B. 65 thousand years   **D.** 101 thousand years

44. Which statement regarding Planck's constant is true?

    A. It relates mass to the amount of energy that can be emitted

    B. It sets a lower limit to the amount of energy that can be absorbed or emitted

    C. It sets an upper limit to the amount of energy that can be absorbed

    D. It sets an upper limit to the amount of energy that can be absorbed or emitted

45. The decay rate of a radioactive isotope will NOT be increased by increasing the:

    I. surface area   II. pressure   III. temperature

    A. I only   **B.** II only   **C.** III only   **D.** I, II and III

46. Why are some smaller nuclei such as ^{14}Carbon often radioactive?

    I. The attractive force of the nucleons has a limited range

    II. The neutron to proton ratio is too large or too small

    III. Most smaller nuclei are not stable

    A. I only   **B.** II only   **C.** III only   **D.** II and III only

47. Scandium ^{44}Sc decays by emitting a positron. What is the resultant nuclide which is produced by this decay?

    A. $^{43}_{21}$Sc   **B.** $^{45}_{21}$Sc   **C.** $^{44}_{20}$Ca   **D.** $^{43}_{20}$Ca

48. A scintillation counter detects radioactivity by:

    A. analyzing the mass and velocity of each electron

    B. ionizing argon gas in a chamber which produces an electrical signal

    C. emitting light from a NaI crystal when radioactivity passes through the crystal

    D. developing film which is exposed by radioactive particles

49. Which of the following is indicated by each detection sound by a Geiger counter?

    A. One half-life   **C.** One neutron being emitted

    B. One nucleus decaying   **D.** One positron being emitted

50. According to the Pauli Exclusion Principle, how many electrons in an atom may have a particular set of quantum numbers?

A. 1 **B.** 2 **C.** 3 **D.** 4

51. The atomic number of an atom identifies the number of:

A. excited states **B.** electron orbits **C.** neutrons **D.** protons

52. Which of the following correctly characterizes gamma radiation?

A. High penetrating power; charge $= -1$; mass $= 0$ amu
B. Low penetrating power; charge $= -1$; mass $= 0$ amu
C. High penetrating power; charge $= 0$; mass $= 0$ amu
D. High penetrating power; charge $= 0$; mass $= 4$ amu

53. The rest mass of a proton is 1.0072764669 amu, and that of a neutron is 1.0086649156 amu. The ^{4}He nucleus weighs 4.002602 amu. What is the total binding energy of the nucleus? (Use the speed of light $c = 3 \times 10^8$ m/s and 1 amu $= 1.6606 \times 10^{-27}$ kg)

A. 2.7×10^{-11} J **C.** 1.6×10^{-7} J
B. 4.4×10^{-12} J **D.** 2.6×10^{-12} J

54. Which is the correct electron configuration for ground state boron ($Z = 5$)?

A. $1s^2 1p^2 2s$ **B.** $1s^2 2p^2 3s$ **C.** $1s^2 2p^3$ **D.** $1s^2 2s^2 2p$

55. The Sun produces 3.85×10^{26} J each second. How much mass does it lose per second from nuclear processes alone? (Use the speed of light $c = 3 \times 10^8$ m/s)

A. 9.8×10^1 kg **B.** 2.4×10^9 kg **C.** 4.3×10^9 kg **D.** 1.1×10^8 kg

56. The damaging effects of radiation on the body are a result of:

A. extensive damage to nerve cells
B. transmutation reactions in the body
C. the formation of radioactive particles in the body
D. the formation of unstable ions or radicals in the body

57. How does the emission of a gamma ray affect the radioactive atom?

I. The atomic mass increases
II. The atom has a smaller amount of energy
III. The atom gains energy for further radioactive particle emission

A. I only **B.** II only **C.** III only **D.** I and II only

58. The nuclear particle, which is described by the symbol $_{0}^{1}n$ is a(n):

    A. neutron   **B.** gamma ray   **C.** beta particle   **D.** electron

59. Heisenberg's uncertainty principle states that:

    A. at times a photon appears to be a particle, and at other times it appears to be a wave

    B. whether a photon is a wave or a particle cannot be determined with certainty

    C. the position and the momentum of a particle cannot be simultaneously known with absolute certainty

    D. the properties of an electron cannot be known with absolute certainty

Atomic Nucleus & Electronic Structure

1: A	11: B	21: D	31: A	41: D	51: D
2: C	12: D	22: C	32: C	42: D	52: C
3: D	13: A	23: B	33: D	43: D	53: B
4: B	14: C	24: D	34: B	44: B	54: D
5: C	15: C	25: A	35: C	45: D	55: C
6: D	16: A	26: C	36: D	46: B	56: D
7: B	17: B	27: D	37: B	47: C	57: B
8: D	18: D	28: D	38: C	48: C	58: A
9: C	19: B	29: C	39: C	49: B	59: C
10: A	20: A	30: D	40: B	50: A	

Diagnostic Tests

Answer Keys
&
Detailed Explanations

Diagnostic Test #1 – Explanations

1. C is correct.

The slope of a tangent line of a position vs. time graph at a specific time value is the instantaneous velocity. This is equivalent to taking the derivative of the graph at this same time value.

2. A is correct.

An object in motion with constant nonzero velocity experiences no acceleration and thus cannot have any net force upon it.

If v = constant, then:

$$a = 0$$

$$F = ma$$

$$F = m(0 \text{ m/s}^2)$$

$$F = 0 \text{ N}$$

3. B is correct.

Heat conduction equation:

$$Q / t = (kA\Delta T) / d$$

where k is the thermal conductivity of the wall material, A is the surface area of the wall, d is the wall's thickness, and ΔT is the temperature difference on either side.

Assume heat flow is lengthwise so barrier distance:

$$d = 2d_0$$

The important value here is A ($A = \pi r^2$), which is the surface area of the object with respect to the direction of heat flow and d, which is barrier thickness.

The surface area with respect to heat flow:

$$A_0 = (\pi / 4)D_0^2$$

$$A = (\pi / 4) \cdot (2D_0)^2$$

$$A = 4(\pi / 4) D_0^2$$

$$A = 4A_0$$

Substitute values into original equation:

$$Q / t = (k\Delta T) \cdot (4A_0 / 2d_0)$$

$$Q / t = 2(kA_0\Delta T / d_0)$$

$$Q / t = 2(Q_0 / t)$$

$$Q / t = 2(30 \text{ W})$$

$$Q / t = 60 \text{ W}$$

4. A is correct.

The spring already has the 0.9 kg mass attached to it, so its original equilibrium length is the length needed to counteract the force of gravity.

If the spring is stretched further, then the net force only includes the component from the spring force:

$F_{spring} = k\Delta x$

$F_{spring} = (3 \text{ N/m}) \cdot (0.18 \text{ m})$

$F_{spring} = 0.54 \text{ N}$

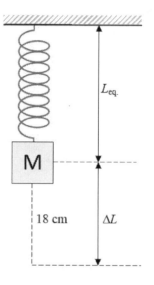

5. B is correct.

Convert weight to mass:

$F = ma$

$m = F / a$

$m = 30 \text{ N} / (9.8 \text{ m/s}^2)$

$m = 3.061 \text{ kg}$

Frequency of a spring system:

$\omega = \sqrt{(k / m)}$

$\omega = \sqrt{(40.0 \text{ N/m} / 3.061 \text{ kg})}$

$\omega = 3.615 \text{ rad/s}$

$f = \omega / 2\pi$

$f = (3.615 \text{ rad/s}) / 2\pi$

$f = 0.58 \text{ Hz}$

6. C is correct.

$f_{beat} = |f_2 - f_1|$

$f_{beat} = |786.3 \text{ Hz} - 785.8 \text{ Hz}|$

$f_{beat} = 0.5 \text{ Hz}$

7. D is correct.

The weight of the piston surface area is a ratio:

$F_1 / A_1 = F_2 / A_2$

$F_2 = F_1 \times A_2 / A_1$

$F_2 = (600 \text{ N}) \cdot (50 \text{ cm}^2) / 5 \text{ cm}^2$

$F_2 = 6,000 \text{ N}$

8. D is correct. Equation for potential energy:

$$\Delta PE = q\Delta V$$

Note: q is negative because electrons are negatively charged

$$\Delta PE = (-1.6 \times 10^{-19} \text{ C}) \cdot (-500 \text{ V} - 500 \text{ V})$$
$$\Delta PE = (-1.6 \times 10^{-19} \text{ C}) \cdot (-1{,}000 \text{ V})$$
$$\Delta PE = 1.6 \times 10^{-16} \text{ J}$$

Moving this electron increases its PE energy.

9. B is correct. $P = VI$

$V = IR$, substituting into the equation

$$P = (IR) \times I$$
$$P = I^2 \times R$$

If P is on y-axis and R is on x-axis,

$$\text{slope} = P / R$$
$$\text{slope} = I^2$$

10. B is correct. The resolution is the smallest distance between two objects where they are still capable of being distinguished as separate objects.

Therefore, the light with a shorter wavelength gives a smaller distance between peaks and therefore a higher resolution.

11. D is correct. The photoelectric effect is the phenomenon where light incident upon a metallic surface causes electrons to be emitted.

The photoelectric effect is described by the equation:

$$KE_{max} = hf - \phi$$

where h = Planck's constant, f = frequency and ϕ = work function.

If the light of a threshold frequency such that $hf > \phi$ shines upon a metallic surface, the electrons will be ejected with KE. Increasing frequency increases the KE.

Note: hf is the energy carried by one incident photon. Since the incident intensity remains constant, but the energy per photon has increased, the rate of incident photons must decrease, resulting in a decrease in the rate of ejection events.

12. B is correct.

Distance traveled is represented by the area under the velocity vs. time curve.

At the point where each of those curves intersects on this plot, there is more area under the curve of the truck velocity than there is under the curve of the car velocity.

13. D is correct. Find kinetic energy and set equal to the work done by friction:

$KE = W_f$

$\frac{1}{2}mv^2 = F_f \times d$

$\frac{1}{2}m / F_f = d / v^2$

Because the mass is constant, d / v^2 = constant regardless of velocity.

Solve for the new skid distance:

$d_1 / v_1^2 = d_2 / v_2^2$

$d_2 = (d_1) \cdot (v_2^2) / (v_1^2)$

$d_2 = (30 \text{ m}) \cdot (150 \text{ km/h})^2 / (45 \text{ km/h})^2$

$d_2 = 333 \text{ m}$

14. A is correct. The time it takes to complete one cycle is the period T.

$T = 1 / f$

Period is measured in seconds.

$\text{Frequency} = s^{-1} \text{ or Hz}$

15. B is correct.

$\text{One mosquito} = 1.5 \times 10^{-11} \text{ W}$

To power a 30 W bulb:

$(30 \text{ W}) / (1.5 \times 10^{-11} \text{ W}) = 2 \times 10^{12} \text{ mosquitoes}$

16. C is correct. First, find the total mass of the mixture once the ethanol has been added to the chloroform:

$\text{Total Mass} = x + 5 \text{ grams}$

where x is the mass of the ethanol added.

Then, find the volume of the resulting mixture. Volume is found using the specific gravity formula:

$\text{Volume (mL)} = \text{Mass (g)} / SG$

Therefore:

$V_e = x / 0.8$

$V_c = 5 \text{ g} / 1.5$

$\text{Total Volume} = V_e + V_c$

$\text{Total Volume} = (x / 0.8) + (5 \text{ g} / 1.5)$

$\text{Total Volume} = 1.25x + 3.33 \text{ mL}$

Find the mass of added ethanol using the given specific gravity of the mixture:

$SG_{mixture}$ = Total Mass / Total Volume

$1.2 = (x + 5 \text{ g}) / (1.25x + 3.33 \text{ mL})$

$(1.2) \cdot (1.25x + 3.33 \text{ mL}) = (x + 5 \text{ g})$

$1.5x + 3.96 \text{ g} = x + 5 \text{ g}$

$0.5x = 1.04 \text{ g}$

$x = 2.08 \text{ g} \approx 2 \text{ g}$

17. A is correct. Power = current × voltage

$P = IV$

Power is measured in watts (W), current in amps (A) and voltage in volts (V).

$W = A \times V$

18. B is correct.

The equivalent resistance of resistors in parallel:

$R_{eq} = 1 / (1 / R_1 + 1 / R_2 + 1 / R_3 \ldots)$

The equivalent resistance is always smaller than the smallest resistance:

For example:

$R_1 = 20 \ \Omega, R_2 = 30 \ \Omega, R_3 = 30 \ \Omega$

$R_{eq} = 1 / (1 / 20 \ \Omega + 1 / 30 \ \Omega + 1 / 30 \ \Omega \ldots)$

$R_{eq} = 8.75 \ \Omega$

$R_{eq} < R_1$

19. C is correct.

First, assume that the distance of the Moon from the lens is ∞.

$d_o = \infty$

Next, assume d_i is the distance from the lens where the image forms.

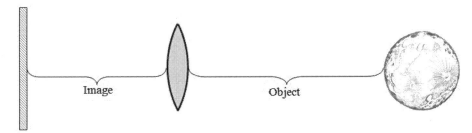

By the thin lens equation:

$$1/d_i + 1/d_o = 1/f$$

$$1/d_i + 1/\infty = 1/f$$

$$1/d_i + 0 = 1/f$$

$$1/d_i = 1/f$$

$$d_i = f$$

20. D is correct. The superscript is the mass number (# protons and # neutrons).

The subscript is the atomic number (# protons).

Thus, ^1_1H depicts a hydrogen atom with 1 proton, 1 electron, and 0 neutrons.

21. C is correct. Foods with high specific heat capacities tend to burn more than foods with lower specific heat capacities. This is because specific heat is a measure of how much thermal energy a material can absorb (or loose) before changing temperature.

Thus, high specific heat foods can deliver more energy and burn a person's mouth before cooling down (compared to low specific heat foods).

22. C is correct.

The coefficient of static friction (object at rest) is larger than the coefficient of kinetic friction (object in motion). It is proportional to the force needed to take a stationary object out of static equilibrium and accelerate it. The coefficient of kinetic friction is proportional to the force needed to maintain dynamic equilibrium in an object moving at constant speed.

Therefore, the force required to take a stationary object out of static equilibrium and accelerate it is greater than the force required to keep a moving object in dynamic equilibrium. It is more difficult to set an object in motion than it is to keep it in motion.

23. B is correct.

The two ends count as nodes. From a standing wave with four nodes, there are three antinodes.

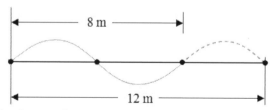

Therefore, there are three half-wavelengths.

Each dot on the curve represents one of the four nodes.

One complete wave (the solid line) includes three nodes.

$$1 \text{ wave} = (2/3) \text{ entire string}$$

$$1 \text{ wave} = (2/3)\cdot(12 \text{ m}) = 8 \text{ m}$$

24. A is correct.

The reading on the meter is the net force between the necklace weight and buoyant force.

$$F_{total} = F_O - F_B$$

$$F_{total} = mg - \rho Vg$$

$$F_{total} = g(m - \rho V)$$

$$F_{total} = (9.8 \text{ m/s}^2) \cdot [(0.06 \text{ kg}) - (1 \text{ g/cm}^3) \cdot (5.7 \text{ cm}^3) \cdot (1 \text{ kg/1,000 g})]$$

$$F_{total} = 0.53 \text{ N}$$

25. D is correct.

Centripetal force F_C on a charged particle in a magnetic field is the magnetic Lorentz force:

$$F_M = qvB$$

Therefore:

$$F_C = F_M$$

$$mv^2 / r = qvB$$

or

$$r = mv / qB$$

Increasing the speed by a factor of two increases the radius by a factor of two.

26. B is correct.

The equation for force in a magnetic field (B):

$$F = qv \times B$$

The direction of B is given by the right-hand rule.

If the thumb is oriented upward as shown for F, the magnetic field B points into the page.

27. C is correct.

According to the law of reflection, the angle of incidence is always equal to the angle of reflection.

$$\theta_{incidence} = \theta_{reflection}$$

28. D is correct.

The sum of subscripts and superscripts must be balanced:

$$^{14}_{7}\text{N} + ^{1}_{0}\text{n} \rightarrow ^{14}_{6}\text{C} + ^{1}_{1}\text{p}$$

A proton is necessary to balance the subscripts to 7 and the superscripts to 15 on each side of the expression.

29. B is correct.

The maximum and minimum of position vs. time are always equal to zero velocity.

30. D is correct.

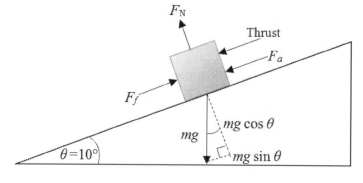

$$F_f = \mu_k F_N$$

$$F_f = \mu_k mg \cos \theta$$

Find the length of travel:

$$L = 50 \text{ m} / \sin 10°$$

$$L = 50 \text{ m} / 0.174$$

$$L = 288 \text{ m}$$

Find acceleration to reach 40 m/s:

$$v_f^2 = v_i^2 + 2ad$$

$$(40 \text{ m/s})^2 = 0 + 2a(288 \text{ m})$$

$$1{,}600 \text{ m}^2/\text{s}^2 = a(576 \text{ m})$$

$$a = (1{,}600 \text{ m}^2/\text{s}^2) / (576 \text{ m})$$

$$a = 2.8 \text{ m/s}^2$$

Find normal (F_N) and gravitational (F_G) forces:

$$F_N = mg \cos \theta$$

$$F_N = (50 \text{ kg}) \cdot (9.8 \text{ m/s}^2) \cos 10°$$

$$F_N = (50 \text{ kg}) \cdot (9.8 \text{ m/s}^2) \cdot (0.985)$$

$$F_N = 483 \text{ N}$$

$$F_G = mg \sin \theta$$

$$F_G = (50 \text{ kg}) \cdot (9.8 \text{ m/s}^2) \sin 10°$$

$$F_G = (50 \text{ kg}) \cdot (9.8 \text{ m/s}^2) \cdot (0.174)$$

$$F_G = 85 \text{ N}$$

$$F_{total} = (260 \text{ N} + 85 \text{ N})$$

$$F_{total} = 345 \text{ N, total force experienced by the skier}$$

The skier experiences acceleration down the slope that was reduced by friction.

The coefficient of kinetic friction can be calculated by:

$$F_{total} - F_{friction} = F_{experienced}$$

$$F_{total} - \mu F_N = F_{experienced}$$

$$345 \text{ N} - \mu_k 483 \text{ N} = (2.8 \text{ m/s}^2 \times 50 \text{ kg})$$

$$345 \text{ N} - \mu_k 483 \text{ N} = 140 \text{ N}$$

$$345 \text{ N} - 140 \text{ N} = \mu_K 483 \text{ N}$$

$$205 \text{ N} = \mu_k 483 \text{ N}$$

$$205 \text{ N} / 483 \text{ N} = \mu_k$$

$$\mu_k = 0.42$$

31. A is correct.

Since the velocity is constant, the acceleration is $a = 0$.

$$F_{net} = ma$$

$$F_{net} = 0$$

32. B is correct.

Upward force due to the spring (Hooke's law):

$$F = k\Delta x$$

where k is the spring constant and Δx is the distance the spring is stretched

The downward force due to gravity:

$$F = mg$$

System is in equilibrium so set the expressions equal to each other:

$$k\Delta x = mg$$

$$\Delta x = mg / k$$

$$\Delta x = (4 \text{ kg}) \cdot (10 \text{ m/s}^2) / (10 \text{ N/m})$$

$$\Delta x = 4 \text{ m}$$

33. B is correct.

The overtone or harmonic can be found by the following:

harmonic	overtone
n^{th} harmonic	$(n^{th} - 1)$ overtone

Thus, the third harmonic has the

$$(3 - 1) = 2^{nd} \text{ overtone}$$

34. B is correct.

Heat can never flow from a cold body to a hot body without some other change. This violates the Clausius Statement of the Second Law of Thermodynamics.

35. A is correct.

$m = -d_i / d_o$

$m = -(-6 \text{ m}) / (2 \text{ m})$

$m = 3$

Positive magnification means an upright image.

36. B is correct.

Calculate impedance for each circuit element.

Resistor:

$Z_r = 30 \ \Omega$

Inductor:

$Z_i = j2\pi fL$

where j is an imaginary number used in calculating complex impedance.

$Z_i = j2\pi(50 \text{ Hz})\cdot(0.4 \text{ H})$

$Z_i = j125.6 \ \Omega$

Capacitor:

$Z_c = -j / (2\pi fC)$

$Z_c = -j / [2\pi(50 \text{ Hz})\cdot(50 \times 10^{-6} \text{ F})]$

$Z_c = -j63.7 \ \Omega$

Adding in series:

$Z_{total} = 30 \ \Omega + j(125.6 \ \Omega - 63.7 \ \Omega)$

To find magnitude, use Pythagorean Theorem:

$|Z| = \sqrt{[(30 \ \Omega)^2 + (61.9 \ \Omega)^2]}$

$|Z| = 68.79 \ \Omega$

$V = IR$

Using impedance (Z) as resistance:

$V = (1.8 \text{ A})\cdot(68.79 \ \Omega)$

$V = 124 \text{ V}$

37. D is correct.

Coulomb's Law, which describes repulsive force between two particles, is given as:

$F = kq_1q_2 / r^2$

The expression does not include mass, so the repulsive force remains the same when m changes.

Note: gravitational (attractive) forces do rely on the masses of the objects.

38. A is correct. The gauge pressure is referenced at ambient air pressure thus:

$P = \rho g h$

$P = (1{,}000 \text{ kg/m}^3){\cdot}(9.8 \text{ m/s}^2){\cdot}(6 \text{ m} + 22 \text{ m})$

$P = 2.7 \times 10^5 \text{ N/m}^2$

39. C is correct.

$f_{\text{beat}} = |f_2 - f_1|$

$\pm f_{\text{beat}} = f_2 - f_1$

$f_2 = \pm f_{\text{beat}} + f_1$

$f_2 = \pm 5 \text{ Hz} + 822 \text{ Hz}$

$f_2 = 817 \text{ Hz}, 827 \text{ Hz}$

Only 827 Hz is an answer choice.

40. D is correct. A phase change occurs when waves reflect from the surface of a medium with a higher refractive index than the medium they are traveling in.

Glass has a higher refractive index than air and therefore, when the light ray moves from glass to air, no change occurs.

41. A is correct.

Convert PE (before release) into KE (as it is about to strike the ground):

$mgh = \text{KE}$

KE is proportional to h.

42. A is correct. Beam A is due to high energy electrons because it deflects towards the positive plate indicating attraction.

43. C is correct. $F_{\text{net}} = ma$

The only acceleration is centripetal:

$a_{\text{cent}} = v^2 / r$

$a_{\text{cent}} = (4 \text{ m/s})^2 / 16 \text{ m}$

$a_{\text{cent}} = (16 \text{ m}^2/\text{s}^2) / 16 \text{ m}$

$a_{\text{cent}} = 1 \text{ m/s}^2$

$F_{\text{net}} = ma$

$F_{\text{net}} = (40 \text{ kg}){\cdot}(1 \text{ m/s}^2)$

$F_{\text{net}} = 40 \text{ kg}{\cdot}\text{m/s}^2 = 40 \text{ N}$

44. B is correct.

When an object is accelerating its velocity must change in either speed or direction.

The speed or direction do not always change, but velocity does.

45. C is correct.

Solve for heat required:

$Q = cm\Delta T$

$Q = (113 \text{ cal/kg·°C})·(1.14 \text{ kg})·(90 \text{ °C} - 18 \text{ °C})$

$Q = 9{,}275 \text{ cal}$

Convert to Joules:

$Q = (9{,}275 \text{ cal} / 1)·(4.186 \text{ J} / \text{cal})$

$Q = 38{,}825 \text{ J}$

46. A is correct.

Include the term for work done by air resistance in the conservation of energy equation.

$KE_i + PE_i + W_{\text{air resis}} = KE_f + PE_f$

$0 + mgh + (-F_{\text{air}} \times d) = \frac{1}{2}mv_f^2 + 0$

$mgh + (-mad) = \frac{1}{2}mv_f^2$

$(1.2 \text{ kg})·(10 \text{ m/s}^2)·(6 \text{ m}) + (-3.4 \text{ kg·m/s}^2)·(6 \text{ m}) = \frac{1}{2}(1.2 \text{ kg})v_f^2$

$v_f^2 = 86 \text{ m}^2/\text{s}^2$

$v_f = 9.2 \text{ m/s}$

47. D is correct. Sound intensity is expressed as power / area:

Units of intensity: $W/m^2 = J/s/m^2 = J/m^2/s$

which is the unit of energy per unit area per unit time.

48. A is correct. Unit of watt = work / time

Multiply by time, time cancels, and work is left.

Alternatively, 1 kilowatt-hour:

1 watt = 1 J/s

1 watt·second = 1 J

$(1 \text{ hr}/60 \text{ s})·(60 \text{ min}/1 \text{ hr})·(60 \text{ s}/1\text{min}) = 60^2 \text{ s}$

$1 \times 10^3 \text{ Watt} \times (1 \text{ hour})·(60^2 \text{ s}/1 \text{ hour}) = 36 \times 10^5 \text{ J}$

Work = force × distance

Joule is a unit of work.

49. D is correct.

Critical angle = $\sin^{-1}(n_2 / n_1)$

Critical angle = $\sin^{-1}(1.3 / 1.6)$

Critical angle = $\sin^{-1}(0.81)$

Critical angle = $54°$

50. A is correct.

If acceleration is constant, then velocity is always increasing or decreasing and results in a sloped line (not a straight line).

51. D is correct. Heat required to melt a solid:

$Q = mL_f$

$Q = (70 \text{ kg}) \cdot (334 \times 10^3 \text{ J/kg})$

$Q = 2.3 \times 10^4 \text{ kJ}$

52. C is correct.

Frequency = # cycles / time

$f = 2$ cycles / 1 s

$f = 2 \text{ s}^{-1}$

$v = \lambda f$

where λ is wavelength

$v = (12 \text{ m}) \cdot (2 \text{ s}^{-1})$

$v = 24 \text{ m/s}$

53. B is correct. Atmospheric pressure is not taken into account because it acts at the surface of the water and all around Mike's finger, so it cancels.

$P_{water} = \rho g h$

$P_{water} = (10^3 \text{ kg/m}^3) \cdot (10 \text{ m/s}^2) \cdot (1 \text{ m})$

$P_{water} = 10^4 \text{ N/m}^2$

Area of hole:

$A = (0.01 \text{ m}) \cdot (0.01 \text{ m})$

$A = 10^{-4} \text{ m}^2$

$F = PA$

$F = (10^4 \text{ N/m}^2) \cdot (10^{-4} \text{ m}^2)$

$F = 1 \text{ N}$

54. C is correct.

$$P = IV$$

Voltage is considered potential in a DC circuit.

Slope = Voltage / Power

Slope = V / IV

Slope = 1 / I

Slope = 1 / current

55. C is correct.

Energy needed to change hydrogen from one state to another:

$$E = -13.6 \text{ eV}[(1 / n_1^2) - (1 / n_2^2)]$$

To ionize hydrogen, the electron must be removed to the n = ∞ state.

Energy needed to change from the ground state:

$$E = -13.6[(1 / 1) - (1 / \infty)]$$

$$E = -13.6 \text{ eV}$$

Energy is expressed as a negative number to indicate that this much energy is needed to be input to the atom.

Diagnostic Test #2 – Explanations

1. D is correct.

When an object is thrown into the air, the acceleration vector is always equal to gravity (for objects in free fall).

The velocity vector changes direction when the object starts to come down.

2. D is correct.

A larger coefficient of thermal expansion causes a greater size increase compared to materials with smaller coefficients of thermal expansion.

If the pin were removed easily while hot, it did not expand as much as material X and must have a smaller coefficient.

3. B is correct.

The sun warms the Earth only through radiation because space is a vacuum and contains no matter to transfer heat through convection or conduction.

4. C is correct.

$$P = W / t$$
$$W = Fd$$
$$P = (Fd) / t$$
$$F = mg$$
$$P = (mgd \sin \theta) / t$$
$$P = [(54 \text{ kg}) \cdot (9.8 \text{ m/s}^2) \cdot (10 \text{ m}) \sin 30°] / (4 \text{ s})$$
$$P = [(54 \text{ kg}) \cdot (9.8 \text{ m/s}^2) \cdot (10 \text{ m}) \cdot (0.5)] / (4 \text{ s})$$
$$P = 2,646 \text{ J} / (4 \text{ s})$$
$$P = 661 \text{ J/s}$$
$$P = 661 \text{ W}$$

Convert watts into horsepower:

$$1 \text{ hp} = 745 \text{ W}$$
$$P = (661 \text{ W}) \cdot (1 \text{ hp} / 745 \text{ W})$$
$$P = 0.89 \text{ hp}$$

5. A is correct.

The amplitude of a wave is a measure of the energy of the wave. Thus, if energy is dissipated the amplitude is reduced.

6. B is correct.

To determine the frequency of the fundamental:

$f_n = nf_1$

where f_1 = fundamental

$f_1 = f_3 / 3$

$f_1 = 783\ \text{Hz} / 3$

$f_1 = 261\ \text{Hz}$

7. C is correct.

To calculate the buoyant force due to the water:

$F_B = 7.86\ \text{N} - 6.92\ \text{N}$

$F_B = 0.94\ \text{N}$

Volume of displaced water is equal to volume of object:

$F_B = \rho g V$

$V = F_B / \rho g$

$V = 0.94\ \text{N} / (1{,}000\ \text{kg/m}^3)\cdot(9.8\ \text{m/s}^2)$

$V = 9.6 \times 10^{-5}\ \text{m}^3$

Mass of the object:

$m = W / g$

$m = 7.86\ \text{N} / 9.8\ \text{m/s}^2$

$m = 0.8\ \text{kg}$

$\rho = \text{mass / volume}$

$\rho = 0.8\ \text{kg} / 9.6 \times 10^{-5}\ \text{m}^3$

$\rho = 8{,}333\ \text{kg/m}^3$

8. A is correct.

Height determines the energy per mass required to position the water at a particular point.

This is analogous to an electric potential, as a measure of energy per charge required to position the charge at a particular point.

9. C is correct.

As the copper sheet is quickly passed through the magnetic field eddy currents form.

According to Lenz's Law, the eddy currents rotate in such a way to produce magnetic fields that oppose the changing magnetic flux.

This opposing magnetic force acts to impede the motion of the copper sheet.

10. A is correct.

$n_1 \sin \theta_1 = n_2 \sin \theta_2$

$1.33 \sin 42° = 1 \sin \theta_2$

$1.33 \times (0.67) = 1 \sin \theta_2$

$\sin \theta_2 = 0.89$

$\theta_2 = \sin^{-1}(0.89)$

$\theta_2 = 63°$

11. B is correct. Half-life is the time it takes for ½ of the quantity to decay.

1st half-life: 3,200 µg / 2 = 1,600 µg

2nd half-life: 1,600 µg / 2 = 800 µg

If two periods took 24.6 years, then one cycle takes 12.3 years.

Mathematically solving for half-life:

$A_{final} = A_{initial} \times (½)^{t/h}$

where t = time and h = half-life

$800 \text{ µg} = (3,200 \text{ µg}) \cdot (½)^{24.6 \text{ yr}/h}$

$(800 \text{ µg}) / (3,200 \text{ µg}) = (½)^{24.6 \text{ yr}/h}$

$0.25 = (½)^{24.6 \text{ yr}/h}$

$\ln(0.25) = (24.6 \text{ yr}/h) \ln(½)$

$h = 12.3 \text{ yr}$

12. C is correct.

If the object's velocity is constant, then the net force is zero.

In the y-direction:

$0 = F_N + F_g$

In the x-direction:

$0 = F_{friction} + F$

$F_N + F_g = F_{friction} + F$

$-F = F_{friction}$

Since kinetic friction is exerting a force opposing the object's motion, there must be an equal and opposing force propelling it forward for net force to be zero.

13. B is correct.

According to the principle of conservation of mechanical energy: total mechanical energy in a system remains constant as long as the only forces acting are conservative forces.

14. D is correct.

This is a thin film interference problem.

When light strikes the surface of the oil, some will be transmitted, and some light will be reflected off the surface.

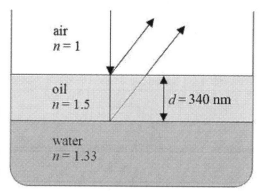

This process is repeated when the light reaches the oil-water interface.

However, the light reflected from the oil-water interface may combine with the light originally reflected off the oil from before in either constructive or destructive interference.

The light which is strongly reflected is formed through constructive interference, the rays that destructively interfere with the originally reflected light cannot be seen.

Use the thin film constructive interference equation:

$$2n_{oil}d = (m + \tfrac{1}{2})\lambda \qquad (m = 0, 1, 2...)$$

where m is the order of the reflected light.

$$\lambda = (2n_{oil}d) / (m + \tfrac{1}{2})$$

Solve for range: $400 \text{ nm} \leq \lambda \leq 800 \text{ nm}$

Use m = 0

$$\lambda_0 = (2)\cdot(1.5)\cdot(340 \times 10^{-9} \text{ m}) / (0 + \tfrac{1}{2}),$$

$$\lambda_0 = 1{,}020 \times 10^{-9} \text{ m} = 1{,}020 \text{ nm}$$

λ_0 is out of range

Use m = 1

$$\lambda_1 = (2)\cdot(1.5)\cdot(340 \times 10^{-9} \text{ m}) / (1 + \tfrac{1}{2})$$

$$\lambda_1 = 680 \times 10^{-9} \text{ m} = 680 \text{ nm}$$

λ_1 is in range

Use m = 2

$$\lambda_2 = (2)\cdot(1.5)\cdot(340 \times 10^{-9} \text{ m}) / (2 + \tfrac{1}{2})$$

$$\lambda_2 = 408 \times 10^{-9} \text{ m} = 408 \text{ nm}$$

λ_2 is in range

If m is a value greater than 2, it produces wavelength outside the 400 nm to 800 nm range.

Thus, the two most strongly reflected wavelengths are:

$$\lambda_1 = 680 \text{ nm}$$

$$\lambda_2 = 408 \text{ nm}$$

15. B is correct.

The harmonic wavelength λ_n occurs when:

$\lambda_n = (2L) / n$

where L is the length of the string and n is the harmonic (n = 1, 2, 3…).

The fourth harmonic wavelength occurs at n = 4.

$\lambda_4 = (2L) / 4$

$\lambda_4 = (2 \times 1 \text{ m}) / 4$

$\lambda_4 = 0.5 \text{ m}$

16. C is correct.

$v_f = v_0 + at$

The only force causing acceleration acting on the ball after it has been thrown is gravity.

Thus, acceleration due to gravity is -10 m/s^2 because it acts opposite the upward direction.

The acceleration due to gravity points downwards, giving a negative value

17. D is correct.

Electric field at a distance:

$E = kQ / d^2$

Solve for $Q_1 = 18$ μC, where d is half the distance:

$E_1 = (9 \times 10^9 \text{ N·m}^2\text{·C}^{-2})\cdot(18 \times 10^{-6} \text{ C}) / (0.075 \text{ m})^2$

$E_1 = 28.8 \times 10^6 \text{ N/C}$

Solve for Q_2:

$E_2 = (9 \times 10^9 \text{ N·m}^2\text{·C}^{-2})\cdot(-6 \times 10^{-6} \text{ C}) / (0.075 \text{ m})^2$

$E_2 = -9.6 \times 10^6 \text{ N/C}$

Note that the negative sign indicates that the electric field goes into the charge because the charge is negative.

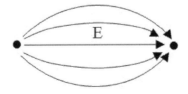

Because the electric fields generated by both charges point in the same direction, sum E_1, and E_2 to find the strength halfway between the charges:

$E_{total} = E_1 + E_2$

$E_{total} = (28.8 \times 10^6 \text{ N/C}) + (9.6 \times 10^6 \text{ N/C})$

$E_{total} = 38.4 \times 10^6 \text{ N/C}$ toward the negative charge.

18. A is correct.

$$P = I^2R$$

$$P = (4I)^2R$$

$$P = (16)I^2R$$

Power increased by a factor of 16

19. C is correct.

$$1/f = 1/d_o + 1/d_i$$

$$1/d_i = 1/f - 1/d_o$$

Since $d_o > f$,

$1/f - 1/d_o$ is always positive, so the image is real.

$$m = -d_i/d_o$$

Since i is positive, $m = -(+i/o)$ is negative, so the image is inverted.

If the resulting magnification is positive, the image is upright.

If the magnification is negative, the image is inverted (upside down).

20. D is correct.

The effect of nuclear radiation on living tissue is measured by biological radiation units.

Gray (Gy) is the SI unit of biological radiation effect and one gray corresponds to the transfer of one joule of energy to one kilogram of tissue.

The rad is an older unit not in use today and equals 0.01 Gy.

Another the older unit of roentgen (R) is still commonly used and was originally devised as a measurement unit for use with X-rays or gamma rays. Roentgen is the quantity of radiation that generates 2.1×10^9 ion pairs per 1 cm^3 of dry air. It is also 1.8×10^{12} ion pairs per gram of tissue. 1 R roentgen = 0.0096 Gy ≈ 1 rad.

21. B is correct. Solve for heat required:

$$Q = cm\Delta T$$

$$Q = (92 \text{ cal/kg·°C})·(0.5 \text{ kg})·(70 \text{ °C} - 20 \text{ °C})$$

$$Q = 2{,}300 \text{ cal}$$

Convert to Joules:

$$Q = (2{,}300 \text{ cal} / 1 \text{ J})·(4.186 \text{ J/cal})$$

$$Q = 9{,}628 \text{ J}$$

22. D is correct.

The force of gravity depends only on the *m* and the distance between their centers.

$$F_{grav} = GM_1M_2 / d^2$$

If one *m* decreases by a factor of 2, then F_{grav} decreases by a factor of 2.

23. B is correct.

The Doppler effect for a receding source:

$$f_{observed} = [v_{sound} / (v_{sound} + v_{source})]f_{source}$$

Thus, a receding source has a lower pitch (higher frequency) and decreases further as he falls due to the increase in the source velocity.

24. C is correct.

As the block just enters the water, the total pressure will be the sum of atmospheric pressure and the pressure produced by submersion.

$$P_{total} = P_{atmosphere} + \rho gh$$

When the block just enters the water:

$$P_{total} = P_{atmosphere} + 0$$

Graph C depicts the scenario as the block will experience an initial pressure of $P_{atmosphere}$ and this will linearly increase (from ρgh) as the block is lowered further into the water.

25. A is correct.

$$F = qE$$

where *q* is the charge and *E* is the electric field

They both act in the same direction because they have a positive charge and are moving opposite the negative charge generated by the plates.

Since *E* is constant, and *q* is twice as large for the α particle (He has two protons and two neutrons), the charge is multiplied by +2.

$$F \propto q$$

F is twice as large.

26. C is correct.

Resistance = resistivity × (length / area)

$$A = \pi r^2$$

$$R = (1.68 \times 10^{-8} \ \Omega \cdot m) \cdot [(57 \ m) / \pi(5.7 \times 10^{-3} \ m)^2]$$

$$R = 9.4 \times 10^{-3} \ \Omega$$

$$V = IR$$

$$I = V / R$$

$$I = 70 \text{ V} / 9.4 \times 10^{-3} \, \Omega$$

$$I = 7{,}447 \text{ A}$$

27. D is correct. Virtual images can be seen (image in a plane mirror) but cannot be projected onto a screen.

28. C is correct. Beta Decay (plus): the parent nuclide ejects a positron and neutrino. However, in the process, a proton converts to a neutron, so the mass number remains the same, but the atomic number decreases by 1.

$$^A_Z X \rightarrow \,^{A}_{Z-1} Y + \,^0_{+1} e^+ + \,^0_0 v$$

29. D is correct. All external forces are balanced for a system of a bicycle and a rider as the rider pedals at a constant speed in a straight line? (Ignore friction in the bearings of the bicycle)

30. A is correct.

$$F_{net} = ma$$

The suitcase is moving in a straight line, at a constant speed, so the suitcase's velocity is constant. Therefore,

$$a = 0$$

$$F_{net} = 0$$

31. B is correct.

$$a = \Delta v / \Delta t$$

$$a = (0.9 \text{ m/s}) / (8 \text{ s})$$

$$a = 0.1125 \text{ m/s}^2$$

$$F = ma$$

Total mass:

$$m = F_{net} / a$$

$$m = 900 \text{ N} / 0.1125 \text{ m/s}^2$$

$$m = 8{,}000 \text{ kg}$$

The mass of the rocket:

$$m_{rocket} = m - m_{spacecraft}$$

$$m_{rocket} = (8{,}000 \text{ kg} - 3{,}500 \text{ kg})$$

$$m_{rocket} = 4{,}500 \text{ kg}$$

32. A is correct.

Power = current × voltage

$P = I\Delta V$

$P = (5 \text{ A})\cdot(25 \text{ V})$

$P = 125 \text{ W}$

Energy = power × time

Energy = $(125 \text{ W})\cdot(60 \text{ s})$

Energy = 7,500 J

At 30% efficiency, the energy converted into PE:

7,500 J × 30% = 2,250 J

Set PE equal to *mgh*:

$2{,}250 \text{ J} = mgh$

$2{,}250 \text{ J} = (50 \text{ kg})\cdot(10 \text{ m/s}^2)h$

$2{,}250 \text{ J} = (500 \text{ kg m/s}^2)h$

$2{,}250 \text{ J} = (500 \text{ J/m})h$

$h = 2{,}250 \text{ J} / (500 \text{ J/m})$

$h = 4.5 \text{ m}$

33. D is correct.

Gravitational PE is converted into KE as the pendulum swings back from its maximum height.

To calculate the pendulum's speed as it passes through its lowest point:

$mgh = \frac{1}{2}mv^2$, cancel *m* from both sides of the expression

$gh_0 = \frac{1}{2}v_0^2$

$v_0 = \sqrt{(2gh_0)}$

If h_0 is doubled the velocity is:

$v = \sqrt{[2g(2h_0)]}$

$v = \sqrt{(2gh_0)} \times \sqrt{2}$

$v = v_0\sqrt{2}$

The velocity increases by a factor of $\sqrt{2}$.

34. B is correct.

$\Delta L / L = \alpha\Delta T$

where α is coefficient of linear expansion

$\Delta L = \alpha\Delta T L$

Using $3L$ for L:

$\Delta L = \alpha \Delta \mathrm{T}(3L)$

$\Delta L = 3(\alpha \Delta \mathrm{T}L)$

ΔL is 3 times larger

35. D is correct.

$n_1 \sin \theta_1 = n_2 \sin \theta_2$

When the critical angle is reached:

$\theta_2 = 90°$

$\sin \theta_\mathrm{C} = (n_2 / n_1)$

For this statement to be valid:

$n_1 > n_2$

36. B is correct. Semiconductors have electrical conductivity between metals and insulators (i.e., poor conductors). The resistance for a semiconductor decreases as their temperature increases.

Therefore, the graph for a semiconductor for a resistivity vs temperature graph has a negative slope for resistivity (y-axis) as the temperature (x-axis) increases.

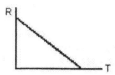

37. C is correct. A volt is equal to the difference in electric potential between two points of a conductor.

A volt is also defined as the potential difference between two parallel infinite plates with an electric field between them.

38. A is correct. $F_\mathrm{B} = \rho g \mathrm{V}$

Buoyant force is directly proportional to volume.

Volume of a sphere is given as:

$\mathrm{V} = 4 / 3\pi r^3$

If radius doubles:

$\mathrm{V} = 4 / 3\pi(2r)^3$

$\mathrm{V} = (8){\cdot}(4 / 3\pi r^3)$

Therefore, when r doubles, F_B increase by a factor of 8 times.

39. C is correct.

Speed of sound in a gas:

$$V_{sound} = \sqrt{(\gamma R T) / M}$$

where γ = adiabatic constant, R = gas constant, T = temperature and M = molar mass of a gas

$$V_{sound\,H} = \sqrt{(\gamma R T) / M}$$

If M is doubled, the speed of sound in He compared to in H is:

$$V_{sound\,He} = \sqrt{(\gamma R T) / 2\,M}$$

$$V_{sound\,He} = (1 / \sqrt{2}) \cdot \sqrt{(\gamma R T) / M}$$

$$V_{sound\,He} = (0.707) \cdot \sqrt{(\gamma R T) / M}$$

Comparing the two with respect to He:

$$V_{sound\,He} = (0.707) \cdot (V_{sound\,H})$$

$$(1 / 0.707) V_{sound\,He} = V_{sound\,H}$$

$$V_{sound\,H} = 1.41\ V_{sound\,He}$$

40. D is correct.

The amplitude of a wave is a measure of the energy of the wave. If energy increases, the amplitude increases.

41. D is correct.

I: PE = work

II: PE = $(mg)h$

III: PE = (weight)h

All the statements are measurements of potential energy of the box.

42. A is correct.

The Bohr model of the atom has two major failures:

1. It could not explain why some spectral emission lines were brighter than others.

2. It defines a radius and momentum for the electron which violates the Heisenberg uncertainty principle.

43. C is correct.

$$(m_1 + m_2)a = m_1 g$$

$$(70\ kg + 10\ kg)a = (70\ kg) \cdot (10\ m/s^2)$$

$$a = 8.8\ m/s^2$$

Or another method to solve this problem:

Sum of forces for each system equals zero:

(A)　　$0 = T + ma$

　　　　$T = -(10 \text{ kg})a$

(B)　　$0 = T - ma - mg$

　　　　$0 = T - (70 \text{ kg})a - (70 \text{ kg})\cdot(10 \text{ m/s}^2)$

　　　　$0 = T - (70 \text{ kg})a - 700 \text{ N}$

Substituting (A) into (B):

　　　　$0 = [(-10 \text{ kg})a] - (70 \text{ kg})a - 700 \text{ N}$

　　　　$0 = (-80 \text{ kg})a - 700 \text{ N}$

　　　　$700 \text{ N} / 80 \text{ kg} = a$

　　　　$a = 8.8 \text{ m/s}^2$

44. B is correct.

　　　　$v_f = v_i + at$

　　　　$a = (v_f - v_i) / t$

　　　　$a = (16 \text{ m/s} - 4 \text{ m/s}) / 2 \text{ s}$

　　　　$a = 6 \text{ m/s}^2$

　　　　$d = d_i + v_i t + \frac{1}{2}(6 \text{ m/s}^2)\cdot(2 \text{ s})^2$

　　　　$d = 0 + (4 \text{ m/s})\cdot(2 \text{ s}) + \frac{1}{2}(6 \text{ m/s}^2)\cdot(2 \text{ s})^2$

　　　　$d = (8 \text{ m}) + \frac{1}{2}(6 \text{ m/s}^2)\cdot(4 \text{ s}^2) = 20 \text{ m}$

45. A is correct.

　　　　$Q = m_s c_p \Delta T$

　　　　$Q = (70 \text{ g})\cdot(0.11 \text{ cal/g}\cdot°\text{C})\cdot(450 °\text{C} - 100 °\text{C})$

　　　　$Q = 2{,}695 \text{ cal}$

　　　　$Q = m_w c_p \Delta T$

　　　　$m_w = Q / c_p \Delta T$

　　　　$m_w = 2{,}695 \text{ cal} / [(1 \text{ cal/g}\cdot°\text{C})\cdot(100 °\text{C} - 25 °\text{C})]$

　　　　$m_w = 36 \text{ g}$

46. C is correct.

　　　　$PE_{spring} = KE_{mass}$

　　　　$\frac{1}{2}kx^2 = \frac{1}{2}mv^2$

　　　　$x = \sqrt{[(m / k) / v^2]}$

　　　　$m / k = 0.031 \text{ kg}\cdot\text{m/N}$

　　　　$x = \sqrt{[(0.031 \text{ kg}\cdot\text{m/N})\cdot(30 \text{ m/s})^2]}$

　　　　$x = 5.3 \text{ m}$

47. B is correct. A guitar is louder because the sounding board resonates at the frequency of the strings and produces a louder sound.

48. D is correct.

According to Coulomb's Law, like charges repel with equal and opposite force:

$F_1 = F_2 = kq_1q_2 / r^2$

49. B is correct.

$1 / f = 1 / d_i + 1 / d_o$

$1 / 10$ m $= 1 / d_i + 1 / 20$ m

$1 / 10$ m $- 1 / 20$ m $= 1 / d_i$

$1 / 20$ m $= 1 / d_i$

$d_i = 20$ m, positive so it must be in front of the mirror

Image is 20 m in front of mirror – same position as the object (i.e., in front), only inverted.

50. A is correct.

The speed of an object with reference to direction is the velocity of the object. Velocity is a vector and includes a component of direction whereas speed is a scalar and has no direction component.

51. D is correct.

$Q = mc_p\Delta T$

$c_p = Q / m\Delta T$

$c_p = (14$ J$) / (0.185$ kg$) \cdot (10$ °C$)$

$c_p = 7.6$ J/kg·C

1 °C $= 1$ K

$c_p = 7.6$ J/kg·K

52. C is correct.

$T = 2\pi\sqrt{(L / g)}$

When L is tripled:

$T_2 = 2\pi\sqrt{(3L / g)}$

$T_2 = 2\pi\sqrt{3}\sqrt{(L / g)}$

$T_2 / T_1 = [2\pi\sqrt{3}\sqrt{(L / g)}] / [2\pi\sqrt{(L / g)}]$

$T_2 / T_1 = \sqrt{3}$

53. D is correct.

Static fluid pressure only depends on fluid density, height and acceleration

$P = \rho g h$

$P = (1{,}000 \text{ kg/m}^3) \cdot (9.8 \text{ m/s}^2) \cdot (15 \text{ m} + 30 \text{ m})$

$P = 4.4 \times 10^5 \text{ N/m}^2$

54. A is correct.

The resistance of a wire is given by:

$R = \rho L / A$

where ρ = resistivity, L = length and A = cross-sectional area

Resistance of thin wire:

$R_0 = \rho L / A_0$

Resistance of thicker wire:

$A = 2A_0$

$R = \rho L / 2A_0$

$R = \frac{1}{2}R_0$

The thicker wire has ½ the resistance of the thinner wire.

55. B is correct.

The orbital angular momentum is given by:

$L = \sqrt{[\ell(\ell + 1)]}\, h$

Allowable angular momentum quantum numbers: $\ell = 0, 1, 2 \ldots n - 1$

Diagnostic Test #3 – Explanations

1. A is correct.

Involves proportions: what change in h (distance) is required for t to double?

$$t = (v_f - v_i) / a$$

$$t = v_f / g$$

If t is doubled, then v_f is also doubled:

$$2t = 2(v_f / g)$$

$$2t = (2v_f) / g$$

The height h is related to the velocity v_f through the equation for conservation of energy:

$$mgh = \tfrac{1}{2}mv_f^2$$

Cancel m from both sides and rearrange for h:

$$h = v_f^2 / 2g$$

Since v_f was doubled when t was doubled, the new height is:

$$h = (2v_f)^2 / 2g$$

$$h = (4)v_f^2 / 2g$$

If t is doubled, h increases by a factor of $2^2 = 4$.

2. D is correct.

Take the system to comprise both the lower block and Rope 2.

There are two forces on this system: the tension due to Rope 1 (pointing up) and gravity (pointing down).

The net force is:

$$F_{net} = T - m_{system}\,g$$

The mass of the system is the sum of the mass of the lower block and Rope 2:

$$m_{system} = m_{block} + m_{Rope2}$$

By Newton's second law:

$$F_{net} = m_{system}\,a$$

Combine these:

$$T - (m_{block} + m_{Rope2})g = (m_{block} + m_{Rope2})a$$

Or:

$$T = (m_{block} + m_{Rope2}) \cdot (g + a)$$

$$T = (1.0\ \text{kg} + 0.35\ \text{kg}) \cdot (9.8\ \text{m/s}^2 + 5.5\ \text{m/s}^2)$$

$$T = (1.35\ \text{kg}) \cdot (15.3\ \text{m/s}^2)$$

$$T = 20.7\ \text{N} \approx 21\ \text{N}$$

3. C is correct.

$$Q = 9 \text{ kJ}$$

$$W = -5 \text{ kJ}$$

By the first law of thermodynamics:

$$\Delta U = Q + W$$

$$\Delta U = 9 \text{ kJ} - 5 \text{ kJ}$$

$$\Delta U = 4 \text{ kJ}$$

4. B is correct.

The force of gravity and the normal force on the table sum to zero.

The spring provides the centripetal force:

$$F_{\text{spring}} = mv^2 / r$$

$$20 \text{ N} = (5 \text{ kg})v^2 / (4 \text{ m})$$

$$80 \text{ N·m} = (5 \text{ kg})v^2$$

$$v^2 = 16 \text{ m}^2/\text{s}^2$$

$$v = 4 \text{ m/s}$$

One revolution is equivalent to the circumference:

$$C = 2\pi r$$

$$C = 2\pi(4 \text{ m})$$

$$C = 25.1 \text{ m}$$

$$t = C / v$$

$$t = (25.1 \text{ m}) / (4 \text{ m/s})$$

$$t = 6.3 \text{ s}$$

5. A is correct.

Waves transport energy from one region to another but do not transport matter.

6. A is correct.

An organ pipe produces sounds of wavelength:

$$\lambda_n = (2L / n)$$

where n is harmonic number: n = 1, 2, 3…

The lowest tone is the fundamental where n = 1.

$$\lambda_1 = (2L / 1)$$

$$\lambda_1 = 2L$$

The next lowest tone is the second harmonic where n = 2.

$\lambda_2 = (2L / 2)$

$\lambda_2 = L$

The next lowest tone is the third harmonic where n = 3.

$\lambda_3 = (2L / 3)$

$\lambda_3 = 2L/3$

7. C is correct.

Draw a free body diagram:

4 N

10 N

Find sum of forces to get net force:

$F_{net} = 10\ N - 4\ N$

$F_{net} = 6\ N$

8. D is correct.

Parallel to the field direction.

Faraday's Law (induced emf in a coil with changing magnetic flux):

$V_{generated} = -N\Delta(BA) / \Delta t$

where N = number of turns, B = magnetic field, A = area of coil and t = time

Positioning the loop such that the area vector is parallel to the magnetic field maximizes the flux through the loop (BA) and maximizes $V_{generated}$.

9. C is correct.

The nuclei have the same charge because each has one proton.

Therefore, the forces are the same.

10. B is correct.

A diverging thin lens always produces images that are virtual, erect and reduced in size.

A converging thin lens produces images that are real or virtual, erect or inverted and reduced or magnified.

11. A is correct.

Beta Decay (plus): the parent nuclide ejects a positron and neutrino.

However, in the process, a proton converts to a neutron, so the mass number remains the same, but the atomic number decreases by 1.

$$^A_Z X \rightarrow {}^A_{Z-1} Y + {}^0_{+1} e^+ + {}^0_0 v_e$$

12. B is correct.

Velocity is a vector that comprises both speed (magnitude of movement) and direction.

    7 m represents distance only.

    7 m to the North is a displacement.

    7 m/s represents speed.

13. D is correct.

Potential energy is equal to the work performed:

    PE = W

    PE = *mgh*

    mgh = W

    m = W / *gh*

    m = 400 J / (9.8 m/s^2)·(4 m)

    m = 10.2 kg

14. A is correct.

Frequency to period relation:

    f = 1 / *T*

    f = 1 / 2 s

    f = 0.5 Hz

15. D is correct.

The diagram represents the Doppler effect for a source with velocity with respect to the observer (positioned to the right).

The siren on truck changes pitch because as the source approaches, the pitch is higher.

As the source is receding, the pitch is lower.

16. C is correct.

$P = F / A$

$F = PA$

$F = (3 \text{ atm}) \cdot (1.01 \times 10^5 \text{ Pa/1 atm}) \cdot (0.2 \text{ m})^2$

$F = 12{,}120 \text{ N} = 1.2 \times 10^4 \text{ N}$

17. A is correct.

Force from a magnetic field on a charged particle equals the electric field force on the charged particle.

For an electromagnetic wave:

$B = E / c$

$B = (1{,}200 \text{ V/m}) / (3 \times 10^8 \text{ m/s})$

$B = 4 \times 10^{-6} \text{ T}$

18. A is correct.

$V_{rms} = V_{max} / \sqrt{2}$

$V_{rms} = 200 \text{ V} / 1.41$

$V_{rms} = 142 \text{ V}$

19. C is correct.

For diverging lens, the image is always located on the same side as the object.

The equation is:

$1 / f = 1 / d_i + 1 / d_o$

For a diverging lens, the focal length is negative by convention.

$-1 / 3 \text{ m} = 1 / d_i + 1 / 4 \text{ m}$

$1 / d_i = -1 / 3 \text{ m} - 1 / 4 \text{ m}$

$1 / d_i = -4 / 12 \text{ m} - 3 / 12 \text{ m}$

$1 / d_i = -7 / 12 \text{ m}$

$d_i = -12 / 7 \text{ m}$

For a diverging lens, the image distance is always negative.

For a concave or diverging lens, the focal length is negative because the focus used in the ray diagram is located on the left side (x- and y-axis coordinate system) of the lens.

The image distance will be negative because it is also formed on the left-hand side.

20. D is correct.

The transition from level 3 to 2 produces a wavelength λ so that wavelength has energy of:

$$E_{3,2} = hf$$

$$f = c / \lambda$$

$$E_{3,2} = h(c / \lambda)$$

$$E_{3,2} = (1 / \lambda){\cdot}(hc)$$

Then the energy from 2 to 1 is:

$$E_{2,1} = 2E_{3,2}$$

Then the energy from 3 to 1 is:

$$E_{3,1} = 3E_{3,2}$$

Because the energy and wavelength are inversely related, the transition from 2 to 1 must have ½ λ and the transition from 3 to 1 must have 1/3 λ.

21. A is correct. PE = *mgh*

Energy used in one repetition:

$$PE = (2){\cdot}(3 \text{ kg}){\cdot}(9.8 \text{ m/s}^2){\cdot}(0.5 \text{ m})$$

$$PE = 29.4 \text{ J}$$

Convert 19 kcal to joules:

$$PE = (19 \text{ kcal} / 1){\cdot}(1{,}000 \text{ cal} / \text{kcal}){\cdot}(4.186 \text{ J} / \text{cal})$$

$$PE = 79{,}534 \text{ J}$$

Divide by 29.4 J to find the # of repetitions

$$\# = (79{,}534 \text{ J}) / (29.4 \text{ J})$$

$$\# = 2{,}705 \text{ repetitions}$$

22. C is correct.

Find force due to gravity on 18 kg block:

$$F_{g1} = mg \sin \theta$$

$$F_{g1} = (18 \text{ kg}){\cdot}(9.8 \text{ m/s}^2) \sin 20°$$

$$F_{g1} = 60.3 \text{ N}$$

Find force due to gravity on 21 kg block:

$$F_{g2} = m_2 g$$

$$F_{g2} = (21 \text{ kg}){\cdot}(9.8 \text{ m/s}^2)$$

$$F_{g2} = 205.8 \text{ N}$$

Sum forces (note opposite signs so the F_{g1} values is subtracted):

$$F_{tot} = F_{g2} - F_{g1}$$

$$F_{tot} = (205.8 \text{ N} - 60.3 \text{ N})$$

$$F_{tot} = 145.5 \text{ N}$$

Find the acceleration of system:

$$F = m_{tot}a$$

$$a = F / m_{tot}$$

$$a = 145.5 \text{ N} / (18 \text{ kg} + 21 \text{ kg})$$

$$a = 3.7 \text{ m/s}^2$$

23. A is correct.

The time it takes for the point on the string to move from $+x$ to $-x$ is half a period, or $T / 2$.

$$\lambda = vT$$

where v is the velocity of the wave

$$T = \lambda / v$$

$$T = (8 \text{ m}) / (4 \text{ m/s})$$

$$T = 2 \text{ s}$$

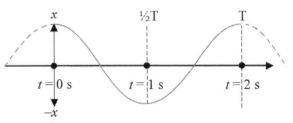

In general, calculating the frequency of a repeating event is accomplished by counting the number of times that event occurs within a specific period, then dividing the count by the period.

$$t = \tfrac{1}{2}T$$

$$t = 1 \text{ s}$$

24. B is correct.

The equation of continuity:

$f = Av$ remains constant

$$A_2V_2 = A_1V_1$$

$$V_2 = A_1V_1 / A_2$$

$$V_2 = \pi(16 \text{ cm})^2 \cdot (V_1) / \pi(4 \text{ cm})^2$$

$$V_2 = 16V_1$$

If the radius decreases by a factor of 4 then the velocity increases by a factor of 16.

25. B is correct.

Coulomb's Law equation:

$$F = kQ_1Q_2 / d$$

Because of the multiplication of Q_1 and Q_2 by Coulomb's Law, each ball experiences the same force regardless of the magnitude of its charge.

$$F_1 = k(2Q_1)Q_2 / d$$
$$F_2 = k(2Q_1)Q_2 / d$$
$$F_1 = F_2$$

26. B is correct.

Ohm's Law:

$$I = V / R$$

Rearrange:

$$R = V / I$$
$$R = \text{volts} / \text{amps}$$
$$R = \Omega$$
$$\Omega = V / A$$

27. B is correct.

Linear magnification of lens:

$$m = -d_i / d_o$$

The negative in the image distance is because all real images are inverted.

If the image distance value is negative, the image is virtual, m is positive and the image is erect:

m	Image	Inverted / Erect
+	virtual	erect
–	real	inverted

28. C is correct.

All the masses of the elements are determined relative to ^{12}C (Carbon-12), which is defined as the exact number of 12 amu.

Elements exist as a variety of isotopes, and two major isotopes of carbon are ^{12}C and ^{13}C.

Each carbon atom has the same number of protons and electrons – 6.

^{12}C has 6 neutrons, ^{13}C has 7 neutrons.

29. B is correct.

Kinetic energy is equal to potential energy at top of flight:

$PE = KE$

$mgh = \frac{1}{2}mv^2$, cancel m from the expression

$gh = \frac{1}{2}v^2$

$h = \frac{1}{2}v^2 / g$

$h = v^2 / 2g$

Thus, height does not depend on mass.

Objects thrown at the same velocity travel to equal heights, regardless of mass.

30. D is correct.

According to Newton's First Law:

"An object at rest, or in uniform motion, remains that way unless acted upon by an outside force."

Because no outside forces are acting on the puck, no force is required to keep the puck in uniform motion.

31. D is correct.

Final velocity of an object with respect to time:

$v_f = v_i + at$

Solve for acceleration:

$0 = 16 \text{ m/s} + a(0.091 \text{ s})$

$a = -175.8 \text{ m/s}^2$

The acceleration is negative because it acts opposite the velocity vector. Calculate force using the magnitude of acceleration:

$F = ma$

$F = (0.24 \text{ kg}) \cdot (175.8 \text{ m/s}^2)$

$F = 42 \text{ N}$

32. A is correct.

$d_{tot} = d_1 + d_2 + d_3$

$d_{tot} = (5 \text{ km} + 7.3 \text{ km} + 3.4 \text{ km})$

$d_{tot} = 15.7 \text{ km}$

$d_{tot} = 15.7 \times 10^3 \text{ m}$

Force to work relationship:

$W = Fd$

$F = W / d$

$F = (2.6 \times 10^6 \text{ J}) / (15.7 \times 10^3 \text{ m})$

$F = 1.7 \times 10^2 \text{ N}$

33. C is correct.

A redshift is created when a light source moves away from the observer and thereby its wavelength is perceived to be longer due to the Doppler effect.

A blueshift occurs when the light source moves towards the observer and the perceived wavelength is shorter.

34. D is correct.

Stefan-Boltzmann Law:

$P = A\varepsilon\sigma T^4$

Temperature is doubled:

$P = A\varepsilon\sigma(2T)^4$

$P = A\varepsilon\sigma(16)T^4$

The power increases by a factor of 16.

$P_2 = P(16)$

$P_2 = (15 \text{ W})\cdot(16)$

$P_2 = 240 \text{ W}$

35. A is correct. Angular magnification equation:

$M_\alpha = NP / f$

where NP = near point

$M_\alpha = (250 \text{ mm} / 50 \text{ mm})$

$M_\alpha = 5$

36. D is correct.

Faraday's Law states that a voltage will be induced in a coil exposed to a magnetic field:

$V = -N\Delta(BA) / \Delta t$

All three choices are correct because options I and III would increase the rate of change of the magnetic field (B) and thereby increase the voltage.

Option II is correct because it would increase the number of turns (N) and therefore increase the induced voltage.

37. C is correct.

Ampere is used to express the flow rate of electric charge (i.e., current).

38. B is correct.

Boltzmann's constant relates energy at the individual particle level with temperature, where N is the number of molecules of gas.

39. D is correct. Standing wave: relationship of wavelength to length and harmonic number.

$$\lambda = 2L / n$$

$$\lambda = 2(0.2 \text{ m}) / 5$$

$$\lambda = 0.08 \text{ m}$$

In a wave, the length between a node and antinode is ¼λ:

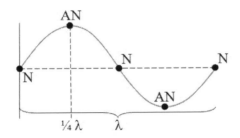

$$d = \frac{1}{4}\lambda$$

$$d = \frac{1}{4}(0.08 \text{ m})$$

$$d = 0.02 \text{ m} = 20 \text{ mm}$$

40. B is correct.

Notice that every time the position graph reads a maximum, it must be changing direction. Therefore, velocity must be zero at these points.

Graphs B and C have zero velocity at the maximum of the position graph.

Graph C displays a negative velocity while the position graph is increasing which is not possible. Graph B is correct because it has positive velocity as the position increases and negative velocity as the position decreases.

41. D is correct.

Potential energy:

$$PE = mgh$$

$$PE = (2 \text{ kg}) \cdot (9.8 \text{ m/s}^2) \cdot (4 \text{ m})$$

$$PE \approx 80 \text{ J}$$

42. C is correct.

Heavy nuclei tend to have more neutrons than protons because neutrons contribute to the nuclear strong force but do not contribute to the electrostatic repulsion (i.e., protons) because of their neutral charge.

Thus, an excess of neutrons helps keep the nuclei together without adding repulsion forces within the nuclei.

43. C is correct.

Force equation:

$$F = ma$$

$$F = (400 \text{ kg}) \cdot (1.5 \text{ m/s}^2)$$

$$F = 600 \text{ N}$$

44. B is correct.

Constant velocity means balanced forces are acting on the box. Therefore, the horizontal forces must be equal.

45. D is correct.

Isometric refers to constant volume. Since the container does not expand when heat energy is added, it undergoes an isometric process.

46. A is correct.

A watt is a J/s

$$J = N \cdot m$$

$$N = kg \cdot m/s^2$$

$$J = (kg \cdot m/s^2)m$$

$$W = J/s$$

$$W = N \cdot m/s$$

$$W = kg \cdot m^2/s^3$$

47. D is correct.

Sound speed and frequency are related:

$$f = v / \lambda$$

where λ is twice the length of the organ pipe.

If sound speed is 3% slower, then v decreases by a factor of 0.97, and f decreases by a factor of 0.97 because f is directly proportional to v.

Thus, f decreases by 3%.

48. B is correct.

Particle 1 is negative because it is deflected in the magnetic field but goes in the opposite direction of the right-hand rule.

Particle 2 is neutral because it is unaffected by the magnetic field.

Particle 3 is positive because it is deflected in the presence of the magnetic field and obeys the right-hand rule.

49. C is correct.

Among the choices listed, radio waves have the lowest frequency.

$$f_{radio} < f_{microwave} < f_{infrared} < f_{X\text{-ray}} < f_{\gamma\ rays}$$

50. B is correct.

If both marbles are thrown with speed v_0, then both marbles have equal KE_0.

When they reach the ground their final KE is:

$$KE_0 + PE_0 = KE_{final}$$

Because the height of the cliff is the same, the PE_0 of both marbles is equal.

Thus, both marbles have equal KE_{final} and equal speed at the bottom.

51. D is correct.

$$10\ °C = 10\ K$$
$$Q = mc\Delta T$$
$$Q = (0.3\ kg)·(128\ J/kg·K)·(10\ K)$$
$$Q = 384\ J$$

52. D is correct.

Calculate cable tension:

$$T = mg$$
$$T = (2{,}500\ kg)·(9.8\ m/s^2)$$
$$T = 24{,}500\ N$$

Calculate wave velocity:

$$v = \sqrt{[T / (m / L)]}$$
$$v = \sqrt{(24{,}500\ N / 0.65\ kg/m)}$$
$$v = 194\ m/s$$

53. A is correct.

Volumetric flow rate:

$$V_f = Av$$

$$A = \pi d^2 / 4$$

So, for the original pipe:

$$V_f = (\pi d^2 / 4) \cdot v$$

If diameter is doubled:

$$V_f = [\pi (2d)^2 / 4] v$$

$$V_f = (\pi / 4) \cdot (4d^2) v$$

$$V_f = 4 [(\pi d^2 / 4) v]$$

where the term in square brackets is identical to the original flow rate.

Thus, the flow rate increases by a factor of 4.

54. B is correct.

In a current-carrying wire, the magnetic field circles the wire in closed loops in the direction according to the right-hand rule.

55. C is correct.

Because protons are positively charged, they repel each other in the nucleus due to the forces from electrostatic repulsion.

The strong nuclear force keeps the protons together because it overcomes the electrostatic repulsion and thus binds the nucleus together.

Diagnostic Test #4 – Explanations

1. D is correct.

$$v_f = v_0 + at$$

$$5 \text{ m/s} = (0 \text{ m/s}) + a(1 \text{ s})$$

$$a = 5 \text{ m/s}^2$$

$$x = x_0 + v_0 t + \frac{1}{2}at^2$$

$$x = (0 \text{ m}) + (0 \text{ m/s}) \cdot (3 \text{ s}) + \frac{1}{2}(5 \text{ m/s}^2) \cdot (3 \text{ s})^2$$

$$x = 22.5 \text{ m}$$

2. A is correct.

The component of the block's weight (w) that is perpendicular to the inclined plane equals the normal force (N) on the block.

N is given by the expression $w \cos \theta$, where θ is the angle of incline.

As the angle increases toward 90°, $\cos \theta$ decreases.

Therefore, N also decreases.

3. C is correct.

Linear expansion:

$$\Delta L = L_i \alpha \Delta T$$

Total linear expansion of two rods:

$$\Delta L_{total} = \Delta L_A + \Delta L_S$$

$$\Delta L_{total} = L_{iA} \alpha_A \Delta T + L_{iS} \alpha_S \Delta T$$

$$\Delta L_{total} = \Delta T (L_{iA} \alpha_A + L_{iS} \alpha_S)$$

$$\Delta L_{total} = (90 \text{ °C} - 15 \text{ °C}) \cdot [(0.1 \text{ m}) \cdot (2.4 \times 10^{-5} \text{ K}^{-1}) + (0.8 \text{ m}) \cdot (1.2 \times 10^{-5} \text{ K}^{-1})]$$

$$\Delta L_{total} = 9 \times 10^{-4} \text{ m}$$

Convert to mm:

$$\Delta L_{total} = (9 \times 10^{-4} \text{ m}/1) \cdot (1{,}000 \text{ mm}/1 \text{ m})$$

$$\Delta L_{total} = 0.9 \text{ mm}$$

4. B is correct.

The object's KE and momentum become zero after impact.

The total energy of the system (including heat, sound, etc.) remains constant.

5. D is correct.

Frequency is the number of cycles per second.

f = cycles / sec

$2f$ = 2 cycles / sec

By doubling the frequency, the number of cycles per second is doubled.

The speed increases by a factor of two to accomplish this in the same amount of time.

6. B is correct.

For a pipe that has one end closed and one end open, the diagram for the 3rd overtone is:

Note that the closed end of the pipe must have an antinode and the open end has a node. Because the open end can't have an antinode, the even-numbered harmonics can't occur in a pipe like this. That means that the 3rd overtone corresponds to the *seventh* harmonic in this case.

The fundamental frequency for this pipe is 1/7 the frequency of the 3rd overtone.

From the diagram, the number of antinodes (points on the waveform that have zero displacement) can be counted – there are four of them.

7. C is correct.

Both the solid circle and wire circle have the same diameters, but the wire has two surface areas exposed to the water (i.e., inner and outer circumference) where the difference in circumference length is assumed to be negligible.

The solid circle only has the outer edge exposed to the water's surface (i.e., circumference).

$L_{wire} = 2(2\pi r)$ = the relevant length for the wire circle

$2\pi r$ = the relevant length for the solid circle

Solid circle on water:

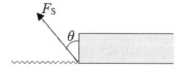

$F_{s1} = y \cos \theta \, L$

Wire on water:

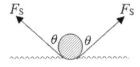

$$F_{s2} = 2y \cos \theta \, L$$

$$F_{s2} = 2F_{s1}$$

Balance weight vs. surface tension where F_s point up and F_w points down.

For solid circle:

$$F_{w1} = F_{s1}$$

For wire circle:

$$F_{w2} = F_{s2}$$

$$F_{w2} = 2F_{s1}$$

$$F_{w2} = 2F_{w1}$$

The wire circle can have double the mass without sinking.

8. A is correct.

The volt is expressed in Joules per Coulomb:

$$1 \, V = 1 \, J \, / \, 1 \, C$$

Thus, 120 V is 120 J per Coulomb of charge.

9. C is correct.

Current:

$$6 \, mA = 0.006 \, A$$

$$0.006 \, A = 0.006 \, Coulombs/sec$$

During 1 minute (60 sec), calculate the charge that has flowed:

$$0.006 \, C/s \times 60 \, s = 0.36 \, C$$

Each electron carries: 1.602×10^{-19} C

Calculate the # of electrons:

$$(0.36 \, C) \cdot (1 \text{ electron} / 1.602 \times 10^{-19} \, C) = 2.25 \times 10^{18} \text{ electrons}$$

10. A is correct.

A convex mirror always produces an image that is upright, virtual and smaller regardless of object location.

11. C is correct.

According to the de Broglie hypothesis, the idea of matter waves describes the wave-like behavior of particles that are moving.

12. B is correct.

Assume that the system is the massless spring and the two masses.

Although KE is not conserved, the sum of KE and spring PE is conserved because KE is converted into PE.

Momentum is conserved only if the system is isolated. The fixed wall provides an external force on the back of the spring, therefore the system is not isolated, and momentum is not conserved.

This results in the changing speed of the massive objects.

13. D is correct.

The potential energy of the pebble at the top of its flight is equal to its kinetic energy right as it is being thrown.

KE = PE

$\frac{1}{2}mv_0{}^2 = mgh_0$, cancel *m* from both sides of the expression

$v_0 = \sqrt{(2gh_0)}$

When the height doubles:

$v = \sqrt{(2g2h_0)}$

$v = \sqrt{2}\,\sqrt{2gh_0}$

$v = \sqrt{2} \times v_0$

14. B is correct.

Period of a simple pendulum only depends on the length:

$T = 2\pi\sqrt{(L\,/\,g)}$

Double the length:

$T = 2\pi\sqrt{(2L\,/\,g)}$

When the length is doubled, the period increases by a factor of $\sqrt{2}$.

15. C is correct.

Open pipes can produce even and odd # harmonics.

Closed pipes only produce odd # harmonics.

16. A is correct.

Bernoulli's Equation:

$$P_1 + \tfrac{1}{2}\rho v_1{}^2 + \rho g h_1 = P_2 + \tfrac{1}{2}\rho v_2{}^2 + \rho g h_2$$

When simplifying Bernoulli's Equation, both the top opening and the bottom opening experience atmospheric pressure, so P_1 and P_2 cancel.

Likewise, $v_1 << v_2$ so it can be assumed to be negligible and go to zero.

Finally, $h_2 = 0$ because it is at the bottom of the tank and is the reference for all further heights in the problem

This results in the simplified expression:

$\rho g h_1 = \tfrac{1}{2}\rho v_2{}^2$, cancel ρ from both sides of the expression

$g h_1 = \tfrac{1}{2} v_2{}^2$

$v_2 = \sqrt{(2 g h_1)}$

$v_2 = \sqrt{[(2) \cdot (9.8 \text{ m/s}^2) \cdot (0.5 \text{ m})]}$

$v_2 = 3.1$ m/s

17. B is correct.

Electric field strength of parallel-plate capacitors: energy = voltage / distance

$E = V / d$

If V remains constant and d increases, E decreases

18. C is correct.

The force on a charged particle due to an electric field:

$F = q E_0$

The charge on the deuteron (1 proton and 1 neutron) has a charge equal and opposite to that of an electron.

The forces on the two particles have the same magnitude but opposite directions.

19. D is correct.

When a wave enters a different medium, both its speed and wavelength change.

An electromagnetic wave always transports its energy in a vacuum at a speed of approximately 3.00×10^8 m/s (speed of light or c).

The frequency remains constant and is related to wavelength by:

$\lambda = c / f$

$\lambda = (3 \times 10^8 \text{ m/s}) / (1.8 \times 10^{14} \text{ Hz})$

$\lambda = 1.667 \times 10^{-6}$ m $= 1,667$ nm

20. C is correct.

Wavelength relates to photon energy:

$$E = hc / \lambda$$

$$E = [(6.626 \times 10^{-34}\,\text{J·s}) \cdot (3 \times 10^8\,\text{m/s})] / (580 \times 10^{-9}\,\text{m})$$

$$E = 3.4 \times 10^{-19}\,\text{J}$$

21. A is correct.

Graham's Law:

$$\text{rate}_1 / \text{rate}_2 = \sqrt{(m_2 / m_1)}$$

22. B is correct.

$$W = mg$$

On a slope, the force on an object due to the acceleration of gravity:

$$F = mg \sin \theta$$

$$F = W \sin \theta$$

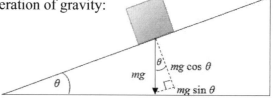

23. B is correct.

Velocity of sound in ideal gas:

$$v_0 = \sqrt{(\text{YRT} / \text{M})}$$

where Y = adiabatic constant, R = gas constant, T = temperature and M = molecular mass.

if T is doubled:

$$v_1 = \sqrt{(\text{YR2T} / \text{M})}$$

$$v_1 = \sqrt{2}\, v_0$$

The velocity increases by $\sqrt{2}$

24. B is correct.

The flow rate must be constant along the flow because water is incompressible.

Volumetric Flow Rate is:

$$\upsilon = Av$$

Volumetric Flow Rate at different points in a pipe with different areas:

$$A_1 v_1 = A_2 v_2$$

Thus, the Volumetric Flow Rate at one point must match that of the other.

$$A_2 v_2 = 0.09\,\text{m}^3/\text{s}$$

25. A is correct.

According to the right-hand rule for a negative charge, the magnetic field causes the electron to curve by path X.

If the charge were positive, the charge would curve by path Z.

26. C is correct.

For the magnetic field around a current-carrying wire, the magnetic field strength is:

$B = (\mu_0 I) / (2\pi r)$

where B is the magnetic field strength, μ_0 is the magnetic constant, I is the current in the wire and r is the distance of the particle from the wire.

According to the equation for magnetic field strength, there are two ways to increase B:

1) increase the current I through the wire, or

2) decrease the distance r from the wire

Changing particle's charge does not affect the field, nor does changing the particle's speed.

The field becomes weaker as the particle moves away from the wire (r increases).

27. C is correct. Relationship between lens power and focal length:

$P = 1 / f$, with f expressed in meters

$f = 1 / P$

$f = 1/4$ m

The lens is a converging lens because the focal length of ¼ m is more than 0.

28. D is correct.

An alpha particle is more massive than a beta particle and thus has more inertia.

An alpha particle deflects less in a magnetic field because its extra inertia requires more force to change it from its path.

29. A is correct. The marble and sponge balls should fall at the same rate. Air resistance prevents this from happening because it causes more friction that increases the time for the sponge ball to reach the ground.

30. A is correct.

$a = (v_2 - v_1) / \Delta t$

$a = [12 \text{ m/s} - (-6 \text{ m/s})] / 10 \text{ s}$

$a = 1.8 \text{ m/s}^2$

31. B is correct.

During beta minus decay, the parent nuclide ejects an electron and electron antineutrino.

However, in the process, a neutron converts to a proton, so the mass number remains the same, but the atomic number increases by 1.

$$_{Z}^{A}X \rightarrow \,_{Z+1}^{\,A}Y + \,_{-1}^{\,0}e^{-} + \,_{0}^{0}v_{e}$$

32. C is correct. The KE of the car must be completely dissipated by work due to friction.

Additionally, the friction is static friction and has a constant normal force involved, so the frictional force is constant in both scenarios.

So: $\frac{1}{2}mv^2 = F_f \times d$

where d is the distance of the skid

$\frac{1}{2}mv_0^2 = F_f \times d_0$

When the velocity is doubled,

$d = \frac{1}{2}m(2v_0)^2 / F_f$

$d = \frac{1}{2}mv_0^2\,(4) / F_f$

$d = 4d_0$

If the velocity is doubled, the car will skid 4 times further.

33. A is correct.

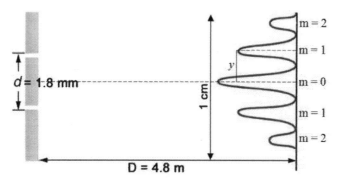

Double slit interference equation:

$y = (m\lambda D) / d$

$\lambda = (yd) / (mD)$

Because 5 bright spots are visible in 1 cm, the first order fringe $m = 1$ will be separated by a distance y from the central fringe $m = 0$.

$y = (1 \text{ cm}) / (5)$

$y = 0.2 \text{ cm}$

$\lambda = (yd) / (mD)$

Solve:

$$\lambda = (0.002 \text{ m}) \cdot (0.0018 \text{ m}) / (1) \cdot (4.8 \text{ m})$$

$$\lambda = 7.5 \times 10^{-7} \text{ m} = 750 \text{ nm}$$

34. D is correct.

Heat required to melt a solid:

$$Q_1 = mL_f$$

$$Q_1 = (0.4 \text{ kg}) \cdot (334 \times 10^3 \text{ J/kg})$$

$$Q_1 = 133.6 \text{ kJ}$$

Heat required to raise temperature of water from 0 °C to 60 °C:

$$Q_2 = mc\Delta T$$

$$Q_2 = (0.4 \text{ kg}) \cdot (4.186 \times 10^3 \text{ J/Kg·°C}) \cdot (60 \text{ °C})$$

$$Q_2 = 100.5 \text{ kJ}$$

Total heat added:

$$Q_1 + Q_2 = Q_{total}$$

$$Q_{total} = (133.6 \text{ kJ} + 100.5 \text{ kJ})$$

$$Q_{total} = 234.1 \text{ kJ}$$

35. D is correct.

Lens equation:

$$1 / f = 1 / d_i + 1 / d_o$$

$$1 / 20 \text{ cm} = 1 / d_i + 1 / 10 \text{ cm}$$

$$-1 / 20 \text{ cm} = 1 / d_i$$

$$d_i = -20 \text{ cm}$$

The negative sign indicates the image should be on the object side of the mirror.

By the sign convention for mirrors, a negative value places the image behind the mirror.

36. B is correct.

For a DC circuit, the slope of the current vs. power graph represents the work per unit of time.

37. A is correct.

$$W = Q\Delta V \text{ (for work or energy with charges)}$$

The charge transferred is:

$$Q = 10^{-10} \text{ C}$$

A positive charge moving from 8,000 V to –8,000 V is a negative sign.

$$W = (10^{-10} \text{ C}) \cdot (-8,000 \text{ V} - 8,000 \text{ V})$$

$$W = (10^{-10} \text{ C}) \cdot (-1.6 \times 10^4 \text{ V})$$

$$W = -1.6 \times 10^{-6} \text{ J}$$

38. B is correct.

Archimedes Principle:

$$\rho_{object} / \rho_{fluid} = W_{object} / W_{fluid}$$

$$\rho_{object} / \rho_{fluid} = (11.3 \text{ g/cm}^3) / (13.6 \text{ g/cm}^3)$$

$$\rho_{object} / \rho_{fluid} = 0.83$$

83% of the lead ball is below the surface by weight. The ball is 17% above the surface because the density is assumed to be consistent throughout the sphere.

The weight is directly correlated to volume.

39. D is correct.

For an approaching sound source, the Doppler equation becomes:

$$f_{observed} = [v / (v - v_{source})] \cdot (f_{source})$$

$$f_{observed} = [350 \text{ m/s} / (350 \text{ m/s} - 50 \text{ m/s})] \cdot (420 \text{ Hz})$$

$$f_{observed} = (1.17) \cdot (420 \text{ Hz})$$

$$f_{observed} = 490 \text{ Hz}$$

40. C is correct. The period T of a pendulum is:

$$T = 2\pi\sqrt{(L / g)}$$

where L is the length of the pendulum and g is the acceleration due to gravity.

Since the gravity on the Moon is 1/6 of that on Earth, the period of the pendulum on the Moon is:

$$T_M = 2\pi\sqrt{(L / (1/6)g)}$$

$$T_M = 2\pi\sqrt{(6L / g)}$$

$$T_M = (\sqrt{6}) \cdot 2\pi \cdot \sqrt{(L / g)}$$

Since $T = 2\pi\sqrt{(L / g)}$, the period of the pendulum on the Moon can be rewritten as:

$$T_M = (\sqrt{6})T$$

$$T_M = (\sqrt{6}) \cdot (3 \text{ s})$$

$$T_M = 7.3 \text{ s}$$

41. D is correct.

The gravitational force and the spring force add to zero; they are equal in magnitude (Newton's Second Law of Motion).

The magnitude of the force is:

$F_{grav} = mg$

$F_{grav} = (1.2 \text{ kg}) \cdot (10 \text{ m/s}^2)$

$F_{grav} = 12 \text{ N}$

Use the spring equation:

$F_{spring} = kx$

$x = F_{spring} / k$

$x = (12 \text{ N}) / (3 \text{ N/m})$

$x = 4 \text{ m}$

Add the amount that the spring stretches to the resting length of 0.25 m.

Total length = (0.25 m + 4 m) = 4.25 m

42. C is correct. The horizontal component of velocity is:

$v_x = v \cos \theta$

$v_x = (20 \text{ m/s}) \cos 25°$

$v_x = 18.1 \text{ m/s}$

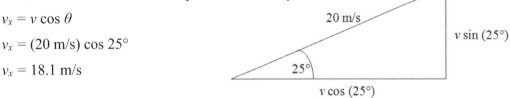

43. A is correct. Force due to friction is expressed as:

$F_f = \mu F_N$

where μ = coefficient of friction and F_N = the normal force on the block.

$F_N = W \cos \theta$

As θ decreases, $\cos \theta$ becomes larger.

F_N increases, and substituting F_N back into the equation for frictional force, the value of F_f increases.

Weight is the force of the mass due to gravity, which are both constants.

Therefore, weight remains constant.

44. B is correct.

If the velocity of an object is constant, then the instantaneous velocity at any arbitrary time equals the average velocity.

However, if the velocity is increasing or decreasing at a constant rate, then the instantaneous velocity at an arbitrary time will not equal the average velocity.

45. A is correct.

Stefan-Boltzmann Law:

$$P = \varepsilon A\sigma T^4$$

$$P = (1)\cdot(1.25 \text{ m}^2)\cdot(5.67 \times 10^{-8} \text{ W/m}^2\text{K}^4)\cdot(100 + 273 \text{ K})^4$$

$$P = 1{,}371.9 \text{ W} \approx 1.4 \text{ kW}$$

46. D is correct.

Power can be expressed as the rate at which work is done, the work per unit of time and the rate at which energy is expended.

47. A is correct.

Sound intensity (loudness) in decibels:

$$I (dB) = 10 \log_{10}(I / I_0) \qquad \text{(equation 1)}$$

$$I (dB) = 10 \log_{10}(P^2 / P_0^{\,2}) \qquad \text{(equation 2)}$$

According to equation 2, the amplitude of the pressure wave P must increase for the sound intensity I (dB) to increase.

48. C is correct.

$$F = kq_1q_2 / r^2$$

If both the charge and the separation distance are doubled:

$$F = k(2q_1)\cdot(2q_2) / (2r)^2$$

$$F = 4kq_1q_2 / 4r^2$$

$$F = kq_1q_2 / r^2 \quad \text{(same as the first expression)}$$

49. D is correct.

For a diverging lens, regardless of the object position, the image is:

- virtual

- upright

- reduced

50. B is correct.

Velocity is a vector and therefore has an associated direction.

Projectile B has an initial velocity that is negative, then becomes positive.

Thus, the direction of Projectile B must have reversed for this to occur.

51. B is correct.

The Carnot cycle is an example of a reversible process?

52. B is correct.

Sound velocity in an ideal gas:

$$v_{sound} = \sqrt{(yRT / M)}$$

where y = adiabatic constant, R = gas constant, T = temp. and M = molecular mass of gas.

Increasing the temperature increases the velocity of sound in air.

53. A is correct.

The Bernoulli Equation originated as a conservation of energy relationship for flowing fluids:

$$P_1 + \tfrac{1}{2}\rho v_1^2 + \rho g h_1 = P_2 + \tfrac{1}{2}\rho v_2^2 + \rho g h_2$$

where P_1 = pressure energy, $\tfrac{1}{2}\rho v_1^2$ = kinetic energy (volumetric) and $\rho g h_1$ = potential energy (volumetric)

Thus, the Bernoulli Equation is a statement of the conservation of pressure energy, kinetic energy and potential energy of a flowing fluid.

54. D is correct.

Resistance in a wire:

$$R = (\rho L) / A$$

where ρ = resistivity, L = length of wire and A = cross-sectional area of wire

If the first wire has resistance R_1:

$$R_1 = \rho L_1 / A_1$$

The second wire has:

$$L_2 = 2L_1$$

$$A_2 = 2A_1$$

$$R_2 = \rho 2L_1 / 2A_1$$

$$R_2 = \rho L_1 / A_1$$

$$R_2 = R_1$$

The resistances are equal.

55. C is correct.

Positron: $^{0}_{1}\beta^+$

The atomic mass remains the same, but the atomic number decreases.

Topical
Practice Questions

Detailed Explanations

Translational Motion – Explanations

1. D is correct.

$$t = (v_f - v_i) / a$$

$$t = (60 \text{ mi/h} - 0 \text{ mi/h}) / (13.1 \text{ mi/h·s})$$

$$t = 4.6 \text{ s}$$

Acceleration is in mi/h·s, so miles and hours cancel, and the answer is in units of seconds.

2. B is correct. At the top of the parabolic trajectory, the vertical velocity $v_{yf} = 0$

The initial upward velocity is the vertical component of the initial velocity:

$$v_{yi} = v \sin \theta$$

$$v_{yi} = (20 \text{ m/s}) \sin 30°$$

$$v_{yi} = (20 \text{ m/s})·(0.5)$$

$$v_{yi} = 10 \text{ m/s}$$

$$t = (v_{yf} - v_{yi}) / a$$

$$t = (0 - 10 \text{ m/s}) / (-10 \text{ m/s}^2)$$

$$t = (-10 \text{ m/s}) / (-10 \text{ m/s}^2)$$

$$t = 1 \text{ s}$$

3. B is correct.

$$\Delta d = 31.5 \text{ km} = 31,500 \text{ m}$$

$$1.25 \text{ hr} \times 60 \text{ min/hr} = 75 \text{ min}$$

$$\Delta t = 75 \text{ min} \times 60 \text{ s/min} = 4,500 \text{ s}$$

$$v_{avg} = \Delta d / \Delta t$$

$$v_{avg} = 31,500 \text{ m} / 4,500 \text{ s}$$

$$v_{avg} = 7 \text{ m/s}$$

4. A is correct. Instantaneous speed is the scalar magnitude of the velocity. It can only be positive or zero (because magnitudes cannot be negative).

5. C is correct.

$$d = (v_f^2 - v_i^2) / 2a$$

$$d = [(21 \text{ m/s})^2 - (5 \text{ m/s})^2] / [2(3 \text{ m/s}^2)]$$

$$d = (441 \text{ m}^2/\text{s}^2 - 25 \text{ m}^2/\text{s}^2) / 6 \text{ m/s}^2$$

$$d = (416 \text{ m}^2/\text{s}^2) / 6 \text{ m/s}^2$$

$$d = 69 \text{ m}$$

6. C is correct.

$$a = (v_f - v_i) / t$$

$$a = [0 - (-30 \text{ m/s})] / 0.15 \text{ s}$$

$$a = (30 \text{ m/s}) / 0.15 \text{ s}$$

$$a = 200 \text{ m/s}^2$$

To represent the acceleration in terms of g, divide a by 9.8 m/s^2:

$$\text{\# of } g = (200 \text{ m/s}^2) / 9.8 \text{ m/s}^2$$

$$\text{\# of } g = 20 \text{ } g$$

The initial velocity (v_i) is negative due to the acceleration of the car being a positive value. Since the car is decelerating, its acceleration is opposite of its initial velocity.

7. D is correct.

When a bullet is fired, it is in projectile motion. The only force in projectile motion (if air resistance is ignored) is the force of gravity.

8. B is correct.

When a car is slowing down, it is decelerating, which is equivalent to acceleration in the opposite direction.

9. A is correct

Uniform acceleration:

$$a = \text{change in velocity} / \text{change in time}$$

$$a = \Delta v / \Delta t$$

$$\Delta v = a\Delta t$$

$$\Delta v = (20 \text{ m/s}^2) \cdot (1 \text{ s})$$

$$\Delta v = 20 \text{ m/s}$$

10. B is correct.

Uniform acceleration:

$$a = \text{change in velocity} / \text{change in time}$$

$$a = \Delta v / \Delta t$$

$$a = (40 \text{ m/s} - 15 \text{ m/s}) / 10 \text{ s}$$

$$a = (25 \text{ m/s}) / 10 \text{ s}$$

$$a = 2.5 \text{ m/s}^2$$

11. C is correct.

$t = d / v$

$t = (540 \text{ mi}) / (65 \text{ mi/h})$

$t = 8.3 \text{ h}$

The time she can stop is the difference between her total allowed time and the time t that it takes to make the trip:

$t_{stop} = 9.8 \text{ h} - 8.3 \text{ h}$

$t_{stop} = 1.5 \text{ h}$

12. B is correct.

Average velocity is the change in position with respect to time:

$v = \Delta x / \Delta t$

After one lap, the racecar's final position is the same as its initial position.

Thus, $x = 0$, which implies the average velocity of 0 m/s.

13. A is correct.

$d = v_i \Delta t + \frac{1}{2} a \Delta t^2$

$d = (0.2 \text{ m/s}) \cdot (5 \text{ s}) + \frac{1}{2}(-0.05 \text{ m/s}^2) \cdot (5 \text{ s})^2$

$d = 1 \text{ m} + \frac{1}{2}(-0.05 \text{ m/s}^2) \cdot (25 \text{ s}^2)$

$d = 1 \text{ m} + (-0.625 \text{ m})$

$d = 0.375 \text{ m} \approx 0.38 \text{ m}$

Decelerating is set to negative.

The net displacement is the difference between the final and initial positions after 5 s.

14. C is correct.

$a = \text{change in velocity} / \text{change in time}$

$a = \Delta v / \Delta t$

15. B is correct.

Convert the final speed from km/h to m/s:

$v_f = (210 \text{ km/h}) \times [(1{,}000 \text{ m/1 km})] \times [(1 \text{ h/3,600 s})]$

$v_f = 58.33 \text{ m/s}$

Calculate the acceleration necessary to reach this speed:

$$a = (v_f^2 - v_i^2) / 2d$$

$$a = [(58.33 \text{ m/s})^2 - (0 \text{ m/s})^2] / 2(1,800 \text{ m})$$

$$a = (3,402.39 \text{ m}^2/\text{s}^2) / (3,600 \text{ m})$$

$$a = 0.95 \text{ m/s}^2$$

16. D is correct.

The distance the rocket travels during its acceleration upward is calculated by:

$$d_1 = \tfrac{1}{2}at^2$$

$$d_1 = \tfrac{1}{2}(22 \text{ m/s}^2)\cdot(4 \text{ s})^2$$

$$d_1 = 176 \text{ m}$$

The distance from when the motor shuts off to when the rocket reaches maximum height can be calculated using the conservation of energy:

$$mgd_2 = \tfrac{1}{2}mv^2, \text{ cancel } m \text{ from both sides of the expression}$$

$$gd_2 = \tfrac{1}{2}v^2$$

where $v = at$

$$gd_2 = \tfrac{1}{2}(at)^2$$

$$d_2 = \tfrac{1}{2}(at)^2 / g$$

$$d_2 = \tfrac{1}{2}[(22 \text{ m/s}^2)\cdot(4 \text{ s})]^2 / (10 \text{ m/s}^2)$$

Magnitudes are not vectors but scalars, so no direction is needed

$$d_2 = 387 \text{ m}$$

For the maximum elevation, add the two distances:

$$h = d_1 + d_2$$

$$h = 176 \text{ m} + 387 \text{ m}$$

$$h = 563 \text{ m}$$

17. A is correct.

Speed is a scalar (i.e., one-dimensional physical property), while velocity is a vector (i.e., has both magnitude and direction).

18. B is correct. Acceleration due to gravity is constant and independent of mass.

19. D is correct.

As an object falls, its acceleration is constant due to gravity.

However, the magnitude of the velocity increases due to the acceleration of gravity and the displacement increases because the object is going further away from its starting point.

20. C is correct.

The man is moving at constant velocity (no acceleration), so it's known immediately that the net force is zero. The only objects interacting with the man directly are Earth and the floor of the elevator.

The cable is not touching the man; it pulls the elevator car up, and the floor of the elevator is what pushes on the man.

21. D is correct.

Horizontal velocity (v_x):

$$v_x = d_x / t$$
$$v_x = (44 \text{ m}) / (2.9 \text{ s})$$
$$v_x = 15.2 \text{ m/s}$$

The x component of a vector is calculated by:

$$v_x = v \cos \theta$$

Rearrange the equation to determine the initial velocity of the ball:

$$v = v_x / \cos \theta$$
$$v = (15.2 \text{ m/s}) / (\cos 45°)$$
$$v = (15.2 \text{ m/s}) / 0.7$$
$$v = 21.4 \text{ m/s}$$

22. A is correct.

Conservation of energy:

$$mgh = \tfrac{1}{2}mv_f^2, \text{ cancel } m \text{ from both sides of the expression}$$
$$gh = \tfrac{1}{2}v_f^2$$
$$(10 \text{ m/s}^2)h = \tfrac{1}{2}(14 \text{ m/s})^2$$
$$(10 \text{ m/s}^2)h = \tfrac{1}{2}(196 \text{ m}^2/\text{s}^2)$$
$$h = (98 \text{ m}^2/\text{s}^2) / (10 \text{ m/s}^2)$$
$$h = 9.8 \text{ m} \approx 10 \text{ m}$$

23. B is correct.

$$d = v_i t + \tfrac{1}{2}at^2$$
$$d = (20 \text{ m/s}) \cdot (7 \text{ s}) + \tfrac{1}{2}(1.4 \text{ m/s}^2) \cdot (7 \text{ s})^2$$
$$d = (140 \text{ m}) + \tfrac{1}{2}(1.4 \text{ m/s}^2) \cdot (49 \text{ s}^2)$$
$$d = 174.3 \text{ m} \approx 174 \text{ m}$$

24. D is correct.

Force is not a scalar because it has a magnitude and direction.

25. B is correct.

$$d = \tfrac{1}{2}at^2$$
$$d_A = \tfrac{1}{2}at^2$$
$$d_B = \tfrac{1}{2}a(2t)^2$$
$$d_B = \tfrac{1}{2}a(4t^2)$$
$$d_B = 4 \times \tfrac{1}{2}at^2$$
$$d_B = 4d_A$$

26. A is correct.

$$d = v_{average} \times \Delta t$$
$$d = \tfrac{1}{2}(v_i + v_f)\Delta t$$
$$d = \tfrac{1}{2}(5 \text{ m/s} + 30 \text{ m/s}) \cdot (10 \text{ s})$$
$$d = 175 \text{ m}$$

27. C is correct.

If there is no acceleration, then velocity is constant.

28. D is correct.

The gravitational force between two objects in space, each having masses of m_1 and m_2, is:

$$F_G = Gm_1m_2 / r^2$$

where G is the gravitational constant and r is the distance between the two objects.

Doubling the distance between the two objects:

$$F_{G2} = Gm_1m_2 / (2r)^2$$
$$F_{G2} = Gm_1m_2 / (4r^2)$$
$$F_{G2} = \tfrac{1}{4}Gm_1m_2 / r^2$$
$$F_{G2} = \tfrac{1}{4}Gm_1m_2 / r^2$$
$$F_{G2} = \tfrac{1}{4}F_G$$

When the distance between the objects is doubled, the force (F_G) is one fourth.

29. D is correct.

I: If the velocity is constant, the instantaneous velocity is always equal to the average velocity.

II and III: If the velocity is increasing, the average value of velocity over an interval must lie between the initial velocity and the final velocity. In going from its initial value to its final value, the instantaneous velocity must cross the average value at one point, regardless of whether or not the velocity is changing at a constant rate or changing irregularly.

30. C is correct. velocity = acceleration × time

$$v = at$$
$$v = (10 \text{ m/s}^2)\cdot(10 \text{ s})$$
$$v = 100 \text{ m/s}$$

31. B is correct.

velocity = distance / time

$$v = d / t$$

d is constant, while t decreases by a factor of 3

32. C is correct. The equation for distance, given a constant acceleration and both the initial and final velocity, is:

$$d = (v_i^2 + v_f^2) / 2a$$

Since the car is coming to rest, $v_f = 0$

$$d = v_i^2 / 2a$$

If the initial velocity is doubled while acceleration and final velocity remain unchanged, the new distance traveled is:

$$d_2 = (2v_i)^2 / 2a$$
$$d_2 = 4(v_i^2 / 2a)$$
$$d_2 = 4d_1$$

Another method to solve this problem:

$$d_1 = (29 \text{ mi/h})^2 / 2a$$
$$d_2 = (59 \text{ mi/h})^2 / 2a$$
$$d_2 / d_1 = [(59 \text{ mi/h})^2 / 2a] / [(29 \text{ mi/h})^2 / 2a]$$
$$d_2 / d_1 = (59 \text{ mi/h})^2 / (29 \text{ mi/h})^2$$
$$d_2 / d_1 = (3{,}481 \text{ mi/h}) / (841 \text{ mi/h})$$
$$d_2 / d_1 = 4$$

33. D is correct.

speed$_{average}$ = total distance / time

speed = (400 m) / (20 s)

speed = 20 m/s

If this were velocity, it would be 0.

34. A is correct.

$\Delta v = a\Delta t$

$(v_f - v_i) = a\Delta t$, where $v_f = 0$ m/s (when the car stops)

$a = -0.1$ m/s^2 (negative because deceleration), $\Delta t = 5$ s

$v_i = v_f - a\Delta t$

$v_i = [(0$ m/s$) - (-0.1$ m/s$^2)] \cdot (5$ s$)$

$v_i = (0.1$ m/s$^2) \cdot (5$ s$)$

$v_i = 0.5$ m/s

35. C is correct.

If acceleration is constant, then the velocity vs. time graph is linear.

The average velocity is the average of the final and initial velocity.

$v_{average} = v_f - v_i / \Delta t$

If acceleration is not constant, then the velocity vs. time graph is nonlinear.

$v_{average} \neq v_f - v_i / \Delta t$

36. D is correct. Find velocity of thrown rock:

$v_{f1}^2 - v_i^2 = 2ad$

$v_{f1}^2 = v_i^2 + 2ad$

$v_{f1}^2 = (10$ m/s$)^2 + [2(9.8$ m/s$^2) \cdot (300$ m$)]$

$v_{f1}^2 = 100$ m^2/s^2 + 5,880 m^2/s^2

$v_{f1}^2 = 5,980$ m^2/s^2

$v_{f1} = 77.33$ m/s

$t_1 = (v_f - v_i) / a$

$t_1 = (77.33$ m/s $- 10$ m/s$) / 9.8$ m/s^2

$t_1 = (67.33$ m/s$) / (9.8$ m/s$^2)$

$t_1 = 6.87$ s

Find velocity of dropped rock:

$$v_{f2} = \sqrt{2ad}$$

$$v_{f2} = \sqrt{[(2)\cdot(9.8 \text{ m/s}^2)\cdot(300 \text{ m})]}$$

$$v_{f2} = 76.7 \text{ m/s}$$

$$t_2 = (76.7 \text{ m/s}) / (9.8 \text{ m/s}^2)$$

$$t_2 = 7.82 \text{ s}$$

$$\Delta t = (7.82 \text{ s} - 6.87 \text{ s})$$

$$\Delta t = 0.95 \text{ s}$$

37. D is correct. $F = ma$

Force and acceleration are directly proportional so doubling force doubles acceleration.

38. B is correct.

Velocity is defined as having speed and direction. If either, or both, of these change, then the object is experiencing acceleration.

39. C is correct.

The acceleration is negative because it acts to slow the car down against the $+y$ direction.

It is unclear if the acceleration decreases in magnitude from the data provided.

40. A is correct.

Total distance is the area under the velocity-time curve with respect to the x-axis.

This graph can be broken up into sections; calculate the area under the curve.

$$d_{total} = d_A + d_B + d_C + d_D$$

$$d_A = \frac{1}{2}(4 \text{ m/s})\cdot(2 \text{ s}) = 4 \text{ m}$$

$$d_B = \frac{1}{2}(4 \text{ m/s} + 2 \text{ m/s})\cdot(2 \text{ s}) = 6 \text{ m}$$

$$d_C = (2 \text{ m/s})\cdot(4 \text{ s}) = 8 \text{ m}$$

Since the total distance traveled needs to be calculated, the area under the curve when the velocity is negative is calculated as a positive value. Distance is a scalar quantity and therefore has no direction.

$$d_D = \frac{1}{2}(2 \text{ m/s})\cdot(1 \text{ s}) + \frac{1}{2}(2 \text{ m/s})\cdot(1 \text{ s}) = 2 \text{ m}$$

$$d_{total} = 4 \text{ m} + 6 \text{ m} + 8 \text{ m} + 2 \text{ m} = 20 \text{ m}$$

If the question was asking to find the displacement, the area under the curve would be calculated as negative and the answer would be 18 m.

41. C is correct.

The two bullets have different velocities when hitting the water, but they both only experience the force due to gravity.

Thus, the acceleration due to gravity is the same for each bullet.

42. A is correct.

$v_f = v_i + at$

$v_f = 0 + (2.5 \text{ m/s}^2) \cdot (9 \text{ s})$

$v_f = 22.5 \text{ m/s}$

43. D is correct.

The equation for impulse is used for contact between two objects over a specified time period:

$F\Delta t = m\Delta v$

$ma\Delta t = m(v_f - v_i)$, cancel m from both sides of the expression

$a\Delta t = (v_f - v_i)$

$a = (v_f - v_i) / \Delta t$

$a = (-2v - v) / (0.45 \text{ s})$

$a = (-3v) / (0.45 \text{ s})$

$a = (-6.7 \text{ s}^{-1})v$

Ratio $a : v = -6.7 \text{ s}^{-1} : 1$

44. B is correct.

The time for the round trip is 4 s.

The weight reaches the top of its path in ½ time:

½(4 s) = 2 s, where $v = 0$

$a = \Delta v / t$ for the first half of the trip

$a = (v_f - v_i) / t$

$a = (0 - 3.2 \text{ m/s}) / 2 \text{ s}$

$a = -1.6 \text{ m/s}^2$

$|a| = 1.6 \text{ m/s}^2$

Acceleration is a vector and the negative direction only indicates direction.

45. A is correct.

$\Delta v = a \Delta t$

$\Delta v = (0.3 \text{ m/s}^2) \cdot (3 \text{ s})$

$\Delta v = 0.9 \text{ m/s}$

46. D is correct.

Velocity, displacement and acceleration are all vectors. Mass is not a vector quantity.

47. B is correct.

$d = d_0 + (v_i^2 + v_f^2) / 2a$

$d = 64 \text{ m} + (0 \text{ m/s} + 60 \text{ m/s})^2 / 2(9.8 \text{ m/s}^2)$

$d = 64 \text{ m} + (3{,}600 \text{ m}^2/\text{s}^2) / (19.6 \text{ m/s}^2)$

$d = 64 \text{ m} + 184 \text{ m}$

$d = 248 \text{ m}$

48. C is correct.

$a = (v_f^2 + v_i^2) / 2d$

$a = [(60 \text{ m/s})^2 + (0 \text{ m/s})^2] / [2(64 \text{ m})]$

$a = (3{,}600 \text{ m}^2/\text{s}^2) / 128 \text{ m}$

$a = 28 \text{ m/s}^2$

49. D is correct.

Expression for the time interval during constant acceleration upward:

$d = \frac{1}{2}at^2$

Solving for acceleration:

$a = (v_f^2 + v_i^2) / 2d$

$a = [(60 \text{ m/s})^2 + (0 \text{ m/s})^2] / [2(64 \text{ m})]$

$a = (3{,}600 \text{ m}^2/\text{s}^2) / (128 \text{ m})$

$a = 28.1 \text{ m/s}^2$

Solving for time:

$t^2 = 2d / a$

$t^2 = 2(64 \text{ m}) / 28.1 \text{ m/s}^2$

$t^2 = 4.5 \text{ s}^2$

$t = 2.1 \text{ s}$

50. C is correct.

$$d = (v_i^2 + v_f^2) / 2a, \text{ where } v_i = 0$$

$$d = v_f^2 / 2a$$

For half the final velocity:

$$d_2 = (v_f / 2)^2 / 2a$$

$$d_2 = \tfrac{1}{4}v_f^2 / 2a$$

$$d_2 = \tfrac{1}{4}d$$

51. A is correct.

$$v_{\text{average}} = \Delta d / \Delta t$$

52. A is correct.

Use an equation that relates v, d and t:

$$d = vt$$

$$v = d / t$$

If v increases by a factor of 3, then t decreases by a factor of 3.

Another method to solve this problem:

$$d = vt, \ t = \text{original time and } t_N = \text{new time}$$

$$d = 3vt_N$$

$$vt = d = 3vt_N$$

$$vt = 3vt_N$$

$$t = 3t_N$$

$$t / 3 = t_N$$

Thus, if v increases by a factor of 3, then the original time decreases by a factor of 3.

53. B is correct.

$$v_f = v_i + at$$

$$t = (v_f - v_i) / a$$

Since the ball is thrown straight up, its initial speed upward equals its final speed downward (just before hitting the ground): Therefore:

$$v_f = -v_i$$

$$t = [39 \text{ m/s} - (-39 \text{ m/s})] / 9.8 \text{ m/s}^2$$

$$t = (78 \text{ m/s}) / 9.8 \text{ m/s}^2$$

$$t = 8 \text{ s}$$

54. D is correct.

Since the speed is changing, the velocity is changing, and therefore there *is* an acceleration.

Since the speed is *decreasing*, the acceleration must be *in the reverse direction* (i.e., opposite to the direction of travel).

Since the particle is moving to the right, the acceleration vector points to the left.

If the speed were increasing, the acceleration is in the *same* direction as the direction of travel, and the acceleration vector points to the right.

55. A is correct.

The only force that Larry applies to the package is the normal force due to his hand;

There is no horizontal force as the package moves with constant velocity.

The normal force due to his hand points upward.

The displacement of the package is horizontal:

$$W = Fd \cos \theta,$$

where θ is the angle between the force and the displacement.

$$\theta = 90°$$

Since $\cos 90° = 0$,

$$W = 0 \text{ J}$$

56. A is correct.

The slope of a tangent line on a velocity vs. time graph is the acceleration at that time point.

This is equivalent to taking the derivative of the velocity with respect to time to find the instantaneous acceleration.

57. C is correct.

Since the car is initially traveling North, let North be the positive direction and South be the negative direction:

$$a = (v_f - v_i) / t$$
$$a = (14.1 \text{ m/s} - 17.7 \text{ m/s}) / 12 \text{ s}$$
$$a = (-3.6 \text{ m/s}) / 12 \text{ s}$$
$$a = -0.3 \text{ m/s}^2$$
$$a = 0.3 \text{ m/s}^2 \text{ South}$$

58. C is correct.

Speed is represented by the magnitude of the slope of a position vs. time plot. A steeper slope equates to a higher speed.

59. B is correct.

If the object has not reached terminal velocity, it continues to accelerate but at an ever decreasing rate until terminal velocity is reached.

60. D is correct.

Approach the problem by finding the distance traveled in each of the three segments.

$$d_1 = \tfrac{1}{2}a_1\Delta t_1{}^2$$

$$d_1 = (0.5) \cdot (2 \text{ m/s}^2) \cdot (10 \text{ s})^2 = 100 \text{ m}$$

The second segment:

$$d_2 = v_2\Delta t_2$$

where $\Delta t_2 = 10$ s, the duration of interval 2 and v_2 is the speed during interval 2, which is the speed at the end of interval 1.

$$v_2 = v_{1f} = a_1\Delta t_1$$

$$v_2 = (2 \text{ m/s}) \cdot (10 \text{ s}) = 20 \text{ m/s}$$

So:

$$d_2 = (20 \text{ m/s}) \cdot (10 \text{ s}) = 200\text{m}$$

Next, the third segment:

$$d_3 = (v^2{}_{3f} - v^2{}_{3i}) / 2a_3$$

$$d_3 = [(0 \text{ m/s})^2 - (20 \text{ m/s})^2] / 2(-2 \text{ m/s}^2)$$

$$d_3 = 100 \text{ m}$$

The total distance traveled is the sum of d_1, d_2 and d_3:

$$d = 100 \text{ m} + 200 \text{ m} + 100 \text{ m}$$

$$d = 400 \text{ m}$$

Force and Motion – Explanations

1. B is correct. The tension of the string keeps the weight traveling in a circular path; otherwise it would move linearly on a tangent path to the circle. Without the string, there are no horizontal forces on the weight and no horizontal acceleration. The horizontal motion of the weight is in a straight line at constant speed.

2. D is correct. The vertical force on the garment bag from the left side of the clothesline is:

$$T_{y,\text{left}} = T \cos \theta$$

Similarly, for the right side:

$$T_{y,\text{right}} = T \cos \theta$$

where $T = 10$ N (tension) and $\theta = 60°$.

Since the garment bag is at rest, its acceleration is zero. Therefore, according to Newton's second law:

$$T_{y,\text{left}} + T_{y,\text{right}} - mg = 0 = 2T (\cos \theta) - mg$$

Or: $\quad 2T (\cos \theta) = mg$

$$m = 2T (\cos \theta) / g$$

$$m = 2(10 \text{ N}) \cdot (\cos 60°) / (10.0 \text{ m/s}^2)$$

$$m = 2(10 \text{ N}) \cdot (0.5) / (10.0 \text{ m/s}^2)$$

$$m = 1 \text{ kg}$$

3. A is correct. An object's inertia is its resistance to change in motion. The milk carton has enough inertia to overcome the force of static friction.

4. C is correct.

$$(F_{\text{net}})_y = (F_N)_y - (F_g)_y$$

The car is not moving up or down, so $a_y = 0$:

$$(F_{\text{net}})_y = 0$$

$$0 = (F_N)_y - (F_g)_y$$

$$F_N = (F_g)_y$$

$$F_N = F_g \cos \theta$$

$$F_N = mg \cos \theta$$

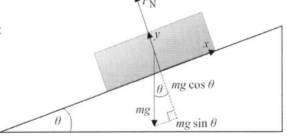

The normal force is a force that is perpendicular to the plane of contact (the slope).

5. B is correct.

$$F = ma$$
$$F = (27 \text{ kg}) \cdot (1.7 \text{ m/s}^2)$$
$$F = 46 \text{ N}$$

6. D is correct.

The mass on the table causes a tension force in the string that acts against the force of gravity.

7. A is correct.

Although the net force acting on the object is decreasing with time and the magnitude of the object's acceleration is decreasing there exists a positive acceleration. Therefore, the object's speed continues to increase.

8. D is correct.

An object moving at constant velocity experiences zero net force.

9. A is correct.

The sine of an angle is equal to the opposite side over the hypotenuse:

$$\sin \theta = \text{opposite} / \text{hypotenuse}$$
$$\sin \theta = h / L$$
$$h = L \sin \theta$$

10. B is correct. The force of the table on the book, the normal force (F_N), is a result of Newton's Third Law of Motion, which states for every action there is an equal and opposite reaction.

A book sitting on the table experiences a force from the table equal to the book's weight:

$$W = mg$$
$$F_N = W$$
$$F_N = mg$$
$$F_N = (2 \text{ kg}) \cdot (10 \text{ m/s}^2)$$
$$F_N = 20 \text{ N}$$

11. A is correct.

$$a = (v_f - v_i) / t$$
$$a = (3.5 \text{ m/s} - 1.5 \text{ m/s}) / (3 \text{ s})$$
$$a = (2 \text{ m/s}) / (3 \text{ s})$$
$$a = 0.67 \text{ m/s}^2$$

12. C is correct.

An object with uniform circular motion (i.e., constant angular velocity) only experiences centripetal acceleration directed toward the center of the circle.

13. B is correct.

$F = ma$, so zero force means zero acceleration in any direction.

14. C is correct.

$$F = ma$$
$$a = F / m$$
$$a = 9 \text{ N} / 9 \text{ kg}$$
$$a = 1 \text{ m/s}^2$$

15. B is correct.

The only force acting on a projectile in motion is the force due to gravity.

Since that force always acts downward, there is always only a downward acceleration.

16. A is correct.

$$F_{\text{net}} = ma$$

If an object moves with constant v; $a = 0$,

So:

$$F_{\text{net}} = 0$$

Since gravity pulls down on the can with a force of mg:

$$F_{\text{g}} = mg$$
$$F_{\text{g}} = (10 \text{ kg}) \cdot (10 \text{ m/s}^2)$$
$$F_{\text{g}} = 100 \text{ N}$$

The rope pulls *up* on the can with the same magnitude of force, so the tension is 100 N, for a net force = 0.

17. D is correct.

$$F = ma$$
$$F = (1{,}000 \text{ kg}) \cdot (2 \text{ m/s}^2)$$
$$F = 2{,}000 \text{ N}$$

18. C is correct.

$a_{cent} = v^2 / r$

$a_{cent} = (4 \text{ m/s})^2 / (4 \text{ m})$

$a_{cent} = (16 \text{ m}^2/\text{s}^2) / (4 \text{ m})$

$a_{cent} = 4 \text{ m/s}^2$

19. A is correct.

Solve for m_1:

$F_{net} = 0$

$m_2 g = F_T$

$m_1 g \sin \theta + F_f = F_T$

$m_1 g \sin \theta + \mu_s m_1 g \cos \theta = m_2 g$

cancel g from both sides

$m_1 (\sin \theta + \mu_s \cos \theta) = m_2$

$m_1 = m_2 / (\sin \theta + \mu_s \cos \theta)$

$m_1 = 2 \text{ kg} / [\sin 20° + (0.55) \cos 20°]$

$m_1 = 2 \text{ kg} / 0.86$

$m_1 = 2.3 \text{ kg}$

Kinetic friction is only used when the mass is in motion.

20. B is correct.

Since the masses are identical, the force of gravity on each is the same. The force of gravity on one of the masses produces the tension force in the string, which in turn pulls on the other mass.

Since this tension force is equal to the force of gravity, there is no net force, and the objects remain at rest.

21. B is correct.

Newton's Third Law states that for every action there is an equal and opposite reaction.

22. A is correct.

Newton's Third Law states that for every action there is an equal and opposite reaction.

23. C is correct.

If w denotes the magnitude of the box's weight, then the component of this force that is parallel to the inclined plane is $w \sin \theta$, where θ is the incline angle.

If θ is less than 90°, then $\sin \theta$ is less than 1.

The component of w parallel to the inclined plane is less than w.

24. B is correct.

The package experiences projectile motion upon leaving the truck, so it experiences no horizontal forces, and its initial velocity of 30 m/s remains unchanged.

25. D is correct.

f = revolutions / unit of time

The time (period) for one complete revolution is:

$T = 1 / f$

Each revolution represents a length of $2\pi r$.

Velocity is the distance traveled in one revolution over duration of one revolution (circumference over period):

$v = 2\pi r / t$

$v = 2\pi r f$

If f doubles, then v doubles.

26. A is correct.

$F = ma$

$m = F / a$

$m = 4{,}500 \text{ N} / 5 \text{ m/s}^2$

$m = 900 \text{ kg}$

27. D is correct.

Newton's First Law states that every object will remain at rest or in uniform motion unless acted upon by an outside force.

In this case, Steve and the bus are in uniform constant motion until the bus stops due to sudden deceleration (the ground exerts no frictional force on Steve). There is no force acting upon Steve. However, his inertia carries him forward because he is still in uniform motion while the bus comes to a stop.

28. D is correct.

The ball is in a state of rest, so $F_{net} = 0$

$$F_{\text{down}} = F_{\text{up}}$$

$$F_{\text{external}} + F_{\text{w}} = F_{\text{buoyant}}$$

$$F_{\text{external}} = F_{\text{buoyant}} - F_{\text{w}}$$

$$F_{\text{external}} = 8.4 \text{ N} - 4.4 \text{ N}$$

$$F_{\text{external}} = 4 \text{ N, in the same direction as the weight}$$

29. A is correct. The luggage and the train move at the same speed, so when the luggage moves forward with respect to the train, it means the train has slowed down while the luggage is continuing to move at the train's original speed.

30. D is correct. The mass does not change by changing the object's location.

Since the object is outside of Earth's atmosphere, the object's weight is represented by the equation:

$$F_{\text{g}} = G m M_{\text{Earth}} / R^2$$

If the altitude is $2R_{\text{Earth}}$, then the distance from the center of the Earth is $3R_{\text{Earth}}$.

The gravitational acceleration decreases by a factor of $3^2 = 9$ ($g = GmM / R^2$).

Weight decreases by a factor of 9.

New weight = 360 N / 9 = 40 N

31. C is correct.

The velocity of the rock just after its release is the same as the truck's. Once in free fall, there are no horizontal forces on the rock. The rock's velocity remains unchanged and is equal to that of the truck.

32. A is correct.

The acceleration of Jason due to thrust is:

$$F_{\text{net}} = ma_1$$

$$ma_1 = F_{\text{ski}} - \mu_k mg$$

$$a_1 = (F_{\text{ski}} - \mu_k mg) / m$$

$$a_1 = [200 \text{ N} - (0.1){\cdot}(75 \text{ kg}){\cdot}(9.8 \text{ m/s}^2)] / 75 \text{ kg}$$

$$a_1 = (126.5 \text{ N}) / 75 \text{ kg}$$

$$a_1 = 1.69 \text{ m/s}^2$$

The distance traveled during the acceleration stage is:

$$d_1 = \tfrac{1}{2} a_1 t^2$$

$$d_1 = \tfrac{1}{2}(1.69 \text{ m/s}^2){\cdot}(67 \text{ s})^2$$

$$d_1 = 3{,}793 \text{ m}$$

The distance traveled after the skis run out of fuel is:

$$d_2 = (v_f^2 - v_i^2) / 2a_2$$

a_2 is Jason's acceleration after the fuel runs out:

$$F_{net} = ma_2$$

$ma_2 = -\mu_k mg$, cancel m from both sides of the expression

$$a_2 = -\mu_k g$$

$$a_2 = -(0.1)\cdot(9.8 \text{ m/s}^2)$$

$$a_2 = -0.98 \text{ m/s}^2$$

The acceleration is negative since the frictional force opposes the direction of motion.

v_i is the velocity at the moment when the fuel runs out:

$$v_i = a_1 t$$

$$v_i = (1.69 \text{ m/s}^2)\cdot(67 \text{ s})$$

$$v_i = 113.2 \text{ m/s}$$

Substitute a_2 and v_i into the equation for d_2:

$$d_2 = [(0 \text{ m/s})^2 - (113.2 \text{ m/s})^2] / 2(-0.98 \text{ m/s}^2)$$

$$d_2 = (-12,814.2 \text{ m}^2/\text{s}^2) / -1.96 \text{ m/s}^2$$

$$d_2 = 6,538 \text{ m}$$

The total distance Jason traveled is:

$$d_{total} = d_1 + d_2$$

$$d_{total} = 3,793 \text{ m} + 6,538 \text{ m}$$

$$d_{total} = 10,331 \text{ m}$$

33. D is correct.

Using the force analysis:

$$F_{net} = F_g + F_{fk}$$

$$F_g = mg \sin \theta$$

$$F_g = (0.2 \text{ kg})\cdot(-9.8 \text{ m/s}^2) \sin 30°$$

$$F_g = (0.2 \text{ kg})\cdot(-9.8 \text{ m/s}^2)\cdot(1/2)$$

$$F_g = -1 \text{ N}$$

$$F_{fk} = \mu_k F_N$$

$$F_{fk} = \mu_k mg \cos \theta$$

$$F_{fk} = (0.3)\cdot(0.2 \text{ kg})\cdot(-9.8 \text{ m/s}^2) \cos 30°$$

$$F_{fk} = (0.3)\cdot(0.2 \text{ kg})\cdot(-9.8 \text{ m/s}^2)\cdot(0.866)$$

$$F_{fk} = -0.5 \text{ N}$$

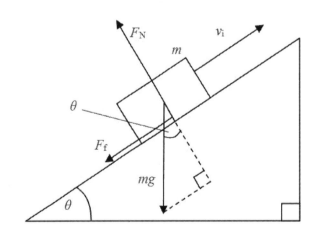

$F_{net} = -1\ N + (-0.5\ N)$

$F_{net} = -1.5\ N$

$a = F_{net} / m$

$a = -1.5\ N / 0.2\ kg$

$a = -7.5\ m/s^2$

The distance it travels until it reaches a velocity of 0 at its maximum height:

$d = (v_f^2 - v_i^2) / 2a$

$d = [(0\ m/s)^2 - (63\ m/s)^2] / 2(-7.5\ m/s^2)$

$d = (-4{,}000\ m^2/s^2) / (-15\ m/s^2)$

$d = 267\ m$

The vertical height is:

$h = d \sin \theta$

$h = (267\ m) \sin 30°$

$h = (267\ m)\cdot(0.5)$

$h = 130\ m$

Using energy to solve the problem:

$KE = PE + W_f$

$\tfrac{1}{2}mv^2 = mgd \sin \theta + \mu_k mgd \cos \theta$, cancel m from the expression

$\tfrac{1}{2}v^2 = gd \sin \theta + \mu_k gd \cos \theta$

$\tfrac{1}{2}v^2 = d(g \sin \theta + \mu_k g \cos \theta)$

$d = v^2 / [2g(\sin \theta + \mu_k \cos \theta)]$

$d = (63\ m/s)^2 / [(2)\cdot(9.8\ m/s^2)\cdot(\sin 30° + 0.3 \times \cos 30°)]$

$d = 267\ m$

$h = d \sin \theta$

$h = (267\ m) \sin 30°$

$h = 130\ m$

34. A is correct.

$F = ma$

$a = F / m$

$a_1 = F / 4\ kg$

$a_2 = F / 10\ kg$

$4a_1 = 10a_2$

$a_1 = 2.5a_2$

35. D is correct.

At $\theta = 17°$, the force of static friction is equal to the force due to gravity:

$F_f = F_g$

$\mu_s mg \cos \theta = mg \sin \theta$

$\mu_s = \sin \theta / \cos \theta$

$\mu_s = \tan \theta$

$\mu_s = \tan 17°$

$\mu_s = 0.31$

36. A is correct.

Newton's Third Law describes that any time one object pushes on another, the second object pushes right back with the same force. Mathematically, it can be expressed as:

$F_{AonB} = -F_{BonA}$

In the described scenario, the force that the truck exerts on the car is in the opposite direction to the force that the car exerts on the truck (since they push on each other) and, crucially, the *magnitudes* of the two forces are the same.

This may seem counterintuitive since it is known that the car will get far more damaged than the truck. To understand this apparent contradiction, remember Newton's Second Law which states that the car will *accelerate* at a much higher rate (since it is less massive than the truck). It is this extreme acceleration that causes the car to be completely destroyed.

Therefore, to understand this situation fully, two Newton's laws must be applied:

The Third Law, which states that each vehicle experiences a force of the same magnitude, and

The Second Law, which describes why the car *responds* to that force more violently due to its smaller mass.

37. D is correct.

$m = F / a_{Earth}$

$m = 20 \text{ N} / 3 \text{ m/s}^2$

$m = 6.67 \text{ kg}$

$F_{Moon} = mg_{Moon}$

$F_{Moon} = (6.67 \text{ kg}) \cdot (1.62 \text{ m/s}^2)$

$F_{Moon} = 11 \text{ N}$

38. A is correct.

If θ is the angle with respect to a horizontal line, then:

$\theta = \frac{1}{2}(40°)$

$\theta = 20°$

Therefore, in order for the third force to cause equilibrium, the sum of all three forces' components must equal zero. Since F_1 and F_2 mirror each other in the y direction:

$F_{1y} + F_{2y} = 0$

Therefore, for F_3 to balance forces in the y direction, its y component must also equal zero:

$F_{1y} + F_{2y} + F_{3y} = 0$

$0 + F_{3y} = 0$

$F_{3y} = 0$

Since the y component of F_3 is zero, the angle that F_3 makes with the horizontal is zero:

$\theta_3 = 0°$

The x component of F_3:

$F_{1x} + F_{2x} + F_{3x} = 0$

$F_1 \cos \theta + F_2 \cos \theta + F_3 \cos \theta = 0$

$F_3 = -(F_2 \cos \theta_2 + F_3 \cos \theta_3)$

$F_3 = -[(2.3 \text{ N}) \cos 20° + (2.3 \text{ N}) \cos 20°]$

$F_3 = -4.3 \text{ N}$

$F_3 = 4.3 \text{ N}$ to the right

39. B is correct.

Need an expression which connects time and mass.

Given information for F, v_1, and d:

$a = F / m$

$d = v_1t + \frac{1}{2}at^2$

Combine the expressions and set $v_i = 0$ m/s because initial velocity is zero:

$d = \frac{1}{2}at^2$

$a = F / m$

$d = \frac{1}{2}(F / m)t^2$

$t^2 = 2dm / F$

$t = \sqrt{(2dm / F)}$

If m increases by a factor of 4, t increases by a factor of $\sqrt{4} = 2$

40. C is correct.

$$a = (v_f^2 - v_i^2) / 2d$$

$$a = [(0 \text{ m/s})^2 - (27 \text{ m/s})^2] / 2(578 \text{ m})$$

$$a = (-729 \text{ m}^2/\text{s}^2) / 1{,}056 \text{ m}$$

$$a = -0.63 \text{ m/s}^2$$

$$F = ma$$

$$F = (1{,}100 \text{ kg}) \cdot (-0.63 \text{ m/s}^2)$$

$$F = -690 \text{ N}$$

The car is decelerating, so the acceleration (and therefore the force) is negative.

41. A is correct.

Constant speed upward means no net force.

Tension = weight (equals Mg)

42. C is correct.

$$\text{Weight} = mg$$

$$75 \text{ N} = mg$$

$$m = 75 \text{ N} / 9.8 \text{ m/s}^2$$

$$m = 7.65 \text{ kg}$$

$$F_{net} = F_{right} - F_{left}$$

$$F_{net} = 50 \text{ N} - 30 \text{ N}$$

$$F_{net} = 20 \text{ N}$$

$$F_{net} = ma$$

$$a = F_{net} / m$$

$$a = 20 \text{ N} / 7.65 \text{ kg}$$

$$a = 2.6 \text{ m/s}^2$$

43. B is correct.

The string was traveling at the same velocity as the plane with respect to the ground outside.

When the plane began accelerating backward (decelerating), the string continued to move forward at its original velocity and appeared to go towards the front of the plane.

Since the string is attached to the ceiling at one end, only the bottom of the string moved.

44. C is correct.

If the object slides down the ramp with a constant speed, velocity is constant.

Acceleration and the net force = 0

$$F_{net} = F_{grav \, down \, ramp} - F_{friction}$$

$$F_{net} = mg \sin \theta - \mu_k mg \cos \theta$$

$$F_{net} = 0$$

$$mg \sin \theta - \mu_k mg \cos \theta = 0$$

$$mg \sin \theta = \mu_k mg \cos \theta$$

$$\mu_k = \sin \theta / \cos \theta$$

45. D is correct.

Each scale weighs the fish at 17 kg, so the sum of the two scales is:

$$17 \text{ kg} + 17 \text{ kg} = 34 \text{ kg}$$

46. C is correct.

$$a = \Delta v / \Delta t$$

$$a = (v_f - v_i) / t$$

$$a = (20 \text{ m/s} - 0 \text{ m/s}) / (10 \text{ s})$$

$$a = (20 \text{ m/s}) / (10 \text{ s})$$

$$a = 2 \text{ m/s}^2$$

47. D is correct.

Since the object does not move, it is in a state of equilibrium, so forces are acting on it that equal and oppose the force F that Yania applies to the object.

48. A is correct.

Newton's Third Law describes that any time one object pushes on another, the second object pushes right back with the same force. Mathematically, it can be expressed as:

$$F_{AonB} = -F_{BonA}$$

In this situation, this means if one pushes on an object with force F, the object must push back on them equally strongly (magnitude is F) and in the opposite direction (hence the negative sign); therefore, the force vector of the object is just $-F$.

49. C is correct.

Find equal and opposite forces:

$$F_{Rx} = -F_1$$

$$F_{Rx} = -(-6.6 \text{ N})$$

$$F_{Rx} = 6.6 \text{ N}$$

$$F_{Ry} = -F_2$$

$$F_{Ry} = -2.2 \text{ N}$$

Pythagorean Theorem ($a^2 + b^2 = c^2$) to calculate the magnitude of the resultant force:

The magnitude of F_R:

$$F_R{}^2 = F_{Rx}{}^2 + F_{Ry}{}^2$$

$$F_R{}^2 = (6.6 \text{ N})^2 + (-2.2 \text{ N})^2$$

$$F_R{}^2 = 43.6 \text{ N}^2 + 4.8 \text{ N}^2$$

$$F_R{}^2 = 48.4 \text{ N}^2$$

$$F_R = 7 \text{ N}$$

The direction of F_R:

$$\theta = \tan^{-1}(-2.2 \text{ N} / 6.6 \text{ N})$$

$$\theta = \tan^{-1}(-1 / 3)$$

$$\theta = 342°$$

The direction of F_R with respect to F_1:

$$\theta = 342° - 180°$$

$$\theta = 162° \text{ counterclockwise of } F_1$$

50. A is correct.

$$m_{Bob} = 4m_{Sarah}$$

Conservation of momentum, since the system (Bob and Sarah combined) initially, had a total momentum of 0, in the final state Sarah's momentum and Bob's momentum must add to 0 (i.e., they will be the same magnitude, but opposite directions):

$$m_{Bob}v_{Bob} = m_{Sarah}v_{Sarah}$$

$$4m_{Sarah}\,v_{Bob} = m_{Sarah}v_{Sarah}$$

$$4v_{Bob} = v_{Sarah}$$

51. C is correct.

For most surfaces, the coefficient of static friction is greater than the coefficient of kinetic friction. Thus, the force needed to overcome static friction and start the object's motion is greater than the amount of force needed to overcome kinetic friction and keep the object moving at a constant velocity.

52. A is correct.

Newton's First Law states that an object at rest tends to stay at rest, and an object in motion tends to maintain that motion unless acted upon by an unbalanced force.

This law depends on a property of an object called inertia, which is inherently linked to the object's mass. More massive objects are more difficult to move and manipulate than less massive objects.

53. D is correct.

Neither Joe nor Bill is moving, so the net force is zero:

$$F_{net} = F_{Joe} - F_T$$

$$0 = F_{Joe} - F_T$$

$$F_{Joe} = F_T$$

$$F_T = 200 \text{ N}$$

54. C is correct.

Tension in the rope is always equal to F_T.

The net force on block A to the right is:

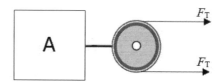

$$F_{right} = m_A a_A = 2F_T$$

The net force of block B downward is:

$$F_{down} = m_B a_B = m_B g - F_T$$

Since block A is connected to both the pulley at the end of the table and the wall, it uses twice the amount of rope length to travel the same distance as block B.

The distance block A moves is half that of block B, the velocity of block A is half the velocity of block B, and the acceleration of block A is half the acceleration of block B:

$$a_A = a_B / 2$$

$$F_{right} = m_A(a_B / 2)$$

$$m_A(a_B / 2) = 2F_T$$

$$m_A a_B = 4F_T$$

$$F_T = \tfrac{1}{4} m_A a_B$$

$$m_B a_B = m_B g - \tfrac{1}{4} m_A a_B$$

$$m_B a_B + \tfrac{1}{4} m_A a_B = m_B g$$

$$a_B[m_B + \tfrac{1}{4} m_A] = m_B g$$

$$a_B = m_B g / [m_B + \tfrac{1}{4} m_A]$$

$$a_B = (5 \text{ kg}) \cdot (9.8 \text{ m/s}^2) / [5 \text{ kg} + \tfrac{1}{4}(4 \text{ kg})]$$

$$a_B = 49 \text{ N} / 6 \text{ kg}$$

$$a_B = 8.2 \text{ m/s}^2$$

$$a_A = a_B / 2$$

$$a_A = (8.2 \text{ m/s}^2) / 2$$

$$a_A = 4.1 \text{ m/s}^2$$

55. B is correct.

The force exerted by one surface on another has a perpendicular component (i.e., normal force) and a parallel component (i.e., friction force).

The force of kinetic friction on an object acts opposite to the direction of its velocity relative to the surface.

56. D is correct.

The scale measures the force of interaction between the person and the floor, the normal force.

The question asks to find the normal force.

Use Newton's Second Law:

$F = ma,$

where the net force is the result of the force of gravity and the normal force.

$F_{net} = F_{normal} - F_{gravity} = N - W$

Here, W is the normal weight of the object, $W = mg$. Therefore, Newton's Law becomes:

$N - W = ma = (W / g) \, a$

Solve for the reading of the scale, N, noting that the acceleration is negative:

$N = W (1 + a / g)$

$N = (600 \text{ N}) \cdot (1 + -6 \text{ m/s}^2 / 9.8 \text{ m/s}^2)$

$N = (600 \text{ N}) \cdot (0.388)$

$N = 233 \text{ N}$

57. B is correct.

If the bureau moves in a straight line at a constant speed, its velocity is constant.

Therefore, the bureau is experiencing zero acceleration and zero net force.

The force of kinetic friction equals the 30 N force that pulls the bureau.

58. D is correct.

Since the crate can only move in the horizontal direction, only consider the horizontal component of the applied force when computing the acceleration.

$F_x = F \cos \theta$

$F_x = (140 \text{ N})\cos 30°$

$F_x = (140 \text{ N}) \cdot (0.866)$

$F_x = 121 \text{ N}$

$a = F_x / m$

$a = 121 \text{ N} / 40 \text{ kg}$

$a = 3 \text{ m/s}^2$

59. C is correct.

Vectors indicate magnitude and direction, while scalars only indicate magnitude.

60. B is correct.

The gravitational force and the direction of travel are perpendicular:

$W = Fd \cos \theta$

$\cos \theta = 0$

61. A is correct.

Work = Force × distance

$W_{\text{rope}} = Fd_x$

$W_{\text{rope}} = Fd \cos \theta$

$d = vt$

$d = (2.5 \text{ m/s}) \cdot (4 \text{ s})$

$W_{\text{rope}} = (30 \text{ N}) \cdot (10 \text{ m})\cos 30°$

$W_{\text{rope}} = 260 \text{ J}$

Work & Energy of Point Object Systems – Explanations

1. D is correct.

The final velocity in projectile motion is related to the maximum height of the projectile through the conservation of energy:

KE = PE

$\frac{1}{2}mv^2 = mgh$

When the stone thrown straight up passes its starting point on its way back down, its downward speed is equal to its initial upward velocity (2D motion). The stone thrown straight downward contains the same magnitude of initial velocity as the stone thrown upward, and thus both the stone thrown upward and the stone thrown downward have the same final speed.

A stone thrown horizontally (or for example, a stone thrown at 45°) does not achieve the same height h as a stone thrown straight up, so it has a smaller final vertical velocity.

2. B is correct.

Work = force × displacement × cos θ

W = Fd cos θ, where θ is the angle between the vectors F and d

W = (5 N)·(10 m) cos 45°

W = (50 J)·(0.7)

W = 35 J

3. A is correct.

KE = $\frac{1}{2}mv^2$

KE is influenced by mass and velocity.

Since velocity is squared, its influence on KE is greater than the influence of mass.

4. B is correct.

Work = force × displacement × cos θ

W = Fd cos θ

cos 90° = 0

W = 0

Since the force of gravity acts perpendicular to the distance traveled by the ball, the force due to gravity does no work in moving the ball.

5. C is correct.

$$KE = \frac{1}{2}mv^2$$

$$KE = \frac{1}{2}(5 \text{ kg}) \cdot (2 \text{ m/s})^2$$

$$KE = 10 \text{ J}$$

6. A is correct.

$$W = Fd \cos \theta$$

$$\cos \theta = 1$$

$$F = W / d$$

$$F = (360 \text{ J}) / (8 \text{ m})$$

$$F = 45 \text{ N}$$

$$F = ma$$

$$m = F / a$$

$$m = (45 \text{ N}) / (10 \text{ m/s}^2)$$

$$m = 4.5 \text{ kg}$$

7. D is correct.

On a displacement (x) vs. force (F) graph, the displacement is the y-axis, and the force is the x-axis.

The slope is x / F, (in units of m/N) which is the reciprocal of the spring constant k, which is measured in N/m.

8. C is correct.

Work done by a spring equation:

$$W = \frac{1}{2}kx^2$$

$$W = \frac{1}{2}(22 \text{ N/m}) \cdot (3 \text{ m})^2$$

$$W = 99 \text{ J}$$

9. A is correct.

The force of gravity always points down. When the ball is moving upwards, the direction of its displacement is opposite of that of the force of gravity, and therefore the work done by gravity is negative.

On the way down, the direction of displacement is the same as that of the force of gravity, and therefore the work done by gravity is positive.

10. B is correct.

Work done by gravity is an object's change in gravitational PE.

$$W = -PE$$

$$A_1 = 400 \text{ J}$$

By the work-energy theorem,

$$W = KE$$

$$B_1 = 400 \text{ J}$$

11. D is correct. Work is calculated as the product of force and displacement parallel to the direction of the applied force:

$$W = Fd \cos \theta$$

where some component of d is in the direction of the force.

12. B is correct.

Work only depends on force and distance:

$$W = Fd \cos \theta$$

Power $= W / t$ is the amount of work done in a unit of time.

13. A is correct.

The area under the curve on a graph is the product of the values of $y \times x$.

Here, the y value is force, and the x value is distance:

$$Fd = W$$

14. C is correct.

This is the conservation of energy. The only force acting on the cat is gravity.

$$KE = PE_g$$

$$KE = mgh$$

$$KE = (3 \text{ kg}) \cdot (10 \text{ m/s}^2) \cdot (4 \text{ m})$$

$$KE = 120 \text{ J}$$

15. B is correct.

Although the book is stationary with respect to the plank, the plank is applying a force to the book causing it to accelerate in the direction of the force. Since the displacement of the point of application of the force is in the same direction as the force, the work done is positive. Choice D is not correct because work is a scalar and has no direction.

16. D is correct.

$$W = Fd$$
$$d = W / F$$
$$d = (350 \text{ J}) / (900 \text{ N})$$
$$d = 0.39 \text{ m}$$

17. A is correct.

Conservation of energy between kinetic energy and potential energy:

$$KE = PE$$
$$KE = \tfrac{1}{2}mv^2 \text{ and } PE = mgh$$

Set the equations equal to each other:

$$\tfrac{1}{2}mv^2 = mgh, \text{ cancel } m \text{ from both sides}$$
$$\tfrac{1}{2}v^2 = gh$$

h is only dependent on the initial v, which is equal between both objects, so the two objects rise to the same height.

18. A is correct.

$$\text{Work} = \text{Power} \times \text{time}$$
$$P_1 = W / t$$
$$P_2 = (3 \text{ W}) / (1/3 \ t)$$
$$P_2 = 3(3/1){\cdot}(W / t)$$
$$P_2 = 9(W / t)$$
$$P_2 = 9(P_1)$$

19. D is correct.

Conservation of energy:

$$KE = PE$$
$$KE = mgh$$
$$W = mg$$
$$KE = Wh$$
$$KE = (450 \text{ N}){\cdot}(9 \text{ m})$$
$$KE = 4{,}050 \text{ J}$$

20. A is correct. $F_1 = -kx_1$

Solve for the spring constant k:

$k = F / x_1$

$k = (160 \text{ N}) / (0.23 \text{ m})$

$k = 696 \text{ N/m}$

$F_2 = -kx_2$

$F_2 = (696 \text{ N/m}) \cdot (0.34 \text{ m})$

$F_2 = 237 \text{ N}$

21. B is correct. There is a frictional force since the net force = 0

The mule pulls in the same direction as the direction of travel so $\cos \theta = 1$

$W = Fd \cos \theta$

$d = v\Delta t$

$W = Fv\Delta t$

22. D is correct.

$W = Fd \cos \theta$

$F_T = W / (d \times \cos \theta)$

$F_T = (540 \text{ J}) / (18 \text{ m} \times \cos 32°)$

$F_T = (540 \text{ J}) / (18 \text{ m} \times 0.848)$

$F_T = 35 \text{ N}$

23. B is correct. The spring force balances the gravitational force on the mass. Therefore:

$F_g = -kx$

$mg = -kx$

By adding an extra 120 grams, the mass is doubled:

$(2m)g = -kx$

Since the weight mg and the spring constant k are constant, only x changes.

Thus, after the addition of 120 g, x doubles:

$PE_1 = \frac{1}{2}kx^2$

$PE_2 = \frac{1}{2}k(2x)^2$

$PE_2 = \frac{1}{2}k(4x^2)$

$PE_2 = 4(\frac{1}{2}kx^2)$

The potential energy increases by a factor of 4.

24. C is correct.

In each case the car's energy is reduced to zero by the work done by the frictional force, or in other words:

$KE + (-W) = 0$

$KE = W$

Each car starts with kinetic energy $KE = (\frac{1}{2})mv^2$. The initial speed is the same for each car, so due to the differences in mass, the Ferrari has the most KE. Thus, to reduce the Ferrari's energy to zero requires the most work.

25. D is correct. The hammer does work on the nail as it drives it into the wood. The amount of work done is equal to the amount of kinetic energy lost by the hammer:

$\Delta KE = \Delta W$

26. A is correct. The only force doing work is the road's friction, so the work done by the road's friction is the total work. This work equals the change in KE.

$W = \Delta KE$

$W = KE_f - KE_i$

$W = \frac{1}{2}mv_2^2 - \frac{1}{2}mv_1^2$

$W = 0 - [\frac{1}{2}(1{,}500 \text{ kg}) \cdot (25 \text{ m/s})^2]$

$W = -4.7 \times 10^5 \text{ J}$

27. D is correct.

$KE = \frac{1}{2}mv^2$

$KE_{car} = \frac{1}{2}(1{,}000 \text{ kg}) \cdot (4.72 \text{ m/s})^2$

$KE_{car} = 11{,}139 \text{ J}$

Calculate the KE of the 2,000 kg truck with 20 times the KE:

$KE_{truck} = KE_{car} \times 20$

$KE_{truck} = (11{,}139 \text{ J}) \times 20$

$KE_{truck} = 222.7 \text{ kJ}$

Calculate the speed of the 2,000 kg truck:

$KE = \frac{1}{2}mv^2$

$v^2 = 2KE / m$

$v^2 = 2(222.7 \text{ kJ}) / (2{,}000 \text{ kg})$

$v_{truck} = \sqrt{[2(222.7 \text{ kJ}) / (2{,}000 \text{ kg})]}$

$v_{truck} = 14.9 \text{ m/s}$

28. C is correct.

Gravity and the normal force are balanced, vertical forces.

Since the car is slowing (i.e., accelerating backward) there is a net force backwards, due to friction (i.e., braking).

Newton's First Law of Motion states that in the absence of any forces, the car would keep moving forward.

29. B is correct.

Energy is always conserved so the work needed to lift the piano is 0.15 m is equal to the work needed to pull the rope 1 m:

$$W_1 = W_2$$

$$F_1d_1 = F_2d_2$$

$$F_1d_1 / d_2 = F_2$$

$$F_2 = (6,000 \text{ N}) \cdot (0.15 \text{ m}) / 1 \text{ m}$$

$$F_2 = 900 \text{ N}$$

30. C is correct.

The area under the curve on a graph is the product of the values of $y \times x$.

Here, the y value is force, and the x value is distance:

$$Fd = W$$

31. B is correct.

The vast majority of the Earth's energy comes from the sun, which produces radiation that penetrates the Earth's atmosphere.

Likewise, radiation is emitted from the Earth's atmosphere.

32. C is correct.

$$W = Fd$$

$$W = \Delta KE$$

$$F \times d = \tfrac{1}{2}mv^2$$

If v is doubled:

$$F \times d_2 = \tfrac{1}{2}m(2v)^2$$

$$F \times d_2 = \tfrac{1}{2}m(4v^2)$$

$$F \times d_2 = 4(\tfrac{1}{2}mv^2)$$

For equations to remain equal to each other, d_2 must be 4 times d.

33. D is correct.

Work = Power × time

$P = W / t$

$W = Fd$

$P = (Fd) / t$

$P = [(2,000 \text{ N})\cdot(320 \text{ m})] / (60 \text{ s})$

$P = 10,667 \text{ W} = 10.7 \text{ kW}$

34. A is correct.

Solution using the principle of conservation of energy.

Assuming the system to consist of the barbell alone, the force of gravity and the force of the hands raising the barbell are both external forces.

Since the system contains only a single object, potential energy is not defined.

The net power expended is:

$P_{net} = W_{ext} / \Delta t$

Conservation of energy requires:

$W_{ext} = \Delta KE$

$W_{ext} = \frac{1}{2}m(v_f^2 - v_i^2)$

For constant acceleration situations:

$(v_f + v_i) / 2 = v_{average} = \Delta y / \Delta t$

$(v_f + 0.0 \text{ m/s}) / 2 = 3.0 \text{ m} / 3.0 \text{ s}$

$v_f = 2.0 \text{ m/s}$

Therefore:

$W_{ext} = \frac{1}{2}(25 \text{ kg})\cdot(2.0 \text{ m/s})^2$

$W_{ext} = 50.0 \text{ J}$

The net power expended is:

$P_{net} = 50.0 \text{ J} / 3.0 \text{ s} = 17 \text{ W}$

$P_{net} = 17 \text{ W}$

Solution using work.

The power expended in raising the barbell is:

$P_{net} = W_{net} / \Delta t$

The net work is defined as:

$W_{net} = F_{net}\Delta y$

By Newton's Second law:

$$F_{net} = ma$$

Find the acceleration:

$$\Delta y = \frac{1}{2}a\Delta t^2$$

$$a = (2)\cdot(3.0 \text{ m}) / (3.0 \text{ s})^2$$

$$a = 0.67 \text{ m/s}^2$$

The net force on the barbell is:

$$F_{net} = (25 \text{ kg})\cdot(0.67 \text{ m/s}^2)$$

$$F_{net} = (50 / 3) \text{ N}$$

The net work is:

$$W_{net} = F_{net}\Delta y$$

$$W_{net} = [(50 / 3) \text{ N}] \cdot (3.0 \text{ m})$$

$$W_{net} = 50.0 \text{ J}$$

The net power expended:

$$P_{net} = 50.0 \text{ J} / 3.0 \text{ s}$$

$$P_{net} = 17 \text{ W}$$

35. B is correct.

The bag was never lifted off the ground and moved horizontally at a constant velocity.

$$F = 0$$

$$W = Fd$$

$$W = 0 \text{ J}$$

Because there is no acceleration, the force is zero, and thus the work is zero.

36. B is correct.

Using energy conservation to solve the problem:

$$W = |\Delta KE|$$

$$Fd = |\frac{1}{2}m(v_f^2 - v_0^2)|$$

$$d = |m(v_f^2 - v_0^2) / 2F|$$

$$d = |(1,000 \text{ kg})\cdot[(22 \text{ m/s})^2 - (30 \text{ m/s})^2] / (2)\cdot(9,600 \text{ N})|$$

$$d = |(1,000 \text{ kg})\cdot(484 \text{ m}^2/\text{s}^2 - 900 \text{ m}^2/\text{s}^2) / 19,200 \text{ N}|$$

$$d = 22 \text{ m}$$

Kinematic approach:

$$F = ma$$

$a = F / m$

$a = (9,600 \text{ N}) / (1,000 \text{ kg})$

$a = 9.6 \text{ m/s}^2$

$v_f^2 = v_0^2 + 2a\Delta d$

$(v_f^2 - v_0^2) / 2a = \Delta d$

Note that acceleration is negative due to it acting opposite the velocity.

$\Delta d = [(22 \text{ m/s})^2 - (30 \text{ m/s})^2] / 2(-9.6 \text{ m/s}^2)$

$\Delta d = (484 \text{ m}^2/\text{s}^2 - 900 \text{ m}^2/\text{s}^2) / (-19.2 \text{ m/s}^2)$

$\Delta d = (-416 \text{ m}^2/\text{s}^2) / (-19.2 \text{ m/s}^2)$

$\Delta d = 21.7 \text{ m} \approx 22 \text{ m}$

37. C is correct.

$W = 100 \text{ J}$

Work = Power × time

$P = W / t$

$P = 100 \text{ J} / 50 \text{ s}$

$P = 2 \text{ W}$

38. D is correct.

All of the original potential energy (with respect to the bottom of the cliff) is converted into kinetic energy.

$mgh = \frac{1}{2} m v_f^2$

Therefore:

$v_f = \sqrt{2gh}$

$v_f = \sqrt{(2) \cdot (10 \text{ m/s}^2) \cdot (58 \text{ m})}$

$v_f = 34 \text{ m/s}$

Kinematic approach:

$v_f^2 = v_0^2 + 2a\Delta x$

$v_f^2 = 0 + 2a\Delta x$

$v_f = \sqrt{2a\Delta x}$

$v_f = \sqrt{[2(10 \text{ m/s}^2) \cdot (58 \text{ m})]}$

$v_f = \sqrt{(1,160 \text{ m}^2/\text{s}^2)}$

$v_f = 34 \text{ m/s}$

39. A is correct.

$PE = mgh$

If height and gravity are constant, then potential energy is directly proportional to mass.

As such, if the second stone has four times the mass of the first, then it must have four times the potential energy of the first stone.

$m_2 = 4m_1$

$PE_2 = 4PE_1$

Therefore, the second stone has four times the potential energy.

40. B is correct.

$W = Fd$

$W = mgh$, work done by gravity

$W = (1.3 \text{ kg}) \cdot (10 \text{ m/s}^2) \cdot (6 \text{ m})$

$W = 78 \text{ J}$

41. A is correct. Potential energy is the energy associated with the relative positions of pairs of objects, regardless of their state of motion.

Kinetic energy is the energy associated with the motion of single particles, regardless of their location.

42. A is correct.

$F_{spring} = F_{centripetal}$

$F_{spring} = kx$

$kx = 15 \text{ N}$

$x = (15 \text{ N}) / (65 \text{ N/m})$

$x = 0.23 \text{ m}$

$PE_{spring} = \frac{1}{2}kx^2$

$PE_{spring} = \frac{1}{2}(65 \text{ N/m}) \cdot (0.23 \text{ m})^2$

$PE_{spring} = 1.7 \text{ J}$

43. C is correct.

total time = $(3.5 \text{ h/day}) \cdot (7 \text{ days}) \cdot (5 \text{ weeks})$

total time = 122.5 h

cost = $(8.16 \text{ cents/kW·h}) \cdot (122.5 \text{ h}) \cdot (0.12 \text{ kW})$

cost = 120 cents = $1.20

44. B is correct.

$x = 5.1 \text{ m} \times (\cos 32°)$

$x = 4.33 \text{ m}$

$h = 5.1 \text{ m} - 4.33 \text{ m}$

$h = 0.775 \text{ m}$

$W = Fd$

$W = mg \times h$

$m = W / gh$

$m = (120 \text{ J}) / (9.8 \text{ m/s}^2) \cdot (0.775 \text{ m})$

$m = 15.8 \text{ kg}$

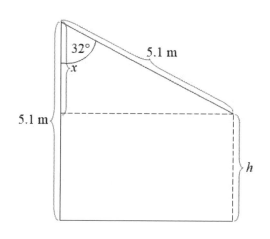

45. D is correct. Potential energy of spring:

$PE_i + W = PE_f$

$\frac{1}{2} k \, x_i^2 + 111\text{J} = \frac{1}{2} k \, x_f^2$

$111\text{J} = \frac{1}{2} k \, (x_f^2 - x_i^2)$

$111\text{J} = \frac{1}{2} k \, [(2.9\text{m})^2 - (1.4\text{m})^2]$

$111\text{J} = \frac{1}{2} k \, [(8.41\text{m}^2) - (1.96\text{m}^2)]$

$111\text{J} = \frac{1}{2} k \, (6.45\text{m}^2)$

$k = 2(111 \text{ J}) / (6.45 \text{ m}^2)$

$k = 34 \text{ N/m}$

Unit check:

$J = \text{kg} \cdot \text{m}^2/\text{s}^2$

$J/\text{m}^2 = (\text{kg} \cdot \text{m}^2/\text{s}^2) \cdot (1/\text{m}^2)$

$J/\text{m}^2 = (\text{kg}/\text{s}^2)$

$N/\text{m} = (\text{kg} \cdot \text{m}/\text{s}^2) \cdot (1/\text{m})$

$N/\text{m} = (\text{kg}/\text{s}^2)$

46. D is correct. Potential energy, kinetic energy and work are all measured in joules:

$J = \text{kg} \cdot \text{m}^2/\text{s}^2$

$KE = \frac{1}{2}mv^2 = \text{kg}(\text{m/s})^2 = J$

$PE = mgh$

$PE = \text{kg}(\text{m/s}^2) \cdot (\text{m}) = J$

$W = Fd = J$

47. A is correct.

Potential energy of spring:

$$PE = \tfrac{1}{2}kx^2$$

Kinetic energy of mass:

$$KE = \tfrac{1}{2}mv^2$$

Set equal to each other and rearrange:

$\tfrac{1}{2}kx^2 = \tfrac{1}{2}mv^2$, cancel $\tfrac{1}{2}$ from both sides of the expression

$$kx^2 = mv^2$$

$$x^2 = (mv^2) / k$$

$$x^2 = (m / k)v^2$$

Since m / k is provided:

$$x^2 = (0.038 \text{ kg·m/N})·(18 \text{ m/s})^2$$

$$x^2 = 12.3 \text{ m}^2$$

$$x = \sqrt{12.3} \text{ m}$$

$$x = 3.5 \text{ m}$$

48. A is correct.

$$m_t = 2m_c$$

$$v_t = 2v_c$$

KE of the truck:

$$KE_t = \tfrac{1}{2}m_t v_t^2$$

Replace mass and velocity of the truck with the equivalent mass and velocity of the car:

$$KE_t = \tfrac{1}{2}(2m_c)·(2v_c)^2$$

$$KE_t = \tfrac{1}{2}(2m_c)·(4v_c^2)$$

$$KE_t = \tfrac{1}{2}(8m_c v_c^2)$$

The truck has 8 times the kinetic energy of the car.

49. C is correct.

When a car stops, the KE is equal to the work done by the force of friction from the brakes.
Through friction, the KE is transformed into heat.

50. B is correct.

When the block comes to rest at the end of the spring, the upward force of the spring balances the downward force of gravity.

$F = kx$

$mg = kx$

$x = mg / k$

$x = (30 \text{ kg}){\cdot}(10 \text{ m/s}^2) / 900 \text{ N/m}$

$x = 0.33 \text{ m}$

51. D is correct.

$KE = \frac{1}{2}mv^2$

$KE = \frac{1}{2}(0.33 \text{ kg}){\cdot}(40 \text{ m/s})^2$

$KE = 264 \text{ J}$

52. C is correct.

Work is the area under a force vs. position graph.

area $= Fd = W$

The area of the triangle as the object moves from 0 to 4 m:

$A = \frac{1}{2}bh$

$A = \frac{1}{2}(4 \text{ m}{\cdot})(10 \text{ N})$

$A = 20 \text{ J}$

$W = 20 \text{ J}$

53. C is correct.

$KE = PE$

$\frac{1}{2}mv^2 = mgh$

$v^2 / 2g = h$

If v is doubled:

$h_\text{B} = v_\text{B}{}^2 / 2g$

$v_\text{J} = 2v_\text{B}$

$(2v_\text{B})^2 / 2g = h_\text{J}$

$4(v_\text{B}{}^2 / 2g) = h_\text{J}$

$4h_\text{B} = h_\text{J}$

James's ball travels 4 times higher than Bob's ball.

54. B is correct. Hooke's Law is given as:

$$F = -kx$$

The negative is only by convention to demonstrate that the spring force is a restoring force.

Graph B is correct because force is linearly increasing with increasing distance.

All other graphs are either constant or exponential.

55. C is correct.

A decrease in the KE for the rocket causes either a gain in its gravitational PE, or the transfer of heat, or a combination.

The rocket loses some KE due to air resistance (friction).

Thus, some of the rocket's KE is converted to heat that causes the temperature of the air surrounding the rocket to increase. Therefore, the average KE of the air molecules increases.

56. D is correct. Kinetic energy is given as:

$$KE_1 = \frac{1}{2}mv^2$$

$$KE_2 = \frac{1}{2}m(4v)^2$$

$$KE_2 = \frac{1}{2}m(16v^2)$$

Increasing the velocity by a factor of 4 increases the KE by a factor of 16.

57. C is correct.

The total energy of the system is conserved. A relationship between the initial compression of the spring and the final speed of the mass can thus be found.

$$E_i = E_f$$

$$KE_i + PE_i = KE_f + PE_f$$

Initially, the spring is compressed and has PE, and the mass is at rest, so the initial KE is zero. At the end, the spring is uncompressed, and the mass is moving, so the final PE is zero, and the mass has KE.

$$PE_i = KE_f$$

$$\frac{1}{2}kx^2 = \frac{1}{2}mv^2$$

$$kx^2 = mv^2$$

$$x\sqrt{k} = v\sqrt{m}$$

The velocity and the compression distance of the spring are directly proportional. Thus, if the spring is compressed by four times the original distance, then the velocity is four times the original.

$$x_2 = 4x_1$$

$$v_2 = 4v_1$$

58. C is correct.

Force: $F = ma$ (N)

Work: $W = Fd$ (N·m)

Power: $P = W / t$ (N·m/s)

59. A is correct.

$W_{net} = \Delta KE$

$\Delta KE = KE_f - KE_i$

$\Delta KE + KE_i = KE_f$

60. D is correct.

$v = (70 \text{ km/h})\cdot(1{,}000 \text{ m/km})\cdot(1 \text{ h/60 min})\cdot(1 \text{ min/60 s})$

$v = 19.4$ m/s

Force acting against the car:

$F = mg \sin \theta$

$F = (1{,}320 \text{ kg})\cdot(9.8 \text{ m/s}^2) \sin 5°$

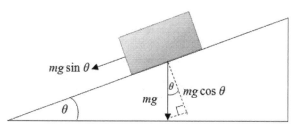

$\sin 5° = 0.0872$, round it to 0.09

$F = (1{,}320 \text{ kg})\cdot(9.8 \text{ m/s}^2)\cdot(0.09)$

$F = 1{,}164$ N

$N = \text{kg·m/s}^2$

Rate of energy is power:

$\text{Watts} = \text{kg·m}^2/\text{s}^3$

Multiply velocity by the downward force:

$P = Fv$

$P = (1{,}164 \text{ N})\cdot(19.4 \text{ m/s})$

$P = 22.6$ kW

Periodic Motion – Explanations

1. B is correct.

Frequency is the measure of the number of cycles per second a wave experiences, which is independent of the wave's amplitude.

2. D is correct.

Hooke's Law:

$$F = kx$$

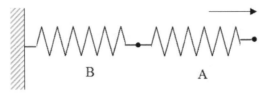

It is known that the force on each spring must be equal if they are in static equilibrium, therefore:

$$F_A = F_B$$

Therefore, the expression can be written as:

$$k_A L_A = k_B L_B$$

Solve for the spring constant of spring B:

$$k_B = (k_A L_A) / L_B$$

3. D is correct.

In a longitudinal wave, particles of a material are displaced parallel to the direction of the wave.

4. C is correct.

speed = wavelength × frequency

$$v = \lambda f$$
$$v = (0.25 \text{ m}) \cdot (1{,}680 \text{ Hz})$$
$$v = 420 \text{ m/s}$$

5. A is correct.

$$E_{stored} = PE = \tfrac{1}{2}kA^2$$

Stored energy is potential energy.

In a simple harmonic motion (e.g., a spring), the potential energy is:

$$PE = \tfrac{1}{2}kx^2 \text{ or } \tfrac{1}{2}kA^2,$$

where k is a constant and A (or x) is the distance from equilibrium

A is the amplitude of a wave in simple harmonic motion (SHM).

6. D is correct.

The spring will oscillate around its new equilibrium position (which is 3 cm below the equilibrium position with no mass hanging) with period $T = 2\pi\sqrt{m/k}$ since it's a mass-spring system undergoing simple harmonic motion.

To find k, consider how much the spring stretched when the mass was hung from it. Since the spring found a new equilibrium point 3 cm below its natural length, the upwards force from the spring (F_s) must balance the downwards gravitational force (F_g) at that displacement:

$$|F_s| = |F_g|$$

$$kd = mg$$

$$k\,(0.03 \text{ m}) = (11 \text{ kg}){\cdot}(9.8 \text{ m/s}^2)$$

$$k = 3593 \text{ N/m}$$

Now, solve for T:

$$T = 2\pi\sqrt{m/k}$$

$$T = 2\pi\sqrt{11 \text{ kg} / 3593 \text{ N/m}}$$

$$T = 0.35 \text{ s}$$

The frequency is the reciprocal of the period:

$$f = 1/T$$

$$f = 1/(0.35 \text{ s})$$

$$f = 2.9 \text{ Hz}$$

7. C is correct.

$$T = 1/f$$

8. D is correct.

The period of a pendulum:

$$T = 2\pi\sqrt{L/g}$$

The period only depends on the pendulum's length and gravity.

In an elevator, the apparent force of gravity only changes if the elevator is accelerating in either direction.

9. A is correct. The period is the reciprocal of the frequency:

$$T = 1 / f$$

$$T = 1 / 100 \text{ Hz} = 0.01 \text{ s}$$

10. B is correct.

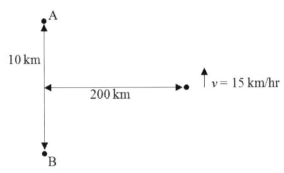

Convert v to m/s:

$$v = (15 \text{ km/1 h}) \cdot (1 \text{ h/60 min}) \cdot (1 \text{ min/60 s}) \cdot (10^3 \text{ m/1 km})$$

$$v = 4.2 \text{ m/s}$$

Convert frequency to λ:

$$\lambda = c / f$$

$$\lambda = (3 \times 10^8 \text{ m/s}) / (4.7 \times 10^6 \text{ Hz})$$

$$\lambda = 63.8 \text{ m}$$

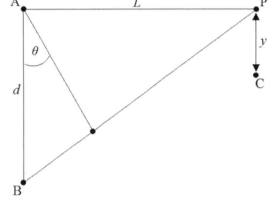

According to Young's Equation:

$$\lambda = yd / mL, \text{ where m} = 0, 1, 2, 3, 4…$$

Solve for y by rearranging to isolate y:

$$y = \lambda Lm / d$$

y = distance travelled by the ship:

$$y = vt$$

Since the first signal came at the point of maximum intensity, m = 0 at that time, at the next maximum m = 1.

Therefore:

$$t = L\lambda / vd$$

$$t = (200,000 \text{ m}) \cdot (63.8 \text{ m}) / (4.2 \text{ m/s}) \cdot (10,000 \text{ m})$$

$$t = 304 \text{ s}$$

Convert time from seconds to minutes:

$$t = (304 \text{ s}) \cdot (1 \text{ min/60 s})$$

$$t = 5.06 \text{ min} \approx 5.1 \text{ min}$$

For all m values greater than 1, the calculated times are beyond the answer choices, so 5.1 min is the correct answer.

11. D is correct.

The tension in the rope is given by the equation:

$T = (mv^2) / L$

where v is the velocity of the wave and L is the length of the rope.

Substituting:

$v = L / t$

$T = [m(L / t)^2] / L$

$T = mL / t^2$

$t^2 = mL / T$

$t = \sqrt{(mL / T)}$

$t = \sqrt{[(2.31 \text{ kg}) \cdot (10.4 \text{ m}) / 74.4 \text{ N}]}$

$t = \sqrt{(0.323 \text{ s}^2)}$

$t = 0.57 \text{ s}$

12. A is correct.

$\omega_A = 2\omega_B$

$\omega_B = \sqrt{g / l_B}$

Therefore:

$l_B = g / \omega^2_B$

Similarly, for A:

$l_A = g / \omega^2_A$

$l_A = g / (2\omega_B)^2$

$l_A = \frac{1}{4}g / \omega^2_B$

$l_A = \frac{1}{4}l_B$

13. B is correct.

$F = -kx$

Since the motion is simple harmonic, the restoring force is proportional to displacement.

Therefore, if the displacement is 5 times greater, then so is the restoring force.

14. C is correct.

Period = (60 s) / (10 oscillations)

$T = 6 \text{ s}$

The period is the time for one oscillation.

If 10 oscillations take 60 s, then one oscillation takes 6 s.

15. A is correct. Conservation of Energy:

total ME = ΔKE + ΔPE = constant

$\frac{1}{2}mv^2 + \frac{1}{2}kx^2$ = constant

16. B is correct.

A displacement from the position of maximum elongation to the position of maximum compression represents *half* a cycle. If it takes 1 s, then the time required for a complete cycle is 2 s.

$f = 1 / T$

$f = 1 / 2$ s

$f = 0.5$ Hz

17. C is correct. Sound waves are longitudinal waves.

18. B is correct.

speed = wavelength $\times$ frequency

speed = wavelength / period

$v = \lambda / T$

$\lambda = vT$

$\lambda = (362$ m/s$)\cdot(0.004$ s$)$

$\lambda = 1.5$ m

19. A is correct.

$a = -A\omega^2 \cos(\omega t)$

where A is the amplitude or displacement from the resting position.

20. D is correct.

The acceleration of a simple harmonic oscillation is:

$a = -A\omega^2 \cos(\omega t)$

Its maximum occurs when cos (ωt) is equal to 1

$a_{max} = -\omega^2 x$

If ω is doubled:

$a = -(2\omega)^2 x$

$a = -4\omega^2 x$

The maximum value of acceleration changes by a factor of 4.

21. B is correct. Resonant frequency of a spring and mass system in any orientation:

$\omega = \sqrt{(k / m)}$

$f = \omega / 2\pi$

$T = 1 / f$

$T = 2\pi\sqrt{(m / k)}$

Period of a spring does not depend on gravity.

The period remains constant because only mass and the spring constant affect the period.

22. C is correct.

$v = \lambda f$

$\lambda = v / f$

An increase in v and a decrease in f must increase λ.

23. B is correct. Frequency is the measure of oscillations or vibrations per second.

frequency = 60 vibrations in 1 s

frequency = 60 Hz

speed = 30 m / 1 s

speed = 30 m/s

24. A is correct.

$T = (mv^2) / L$

$m = TL / v^2$

$m = (60 \text{ N})\cdot(16 \text{ m}) / (40 \text{ m/s})^2$

$m = (960 \text{ N·m}) / (1,600 \text{ m}^2/\text{s}^2)$

$m = 0.6 \text{ kg}$

25. D is correct. Amplitude is independent of frequency.

26. C is correct.

$f = \#$ cycles / time

$f = 60$ drips / 40 s

$f = 1.5$ Hz

27. D is correct. Transverse waves are characterized by their crests and valleys, which are caused by the particles of the wave traveling "up and down" with respect to the lateral movement of the wave.

The particles in longitudinal waves travel parallel to the direction of the wave.

28. B is correct.

The velocity vs. time graph shows that at $t = 0$, the velocity of the particle is positive, and the speed is increasing.

When speed increases, velocity and acceleration point in the same direction.

Therefore, the acceleration is non-zero and positive. Only graph B displays a positive acceleration at $t = 0$.

29. C is correct.

The speed of a wave is determined by the characteristics of the medium (and the type of wave). Speed is independent of amplitude.

30. A is correct.

$f = 1 \,/\, \text{period}$

$f = \#\text{ cycles} \,/\, \text{second}$

$f = 1 \text{ cycle} \,/\, 2 \text{ s}$

$f = \tfrac{1}{2} \text{ Hz}$

31. B is correct.

$f = v \,/\, \lambda$

$\lambda = v \,/\, f$

$\lambda = (340 \text{ m/s}) \,/\, (2{,}100 \text{ Hz})$

$\lambda = 0.16 \text{ m}$

32. D is correct.

$\text{Period (T)} = 2\pi\sqrt{(L \,/\, g)}$

The period is independent of the mass.

33. A is correct.

$v = \omega x$

$\omega = v \,/\, x$

$\omega = (15 \text{ m/s}) \,/\, (2.5 \text{ m})$

$\omega = 6.0 \text{ rad/s}$

34. D is correct.

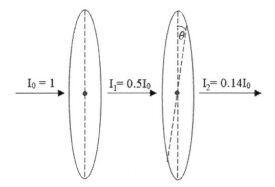

Unpolarized light on a polarizer reduces the intensity by ½.

$$I = (½)I_0$$

After that, the light is further reduced in intensity by the second filter.

Law of Malus:

$$I = I_0 \cos^2 \theta$$

$$(0.14\ I_0) = (0.5\ I_0) \cos^2 \theta$$

$$0.28 = \cos^2 \theta$$

$$\cos^{-1} \sqrt{(0.28)} = \theta$$

$$\theta = 58°$$

35. C is correct.

At a maximum distance from equilibrium, the energy in the system is potential energy, and the speed is zero. Therefore, kinetic energy is also zero. Since there is no kinetic energy, the mass has no velocity.

36. D is correct.

$$v = \lambda f$$

$$f = v / \lambda$$

$$f = (240\ \text{m/s}) / (0.1\ \text{m})$$

$$f = 2,400\ \text{Hz}$$

37. B is correct.

In a transverse wave, the vibrations of particles are perpendicular to the direction of travel of the wave. Transverse waves have crests and troughs that move along the wave.

In a longitudinal wave, the vibrations of particles are parallel to the direction of travel of the wave. Longitudinal waves have compressions and rarefactions that move along the wave.

38. C is correct.

$v = \sqrt{(T / \mu)}$

where μ is the linear density of the wire.

$T = v^2\mu$

$\mu = \rho A,$

where A is the cross-sectional area of the wire and equals πr^2.

$\mu = (2,700 \text{ kg/m}^3)\pi(4.6 \times 10^{-3} \text{ m})^2$

$\mu = 0.18 \text{ kg/m}$

$T = (36 \text{ m/s})^2 \cdot (0.18 \text{ kg/m})$

$T = 233 \text{ N}$

39. D is correct.

Refraction is the change in the direction of a wave, caused by the change in the wave's speed. Examples of waves include sound waves and light waves. Refraction is seen most often when a wave passes from one medium to a different medium (e.g., from air to water and vice versa).

40. C is correct.

$f = \text{\# cycles / second}$

$f = 2 \text{ cycles / 1 s}$

$f = 2 \text{ Hz}$

41. A is correct.

Pitch is how the brain perceives frequency. Pitch becomes higher as frequency increases.

42. C is correct.

The KE is maximum when the spring is neither stretched nor compressed.

If the object is bobbing, KE is maximum at the midpoint between fully stretched and fully compressed because this is where all of the spring's energy is KE rather than a mix of KE and PE.

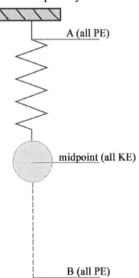

43. B is correct.

Torque $= rF \sin \theta$

$F = ma$, substitute mg for F

$\tau = rmg \sin \theta$

$\tau = (1 \text{ m}) \cdot (0.5 \text{ kg}) \cdot (10 \text{ m/s}^2) \sin 60°$

$\tau = (5 \text{ kg·m}^2/\text{s}^2) \times 0.87$

$\tau = 4.4 \text{ N·m}$

44. D is correct. The Doppler effect can be observed to occur in all types of waves.

45. A is correct.

$v = \sqrt{(T / \mu)}$ where μ is the linear density of the wire.

$F_T = ma$

$F_T = (2{,}500 \text{ kg}) \cdot (10 \text{ m/s}^2)$

$F_T = 25{,}000 \text{ N}$

$v = \sqrt{(25{,}000 \text{ N} / 0.65 \text{ kg/m})}$

$v = 196 \text{ m/s}$

The weight of the wire can be assumed to be negligible compared to the cement block.

46. B is correct.

$f = \frac{1}{2}\pi[\sqrt{(g / L)}]$, frequency is independent of mass

47. A is correct.

$T = 2\pi\sqrt{(L / g)}]$

$T = 2\pi\sqrt{(3.3 \text{ m} / 10 \text{ m/s}^2)}$

$T = 3.6 \text{ s}$

48. C is correct.

$f = (1/2\pi)\sqrt{(k / m)}$

If k increases by a factor of 2, then f increases by a factor of $\sqrt{2}$ (or 1.41).

Increasing by a factor of 1.41 or 41%

49. D is correct. In a simple harmonic motion, the acceleration is greatest at the ends of motions (points A and D) where velocity is zero.

Velocity is greatest at the nadir where acceleration is equal to zero (point C).

50. A is correct.

At the lowest point, the KE is at a maximum, and the PE is at a minimum.

The loss of gravitational PE equals the gain in KE:

$mgh = \frac{1}{2}mv^2$, cancel m from both sides of the expression

$gh = \frac{1}{2}v^2$

$(10 \text{ m/s}^2) \cdot (10 \text{ m}) = \frac{1}{2}v^2$

$(100 \text{ m}^2/\text{s}^2) = \frac{1}{2}v^2$

$200 \text{ m}^2/\text{s}^2 = v^2$

$v = 14 \text{ m/s}$

51. A is correct.

Pitch is a psychophysical phenomenon when the sensation of a frequency is commonly referred to as the pitch of a sound.

A perception of high-pitch sound corresponds to a high-frequency sound wave, and a low-pitch sound corresponds to a low-frequency sound wave.

Amplitude plays no role, and speed is constant.

52. C is correct.

Because wind is blowing in the reference frame of both the train and the observer, it does not need to be taken into account.

$f_{observed} = [v_{sound} / (v_{sound} - v_{source})]f_{source}$

$f_{observed} = [340 \text{ m/s} / (340 \text{ m/s} - 50 \text{ m/s})] \cdot 500 \text{ Hz}$

$f_{observed} = 586 \text{ Hz}$

$\lambda = v / f$

$\lambda = 340 \text{ m/s} / 586 \text{ Hz}$

$\lambda = 0.58 \text{ m}$

53. B is correct.

$PE = \frac{1}{2}kx^2$

Doubling the amplitude x increases PE by a factor of 4.

54. C is correct.

The elastic modulus is given by:

E = tensional strength / extensional strain

$E = \sigma / \varepsilon$

55. D is correct.

Resonance is the phenomenon where one system transfers its energy to another at that system's resonant frequency (natural frequency). It is a forced vibration that produces the highest amplitude response for a given force amplitude.

56. A is correct.

Period of a pendulum:

$$T_P = 2\pi\sqrt{(L / g)}$$

Period of a spring:

$$T_S = 2\pi\sqrt{(m / k)}$$

The period of a spring does not depend on gravity and is unaffected.

57. B is correct.

At the top of its arc, the pendulum comes to rest momentarily; the KE and the velocity equal zero.

Since its height above the bottom of its arc is at a maximum at this point, its (angular) displacement from the vertical equilibrium position is at a maximum also.

The pendulum constantly experiences the forces of gravity and tension and is therefore continuously accelerating.

58. D is correct.

The Doppler effect is the observed change in frequency when a sound source is in motion relative to an observer (away or towards).

If the sound source moves with the observer, then there is no relative motion between the two and the Doppler effect does not occur.

59. C is correct.

The amplitude of a wave is the magnitude of its oscillation from its equilibrium point.

60. A is correct.

$$f = \sqrt{(k / m)}$$

An increase in m causes a decrease in f.

Fluids and Gas Phase – Explanations

1. C is correct.

Refer to the unknown liquid as "A" and the oil as "O."

$\rho_A h_A g = \rho_O h_O g$, cancel g from both sides of the expression

$\rho_A h_A = \rho_O h_O$

$h_A = 5$ cm

$h_O = 20$ cm

$h_A = \frac{1}{4} h_O$

$\rho_A(\frac{1}{4}) h_O = \rho_O h_O$

$\rho_A = 4\rho_O$

$\rho_A = 4(850$ kg/m$^3)$

$\rho_A = 3{,}400$ kg/m^3

2. D is correct.

$P = \rho_{oil} \times V_{oil} \times g \, / \, (A_{tube})$

$P = [\rho_o \pi (r_{tube})^2 \times hg] \, / \, \pi (r_{tube})^2$

cancel $\pi(r_{tube})^2$ from both the numerator and the denominator.

$P = \rho_o g h$

$P = (850$ kg/m$^3) \cdot (9.8$ m/s$^2) \cdot (0.2$ m$)$

$P = 1{,}666$ Pa

3. A is correct.

$m_{oil} = \rho_{oil} V_{oil}$

$V = \pi r^2 h$

$m_{oil} = \rho_{oil} \pi r^2 h$

$m_{oil} = \pi(850$ kg/m$^3) \cdot (0.02$ m$)^2 \times (0.2$ m$)$

$m_{oil} = 0.21$ kg $= 210$ g

4. A is correct.

Gauge pressure is the pressure experienced by an object referenced at atmospheric pressure. When the block is lowered its gauge pressure increases according to:

$P_G = \rho g h$

At $t = 0$, the block just enters the water and $h = 0$ so $P_G = 0$. As time passes, the height of the block below the water increases linearly, so P_G increases linearly as well.

5. D is correct.

Using Bernoulli's principle and assuming the opening of the tank is so large that the initial velocity is essentially zero:

$\rho gh = \frac{1}{2}\rho v^2$, cancel ρ from both sides of the expression

$gh = \frac{1}{2}v^2$

$v^2 = 2gh$

$v^2 = 2 \cdot (9.8 \text{ m/s}^2) \cdot (0.8 \text{ m})$

$v^2 = 15.68 \text{ m}^2/\text{s}^2$

$v = 3.96 \text{ m/s} \approx 4 \text{ m/s}$

Note: the diameter is not used to solve the problem.

6. C is correct.

The ideal gas law is:

$PV = nR\text{T}$

Keeping $n\text{RT}$ constant:

If $P_{final} = \frac{1}{2}P_{initial}$

$V_{final} = \frac{1}{2}V_{initial}$

However, in an isothermal process there is no change in internal energy.

Therefore, because energy must be conserved:

$\Delta U = 0$

7. B is correct.

For most substances, the solid form is denser than the liquid phase. Therefore, a block of most solids sinks in the liquid. With regards to pure water though, a block of ice (solid phase) floats in liquid water because ice is less dense.

Like other substances, when liquid water is cooled from room temperature, it becomes increasingly dense. However, at approximately 4 °C (39 °F), water reaches its maximum density, and as it's cooled further, it expands and becomes less dense. This phenomenon is known as negative thermal expansion and is attributed to strong intermolecular interactions that are orientation-dependent.

The density of water is about 1 g/cm^3 and depends on the temperature. When frozen, the density of water is decreased by about 9%. This is due to the decrease in intermolecular vibrations, which allows water molecules to form stable hydrogen bonds with other water molecules around. As these hydrogen bonds form, molecules are locking into positions similar to form hexagonal structures.

Even though hydrogen bonds are shorter in the crystal than in the liquid, this position locking decreases the average coordination number of water molecules as the liquid reaches the solid phase.

8. C is correct.

The object sinks when the buoyant force is less than the weight of the object.

Since the buoyant force is equal to the weight of the displaced fluid, an object sinks precisely when the weight of the fluid it displaces is less than the weight of the object itself.

9. A is correct.

$$P = \rho g h$$
$$P = (10^3 \text{ kg/m}^3) \cdot (9.8 \text{ m/s}^2) \cdot (100 \text{ m})$$
$$P = 9.8 \times 10^5 \text{ N/m}^2$$

10. C is correct.

Absolute pressure = gauge pressure + atmospheric pressure

$$P_{abs} = P_G + P_{atm}$$
$$P_{abs} = \rho g h + P_{atm}$$

Atmospheric pressure is added to the total pressure at the bottom of a volume of liquid.

Therefore, if the atmospheric pressure increases, absolute pressure increases by the same amount.

11. A is correct.

Surface tension increases as temperature decreases.

Generally, the cohesive forces maintaining surface tension decrease as molecular thermal activity increases.

12. B is correct.

By Poiseuille's Law, the volumetric flow rate of a fluid is given by:

$$V = \Delta P A r^2 / 8\eta L$$

Volumetric flow rate is the volume of fluid that passes a point per unit time:

$$V = Av$$

where v is the speed of the fluid.

Therefore:

$$Av = \Delta P A r^2 / 8\eta L$$
$$v = \Delta P r^2 / 8\eta L$$
$$v = (225 \times 10^3 \text{ Pa}) \cdot (0.0032 \text{ m})^2 / [8 \, (0.3 \text{ Ns/m}^2) \cdot (1 \text{ m})]$$
$$v = 0.96 \text{ m/s}$$

13. A is correct.

The buoyant force upward must balance the weight downward.

Buoyant force = weight of the volume of water displaced

$F_B = W_{object}$

$\rho V g = W_{object}$

$W_{object} = 60$ N

$W_{object} = (\rho_{water}) \cdot (V_{water}) \cdot (g)$

60 N = (1,000 kg/m³)·(V_{water})·(10 m/s²)

V_{water} = 60 N / (1,000 kg/m³)·(10 m/s²)

V_{water} = 0.006 m³

14. B is correct.

Volume flow rate:

Q = vA

Q = (2.5 m/s)πr^2

Q = (2.5 m/s)·(0.015 m)²π

Q = 1.8 × 10⁻³ m³/s

15. C is correct.

Force equation for the cork that is not accelerating:

$F_B - mg = 0$

Let *m* be the mass and V be the volume of the cork.

Replace:

$m = \rho V$

$F_B = (\rho_{water}) \cdot (V_{disp}) \cdot (g)$

$(\rho_{water}) \cdot (V_{disp}) \cdot (g) = (\rho_{cork}) \cdot (V) \cdot (g)$

$V_{disp} = \frac{3}{4} V$

$\rho_{water} (\frac{3}{4} V g) = (\rho_{cork}) \cdot (V) \cdot (g)$, cancel *g* and V from both sides of the expression

$\frac{3}{4} \rho_{water} = \rho_{cork}$

$\rho_{cork} / \rho_{water} = \frac{3}{4} = 0.75$

16. D is correct.

volume = mass / density

V = (600 g) / (0.93 g/cm³)

V = 645 cm³

17. C is correct.

For monatomic gases:

$U = 3/2k_BT$

where U is average KE per molecule and k_B is the Boltzmann constant

18. B is correct.

The object weighs 150 N less while immersed because the buoyant force is supporting 150 N of the total weight of the object.

Since the object is totally submerged, the volume of water displaced equals the volume of the object.

$F_B = 150$ N

$F_B = \rho_{water} \times V_{water} \times g$

$V = F_B / \rho g$

$V = (150$ N$) / (1,000$ kg/m$^3) \cdot (10$ m/s$^2)$

$V = 0.015$ m^3

19. C is correct.

$F_B / \rho_w = (m_c g) / \rho_c$

$F_B = (\rho_w m_c g) / \rho_c$

$F_B = [(1$ g/cm$^3) \cdot (0.03$ kg$) \cdot (9.8$ m/s$^2)] / (8.9$ g/cm$^3)$

$F_B = 0.033$ N

$m_{total} = m_w + (F_B / g)$

$m_{total} = (0.14$ kg$) + [(0.033$ N$) / (9.8$ m/s$^2)]$

$m_{total} = 0.143$ kg $= 143$ g

20. D is correct.

$v_1 A_1 = v_2 A_2$

$v_2 = v_1 A_1 / A_2$

$v_2 = [v_1(\pi/4)d_1^2] / (\pi/4)d_2^2$

cancel $(\pi/4)$ from both the numerator and denominator

$v_2 = v_1(d_1^2 / d_2^2)$

$v_2 = (1$ m/s$) \cdot [(6$ cm$)^2 / (3$ cm$)^2]$

$v_2 = 4$ m/s

21. A is correct.

Static fluid pressure:

$$P = \rho g h$$

Pressure is only dependent on gravity (g), the height (h) of the fluid above the object and density (ρ) of the fluid. It does depend on the depth of the object but does not depend on the surface area of the object.

Both objects are submerged to the same depth, so the fluid pressure is equal.

Note that the buoyant force on the blocks is NOT equal, but pressure (force / area) is equal.

22. C is correct.

Surface tension force acts as the product of surface tension and the total length of contact.

$$F = AL$$

For a piece of thread, the length of contact is l as shown:

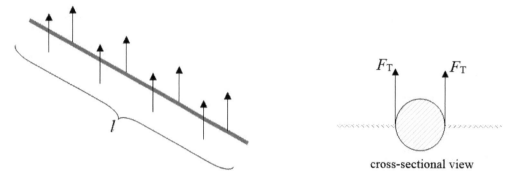

cross-sectional view

$F = 2L$ because the force acts on both sides of the thread.

Thus, for a thread rectangle, the total contact length is the total length times two.

$$L = 2(l + w + l + w)$$
$$F_{max} = 2A(l + w + l + w)$$
$$F_{max} = 2A(2l + 2w)$$
$$F_{max} = 4A(l + w)$$

23. D is correct.

Gauge pressure is the measure of pressure with respect to the atmospheric pressure.

So, if the pressure inside the tire is equal to the air pressure outside, the gauge reads zero.

24. B is correct.

Pressure is measured in force per unit area, which is the force divided by the area.

25. D is correct.

The shear stress is the force per unit area and has units of N/m^2.

26. B is correct.

Because the area of the reservoir is assumed to be essentially infinite, the velocity of the flow at the top of the tank is assumed to be zero.

Using Bernoulli's equation, find the speed through the 3 cm pipe:

$(\frac{1}{2}\rho v^2 + \rho gh)_{out} = (\frac{1}{2}\rho v^2 + \rho gh)_{in}$

$\frac{1}{2}\rho v^2 = \rho gh$, cancel ρ from both sides of the expression

$\frac{1}{2}v^2 = gh$

$v^2 = 2gh$

$v = \sqrt{(2gh)}$

$v = \sqrt{[2(9.8 \text{ m/s}^2)\cdot(4 \text{ m})]}$

$v_{3cm} = 8.9 \text{ m/s}$

To find the speed through the 5 cm pipe use the continuity equation:

$A_{3cm}v_{3cm} = A_{5cm}v_{5cm}$

$(\pi / 4)\cdot(3 \text{ cm})^2\cdot(8.9 \text{ m/s}) = (\pi / 4)\cdot(5 \text{ cm})^2\cdot(v_{5cm})$

$v_{5cm} = 3.2 \text{ m/s}$

27. C is correct.

The ideal gas law is:

$PV = nRT$

where n, R and T are constants.

P is pressure, V is volume, n is the number of particles, R is the ideal gas law constant, and T is temperature.

If $P \rightarrow 3P$,

Then,

$V \rightarrow (1/3)V$ to maintain a constant temperature.

28. D is correct.

$F = PA + F_{cover}$

$P = \rho gh$

$F = \rho ghA + F_{cover}$

$F = [(1,000 \text{ kg/m}^3)\cdot(10 \text{ m/s}^2)\cdot(1 \text{ m})\cdot(1 \text{ m}^2)] + 1,500 \text{ N}$

$F = 11,500 \text{ N}$

29. B is correct.

The buoyant force on a totally submerged object is independent of its depth below the surface (since any increase in the water's density is ignored).

The buoyant force on the ball at a depth of 4 m is 20 N, the same as the buoyant force at 1 m.

When it sits at the bottom of the pool, the two upward forces (i.e., the buoyant force F_B and the normal force F_N), must balance the downward force of gravity.

$$F_B + F_N = F_g$$
$$(20 \text{ N}) + F_N = 80 \text{ N}$$
$$F_N = 80 \text{ N} - 20 \text{ N}$$
$$F_N = 60 \text{ N}$$

30. B is correct.

$$V_{\text{Fluid Displaced}} = \tfrac{1}{2} V_{\text{block}}$$

Buoyant force:

$$F_B = \rho g V$$
$$\rho_F g V_F = \rho_B g V_B, \text{ cancel } g \text{ from both sides of the expression}$$
$$\rho_F V_F = \rho_B V_B$$
$$\rho_F (\tfrac{1}{2} V_B) = \rho_B V_B, \text{ cancel } V_B \text{ from both sides of the expression}$$
$$\tfrac{1}{2} \rho_F = \rho_B$$
$$\rho_F = (1.6) \rho_{\text{water}}$$
$$\rho_B = (1.6) \cdot (10^3 \text{ kg/m}^3) \cdot (\tfrac{1}{2})$$
$$\rho_B = 800 \text{ kg/m}^3$$

31. C is correct.

$$F_{\text{net}} = F_{\text{object}} - F_B$$
$$F_{\text{net}} = mg - \rho_{\text{fluid}} V g$$
$$\rho_{\text{fluid}} = -(F_{\text{net}} - mg) / V_{\text{sphere}} g$$
$$\rho_{\text{fluid}} = -[42 \text{ N} - (9.2 \text{ kg}) \cdot (9.8 \text{ m/s}^2)] / [(9.2 \text{ kg} / 3{,}650 \text{ kg/m3}) \cdot (9.8 \text{ m/s}^2)]$$
$$\rho_{\text{fluid}} = 1{,}950 \text{ kg/m}^3$$

32. A is correct. The pressure due to the density of a fluid surrounding an object submerged at depth *d* below the surface is given by:

$$P = \rho g d$$

Since the distance that the objects are below the surface is not specified, the only conclusion that can be drawn is that object B experiences less fluid pressure than object A. This difference is because object B is higher off the floor of the container and thus its depth is less than object A.

33. B is correct.

$$A_1v_1 = A_2v_2$$
$$A = \pi r^2$$
$$A_2 = \pi(2r)^2$$
$$A_2 = 4\pi r^2$$
$$A_2 = 4A_1$$

If r is doubled, then area is increased by 4 times

$$A_1(14 \text{ m/s}) = (4A_1)v_2$$
$$v_2 = (A_1 \times 14 \text{ m/s}) / (4 \times A_1)$$
$$v_2 = (14 \text{ m/s}) / (4)$$
$$v_2 = 3.5 \text{ m/s}$$

Use Bernoulli's equation to find resulting pressure:

$$P_1 + \tfrac{1}{2}\rho v_1^2 = P_2 + \tfrac{1}{2}\rho v_2^2$$
$$(3.5 \times 10^4 \text{ Pa}) + \tfrac{1}{2}(1{,}000 \text{ kg/m}^3){\cdot}(14 \text{ m/s})^2 = P_2 + \tfrac{1}{2}(1{,}000 \text{ kg/m}^3){\cdot}(3.5 \text{ m/s})^2$$
$$P_2 = (13.3 \times 10^4 \text{ Pa}) - (6.1 \times 10^3 \text{ Pa})$$
$$P_2 = 12.7 \times 10^4 \text{ Pa}$$

34. D is correct.

The pressure due to the atmosphere is equal to its weight per unit area. At an altitude of 2 km, there is less atmosphere pushing down than at the Earth's surface.

Therefore, atmospheric pressure decreases with increasing altitude.

35. C is correct. The buoyant force:

$$F_B = \rho_{air}V_{disp}g, \text{ and } V_{disp} \text{ is the volume of the man } m / \rho_{man}$$
$$F_B = (\rho_{air} / \rho_{man})mg$$
$$F_B = [(1.2 \times 10^{-3} \text{ g/cm}^3) / (1 \text{ g/cm}^3)]{\cdot}(80 \text{ kg}){\cdot}(9.8 \text{ m/s}^2)$$
$$F_B = 0.94 \text{ N}$$

36. D is correct. Graham's law states that the rate at which gas diffuses is inversely proportional to the square root of the density of the gas.

37. D is correct.

$$F_B = \rho Vg$$
$$F_{net} = F_{object} - F_B$$
$$F_{net} = (41{,}800 \text{ N}) - (1{,}000 \text{ kg/m}^3)(4.2 \text{ m}^3)(9.8 \text{ m/s}^2)$$
$$F_{net} = (41{,}800 \text{ N}) - (41{,}160 \text{ N})$$
$$F_{net} = 640 \text{ N}$$

38. D is correct.

$$A = \pi r^2$$

$$A_T v_T = A_P v_P$$

$$v_T = v_P A_P / A_T$$

The ratio of the square of the diameter is equal to the ratio of area:

$$v_T = v_P (d_1 / d_2)^2$$

$$v_T = (0.03 \text{ m/s}) \cdot [(0.12 \text{ m}) / (0.002 \text{ m})]^2$$

$$v_T = 108 \text{ m/s}$$

39. B is correct.

Specific gravity: $\rho_{object} / \rho_{water}$

Archimedes' principle:

$$F = \rho g V$$

$$\rho_{water} = F / g(0.9V)$$

$$\rho_{object} = F / gV$$

$$\rho_{object} / \rho_{water} = (F / gV) / [F / g(0.9V)]$$

$$\rho_{object} / \rho_{water} = 0.9$$

V_{water} is 0.9V because only 90% of the object is in the water, so 90% of the object's volume equals water displaced.

40. C is correct.

The factors considered are length, density, radius, pressure difference, and viscosity.

The continuity equation does not apply here because it can only relate velocity and radius to the flow rate.

Bernoulli's equation does not apply because it only relates density and velocity.

The Hagen-Poiseuille equation is needed because it includes all the terms except for density and therefore is the most applicable to this question.

Volumetric flow rate (Q) is:

$$Q = \Delta P \pi r^4 / 8 \eta L$$

The radius is raised to the fourth power.

A 15% change to r results in the greatest change.

41. A is correct.

A force meter provides a force, and the reading indicates what the force is.

Since the hammer is not accelerating, the force equation is:

$$F_{meter} + F_B - m_h g = 0$$
$$m_h g = (0.68 \text{ kg}) \cdot (10 \text{ m/s}^2)$$
$$m_h g = 6.8 \text{ N}$$

The displaced volume is the volume of the hammer:

$$V_{disp} = m_h / \rho_{steel}$$
$$V_{disp} = (680 \text{ g}) / (7.9 \text{ g/cm}^3)$$
$$V_{disp} = 86 \text{ cm}^3$$
$$F_B = \rho_{water} \times V_{disp} \times g$$
$$F_B = (1 \times 10^{-3} \text{ kg/cm}^3) \cdot (86 \text{ cm}^3) \cdot (10 \text{ m/s}^2)$$
$$F_B = 0.86 \text{ N}$$
$$F_{meter} = m_h g - F_B$$
$$F_{meter} = 6.8 \text{ N} - 0.86 \text{ N}$$
$$F_{meter} = 5.9 \text{ N}$$

42. D is correct.

Pascal's Principle states that pressure is transmitted undiminished in an enclosed static fluid.

43. B is correct.

The normal force exerted by the sea floor is the net force between the weight of the submarine and the buoyant force:

$$F_N = F_{net}$$
$$F_{net} = mg - F_B$$
$$F_{net} = mg - \rho g V$$
$$F_{net} = mg - W_{water}$$
$$F_N = mg - W_{water}$$

44. D is correct.

$$P = \rho g h$$

Because the bottom of the brick is at a lower depth than the rest of the brick, it will experience the highest pressure.

45. A is correct.

Mass flow rate:

$\dot{m}$ = cross-sectional area × density × velocity

$\dot{m} = A_C \rho v$

$\dot{m}$ = (7 m)·(14 m)·(10^3 kg/m^3)·(3 m/s)

$\dot{m} = 2.9 \times 10^5$ kg/s

46. C is correct.

Since the object is motionless:

$a = 0$

$F_{net} = 0$

The magnitude of the buoyant force upward = weight downward:

$F = W$

$F = mg$

F = (3 kg)·(10 m/s^2)

$F = 30$ N

47. A is correct.

$P = P_{atm} + \rho g h$

P = (1.01 × 10^5 Pa) + (10^3 kg/m^3)·(10 m/s^2)·(6 m)

P = (1.01 × 10^5 Pa) + (0.6 × 10^5 Pa)

$P = 1.6 \times 10^5$ Pa

48. B is correct.

density = mass / volume

49. C is correct.

The bulk modulus is defined as how much a material is compressed under a given external pressure:

$B = \Delta P / (\Delta V / V)$

Most solids and liquids compress slightly under external pressure.

However, gases have the highest change in volume and thus the lowest value of B.

50. C is correct.

$$P_1 = P_2 + \rho gh$$

$$F_1 / A_1 = F_2 / A_2 + \rho gh$$

$$F_1 = A_1(F_2 / A_2 + \rho gh)$$

$$F_1 = \pi(0.06 \text{ m})^2 \cdot [(14{,}000 \text{ N}) / \pi(0.16 \text{ m})^2 + (750 \text{ kg/m}^3) \cdot (9.8 \text{ m/s}^2) \cdot (1.5 \text{ m})]$$

$$F_1 = \pi(0.0036 \text{ m}^2) \cdot [(14{,}000 \text{ N}) / \pi(0.0256 \text{ m}^2) + (750 \text{ kg/m}^3) \cdot (9.8 \text{ m/s}^2) \cdot (1.5 \text{ m})]$$

$$F_1 = (0.0036 \text{ m}^2) \cdot [(14{,}000 \text{ N}) / (0.0256 \text{ m}^2) + (11{,}025 \text{ N})\pi]$$

$$F_1 = 1{,}969 \text{ N} + 125 \text{ N}$$

$$F_1 = 2{,}094 \text{ N}$$

51. C is correct.

Solve for density of ice and saltwater:

$$SG = \rho_{substance} / \rho_{water}$$

$$SG_{ice} = 0.98 = \rho_{ice} / 10^3 \text{ kg/m}^3$$

$$\rho_{ice} = 980 \text{ kg/m}^3$$

$$SG_{saltwater} = 1.03 = \rho_{saltwater} / 10^3 \text{ kg/m}^3$$

$$\rho_{saltwater} = 1{,}030 \text{ kg/m}^3$$

Solve for volume of ice:

$$F_B = F_{bear} + F_{ice}$$

$$\rho_{saltwater} V_{ice} g = m_{bear} g + \rho_{ice} V_{ice} g, \text{ cancel } g \text{ from all terms}$$

$$V_{ice} = m_{bear} / (\rho_{saltwater} - \rho_{ice})$$

$$V_{ice} = (240 \text{ kg}) / (1{,}030 \text{ kg/m}^3 - 980 \text{ kg/m}^3)$$

$$V_{ice} = 4.8 \text{ m}^3$$

Solve for area of ice:

$$A = V / h$$

$$A = (4.8 \text{ m}^3) / (1 \text{ m})$$

$$A = 4.8 \text{ m}^2$$

52. B is correct. Absolute pressure is measured relative to absolute zero pressure (perfect vacuum), and gauge pressure is measured relative to atmospheric pressure.

If the atmospheric pressure increases by ΔP, then the absolute pressure increases by ΔP, but the gauge pressure does not change.

Absolute pressure at an arbitrary depth h in the lake:

$$P_{abs} = P_{atm} + \rho_{water} gh$$

Gauge pressure at an arbitrary depth h in the lake:

$P_{gauge} = \rho_{water}gh$

53. C is correct.

$P_{top} = \rho gh$

$P_{top} = 108 \times 10^3$ Pa

$h = (1 / \rho) \cdot (108 \times 10^3$ Pa $/ 9.8$ m/s$^2)$

$h = (1 / \rho) \cdot (11{,}020$ kg/m$^2)$

$P_{bottom} = \rho g(h + 25$ cm$)$

$\rho g(h + 25$ cm$) = 114 \times 10^3$ Pa

$h = (1 / \rho) \cdot (114 \times 10^3$ Pa $/ 9.8$ m/s$^2) - 0.25$ m

$h = (1 / \rho) \cdot (11{,}633) - 0.25$ m

Set equal and solve for ρ:

$(1 / \rho) \cdot (11{,}020$ kg/m$^2) = (1 / \rho) \cdot (11{,}633$ kg/m$^2) - 0.25$ m

$(11{,}020$ kg/m$^2) = (11{,}633$ kg/m$^2) - 0.25$ m(ρ)

0.25 m$(\rho) = 613$ kg/m^2

$\rho = (613$ kg/m$^2) / (0.25$ m$)$

$\rho = 2{,}452$ kg/m^3

54. D is correct.

By Poiseuille's Law:

$v = \Delta Pr^2 / 8\eta L$

$\eta = \Delta Pr^2 / 8Lv_{effective}$

$\eta = (970$ Pa$) \cdot (0.0021$ m$)^2 / 8 \cdot (1.8$ m/s$) \cdot (0.19$ m$)$

$\eta = 0.0016$ N·s/m^2

55. C is correct. Bernoulli's equation:

$P_1 + \frac{1}{2}\rho_1 v_1^2 + \rho_1 gh_1 = P_2 + \frac{1}{2}\rho_2 v_2^2 + \rho_2 gh_2$

There is no height difference, so the equation reduces to:

$P_1 + \frac{1}{2}\rho_1 v_1^2 = P_2 + \frac{1}{2}\rho_2 v_2^2$

If the flow of air across the wing tip is v_1 then:

$v_1 > v_2$

Since the air that flows across the top has a higher velocity, as it travels a larger distance (curved surface of the top) over the same period, then:

$\frac{1}{2}\rho_1 v_1^2 > \frac{1}{2}\rho_2 v_2^2$

To keep both sides equal:

$P_1 < P_2$

$\Delta P = (P_2 - P_1)$

Thus, the lower portion of the wing experiences greater pressure and therefore lifts the wing.

56. A is correct.

57. B is correct.

The Bulk Modulus is expressed as:

$B = \Delta P / (\Delta V / V)$

$B = (\Delta P V) / \Delta V$

Solve for ΔV:

$\Delta V = (\Delta P V) / B$

$\Delta V = (10^7 \text{ N/m}^2) \cdot (1 \text{ m}^3) / (2.3 \times 10^9 \text{ N/m}^2)$

$\Delta V = 0.0043 \text{ m}^3$

58. B is correct.

Pascal's Principle states that pressure is transmitted undiminished in an enclosed static fluid. This principle makes hydraulic lift possible because, for equal pressure across a fluid, force can be multiplied through an area difference:

$P_1 = P_2$

$F_1 / A_1 = F_2 / A_2$

$F_1 = (A_1 / A_2)F_2$

59. A is correct.

Gauge pressure is referenced relative to atmospheric pressure and is calculated by:

$P_{gauge} = \rho g h$

$P_{gauge} = (1{,}025 \text{ kg/m}^3) \cdot (9.8 \text{ m/s}^2) \cdot (11{,}030 \text{ m})$

$P_{gauge} = 1.1 \times 10^8 \text{ Pa}$

60. D is correct.

$P = \rho g h$

$P = (10^3 \text{ kg/m}^3) \cdot (9.8 \text{ m/s}^2) \cdot (1 \text{ m})$

$P = 9{,}800 \text{ Pa} \approx 1 \times 10^4 \text{ Pa}$

Electrostatics and Magnetism – Explanations

1. C is correct. Since charge is quantized, the charge Q must be a whole number (n) times the charge on a single electron:

Charge = # electrons × electron charge

$Q = n(e^-)$

$n = Q / e^-$

$n = (-1 \text{ C}) / (-1.6 \times 10^{-19} \text{ C})$

$n = 6.25 \times 10^{18} \approx 6.3 \times 10^{18}$ electrons

2. D is correct.

In Gaus's Law, the area is a vector perpendicular to the plane. Only the component of the electric field strength parallel is used.

Gaus's Law:

$\Phi = EA \cos \theta$

where Φ is electric flux (scalar), E is electric field strength, and A is area vector.

Solve:

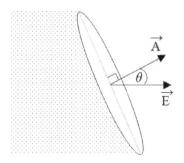

$\Phi = EA \cos (\pi / 6)$

$A = \pi r^2 = \pi D^2 / 4$

$\Phi = (740 \text{ N/C}) \cdot (\pi / 4) \cdot (1 \text{ m})^2 \cos (\pi / 6)$

$\Phi = 160\pi \text{ N·m}^2/\text{C}$

For calculation, use radians mode, not degree mode.

3. A is correct.

The magnitude of the negative charge's electric field:

$|E_2| = kQ_2 / d_2^2$

$|E_2| = (9 \times 10^9 \text{ N·m}^2/\text{C}^2) \cdot [(-1.3 \times 10^{-9} \text{ C}) / (+10^{-3} \text{ m})^2]$

$|E_2| = 1.17 \times 10^7 \text{ N/C}$ to the left

The magnitude of the positive charge's electric field:

$|E_1| = kQ_1 / d_1^2$

$|E_1| = (9 \times 10^9 \text{ N·m}^2/\text{C}^2) \cdot [(1.3 \times 10^{-9} \text{ C}) / (2 \times 10^{-3} \text{ m})^2]$

$|E_1| = 2.9 \times 10^6 \text{ N/C}$ to the right

$\Delta E = E_2 - E_1$

$\Delta E = (1.17 \times 10^7 \text{ N/C}) - (2.9 \times 10^6 \text{ N/C})$

$\Delta E = 8.8 \times 10^6 \text{ N/C}$, to the left

---

4. C is correct. Coulomb's law:

$$F_1 = kQ_1Q_2 / r^2$$

If r is increased by a factor of 4:

$$F_e = kQ_1Q_2 / (4r)^2$$

$$F_e = kQ_1Q_2 / (16r^2)$$

$$F_e = (1/16)kQ_1Q_2 / r^2$$

$$F_e = (1/16)F_1$$

As the distance increases by a factor of 4, the force decreases by a factor of $4^2 = 16$.

5. B is correct. Calculate the distance between two charges using the Pythagorean Theorem:

$$r^2 = (1 \text{ nm})^2 + (4 \text{ nm})^2$$

$$r^2 = 17 \text{ nm}^2$$

$$r = 4.1 \text{ nm}$$

$$F = kQ_1Q_2 / r^2$$

$$F = [(9 \times 10^9 \text{ N·m}^2/\text{C}^2)·(1.6 \times 10^{-19} \text{ C})·(1.6 \times 10^{-19} \text{ C})] / (4.1 \times 10^{-9} \text{ m})^2$$

$$F = 1.4 \times 10^{-11} \text{ N}$$

6. A is correct.

7. D is correct. Use a coordinate system in which a repulsive force is in the positive direction, and an attractive force is in the negative direction.

Gravitational Force: F_g

$$F_g = -Gm_1m_2 / r^2$$

$$F_g = -[(6.673 \times 10^{-11} \text{ N·m}^2/\text{kg}^2)·(54,000 \text{ kg})·(51,000 \text{ kg})] / (180 \text{ m})^2$$

$$F_g = -0.18 \text{ N·m}^2 / (32,400 \text{ m}^2)$$

$$F_g = -5.7 \times 10^{-6} \text{ N}$$

Electrostatic Force: F_e

$$F_e = kQ_1Q_2 / r^2$$

$$F_e = [(9 \times 10^9 \text{ N·m}^2/\text{C}^2)·(-15 \times 10^{-6} \text{ C})·(-11 \times 10^{-6} \text{ C})] / (180 \text{ m})^2$$

$$F_e = (1.49 \text{ N·m}^2) / (32,400 \text{ m}^2)$$

$$F_e = 4.6 \times 10^{-5} \text{ N}$$

Net Force:

$$F_{net} = F_g + F_e$$

$$F_{net} = (-5.7 \times 10^{-6} \text{ N}) + (4.6 \times 10^{-5} \text{ N})$$

$$F_{net} = 4 \times 10^{-5} \text{ N}$$

F_{net} is positive, which means there is a net repulsive force on the asteroids. In other words, the repulsive electrostatic force between them is stronger than the attractive gravitational force.

8. B is correct. Newton's Third Law states for every force there is an equal and opposite reaction force. This also applies to electrostatic forces.

Electrostatic Force:

$$F_1 = kQ_1Q_2 / r^2$$
$$F_2 = kQ_1Q_2 / r^2$$
$$F_1 = F_2$$

9. D is correct. Forces balance to yield:

$$F_{electric} = F_{gravitation}$$
$$F_{electric} = mg$$

The values for an electric field are provided.

$$F_{electric} = QE$$
$$F_{electric} - F_{gravitation} = 0$$
$$QE - mg = 0, \text{ where } Q \text{ is the charge on the ball}$$
$$QE = mg$$
$$Q = mg / E$$
$$Q = (0.008 \text{ kg}) \cdot (9.8 \text{ m/s}^2) / (3.5 \times 10^4 \text{ N/C})$$
$$Q = -2.2 \times 10^{-6} \text{ C}$$

If the electric field points down, then a positive charge experiences a downward force.

The charge must be negative, so the electric force balances gravity.

10. A is correct. $a = qE / m$

The electron moves against the electric field, in the upward direction, so its acceleration:

$$a_e = qE / m_e$$

The proton moves with the electric field, which is down, so:

$$a_p = qE / m_p$$

However, the masses considered are small to where the gravity component is negligible.

$$m_p / m_e = (1.67 \times 10^{-27} \text{ kg}) / (9.11 \times 10^{-31} \text{ kg})$$
$$m_p / m_e = 1,830$$

The mass of an electron is about 1,830 times smaller than the mass of a proton.

$$(1,830)m_e = m_p$$
$$a_p = qE / (1,830)m_e$$
$$a_p = a_e / (1,830)$$
$$a_e = 1,830a_p$$

11. D is correct.

Calculate the strength of the field at point P due to only one charge:

$E = kQ / r^2$

$E_1 = (9 \times 10^9 \text{ N·m}^2/\text{C}^2)\cdot[(2.3 \times 10^{-11} \text{ C}) / (5 \times 10^{-3} \text{ m})^2]$

$E_1 = 8.3 \times 10^3 \text{ N/C}$

Both electric field vectors point toward the negative charge, so the magnitude of each field at point P is doubled:

$E_T = 2E_1$

$E_T = 2(8.3 \times 10^3 \text{ N/C})$

$E_T = 1.7 \times 10^4 \text{ N/C}$

12. A is correct.

charge = # electrons × electron charge

$Q = ne^-$

$n = Q / e^-$

$n = (-10 \times 10^{-6} \text{ C}) / (-1.6 \times 10^{-19} \text{ C})$

$n = 6.3 \times 10^{13}$ electrons

13. C is correct.

Coulomb's law:

$F_e = kQ_1Q_2 / r^2$

If the separation is halved, then r decreases by ½:

$F_2 = kq_1q_2 / (½r)^2$

$F_2 = 4(kq_1q_2 / r^2)$

$F_2 = 4F_e$

14. D is correct.

Coulomb's law:

$F = kQ_1Q_2 / r^2$

Doubling both the charges and distance:

$F = [k(2Q_1)\cdot(2Q_2)] / (2r)^2$

$F = [4k(Q_1)\cdot(Q_2)] / (4r^2)$

$F = (4/4)[kQ_1Q_2 / (r^2)]$

$F = kQ_1Q_2 / r^2$, remains the same

15. D is correct.

Like charges repel each other.

From Newton's Third Law, the magnitude of the force experienced by each charge is equal.

16. A is correct. Coulomb's law:

$$F = kQ_1Q_2 / r^2$$

The Coulomb force between opposite charges is attractive.

Since the strength of the force is inversely proportional to the square of the separation distance (r^2), the force decreases as the charges are pulled apart.

17. B is correct.

Currents occur in a conducting circuit element when there is a potential difference between the two ends of the element, and hence an established electric field.

18. D is correct.

Voltage is related to the number of coils in a wire. More coils yield a higher voltage.

Turns ratio:

$$V_s / V_p = n_s / n_p$$

In this case:

$$n_s < n_p$$

Therefore,

$$V_s < V_p$$

Because the secondary voltage (V_s) is lower than the primary voltage (V_p) the transformer is a step-down transformer.

19. B is correct. Coulomb's Law:

$$F_1 = kQ_1Q_2 / r^2$$
$$F_2 = kQ_1Q_2 / r^2$$
$$F_1 = F_2$$

Newton's Third Law: the force exerted by one charge on the other has the same magnitude as the force the other exerts on the first.

20. C is correct.

$$F_e = kQ_1Q_2 / r^2$$
$$F_e = (9 \times 10^9 \text{ N·m}^2/\text{C}^2) \cdot (-1.6 \times 10^{-19} \text{ C}) \cdot (-1.6 \times 10^{-19} \text{ C}) / (0.03 \text{ m})^2$$
$$F_e = 2.56 \times 10^{-25} \text{ N}$$

21. A is correct.

According to Lenz's Law, inserting a magnet into the coil causes the magnetic flux through the coil to change.

This produces an emf in the coil which drives a current through the coil:

Lenz's Law:

$$\text{emf} = -N\Delta BA / \Delta t$$

The brightness of the bulb changes with a change in the current, but it cannot be known if the bulb gets brighter or dimmer without knowing the orientation of the coil with respect to the incoming magnetic pole of the magnet.

22. C is correct.

Charge = # electrons × electron charge

$$Q = ne^-$$
$$n = Q / e^-$$
$$n = (8 \times 10^{-6}\,\text{C}) / (1.6 \times 10^{-19}\,\text{C})$$
$$n = 5 \times 10^{13} \text{ electrons}$$

23. A is correct.

An object with a charge can attract another object of opposite charge or a neutral charge.

Like charges cannot attract, but the type of charge does not matter otherwise.

24. B is correct.

$$1 \text{ amp} = 1 \text{ C} / \text{s}$$

The ampere is the unit to express flow rate of electric charge known as current.

25. A is correct.

Initially, the current flows clockwise, but after 180° of rotation, the current reverses.

After 360° of rotation, the current will reverse itself again.

Thus, there are 2 current reverses in 1 revolution.

26. D is correct.

$$W = Q\Delta V$$
$$V = kQ / r$$

Consider the charge Q_1 to be fixed and move charge Q_2 from initial distance r_i to final distance r_f.

$$W = Q_2(V_f - V_i)$$

$W = Q_2[(kQ_1 / r_f) - (kQ_1 / r_i)]$

$W = kQ_1Q_2(1 / r_f - 1 / r_i)$

$W = (9 \times 10^9 \text{ N·m}^2/\text{C})·(2.3 \times 10^{-8} \text{ C})·(2.5 \times 10^{-9} \text{ C})·[(1 / 0.01 \text{ m}) - (1 / 0.1 \text{ m})]$

$W = 4.7 \times 10^{-5} \text{ J}$

27. C is correct.

The electric field is oriented in a way that a positively-charged particle would be forced to move to the top because negatively-charged particles move to the bottom of the cube to be closer to the source of the electric field.

Therefore, all the positively charged particles are forced upward and the negatively-charged ones downward, leaving the top surface positively charged.

28. C is correct.

The magnitude of the force between the center charge and each charge at a vertex is 5 N. The net force of these two forces is directed toward the third vertex.

To determine the magnitude of the net force, calculate the magnitude of the component of each force acting in that direction:

$F_{net} = F_1 \sin (\tfrac{1}{2} \theta) + F_2 \sin (\tfrac{1}{2} \theta)$ (see diagram)

Since it is an equilateral triangle $\theta = 60°$,

$F_{net} = (5 \text{ N} \sin 30°) + (5 \text{ N} \sin 30°)$

$F_{net} = (5 \text{ N})·(\tfrac{1}{2}) + (5 \text{ N})·(\tfrac{1}{2})$

$F_{net} = 5 \text{ N}$

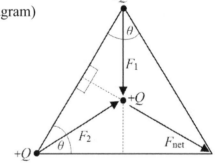

29. D is correct.

Equilibrium:

$F = kq_1q_2 / r_1^2$

$F_{\text{attractive on } q2} = F_{\text{repulsive on } q2}$

$kq_1q_2 / r_1^2 = kq_2Q / r_2^2$

$q_1 = Qr_1^2 / r_2^2$

$q_1 = (7.5 \times 10^{-9} \text{ C})·(0.2 \text{ m})^2 / (0.1 \text{ m})^2$

$q_1 = 30 \times 10^{-9} \text{ C}$

30. A is correct.

Gamma rays have the highest frequency on the electromagnetic spectrum, with frequencies greater than $3 \times 10^{19} \text{ Hz}$.

31. A is correct.

The strength of the electrostatic field due to a single point charge is given by:

$E = kQ / r^2$, assumes that the source charge is in vacuum

E depends on both the magnitude of the source charge Q and the distance r from Q.

The sign of the source charge affects only the direction of the electrostatic field vectors.

The sign of the source charge does not affect the strength of the field.

32. B is correct.

$$F = qvB$$
$$F = mv^2 / r$$
$$mv^2 / r = qvB, \text{ cancel } v \text{ from both sides of the expression}$$
$$mv / r = qB$$
$$r = (mv) / (qB)$$

If the velocity doubles, the radius also doubles.

33. C is correct. Coulomb's law:

$$F_e = kQ_1Q_2 / r^2$$
$$1 \text{ N} = kQ_1Q_2 / r^2$$

Doubling charges and keeping distance constant:

$$k(2Q_1) \cdot (2Q_2) / r^2 = 4kQ_1Q_2 / r^2$$
$$4kQ_1Q_2 / r^2 = 4F_e$$
$$4F_e = 4(1 \text{ N}) = 4 \text{ N}$$

34. D is correct.

The Na^+ ion is positively charged and attracts the oxygen atom.

Oxygen is slightly negative because it is more electronegative than the hydrogen atoms to which it is bonded.

35. C is correct.

Charge = # of electrons × electron charge

$$Q = ne^-$$
$$Q = (30) \cdot (-1.6 \times 10^{-19} \text{ C})$$
$$Q = -4.8 \times 10^{-18} \text{ C}$$

36. A is correct.

Cyclotron frequency is given as:

$f = qB / 2\pi m$

This expression does not consider speed.

37. B is correct.

The repulsive force between two particles is:

$F = kQ_1Q_2 / r^2$

As r increases, F decreases

Using $F = ma$, a also decreases

38. A is correct.

The given unit can be written $[\text{kg·m}^2/\text{s}^2] / \text{C} = \text{J} / \text{C}$, which is the definition of the Volt, the unit of electric potential difference.

39. C is correct.

The Coulomb is the basic unit of electrical charge in the SI unit system.

40. A is correct.

By the Law of Conservation of Charge, a charge cannot be created nor destroyed.

41. B is correct.

Coulomb's Law:

$F = kQ_1Q_2 / r^2$

If both charges are doubled,

$F = k(2Q_1)·(2Q_2) / r^2$

$F = 4kQ_1Q_2 / r^2$

F increases by a factor of 4.

42. C is correct.

Coulomb's law:

$$F = kQ_1Q_2 \,/\, r^2$$

$$Q_1 = Q_2$$

Therefore:

$$Q_1Q_2 = Q^2$$

$$F = kQ^2 \,/\, r^2$$

Rearranging:

$$Q^2 = Fr^2 \,/\, k$$

$$Q = \surd(Fr^2 \,/\, k)$$

$$Q = \surd[(4\text{ N})\cdot(0.01\text{ m})^2 \,/\, (9 \times 10^9\text{ N}\cdot\text{m}^2/\text{C}^2)]$$

$$Q = 2 \times 10^{-7}\text{ C}$$

43. A is correct.

Faraday's law states that electromotive force (emf) is equal to the rate of change of magnetic flux. Magnetic flux is the product of the magnetic field and projected area:

$$\Phi = BA_{\perp},$$

where $A_{\perp}$ is the area of the loop projected on a plane perpendicular to the magnetic field.

In this problem, B is vertical (and constant), so the projection plane is horizontal.

Therefore, find the orientation of the axis of rotation that guarantees that as the loop rotates, the projection of its area on a horizontal plane does not change with time.

Notice that if the orientation of the axis is at an arbitrary angle to the field, the emf can be made to be zero by aligning the axis of rotation with the axis of the loop (i.e., perpendicular to the loop). With this orientation, the projection of the area never changes, which is not true of other alignments to the loop.

Although the emf can be made to be zero, it is not *guaranteed* to be zero.

The only orientation of the axis that *guarantees* that the projected area is constant is the vertical orientation. One way to see this is to notice that because of the high symmetry of the vertical-axis orientation, rotating the loop about a vertical axis is equivalent to changing the perspective of the viewer from one angle to another.

The answer cannot depend on the viewer's perspective. Therefore, the projected area cannot change as the loop is rotated about the vertical axis; the emf is guaranteed to be zero.

44. C is correct.

Coulomb's law:

$$F = kQ_1Q_2 / r^2$$

When each particle has lost ½ its charge:

$$F_2 = k(½Q_1)\cdot(½Q_2) / r^2$$
$$F_2 = (¼)kQ_1Q_2 / r^2$$
$$F_2 = (¼)F$$

F decreases by a factor of ¼

45. B is correct.

The time taken for one revolution around the circular path is $T = 2\pi R/v$, where R is the radius of the circle and v is the speed of the proton.

If the speed is increased, the radius also increases.

The relationship between speed and radius follows from the fact that the magnetic interaction provides the centripetal force:

$$mv^2/ R = qvB$$

Thus:

$$R = mv / qB.$$

If the speed is tripled, the radius triples, all other thigs being equal. The final period for a revolution is:

$$T_f = 2\pi R_f / v_f = 2\pi(3R) / 3v = 2\pi R / v = T$$

46. C is correct.

An electrostatic field shows the path that would be taken by a positively-charged particle.

As this positive particle moves closer to the negatively-charged one, the force between them increases.

Coulomb's law:

$$F = kQ_1Q_2 / r^2$$

By convention, electric field vectors always point towards negative source charges.

Since electrical field strength is inversely proportional to the square of the distance from the source charge, the magnitude of the electric field progressively increases as an object moves towards the source charge.

47. D is correct.

Protons are charges, so they have an electric field.

Protons have mass, so they have a gravitational field.

Protons have an intrinsic magnetic moment, so they have a magnetic field.

48. A is correct.

$$W = Q\Delta V$$

$$V = kq / r$$

$$W = (kQq)\cdot(1 / r_2 - 1 / r_1)$$

$$W = (kQq)\cdot(1 / 2 \text{ m} - 1 / 6 \text{ m})$$

$$W = (kQq)\cdot(1 / 3 \text{ m})$$

$$W = (9 \times 10^9 \text{ N·m}^2/\text{C}^2)\cdot(3.1 \times 10^{-5} \text{ C})\cdot(-10^{-6} \text{ C}) / (1 / 3 \text{ m})$$

$$W = -0.093 \text{ J} \approx -0.09 \text{ J}$$

The negative sign indicates that the electric field does the work on charge q.

49. D is correct.

charge = # electrons × electron charge

$$Q = ne^-$$

$$n = Q / e^-$$

$$n = (-600 \times 10^{-9} \text{ C}) / (-1.6 \times 10^{-19} \text{ C})$$

$$n = 3.8 \times 10^{12} \text{ electrons}$$

50. C is correct.

The analog to N/kg would be N/C, the unit for the electric field.

51. D is correct.

All the electromagnetic waves travel through space (vacuum) at the same speed:

$$c = 3 \times 10^8 \text{ m/s}$$

52. A is correct.

As the proton of charge q moves in the direction of the electric field lines, it moves away from a positive charge (because field lines emanate from positive charge).

Electric Potential Energy:

$$U = kQq / r$$

As distance increases, the potential energy decreases because they are inversely proportional.

Electrical potential:

$$V = kQ / r$$

Electrical potential is inversely proportional to distance and decreases as distance increases.

53. B is correct. 1 watt = 1 J/s

54. D is correct.

An object that is electrically polarized has had its charge separated into opposites and thus rearrange themselves within distinct regions.

55. A is correct.

Because point P is symmetric about Q_1 and Q_2 and both charges have the same positive magnitude, the electric field cancels midway between the charges.

$$E = kQ / r^2$$

$$E_1 = -E_2$$

$$E_{tot} = E_1 + E_2$$

$$E_{tot} = (-E_2 + E_2)$$

$$E_{tot} = 0 \text{ N/C}$$

56. C is correct.

Force due to motion:

$$F = ma$$

$$F = (0.001 \text{ kg}) \cdot (440 \text{ m/s}^2)$$

$$F = 0.44 \text{ N}$$

Force due to charge:

$$F = kQ_1Q_2 / r^2$$

$$Q_1 = Q_2$$

$$Q_1Q_2 = Q^2$$

$$F = kQ^2 / r^2$$

Rearranging:

$$Q^2 = Fr^2 / k$$

$$Q = \sqrt{(Fr^2 / k)}$$

$$Q = \sqrt{[(0.44 \text{ N}) \cdot (0.02 \text{ m})^2 / (9 \times 10^9 \text{ N} \cdot \text{m}^2/\text{C}^2)]}$$

$$Q = 1.4 \times 10^{-7} \text{ C} = 140 \text{ nC}$$

57. D is correct.

A sphere or any conduction object that acquires a net charge has the charge collect on the surface. This is due to excess charge repelling itself and moving to the surface to increase the distance between themselves.

58. B is correct.

$F = kQ_1Q_2 / r^2$

	Force from +	Force from −
x-direction	→	→
y-direction	↑	↓

Net force = →

59. A is correct.

A charged particle only experiences a magnetic force if it moves with a perpendicular velocity component to the field. Thus, there must not be a magnetic field, or the particle moves parallel to the field.

60. B is correct.

Coulomb's law: the strength of the electrostatic force between two point charges.

$F = kQ_1Q_2 / r^2$

$F = [(9 \times 10^9 \text{ N·m}^2/\text{C}^2)·(+3 \text{ C})·(-12 \text{ C})] / (0.5 \text{ m})^2$

$F = -1.3 \times 10^{12} \text{ N}$

F is positive to indicate an attractive force; therefore, the magnitude of the force is: $1.3 \times 10^{12} \text{ N}$.

Circuit Elements – Explanations

1. B is correct.

$R = \rho L / A$, where ρ is the resistivity of the wire material.

If the length L is doubled, the resistance R is doubled.

If the radius r is doubled, the area $A = \pi r^2$ is quadrupled, and resistance R is decreased by ¼.

If these two changes are combined:

$R_{new} = \rho(2L) / \pi(2r)^2$

$R_{new} = (2/4)\cdot(\rho L / \pi r^2)$

$R_{new} = (2/4)R = \frac{1}{2}R$

2. D is correct.

Internal resistance of battery is in series with resistors in circuit:

$R_{eq} = R_1 + R_{battery}$

where R_{eq} is equivalent resistance and R_1 is resistor connected to battery

$V = IR_{eq}$

$V = I(R_1 + R_{battery})$

$R_{battery} = V / I - R_1$

$R_{battery} = (12 \text{ V} / 0.6 \text{ A}) - 6 \text{ } \Omega$

$R_{battery} = 14 \text{ } \Omega$

3. C is correct.

An ohm Ω is defined as the resistance between two points of a conductor when a constant potential difference of 1 V, applied to these points, produces in the conductor a current of 1 A.

A series circuit experiences the same current through all resistors regardless of their resistance.

However, the voltage across each resistor can be different.

Since the light bulbs are in series, the current through them is the same.

4. D is correct.

$V = kQ / r$

$V_B = kQ / r_B$

$V_B = (9 \times 10^9 \text{ N·m}^2/\text{C}^2)\cdot(1 \times 10^{-6} \text{ C}) / 3.5 \text{ m}$

$V_B = 2{,}571 \text{ V}$

$V_A = kQ / r_A$

$V_A = (9 \times 10^9 \text{ N·m}^2/\text{C}^2)\cdot(1 \times 10^{-6} \text{ C}) / 8 \text{ m}$

$$V_A = 1,125 \text{ V}$$

Potential difference:

$$\Delta V = V_B - V_A$$

$$\Delta V = 2,571 \text{ V} - 1,125 \text{ V}$$

$$\Delta V = 1,446 \text{ V}$$

5. D is correct.

The capacitance of a parallel place capacitor demonstrates the influence of material, separation distance and geometry in determining the overall capacitance.

$$C = k\varepsilon_0 A \, / \, d$$

where k = dielectric constant or permittivity of material between the plates, A = surface area of the conductor and d = distance of plate separation.

6. A is correct.

$$E = qV$$

$$E = \tfrac{1}{2}m(\Delta v)^2$$

$$qV = \tfrac{1}{2}m(v_f^2 - v_i^2)$$

$$v_f^2 = (2qV \, / \, m) + v_i^2$$

$$v_f^2 = [2(1.6 \times 10^{-19} \text{ C}) \cdot (100 \text{ V}) \, / \, (1.67 \times 10^{-27} \text{ kg})] + (1.5 \times 10^5 \text{ m/s})^2$$

$$v_f^2 = (1.9 \times 10^{10} \text{ m}^2/\text{s}^2) + (2.3 \times 10^{10} \text{ m}^2/\text{s}^2)$$

$$v_f^2 = 4.2 \times 10^{10} \text{ m}^2/\text{s}^2$$

$$v_f = 2.04 \times 10^5 \text{ m/s} \approx 2 \times 10^5 \text{ m/s}$$

7. C is correct.

$$\text{Power} = \text{current}^2 \times \text{resistance}$$

$$P = I^2 R$$

Double current:

$$P_2 = (2I)^2 R$$

$$P_2 = 4(I^2 R)$$

$$P_2 = 4P$$

Power is quadrupled

8. D is correct.

A magnetic field is created only by electric charges in motion.

A stationary charged particle does not generate a magnetic field.

9. B is correct. Combining the power equation with Ohm's law:

$P = (\Delta V)^2 / R$, where $\Delta V = 120$ V is a constant

To increase power, decrease the resistance.

A longer wire increases resistance, while a thicker wire decreases it:

$A = \pi r^2$

$R = \rho L / A$

Larger radius of the cross-sectional area means A is larger (denominator) which lowers *R*.

10. C is correct.

$W = k q_1 q_2 / r$

$r = \Delta x$

$r = 2$ mm $- (- 2$ mm$)$

$r = 4$ mm

$W = [(9 \times 10^9$ N·m^2/C^2)·$(4 \times 10^{-6}$ C$)$·$(8 \times 10^{-6}$ C$)] / (4 \times 10^{-3}$ m$)$

$W = (0.288$ N·m$^2) / (4 \times 10^{-3}$ m$)$

$W = 72$ J

11. A is correct.

$V = IR$

$I = V / R$

$I = (220$ V$) / (400 \ \Omega)$

$I = 0.55$ A

12. B is correct.

A parallel circuit experiences the same potential difference across each resistor.

However, the current through each resistor can be different.

13. D is correct.

$E = qV$

$E = \tfrac{1}{2}mv^2$

$qV = \tfrac{1}{2}mv^2$

$v^2 = 2qV / m$

$v^2 = [2(1.6 \times 10^{-19}$ C$)$·$(990$ V$)] / (9.11 \times 10^{-31}$ kg$)$

$v^2 = 3.5 \times 10^{14}$ m^2/s^2

$v = 1.9 \times 10^7$ m/s

14. B is correct. Calculate magnetic field perpendicular to loop:

$B_{Perp2} = (12\ T)\cos 30°$

$B_{Perp2} = 10.4\ T$

$B_{Perp1} = (1\ T)\cos 30°$

$B_{Perp1} = 0.87\ T$

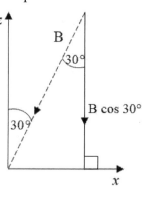

Use Faraday's Law to calculate generated voltage:

$V = N\Delta BA\ /\ \Delta t$

$V = N\Delta B(\pi r^2)\ /\ \Delta t$

$V = [(1)\cdot(10.4\ T - 0.87\ T)\cdot(\pi(0.5\ m)^2)]\ /\ (5\ s - 0\ s)$

$V = [(1)\cdot(10.4\ T - 0.87\ T)\cdot(0.785\ m^2)]\ /\ (5\ s)$

$V = 1.5\ V$

Use Ohm's Law to calculate current:

$V = IR$

$I = V\ /\ R$

$I = (1.5\ V)\ /\ (12\ \Omega)$

$I = 0.13\ A$

15. C is correct. Ohm's Law:

$V = IR$

$V = (10\ A)\cdot(35\ \Omega)$

$V = 350\ V$

16. A is correct.

The magnitude of the acceleration is given by:

$F = ma$

$a = F\ /\ m$

$F = qE_0$

$a = qE_0\ /\ m$

Bare nuclei = no electrons

^{1}H has 1 proton, and ^{4}He has 2 protons and 2 neutrons

Thus, ^{1}H has ½ the charge and ¼ the mass of ^{4}He.

$a_H = q_H E_0\ /\ m_H$

$a_{He} = q_{He}E_0\ /\ m_{He}$

$a_H = (½q_{He})E_0\ /\ (¼m_{He})$

$a_H = 2(q_{He}E_0\ /\ m_{He})$

$a_H = 2a_{He}$

17. B is correct.

The current will change as the choice of lamp arrangement changes.

Since $P = V^2/R$, power increases as resistance decreases.

To rank the power in increasing order, the equivalent resistance must be ranked in decreasing order.

For arrangement B, the resistors are in series, so:

$R_{eq} = R + R = 2R$

For arrangement C, the resistors are in parallel, so:

$1/R_{eq} = 1/R + 1/R$

$R_{eq} = R/2$

The ranking of resistance in decreasing order is B to A to C, which is, therefore, the ranking of power in increasing order.

18. D is correct.

$C = k\varepsilon_0 A / d$

where k = dielectric constant or permittivity of material between the plates, A = area and d = distance of plate separation

$C = (2.1){\cdot}(8.854 \times 10^{-12} \text{ F/m}){\cdot}(0.01 \text{ m} \times 0.01 \text{ m}) / (0.001 \text{ m})$

$C = (1.9 \times 10^{-15} \text{ F/m}) / (0.001 \text{ m})$

$C = 1.9 \times 10^{-12} \text{ F} = 1.9 \text{ pF}$

19. C is correct.

Resistor R_1 is connected directly across the battery.

Thus, the voltage across R_1 is V and is held constant at that value regardless of whatever happens in the circuit.

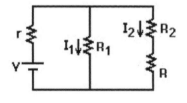

Similarly, the voltage across the series combination of R and R_2 is also held constant at V.

Since the voltage across R_1 will always be V, the current I_1 through R_1 will be unchanged as R changes (since R_1 didn't change, so $I_1 = V / R_1$ remains the same).

Since the voltage across the combination of R and R_2 will always be V, when R is decreased the effective resistance of the series combination $R + R_2$ will decrease, and the current I_2 through R_2 will increase.

20. C is correct.

$$V = IR$$

$$I = V / R$$

Ohm's law states that the current between two points is directly proportional to the potential difference between the points.

21. B is correct.

Root mean square voltage equation:

$$V_{rms} = V_{max} / \sqrt{2}$$

$$V_{rms} = 12 / \sqrt{2}$$

$$V_{rms} = (12 / \sqrt{2}) \cdot (\sqrt{2} / \sqrt{2})$$

$$V_{rms} = (12\sqrt{2}) / 2$$

$$V_{rms} = 6\sqrt{2} \text{ V}$$

22. C is correct.

By definition:

$$V_{rms} = V_{max} / \sqrt{2}$$

Therefore:

$$V_{max} = V_{rms}\sqrt{2}$$

$$V_{max} = (150 \text{ V})\sqrt{2}$$

$$V_{max} = 212 \text{ V}$$

23. D is correct. Kirchhoff's junction rule states that the sum of all currents coming into a junction is the sum of all currents leaving a junction. This is a statement of conservation of charge because it defines that no charge is created nor destroyed in the circuit.

24. A is correct. The capacitance of capacitors connected in parallel is the sum of the individual capacitances:

$$C_{eq} = C_1 + C_2 + C_3 + C_4 = 4C$$

The relationship between the total charge delivered by the battery and the voltage of the battery is:

$$V = Q / C_{eq} = Q / 4C$$

The charge on one capacitor is:

$$Q_1 = CV$$

$$Q_1 = C (Q / 4C)$$

$$Q_1 = Q / 4$$

25. B is correct.

If two conductors are connected by copper wire, each conductor will be at the same potential because current can flow through the wire and equalize the difference in potential.

26. C is correct.

Electromagnetic induction is the production of an electromotive force across a conductor.

When a changing magnetic field is brought near a coil, a voltage is generated in the coil thus inducing a current.

The voltage generated can be calculated by Faraday's Law:

emf = $-N\Delta\phi$ / Δt

where N = number of turns and $\Delta\phi$ = change in magnetic flux

27. A is correct.

Current is constant across resistors connected in series.

28. D is correct.

By convention, the direction of electric current is the direction that a positive charge migrates.

Therefore, current flows from the point of high potential to the point of lower potential.

29. B is correct.

$PE_e = PE_1 + PE_2 + PE_3$

$PE_e = (kQ_1Q_2) / r_1 + (kQ_2Q_3) / r_2 + (kQ_1Q_3) / r_3$

$PE_e = kQ^2 [(1 / r_1) + (1 / r_2) + (1 / r_3)]$

$r_1 = 4$ cm and $r_2 = 3$ cm are known, use Pythagorean Theorem to find r_3:

$r_3^2 = r_1^2 + r_2^2$

$r_3^2 = (4 \text{ cm})^2 + (3 \text{ cm})^2$

$r_3^2 = 16 \text{ cm}^2 + 9 \text{ cm}^2$

$r_3^2 = 25 \text{ cm}^2$

$r_3 = 5$ cm

$PE_e = (9.0 \times 10^9 \text{ N·m}^2/\text{C}^2)\cdot(3.8 \times 10^{-9} \text{ C})^2 \times [(1 / 0.04 \text{ m}) + (1 / 0.03 \text{ m}) + (1 / 0.05 \text{ m})]$

$PE_e = (1.2 \times 10^{-7} \text{ N·m}^2)\cdot(25 \text{ m}^{-1} + 33 \text{ m}^{-1} + 20 \text{ m}^{-1})$

$PE_e = (1.2 \times 10^{-7} \text{ N·m}^2)\cdot(78 \text{ m}^{-1})$

$PE_e = 1.0 \times 10^{-5} \text{ J}$

30. A is correct.

The magnetic force acting on a charge q moving at velocity v in a magnetic field B is given by:

$$F = qv \times B$$

If q, v, and the angle between v and B are the same for both charges, then the magnitude of the force F is the same on both charges.

However, if the charges carry opposite signs, each experiences oppositely-directed forces.

31. C is correct. By convention, the direction of electric current is the direction that a positive charge migrates.

Electrons flow from regions of low potential to regions of high potential.

Electric Potential Energy:

$$U = (kQq) / r$$

Electric Potential:

$$V = (kQ) / r$$

Because the charge of an electron (q) is negative, as the electron moves opposite to the electric field, it must be getting closer to the positive charge Q. As this occurs, an increasingly negative potential energy U is produced; thus, potential energy is decreasing.

Conversely, as the electron approaches Q, the electric potential V increases with less distance. This is because the product is positive and reducing r increases V.

32. D is correct. Magnets provide magnetic forces.

Generators convert mechanical energy into electrical energy, turbines extract energy from fluids (e.g., air and water), and transformers transfer energy between circuits.

33. B is correct. The potential energy of a system containing two point charges is:

$$U = kq_1q_2/r$$

In this problem, one of the charges is positive, and the other is negative. To account for this, write:

$$q_1 = +|q_1| \text{ and } q_2 = -|q_2|$$

The potential energy can be written as:

$$U = -k|q_1||q_2|/r$$

Moreover, the absolute value of the potential energy is:

$$|U| = k|q_1||q_2|/r$$

All quantities are positive. The absolute value of the potential energy is inversely proportional to the orbital radius; therefore, the absolute value of the potential energy decreases as the orbital radius increases.

34. C is correct.

$$R = (\rho L) / (\pi r^2)$$
$$R_A = (\rho L) / (\pi r^2)$$
$$R_B = [\rho(2L)] / [\pi(2r)^2]$$
$$R_B = (2/4)\cdot[(\rho L) / (\pi r^2)]$$
$$R_B = \tfrac{1}{2}[(\rho L) / (\pi r^2)]$$
$$R_B = \tfrac{1}{2}R_A$$

35. D is correct. By convention, current flows from high to low potential, but it represents the flow of positive charges.

Electron flow is in the opposite direction, from low potential to high potential.

36. C is correct.

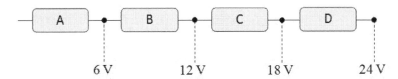

6 V   12 V   18 V   24 V

Batteries in series add voltage like resistors in series add resistance.

The resistances of the lights they power are not needed to solve the problem.

37. B is correct.

$$C = (k\mathcal{E}_0 A) / d$$
$$k = (Cd) / A\mathcal{E}_0$$

If capacitance increases by a factor of 4:

$$k_2 = (4C)d / A\mathcal{E}_0$$
$$k_2 = 4(Cd / A\mathcal{E}_0)$$
$$k_2 = 4k$$

38. C is correct.

$$C = (k\mathcal{E}_0 A) / d$$
$$C = [(1)\cdot(8.854 \times 10^{-12} \text{ F/m})\cdot(0.4 \text{ m}^2)] / (0.04 \text{ m})$$
$$C = 8.854 \times 10^{-11} \text{ F}$$
$$V = Q / C$$
$$V = (6.8 \times 10^{-10} \text{ C}) / (8.854 \times 10^{-11} \text{ F})$$
$$V = 7.7 \text{ V}$$

39. A is correct.

Since force is the cross-product of velocity and magnetic field strength:

$F = qv \times B$

The force is at a maximum when v and B are perpendicular:

$F = qvB \sin 90°$

$\sin 90° = 1$

$F = qvB$

40. D is correct.

Ampere is the unit of current, which is defined as the rate of flow of charge. The current describes how much charge (in Coulombs) passes through a point every second.

So, if the current is multiplied by the number of seconds (the time interval), one can measure just how much charge passed by during that time interval.

Mathematically, the units are expressed as:

$A = C / s$

$C = A \cdot s$

41. C is correct.

$\Delta V = \Delta E / q$

$\Delta V = (1 / q) \cdot (\tfrac{1}{2}mv_f^2 - \tfrac{1}{2}mv_i^2)$

$\Delta V = (m / 2q) \cdot (v_f^2 - v_i^2)$

$\Delta V = [(1.67 \times 10^{-27}\,\text{kg}) / (2) \cdot (1.6 \times 10^{-19}\,\text{C})] \times [(3.2 \times 10^5\,\text{m/s})^2 - (1.7 \times 10^5\,\text{m/s})^2]$

$\Delta V = 384\,\text{V}$

42. D is correct.

$Q = VC$

Even though the capacitors have different capacitances, the voltage across each capacitor is inversely proportional to the capacitance of that capacitor.

Like current, a charge is conserved across capacitors in series.

43. A is correct. Calculate capacitance:

$C = k\varepsilon_o A / d$

$C = [(1) \cdot (8.854 \times 10^{-12}\,\text{F/m}) \cdot (0.6\,\text{m}^2)] / (0.06\,\text{m})$

$C = 8.854 \times 10^{-11}\,\text{F}$

Find potential difference:

$C = Q / V$

$V = Q / C$

$V = (7.08 \times 10^{-10} \text{ C}) / (8.854 \times 10^{-11} \text{ F})$

$V = 8 \text{ V}$

44. B is correct.

"In a perfect conductor" and "in the absence of resistance" have the same meanings, and current can flow in conductors of varying resistances.

A semi-perfect conductor has resistance.

45. C is correct.

Faraday's Law: a changing magnetic environment causes a voltage to be induced in a conductor. Metal detectors send quick magnetic pulses that cause a voltage (by Faraday's Law) and subsequent current to be induced in the conductor.

By Lenz's Law, an opposing magnetic field will then arise to counter the changing magnetic field. The detector picks up the magnetic field and notifies the operator.

Thus, metal detectors use Faraday's Law and Lenz's Law to detect metal objects.

46. A is correct.

$E = qV$

$E = (7 \times 10^{-6} \text{ C}) \cdot (3.5 \times 10^{-3} \text{ V})$

$E = 24.5 \times 10^{-9} \text{ J}$

$E = 24.5 \text{ nJ}$

47. B is correct.

$R_1 = \rho L_1 / A_1$

$R_2 = \rho(4L_1) / A_2$

$R_1 = R_2$

$\rho L_1 / A_1 = \rho(4L_1) / A_2$

$A_2 = 4A_1$

$(\pi / 4)d_2^2 = (\pi / 4) \cdot (4)d_1^2$

$d_2^2 = 4d_1^2$

$d_2 = 2d_1$

48. D is correct.

The total resistance of a network of series resistors increases as more resistors are added.

$V = IR$

An increase in the total resistance results in a decrease in the total current through the network.

49. A is correct.

This is a circuit with two resistors in series. Combine the two resistors into one resistor:

$R_T = R + R_{int}$

$R_T = 0.5\ \Omega + 0.1\ \Omega$

$R_T = 0.6\ \Omega$

Ohm's law:

$V = IR$

$I = V / R$

$I = 9\ V / 0.6\ \Omega$

$I = 15\ A$

50. C is correct.

Energy stored in capacitor:

$U = \frac{1}{2}(Q^2 / C)$

Capacitance:

$C = k\varepsilon_0 A / d$

$U = \frac{1}{2}(Q^2 d) / (k\varepsilon_0 A)$

$Q = \sqrt{[(2U \times k\varepsilon_0 A) / d]}$

$Q = \sqrt{\{[(2)\cdot(10 \times 10^3\ J)\cdot(1)\cdot(8.854 \times 10^{-12}\ F/m)\cdot(2.4 \times 10^{-5}\ m^2)] / 0.0016\ m\}}$

$Q = 52\ \mu C$

51. B is correct.

Potential energy:

$U = (kQq) / r$

Electric Potential:

$V = (kQ) / r$

As r increases, the potential energy U decreases as does the electric potential V.

Movement in the direction of the electric field is a movement away from a positive charge.

52. D is correct. Electric field energy density:

$$\eta_E = \tfrac{1}{2}E^2 \times \mathcal{E}_0$$

$$\eta_E = \tfrac{1}{2}(8.6 \times 10^6 \text{ V/m})^2 \cdot (8.854 \times 10^{-12} \text{ F/m})$$

$$\eta_E = 330 \text{ J/m}^3$$

53. A is correct. Resistance = Ohms

$$\Omega = V / A$$

$$\Omega = [(\text{kg·m}^2/\text{s}^2)/\text{C}] / [\text{C/s}]$$

$$\Omega = \text{kg·m}^2/(\text{C}^2/\text{s})$$

54. C is correct. Ohm's Law:

$$V = IR$$

If V is constant, then I and R are inversely proportional.

An increase in R results in a decrease in I.

55. D is correct.

Electric Potential:

$$V = kQ / r$$

All other positions on the square (1, 2 or 3) are equidistant from point p, as is charge $+Q$.

Thus, a negative charge placed at any of these locations would have equal magnitude potential but an opposite sign because the new charge is negative.

Thus: $|V| = |-V|$

$$V + (-V) = 0$$

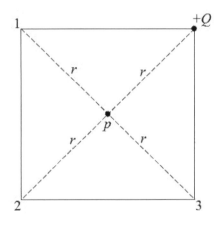

56. B is correct. Electric field energy density:

$$u_E = \tfrac{1}{2}E^2 \mathcal{E}_0$$

$$u_E = \tfrac{1}{2}(6 \text{ N/C})^2 \cdot (8.854 \times 10^{-12} \text{ F/m})$$

$$u_E = 1.6 \times 10^{-10} \text{ J/m}^3$$

57. A is correct.

Ohm's law:

$$V = IR$$

Increasing V and decreasing R increases I.

58. D is correct.

$$C_{Eq1} = C_2 + C_3$$

$$C_{Eq1} = 18 \text{ pF} + 24 \text{ pF}$$

$$C_{Eq1} = 42 \text{ pF}$$

Voltage drops is equal in capacitors in parallel, so:

$$C_{Eq1} = Q_1 / V_1$$

$$Q_1 = C_{Eq1} \times V_1$$

$$Q_1 = (42 \times 10^{-12} \text{ F}) \cdot (240 \text{ V})$$

$$Q_1 = 1 \times 10^{-8} \text{ C}$$

Charge is equal in capacitors in series, so:

$$1 / C_{Eq2} = 1 / C_{Eq1} + 1 / C_1$$

$$1 / C_{Eq2} = 1 / 42 \text{ pF} + 1 / 9 \text{ pF}$$

$$1 / C_{Eq2} = 7.4 \text{ pF}$$

$$1 / C_{Eq2} = V_{system} / Q_1$$

$$V_{system} = Q_1 / C_{Eq2}$$

$$V_{system} = (1 \times 10^{-8} \text{ C}) / (7.4 \times 10^{-12} \text{ F})$$

$$V_{system} = 1{,}350 \text{ V}$$

59. A is correct.

Energy stored in a capacitor:

$$U = \tfrac{1}{2}Q^2 / C$$

$$U_2 = Q^2 / 2(2C)$$

$$U_2 = \tfrac{1}{2}Q^2 / 2C$$

$$U_2 = \tfrac{1}{2}U$$

Decreases by half.

60. C is correct.

The total resistance of a network of series resistors increases as more resistors are added to the network.

An increase in the total resistance results in a decrease in the total current through the network.

A decrease in current results in a decrease in the voltage across the original resistor:

$$V = IR$$

Sound – Explanations

1. B is correct. Intensity is inversely proportional to distance (in W/m², not dB).

$$I_2 / I_1 = (d_1 / d_2)^2$$

$$I_2 / I_1 = (3 \text{ m} / 30 \text{ m})^2$$

$$100 \, I_2 = I_1$$

The intensity is 100 times greater at 3 m away than 30 m away.

Intensity to decibel relationship:

$$I \text{ (dB)} = 10 \log_{10} (I / I_0)$$

The intensity to dB relationship is logarithmic. Thus, if I_1 is 100 times the original intensity then it is two times the dB intensity because:

$$\log_{10} (100) = 2$$

Thus, the decibel level at 3 m away is:

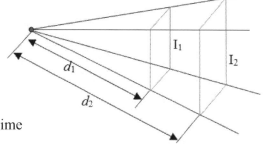

$$I \text{ (dB)} = (2) \cdot (20 \text{ dB})$$

$$I = 40 \text{ dB}$$

2. A is correct. distance = velocity × time

$$d = vt$$

$$t = d / v$$

$$t = (6{,}000 \text{ m}) / (340 \text{ m/s})$$

$$t = 18 \text{ s}$$

3. B is correct. Resonance occurs when a vibrating system is driven at its resonance frequency, resulting in a relative maximum of the vibrational energy of the system. When the force associated with the vibration exceeds the strength of the material, the glass shatters.

4. C is correct. The third harmonic is shown in the figure below:

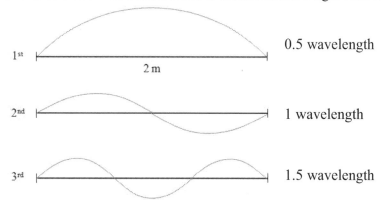

There are $(3/2)\lambda$ in the 2 m wave in the third harmonic

$L = (n / 2)\lambda$ (for n harmonic)

$L = (3 / 2)\lambda$ (for 3rd harmonic)

$L(2 / 3) = \lambda$

$\lambda = (2 \text{ m}) \cdot (2 / 3)$

$\lambda = 4/3 \text{ m}$

5. B is correct.

High-pitched sound has a high frequency.

6. A is correct.

Snell's law:

$n_1 \sin \theta_1 = n_2 \sin \theta_2$

Solve for θ_2:

$(n_1 / n_2) \sin \theta_1 = \sin \theta_2$

$\sin \theta_1 = (n_1 / n_2) \sin \theta_2$

$\theta_2 = \sin^{-1}[(n_1 / n_2) \sin \theta_1]$

Substituting the given values:

$\theta_2 = \sin^{-1}[(1 / 1.5) \sin 60°]$

$\theta_2 = \sin^{-1}(0.67 \sin 60°)$

7. D is correct.

For a standing wave, the length and wavelength are related:

$L = (n / 2)\lambda$ (for n harmonic)

From the diagram, the wave is the 6th harmonic:

$L = (6 / 2)\lambda$

$\lambda = (2 \text{ m}) \cdot (2 / 6)$

$\lambda = 0.667 \text{ m}$

$f = v / \lambda$

$f = (92 \text{ m/s}) / (0.667 \text{ m})$

$f = 138 \text{ Hz}$

8. A is correct.

$v = d / t$

$v = (0.6 \text{ m}) / (0.00014 \text{ s})$

$v = 4{,}286 \text{ m/s}$

$\lambda = v / f$

$\lambda = (4{,}286 \text{ m/s}) / (1.5 \times 10^6 \text{ Hz})$

$\lambda = 0.0029 \text{ m} = 2.9 \text{ mm}$

9. C is correct.

The wave velocity is increased by a factor of 1.3.

$v^2 = T / \rho_L$

$T = v^2 \times \rho_L$

Increasing v by a factor of 1.3:

$T = (1.3v)^2 \rho_L$

$T = 1.69 v^2 \rho_L$

T increases by 69%

10. D is correct.

$\rho_L = \rho A$

$\rho_L = \rho(\pi r^2)$

Thus, if the diameter decreases by a factor of 2, then the radius decreases by a factor of 2, and the area decreases by a factor of 4.

The linear mass density decreases by a factor of 4.

11. B is correct.

The v and period (T) of wire C are equal to wire A so the ρ_L must be equal as well.

$\rho_{LA} = \rho_{LC}$

$\rho_A A_A = \rho_C A_C$

$A_C = (\rho_A A_A) / \rho_C$

$(\pi / 4)\cdot(d_C)^2 = (7 \text{ g/cm}^3)(\pi / 4)\cdot(0.6 \text{ mm})^2 / (3 \text{ g/cm}^3)$

$(d_C)^2 = (7 \text{ g/cm}^3)\cdot(0.6 \text{ mm})^2 / (3 \text{ g/cm}^3)$

$d_C^2 = 0.84 \text{ mm}^2$

$d_C = \sqrt{(0.84 \text{ mm}^2)} = 0.92 \text{ mm}$

12. A is correct.

$$A = \pi r^2$$

If d increases by a factor of 4, r increases by a factor of 4.

A increases by a factor of 16.

13. B is correct.

Since the bird is moving toward the observer, the $f_{observed}$ must be higher than f_{source}.

Doppler shift for an approaching sound source:

$$f_{observed} = (v_{sound} \,/\, v_{sound} - v_{source})f_{source}$$

$$f_{observed} = [340 \text{ m/s} \,/\, (340 \text{ m/s} - 10 \text{ m/s})]f_{source}$$

$$f_{observed} = (340 \text{ m/s} \,/\, 330 \text{ m/s}) \cdot (60 \text{ kHz})$$

$$f_{observed} = (1.03) \cdot (60 \text{ kHz})$$

$$f_{observed} = 62 \text{ kHz}$$

14. C is correct.

When an approaching sound source is heard, the observed frequency is higher than the frequency from the source due to the Doppler effect.

15. D is correct.

Sound requires a medium of solid, liquid or gas substances to be propagated through. A vacuum is none of these.

16. A is correct.

According to the Doppler effect, frequency increases as the sound source moves towards the observer.

Higher frequency is perceived as a higher pitch.

Conversely, as the sound source moves away from the observer, the perceived pitch decreases.

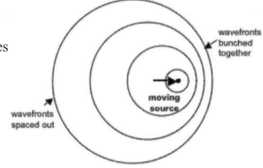

17. C is correct.

If waves are out of phase, the combination has its minimum amplitude of (0.6 – 0.4) Pa = 0.2 Pa.

If waves are in phase, the combination has its maximum amplitude of (0.6 + 0.4) Pa = 1.0 Pa.

When the phase difference has a value between in phase and out of phase, the amplitude will be between 0.2 Pa and 1.0 Pa.

18. B is correct.

$$I = P / A$$

$$I = P / \pi d^2$$

Intensity at 2*d*:

$$I_2 = P / \pi(2d)^2$$

$$I_2 = P / 4\pi d^2$$

$$I_2 = \tfrac{1}{4}P / \pi d^2$$

The new intensity is ¼ the original.

19. A is correct.

speed of sound = √[resistance to compression / density]

$$v_{sound} = \sqrt{(E / \rho)}$$

Low resistance to compression and high density result in low velocity because this minimizes the term under the radical and thus minimizes velocity.

20. B is correct.

A pipe open at each end has no constraint on displacement at the ends.

Furthermore, the pressure at the ends must equal the ambient pressure.

Thus, the pressure is maximum at the ends: an antinode.

21. C is correct.

For a pipe open at both ends, the resonance frequency:

$$f_n = nf_1$$

where n = 1, 2, 3, 4…

Therefore, only a multiple of 200 Hz can be a resonant frequency.

22. D is correct.

Unlike light, sound waves require a medium to travel through, and its speed is dependent upon the medium.

Sound is fastest in solids, then liquids and slowest in the air.

$$v_{solid} > v_{liquid} > v_{air}$$

23. B is correct.

Currents or moving charges induce magnetic fields.

24. C is correct.

$\lambda = v / f$

$\lambda = (5{,}000 \text{ m/s}) / (620 \text{ Hz})$

$\lambda = 8.1 \text{ m}$

25. A is correct.

Sound intensity radiating spherically:

$I = P / 4\pi r^2$

If *r* is doubled:

$I = P / 4\pi(2r)^2$

$I = \frac{1}{4}P / 4\pi r^2$

The intensity is reduced by a factor of ¼.

26. D is correct.

As the sound propagates through a medium, it spreads out in an approximately spherical pattern.

Thus, the power is radiated along the surface of the sphere, and the intensity can be given by:

$I = P / (4\pi r^2)$ ← for the surface area of a sphere

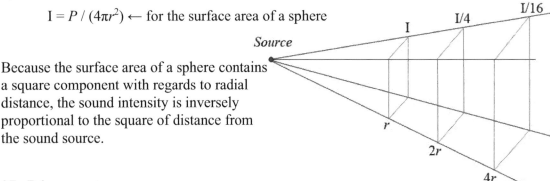

Because the surface area of a sphere contains a square component with regards to radial distance, the sound intensity is inversely proportional to the square of distance from the sound source.

27. B is correct.

The closed end is a node and the open end is an antinode.

$\lambda = (4 / n)L$

where n = 1, 3, 5 …

For the fundamental n = 1:

$\lambda = (4 / 1)\cdot(1.5 \text{ m})$

$\lambda = 6 \text{ m}$

The 1.5 m tube (open at one end) is a quarter of a full wave, so the wavelength is 6 m.

28. A is correct.

The 1.5 m is ¼ a full wave, so the wavelength is 6 m, for the fundamental.

$$f = v / \lambda$$

$$f = (960 \text{ m/s}) / 6 \text{ m}$$

$$f = 160 \text{ Hz}$$

29. B is correct.

For a closed-ended pipe, the wavelength to the harmonic relationship is:

$$\lambda = (4 / n)L$$

where n = 1, 3, 5…

For the 5th harmonic n = 5

$$\lambda = (4 / 5)\cdot(1.5 \text{ m})$$

$$\lambda_n = 1.2 \text{ m}$$

Closed end tube

Harmonic # (n)	# of waves in a tube	# of nodes	# of antinodes	Wavelength to length
1	1/4	1	1	$\lambda = 4 L$
3	3/4	2	2	$\lambda = 4/3 L$
5	5/4	3	3	$\lambda = 4/5 L$
7	7/4	4	4	$\lambda = 4/7 L$

30. A is correct.

$$f = v / \lambda$$

$$f = (340 \text{ m/s}) / (6 \text{ m})$$

$$f = 57 \text{ Hz}$$

31. C is correct.

Wavelength to harmonic number relationship in a standing wave on a string:

$$\lambda = (2L / n)$$

where n = 1, 2, 3, 4, 5 …

For the 3rd harmonic:

$$\lambda = (2)\cdot(0.34 \text{ m}) / 3$$

$$\lambda = 0.23 \text{ m}$$

32. D is correct.

Beat frequency equation:

$$f_{beat} = |f_2 - f_1|$$

If one of the tones increases in frequency, then the beat frequency increases or decreases, but this cannot be determined unless the two tones are known.

33. A is correct.

For a closed-ended pipe, the wavelength to harmonic relationship is:

$\lambda = (4 / n)L$

where n = 1, 3, 5, 7…

The lowest three tones are n = 1, 3, 5

$\lambda = (4 / 1)L; \lambda = (4 / 3)L; \lambda = (4 / 5)L$

34. D is correct.

The sound was barely perceptible, the intensity at Mary's ear is $I_0 = 9.8 \times 10^{-12}$ W/m^2.

Since the mosquito is 1 m away, imagine a sphere 1 m in a radius around the mosquito.

If 9.8×10^{-12} W emanates from each area 1 m^2, then the surface area is $4\pi(1 \text{ m})^2$.

This is the power produced by one mosquito:

$P = 4\pi r^2 I_0$

$P = 4\pi(1 \text{ m})^2 \times (9.8 \times 10^{-12} \text{ W/m}^2)$

$P = 1.2 \times 10^{-10}$ W

energy = power × time

$E = Pt$

Energy produced in 200 s:

$Pt = (1.2 \times 10^{-10} \text{ W}) \cdot (200 \text{ s})$

$E = 2.5 \times 10^{-8}$ J

35. A is correct.

$v = c / n$

where c is the speed of light in a vacuum

$v = \Delta x / \Delta t$

$\Delta x / \Delta t = c / n$

$\Delta t = n\Delta x / c$

$\Delta t = (1.33) \cdot (10^3 \text{ m}) / (3 \times 10^8 \text{ m/s})$

$\Delta t = 4.4 \times 10^{-6}$ s

36. A is correct.

When waves interfere constructively (i.e., in phase), the sound level is amplified. When they interfere destructively (i.e., out of phase), they cancel, and no sound is heard.

Acoustic engineers work to ensure that there are no "dead spots" and the sound waves add.

An engineer should minimize destructive interference which can distort the sound.

37. B is correct.

Velocity of a wave on a string in tension can be calculated by:

$$v = \sqrt{(TL / m)}$$

Graph B gives a curve of a square root relationship which is how velocity and tension are related.

$$y = x^{\frac{1}{2}}$$

38. D is correct.

From the diagram, the wave is a 6th harmonic standing wave.

Find wavelength:

$$\lambda = (2L / n)$$

$$\lambda = (2) \cdot (4 \text{ m}) / (6)$$

$$\lambda = 1.3 \text{ m}$$

Find frequency:

$$f = v / \lambda$$

$$f = (20 \text{ m/s}) / (1.3 \text{ m})$$

$$f = 15.4 \text{ Hz}$$

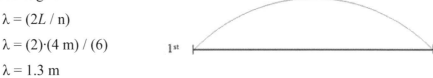

39. B is correct.

Soundwave velocity is independent of frequency and does not change.

40. C is correct.

First, find the frequency of the string, then the length of the pipe excited to the second overtone using that frequency.

The speed of sound in the string is:

$$v_{\text{string}} = \sqrt{T/\mu}$$

where T is the tension in the string, and μ is linear mass density.

$$v_{\text{string}} = \sqrt{[(75 \text{ N}) / (0.00040 \text{ kg})]}$$

$$v_{\text{string}} = 433.01 \text{ m/s}$$

The wavelength of a string of length L_{string} vibrating in harmonic n_{string} is:

$$\lambda_{\text{string}} = 2L_{\text{string}} / n_{\text{string}}$$

Therefore, the vibration frequency of the string is:

$$f = v_{\text{string}} / \lambda_{\text{string}}$$

$$f = [(n_{\text{string}})(v_{\text{string}})] / 2L_{\text{string}}$$

$$f = [(6)(433.01 \text{ m/s})] / (2 \times 0.50 \text{ m})$$

$f = (2{,}598.06 \text{ m/s}) / 1 \text{ m}$

$f = 2{,}598.1 \text{ Hz}$

Now, consider the open pipe.

The relationship between length, wavelength and harmonic number for an open pipe is the same as that for a string.

Therefore:

$L_{\text{pipe}} = \text{n}_{\text{pipe}} (\lambda_{\text{pipe}} / 2)$

However, since $\lambda_{\text{pipe}} = v_{\text{air}} / f$:

$L_{\text{pipe}} = \text{n}_{\text{pipe}} (v_{\text{air}} / 2f)$

Noting that the second overtone is the third harmonic ($\text{n}_{pipe} = 3$):

$L_{pipe} = (3 \times 345 \text{ m/s}) / (2 \times 2{,}598.1 \text{ Hz})$

$L_{pipe} = 0.20 \text{ m}$

Note that it is not necessary to calculate the frequency; its value cancels out.

There is less chance for error if the two steps that use frequency are skipped.

In $L_{\text{pipe}} = \text{n}_{\text{pipe}} (v_{\text{air}} / 2f)$ substitute $f = [(\text{n}_{\text{string}})(v_{\text{string}})] / 2L_{\text{string}}$

which gives:

$L_{\text{pipe}} = L_{\text{string}} (v_{\text{air}} / v_{\text{string}}) \cdot (\text{n}_{\text{pipe}} / \text{n}_{\text{string}})$

It yields the same answer but with fewer calculations.

41. A is correct.

$v = \sqrt{(T / \mu)}$

$\mu = m / L$

$v = \sqrt{(TL / m)}$

$v_2 = \sqrt{(T(2L) / m)}$

$v_2 = \sqrt{2} \sqrt{(TL / m)}$

$v_2 = v\sqrt{2}$

42. C is correct.

For a standing wave, the resonance frequency:

$f_{\text{n}} = \text{n}f_1$

where n is the harmonic number, $\text{n} = 1, 2, 3, 4 \ldots$

Therefore, only a multiple of 500 Hz can be a resonant frequency.

43. D is correct.

The angle of incidence always equals the angle of reflection.

A light beam entering a medium with a greater refractive index than the incident medium refracts *toward* the normal.

Thus, the angle of refraction is less than the angles of incidence and reflection.

Snell's law:

$$n_1 \sin \theta_1 = n_2 \sin \theta_2$$

where $n_1 < n_2$

For Snell's law to be true, then:

$$\theta_1 > \theta_2$$

44. A is correct.

Speed of sound in gas:

$$v_{sound} = \sqrt{(yRT / M)}$$

where y = adiabatic constant, R = gas constant, T = temperature and M = molecular mass

The speed of sound in a gas is only dependent upon temperature and not frequency or wavelength.

45. B is correct.

Waves only transport energy and not matter.

46. D is correct.

$$v = \lambda f$$

$$\lambda = v / f$$

$$\lambda = (344 \text{ m/s}) / (700 \text{ s}^{-1})$$

$$\lambda = 0.5 \text{ m}$$

The information about the string is unnecessary, as the only contributor to the wavelength of the sound in air is the frequency and the speed.

47. C is correct.

$$v = \lambda f$$

$$f = v / \lambda$$

Distance from a sound source is not part of the equation for frequency.

48. A is correct.

Velocity of a wave in a rope:

$v = \sqrt{[T / (m / L)]}$

$t = d / v$

$d = L$

$t = d / \sqrt{[T / (m / L)]}$

$t = (8 \text{ m}) / [40 \text{ N} / (2.5 \text{ kg} / 8 \text{ m})]^{\frac{1}{2}}$

$t = 0.71 \text{ s}$

49. C is correct.

Intensity to decibel relationship:

$I \text{ (dB)} = 10 \log_{10} (I_1 / I_0)$

where I_0 = threshold of hearing

$dB = 10 \log_{10}[(10^{-5} \text{ W/m}^2) / (10^{-12} \text{ W/m}^2)]$

$I = 70$ decibels

50. B is correct. The diagram represents the described scenario.

The wave is in the second harmonic with a wavelength of:

$\lambda = (2 / n)L$

$\lambda = (2 / 2) \cdot (1 \text{ m})$

$\lambda = 1 \text{ m}$

$f = v / \lambda$

$f = (3.8 \times 10^4 \text{ m/s}) / (1 \text{ m})$

$f = 3.8 \times 10^4 \text{ Hz}$

The lowest frequency corresponds to the lowest possible harmonic number.

For this problem, n = 2.

51. D is correct.

The speed of light traveling in a vacuum is c.

$c = \lambda v$

$c = \lambda f$

$f = c / \lambda$

Frequency and wavelength are inversely proportional, so an increase in frequency results in a decreased wavelength.

52. B is correct.

Radio waves are electromagnetic waves while all other choices are mechanical waves.

53. D is correct.

Since the microphone is exactly equidistant from each speaker (i.e., equal path lengths), the sound waves take equal time to reach the microphone.

The speakers are emitting sound waves in phase with each other (i.e., peaks are emitted simultaneously), and since those peaks reach the microphone at the same time (because of the equal path length), they combine constructively and add, forming a large peak, or antinode.

54. C is correct. Doppler equation for receding source of sound:

$$f_{observed} = [v_{sound} / (v_{sound} + v_{source})]f_{source}$$

$$f_{observed} = [(342 \text{ m/s}) / (342 \text{ m/s} + 30 \text{ m/s})] \cdot (1,200 \text{ Hz})$$

$$f_{observed} = 1,103 \text{ Hz}$$

The observed frequency is always lower when the source is receding.

55. D is correct.

$$f_1 = 600 \text{ Hz}$$

$$f_2 = 300 \text{ Hz}$$

$$f_2 = \tfrac{1}{2}f_1$$

$$\lambda_1 = v / f_1$$

$$\lambda_2 = v / (\tfrac{1}{2}f_1)$$

$$\lambda_2 = 2 (v / f_1)$$

Wavelength of 300 Hz frequency is twice as long as wavelength of the 600 Hz frequency.

56. C is correct.

$$f_2 = 2f_1$$

$$f = v / \lambda$$

$v / \lambda_2 = (2)v / \lambda_1$, cancel v from both sides of the expression

$$1 / \lambda_2 = 2 / \lambda_1$$

$\lambda = (2 / n)L$, for open-ended pipes

$$1 / (2 / n)L_2 = 2 / (2 / n)L_1$$

$$L_1 = 2L_2$$

$$L_1 / L_2 = 2$$

57. A is correct.

Resonance occurs when energy gets transferred from one oscillator to another of similar f by a weak coupling.

Dispersion is the spreading of waves due to the dependence of wave speed on frequency.

Interference is the addition of two waves in the same medium, which is what happens when waves from both strings combine, but that is not the excitation of the C_4 string.

58. C is correct.

> frequency = 1 / period
>
> $f = 1 / T$
>
> $f = 1 / 10$ s
>
> $f = 0.1$ Hz

Find wavelength:

> $\lambda = v / f$
>
> $\lambda = (4.5 \text{ m/s}) / (0.1 \text{ Hz}) = 45$ m

59. D is correct.

> $v = \sqrt{K / \rho}$

where K = bulk modulus (i.e., resistance to compression) and ρ = density.

Since ρ for water is greater than for air, the greater v for water implies that water's bulk modulus (K) must be much greater than for air.

60. C is correct.

When visible light strikes glass, it causes the electrons of the atoms in the glass to vibrate at their non-resonant frequency.

The vibration is passed from one atom to the next transferring the energy of the light.

Finally, the energy is passed to the last atom before the light is re-mitted out of the glass at its original frequency.

If the light energy were converted into internal energy, the glass would heat up and not transfer the light.

Light and Geometrical Optics – Explanations

1. A is correct.

Soap film that reflects a given wavelength of light exhibits constructive interference.

The expression for constructive interference of a thin film:

$2t = (m + \frac{1}{2})\lambda$

where t = thickness, m = 0, 1, 2, 3… and λ = wavelength

To find the minimum thickness set m = 0:

$2t = (0 + \frac{1}{2})\lambda = \frac{1}{2}\lambda$

$t = \frac{1}{4}\lambda$

2. A is correct.

By the law of reflection, the angle of incidence = angle of reflection.

Thus, as the angle of incidence increases, the angle of reflection increases as well to be equal to the angle of incidence.

3. B is correct.

If image is twice her height and upright, then:

$2h_o = h_i$

$m = h_i / h_o$

$m = -d_i / d_o$

$m = 2h_o / h_o$

$m = 2$

$2 = -d_i / d_o$

$-2d_o = d_i$

Use lens equation to solve:

$1 / f = 1 / d_o + 1 / d_i$

$1 / 100 \text{ cm} = 1 / d_o + (-1 / 2 d_o)$

$1 / 100 \text{ cm} = 1 / 2 d_o$

$2d_o = 100 \text{ cm}$

$d_o = 50 \text{ cm}$

4. D is correct.
If a person's eye is too long, the light entering the eye is focused in front of the retina causing myopia. This condition is also referred to as nearsightedness.

Hyperopia is also referred to as farsightedness.

5. C is correct.

Visible light:

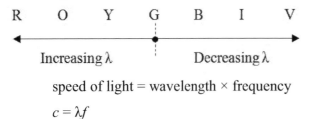

speed of light = wavelength × frequency

$$c = \lambda f$$

Wavelength to frequency:

$$f = c / \lambda$$

Frequency and wavelength are inversely proportional:

As λ increases, f decreases.

As λ decreases, f increases.

Thus, because $E = hf$:

6. B is correct.

The lens equation:

$$1 / f = 1 / d_o + 1 / d_i$$

$$1 / d_i = 1 / f - 1 / d_o$$

$$1 / d_i = -1 / 3 \text{ m} - 1 / 4 \text{ m}$$

$$1 / d_i = (-3 \text{ m} - 4 \text{ m}) / 12 \text{ m}$$

$$1 / d_i = -7 \text{ m} / 12 \text{ m}$$

$$d_i = -12 / 7 \text{ m}$$

Magnification:

$$m = -d_i / d_o$$

$$m = -(-12 / 7 \text{ m}) / 4 \text{ m}$$

$$m = 3 / 7$$

Height of the candle image:

$$h_i = m h_o$$

$$h_i = (3/7) \cdot (18 \text{ cm})$$

$$h_i = 54 / 7 \text{ cm}$$

$$h_i = 7.7 \text{ cm}$$

7. C is correct.

$\theta_{syrup} = \tan^{-1}(0.9 \text{ m} / 0.66 \text{ m})$

$\theta_s = \tan^{-1}(1.36)$

$\theta_s = 53.7°$

$\theta_{oil} = \tan^{-1}[(2 \text{ m} - 0.9 \text{ m}) / 1.58 \text{ m}]$

$\theta_o = \tan^{-1}(0.7)$

$\theta_o = 34.8°$

$n_o \sin \theta_o = n_{air} \sin \theta_{air}$

$n_o \sin 34.8° = (1) \sin 90°$

$n_o = 1 / (\sin 34.8°)$

$n_o = 1.75$

8. D is correct.

$\theta_{syrup} = \tan^{-1}(0.9 \text{ m} / 0.66 \text{ m})$

$\theta_s = \tan^{-1}(1.36)$

$\theta_s = 53.7°$

$\theta_{oil} = \tan^{-1}[(2 \text{ m} - 0.9 \text{ m}) / 1.58 \text{ m}]$

$\theta_o = \tan^{-1}(0.7)$

$\theta_o = 34.8°$

$n_o \sin \theta_o = n_{air} \sin \theta_{air}$

$n_o \sin 34.8° = (1) \sin 90°$

$n_o = 1 / (\sin 34.8°)$

$n_o = 1.75$

$n_s \sin \theta_s = n_o \sin \theta_o$

$n_s = n_o \sin \theta_o / \sin \theta_s$

$n_s = (1.75) \cdot (\sin 34.8°) / (\sin 53.7°)$

$n_s = 1.24$

9. A is correct.

The photoelectric effect (i.e., emission of electrons when light shines on a material) cannot be explained with the wave theory of light.

10. D is correct.

Geometrical optics, or ray optics, describes light propagation in terms of rays and fronts to approximate the path along which light propagates in certain circumstances.

11. D is correct.

First find the critical angle:

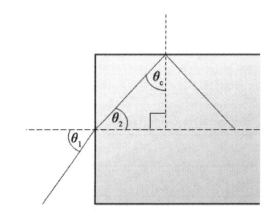

$$n_{\text{fiber}} \sin \theta_c = n_{\text{air}} \sin \theta_{\text{air}}$$

$$(1.26) \sin \theta_c = (1) \sin 90°$$

$$\sin \theta_c = 1 / 1.26$$

$$\theta_c = \sin^{-1} (1 / 1.26)$$

$$\theta_c = 52.5°$$

Find θ_2:

$$\theta_2 + \theta_c + 90° = 180°$$

$$(\theta_2 + 52.5° + 90°) = 180°$$

$$\theta_2 = 37.5°$$

Find θ_1:

$$n_{\text{air}} \sin \theta_1 = n_{\text{fiber}} \sin \theta_2$$

$$(1) \sin \theta_1 = (1.26) \sin 37.5°$$

$$\sin \theta_1 = 0.77$$

$$\theta_1 = \sin^{-1} (0.77)$$

$$\theta_1 = 50°$$

12. A is correct.

If the power of the lens is 10 diopters,

$$1 / f = 10 \text{ D}$$

where f is the focal length in m

Thin Lens Equation:

$$1 / f = 1 / d_o + 1 / d_i$$

$$10 \text{ m}^{-1} = 1 / 0.5 \text{ m} + 1 / d_i$$

$$1 / d_i = 10 \text{ m}^{-1} - 1 / 0.5 \text{ m}$$

$$1 / d_i = 8 \text{ m}^{-1}$$

$$d_i = 1 / 8 \text{ m}$$

$$d_i = 0.13 \text{ m}$$

13. D is correct.

Most objects observed by humans are virtual images or objects which reflect incoming light to project an image.

14. D is correct.

An image from a convex mirror will always have the following characteristics, regardless of object distance:

- located behind the convex mirror
- virtual
- upright
- reduced in size from the object (image < object)

15. A is correct.

The mirror has a positive focal length which indicates that the mirror is concave.

The object is at a distance greater than the focal length.

Therefore, it is inverted.

Use lens equation to solve image distance:

$1 / f = 1 / d_o + 1 / d_i$

$1 / 10 \text{ m} = 1 / 20 \text{ m} + 1 / d_i$

$d_i = 20 \text{ cm}$

The image distance is positive so the image is real.

Use the magnification equation to determine if it is upright or inverted.

$m = -d_i / d_o$

$m = h_i / h_o$

$-(20 \text{ m} / 20 \text{ m}) = h_i / h_o$

$-1 = h_i / h_o$

The object height h_o is always positive so the image height h_i must be negative to satisfy the equation.

A negative image height indicates an inverted image.

16. B is correct.

For a converging lens, if an object is placed beyond $2f$ from the lens, the image is real, inverted and reduced.

Use the lens equation to determine if the image is real (or virtual):

Assume $f = 1 \text{ m}$ and $d_o = 3f$ (because $d_o > 2f$)

$1 / f = 1 / d_o + 1 / d_i$

$1 / f = 1 / 3f + 1 / d_i$

$d_i = 1.5$

A positive d_i indicates a real image.

Use the magnification equation to determine if the image is inverted and reduced.

$$m = -d_i / d_o$$

$$m = -(1.5 \text{ m} / 3 \text{ m})$$

$$m = -\frac{1}{2}$$

$$|m| = \frac{1}{2}$$

$$|m| < 1$$

A negative magnification factor with an absolute value less than 1 is a reduced and inverted image.

17. C is correct.

Radio waves range from 3 kHz to 300 GHz, which is lower than all forms of radiation listed.

Since the energy of radiation is proportional to frequency ($E = hf$), radio waves have the lowest energy.

18. B is correct.

A medium's index of refraction is the ratio of the speed of refracted light in a vacuum to its speed in the reference medium.

$$n = c / v$$

$$n = 2.43$$

$$2.43 = c / v_{\text{diamond}}$$

$$c = 2.43(v_{\text{diamond}})$$

19. D is correct.

$$1 / f = 1 / d_o + 1 / d_i$$

$$1 / 20 \text{ cm} = 1 / 15 \text{ cm} + 1 / d_i$$

$$3 / 60 \text{ cm} - 4 / 60 \text{ cm} = 1 / d_i$$

$$-1 / 60 \text{ cm} = 1 / d_i$$

$$d_i = -60 \text{ cm}$$

The negative sign indicates that the image is projected back the way it came.

20. B is correct.

Red paper absorbs all colors but reflects only red light giving it the appearance of being red.

Cyan is the complementary color to red, so when the cyan light shines upon the red paper, no light is reflected, and the paper appears black.

21. B is correct.

$$1/f = 1/d_o + 1/d_i$$

If $d_i = f$,

$$1/d_o = 0$$

Thus, d_o must be large.

22. A is correct.

Since the index of refraction depends on the frequency, and the focal length depends on the refraction of the beam in the lens, dispersion causes the focal length to depend on frequency.

23. C is correct.

Use the equation for magnification:

$$m = -d_i / d_o$$

$$d_i = d_o$$

$$m = 1$$

Thus, there is no magnification, so the image is the same size as the object.

24. D is correct.

When viewed straight down (90° to the surface), an incident light ray moving from water to air is refracted 0°.

25. C is correct.

The rotating of one polarized lens 90° with respect to the other lens results in complete darkness, since no light would be transmitted.

26. C is correct. First, find the angle that the ray makes with the normal of the glass:

$$180° = x + 90° + 54°$$

$$x = 36°$$

Find θ_1:

$$\theta_1 = 90° - 36°$$

$$\theta_1 = 54°$$

Referring to the diagram, $\theta_1 = 54°$

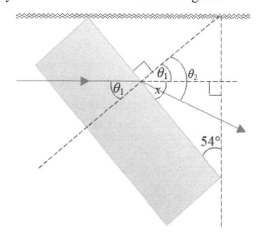

Snell's Law:

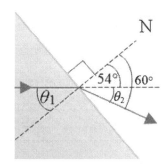

$$n_1 \sin \theta_1 = n_2 \sin \theta_2$$

$$\sin^{-1}\left[(n_1 / n_2) \sin \theta_1\right] = \theta_2$$

$$\theta_2 = \sin^{-1}\left[(1.45 / 1.35) \sin 54°\right]$$

$$\theta_2 = 60°$$

Solve for the angle with the horizontal:

$$\theta_H = 60° - 54°$$

$$\theta_H = 6°$$

27. A is correct.

The angle at which the ray is turned is the sum of the angles if reflected off each mirror once:

$$\theta_{turned} = \theta_1 + \theta_2 + \theta_3 + \theta_4$$

By law of reflection:

$$\theta_1 = \theta_2$$

$$\theta_3 = \theta_4$$

Note the triangle formed (sum of interior angles is 180°):

$$30° + (90° - \theta_2) + (90° - \theta_3) = 180°$$

$$\theta_2 + \theta_3 = 30°$$

Given:

$$\theta_2 + \theta_3 = \theta_1 + \theta_4$$

Thus:

$$\theta_{turned} = 30° + 30°$$

$$\theta_{turned} = 60°$$

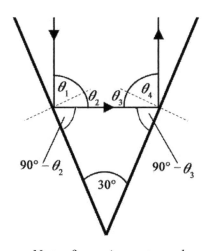

Note: figure is not to scale

In general: for two plane mirrors that meet at an angle of $\theta \le 90°$ the ray that is deflected off both mirrors is deflected through an angle of 2θ.

28. D is correct.

All of the following statements about light are true: a packet of light energy is known as a photon, color can be used to determine the approximate energy of visible light and light travels through space at a speed of 3.0×10^8 m/s.

29. A is correct.

The angle of incidence is < the angle of refraction if the light travels into a less dense medium.

The angle of incidence is > the angle of refraction if the light travels into a denser medium.

The angle of incidence is = the angle of refraction if the densities of the mediums are equal.

30. B is correct.

Plane mirrors do not distort the size or the shape of an object since light is reflected at the same angle the mirror received it.

Magnification equation:

$$m = h_i / h_o$$

For a plane mirror m = 1:

$$1 = h_i / h_o$$

$$h_i = h_o$$

Therefore, the image size is the same as object size, and the image is virtual since it is located behind the mirror.

31. C is correct.

A spherical concave mirror has a focal length of:

$$f = R / 2$$

32. B is correct.

Refracted rays bend further from the normal than the original incident angle when the refracting medium is optically less dense than the incident medium.

Therefore, $n_1 > n_2$.

The index of refraction for a medium can never be less than 1.

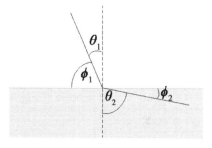

33. B is correct.

If a person's eye is too short, then the light entering the eye is focused behind the retina causing farsightedness (hyperopia).

34. A is correct.

Hot air is less dense than cold air.

Light traveling through both types of air experiences refractions, which appear as shimmering or "wavy" air.

35. C is correct.

Chromatic aberration occurs when a lens focuses different wavelengths of color at different positions in the focal plane.

It always occurs in the following pattern for converging lens:

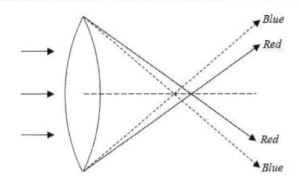

36. B is correct.

$$1 / f_{total} = 1 / f_1 + 1 / f_2$$
$$1 / f_{total} = 1 / 2 \text{ m} + 1 / 4 \text{ m}$$
$$1 / f_{total} = 3 / 4 \text{ m}$$
$$f_{total} = 4 / 3 \text{ m}$$

37. C is correct.   The angle in the water respective to the normal:

$$\theta = \tan^{-1} (37.5 \text{ ft} / 50 \text{ ft})$$
$$\theta = \tan^{-1} (0.75)$$
$$\theta = 36.9°$$
$$n_{air} \sin (90 - \theta) = n_{water} \sin \theta$$
$$(1) \sin (90 - \theta) = (1.33) \sin 36.9°$$
$$\sin (90 - \theta) = 0.8$$
$$(90 - \theta) = \sin^{-1} (0.8)$$
$$(90 - \theta) = 52.9$$
$$\theta = 37.1° \approx 37°$$

38. A is correct. Violet light has the highest energy and frequency; the shortest wavelength.

39. D is correct.

Objects directly in front of plane mirrors are reflected in their likeness since plane mirrors are not curved and therefore reflect light perpendicularly to their surface.

40. B is correct.

A virtual image is always upright and can be formed by both a diverging lens and a converging lens.

Diverging lens → reduced and virtual image

Converging lens → enlarged and virtual image

41. B is correct.

Neon light is the light emitted from neon atoms as their energized electrons cascade back down to ground level. When this occurs, energy is released in the form of light at very specific wavelengths known as the emission spectrum.

When this light is passed through a prism, a series of bright discontinuous spots or lines will be seen due to the specific wavelengths of the emission spectrum of neon.

42. D is correct.

The law of reflection states that the angle of incidence is equal to the angle of reflection (with respect to the normal) and is true for all mirrors.

$$\theta_i = \theta_r$$

43. C is correct.

A concave lens always forms an image that is virtual, upright and reduced in size.

44. B is correct.

Virtual images are always upright.

There is no correlation between the size and nature – virtual or real – of an image.

Images may be larger, smaller, or the same size as the object.

45. A is correct.

From all choices listed, red is the light with the lowest frequency (longest wavelength) detected by your eyes. (ROY G BIV)

46. D is correct.

$$1 / f = 1 / d_o + 1 / d_i$$
$$1 / 6 \text{ m} = 1 / 3 \text{ m} + 1 / d_i$$
$$1 / d_i = 1 / 6 \text{ m} - 1 / 3 \text{ m}$$
$$1 / d_i = -1 / 6 \text{ m}$$
$$d_i = -6 \text{ m}$$

where the negative sign indicates the image is on the same side as the object.

The image is upright and virtual since the rays must be extended to intersect.

47. A is correct.

A diverging lens (concave) always produces an image that is virtual, upright and reduced in size.

48. C is correct.

Thin lens formula:

$$1 / f = 1 / d_o + 1 / d_i$$

d_i is negative because the image is virtual

$$1 / f = 1 / 14 \text{ cm} + 1 / {-5} \text{ cm}$$

$$f = -7.8 \text{ cm}$$

The focus is negative because the lens is diverging.

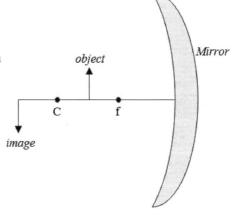

Lens maker formula:

$$1 / f = (n - 1) \cdot (1 / R_1 - 1 / R_2)$$

R_1 is negative by convention because the light ray passes its center of curvature before the curved surface.

$$1 / (-7.8 \text{ cm}) = (n - 1) \cdot (1 / {-15} \text{ cm} - 1 / 15 \text{ cm})$$

$$(1 / {-7.8} \text{ cm}) \cdot (15 \text{ cm} / {-2}) + 1 = n$$

$$n = 2$$

49. B is correct.

The magnification equation relates the image and object distance:

$$m = -d_i / d_o$$

or

The magnification equation relates the image and object height:

$$m = h_i / h_o$$

50. D is correct.

For a concave mirror, if an object is located between the focal point and center of curvature, the image is formed beyond the center of curvature.

In this problem, Mike (i.e., object) does not see his image because he is in front of where it forms.

51. D is correct.

For a concave spherical mirror, the produced image characteristics depend upon the placement of the object in relation to the focal point and center of curvature.

The image can be smaller, larger or the same size as the object.

52. A is correct.

Lens power is the reciprocal of the focal length in meters:

$$P = 1 / f$$

If the effective focal length of the lens combination is less than the focal length of either individual lens, then the power of the combination must be greater than the power of either individual lens.

53. B is correct.

A medium's index of refraction is the ratio of the speed of refracted light in a vacuum to its speed in the reference medium.

$$n = c / v$$

54. D is correct. As it is a plane mirror, the image is not distorted.

Only some of the light rays are reflected, the others create an image behind the mirror's surface.

For a plane mirror:

$$m = 1$$

$$m = -d_i / d_o$$

$$1 = -d_i / d_o$$

$$d_o = -d_i$$

The negative indicates the image is virtual and behind the mirror.

55. C is correct.

The radius length is the center of curvature, $r = 50$ cm

Find the focal length:

$$f = r / 2$$

$$f = 50 \text{ cm} / 2$$

$$f = 25 \text{ cm}$$

For a concave mirror with an object between the center of curvature and the focal length, the resulting image is real and inverted.

56. B is correct. Find index of refraction of glass:

Snell's Law:

$$n_1 \sin \theta_1 = n_2 \sin \theta_2$$

$$n_g \sin 48° = (1.33) \sin 68°$$

$$n_g = (1.33) \sin 68° / \sin 48°$$

$$n_g = 1.66$$

Find refracted angle of ray:

$$(1.66) \sin 29° = (1.33) \sin \theta$$

$$\sin \theta = (1.66) \sin 29° / (1.33)$$

$$\sin \theta = 0.605$$

$$\theta = \sin^{-1}(0.605)$$

$$\theta = 37°$$

57. A is correct.

In a compound microscope, the image of the objective serves as the object for the eyepiece.

58. D is correct.

The refractive index is given by:

$$n = c / v$$

Because $v \approx c$ in air,

$$n_{air} \approx n_{vacuum}$$

$$n_{air} = 1$$

$$n_{vacuum} = 1$$

All other transparent materials slow the speed of light.

Thus, n is greater than 1 because $v_{other\ materials} < c$.

59. D is correct.

Lens maker formula:

$$1 / f = (n - 1) \cdot (1 / R_1 - 1 / R_2)$$

For a flat surface:

$$R_2 = \infty$$

$$1 / f = (1.64 - 1) \cdot [(1 / 33 \text{ cm}) - (1 / \infty)]$$

$$1 / f = (0.64) \cdot (1 / 33 \text{ cm})$$

$$f = 51.6 \text{ cm} \approx 52 \text{ cm}$$

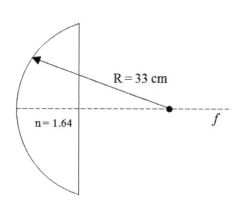

60. C is correct.

Water doesn't absorb visible light very easily (λ = 400 to 700 nm) but absorbs infrared light (λ = 700 nm to 1 mm) from vibrational motion of the molecule.

Water also absorbs microwaves through rotational motion.

Thermodynamics – Explanations

1. B is correct. Ideal gas law:

$$PV = nRT$$

$$P_0 = nRT / V_0$$

If isothermal expansion, then n, R and T are constant

$$P = nRT / (1/3\ V_0)$$

$$P = 3(nRT / V_0)$$

$$P = 3P_0$$

2. C is correct.

Area expansion equation:

$$\Delta A = A_0(2\alpha\Delta T)$$

$$\Delta A = (\pi / 4)\cdot(1.2\ \text{cm})^2\cdot(2)\cdot(19 \times 10^{-6}\ \text{K}^{-1})\cdot(200\ °\text{C})$$

$$\Delta A = 8.6 \times 10^{-3}\ \text{cm}^2$$

$$\Delta A = A_f - A_0$$

$$8.6 \times 10^{-3}\ \text{cm}^2 = (\pi / 4)\cdot[d_f^2 - (1.2\ \text{cm})^2]$$

$$d_f = 1.2\ \text{cm}$$

3. D is correct.

$$1\ \text{Watt} = 1\ \text{J/s}$$

$$\text{Power} \times \text{Time} = Q$$

$$Q = mc\Delta T$$

$$P \times t = mc\Delta T$$

$$t = (mc\Delta T) / P$$

$$t = (90\ \text{g})\cdot(4.186\ \text{J/g}\cdot°\text{C})\cdot(30\ °\text{C} - 10\ °\text{C}) / (50\ \text{W})$$

$$t = 151\ \text{s}$$

4. A is correct.

Convert 15 minutes to seconds:

$$t = (15\ \text{min}/1)\cdot(60\ \text{s}/1\ \text{min})$$

$$t = 900\ \text{s}$$

Find total energy generated:

$$Q = P \times t$$

$$Q = (1{,}260 \text{ J/s}){\cdot}(900 \text{ s})$$

$$Q = 1{,}134 \text{ kJ}$$

Find mass of water needed to carry away energy:

$$Q = mL_v$$

$$m = Q / L_v$$

$$m = (1{,}134 \text{ kJ}) / (22.6 \times 10^2 \text{ kJ/kg})$$

$$m = 0.5 \text{ kg} = 500 \text{ g}$$

5. C is correct.

Phase changes occur at a constant temperature.

Once the phase change is complete the temperature of the substance then either increases or decreases.

For example, water remains at 0 °C until it has completely changed phase to ice before the temperature decreases further.

6. B is correct.

The amount of energy needed to melt a sample of mass m is:

$$Q = m L_f$$

Where L_f is the latent heat of fusion.

$$Q = (55 \text{ kg}){\cdot}(334 \text{ kJ/kg})$$

$$Q = 1.8 \times 10^4 \text{ kJ}$$

7. D is correct.

Metals are good heat and electrical conductors because of their bonding structure. In metallic bonding, the outer electrons are held loosely and can travel freely.

Electricity and heat require high electron mobility.

Thus, the looseness of the outer electrons in the materials allows them to be excellent conductors.

8. A is correct. Find heat of phase change from steam to liquid:

$$Q_1 = mL_v$$

Find heat of phase change from liquid to solid:

$$Q_2 = mL_f$$

Find heat of temperature from 100 °C to 0 °C:

$$Q_3 = mc\Delta T$$

Total heat:

$$Q_{net} = Q_1 + Q_2 + Q_3$$

$$Q_{net} = mL_v + mL_f + mc\Delta T$$

To find mass:

$$Q_{net} = m(L_v + c\Delta T + L_f)$$

$$m = Q_{net} / (L_v + c\Delta T + L_f)$$

Solve:

$$Q_{net} = 200 \text{ kJ}$$

$$Q_{net} = 2 \times 10^5 \text{ J}$$

$$m = (2 \times 10^5 \text{ J}) / [(22.6 \times 10^5 \text{ J/kg}) + (4{,}186 \text{ J/kg·K})\cdot(100 \text{ °C} - 0 \text{ °C}) + (33.5 \times 10^4 \text{ J/kg})]$$

$$m = 0.066 \text{ kg}$$

9. C is correct.

Fusion is the process whereby a substance changes from a solid to liquid (i.e., melting).

Condensation is the process whereby a substance changes from a vapor to liquid.

Sublimation is the process whereby a substance changes directly from a solid to the gas phase without passing through the liquid phase.

10. D is correct.

$$Q = mc\Delta T$$

$$Q = (0.2 \text{ kg})\cdot(14.3 \text{ J/g·K})\cdot(1{,}000 \text{ g/kg})\cdot(280 \text{ K} - 250 \text{ K})$$

$$Q = 86{,}000 \text{ J} = 86 \text{ kJ}$$

11. B is correct.

Heat needed to raise temperature of aluminum:

$$Q_A = m_A c_A \Delta T$$

Heat needed to raise temperature of water:

$$Q_W = m_W c_W \Delta T$$

Total heat to raise temperature of system:

$$Q_{net} = Q_A + Q_W$$

$$Q_{net} = m_A c_A \Delta T + m_W c_W \Delta T$$

$$Q_{net} = \Delta T(m_A c_A + m_W c_W)$$

$$Q_{net} = (98 \text{ °C} - 18 \text{ °C})\cdot[(0.5 \text{ kg})\cdot(900 \text{ J/kg·K}) + (1 \text{ kg})\cdot(4{,}186 \text{ J/kg·K})]$$

$$Q_{net} = 370{,}880 \text{ J}$$

Time to produce Q_{net} with 500 W:

$$Q_{net} = (500 \text{ W})t$$

$$t = Q_{net} / (500 \text{ W})$$

$$t = (370{,}880 \text{ J}) / 500 \text{ W}$$

$$t = 741.8 \text{ s}$$

Convert to minutes:

$$t = (741.8 \text{ s}/1) \cdot (1 \text{ min}/60 \text{ s})$$

$$t = 12.4 \text{ min} \approx 12 \text{ min}$$

12. A is correct.

When a substance goes through a phase change, the temperature doesn't change.

It can be assumed that the lower plateau is L_f and the upper plateau is L_v.

Count the columns: $L_f = 2$, $L_v = 7$

$$L_v / L_f = 7 / 2$$

$$L_v / L_f = 3.5$$

13. B is correct.

Specific heat is the amount of heat (i.e., energy) needed to raise the temperature of the unit mass of a substance by a given amount (usually one degree).

14. D is correct. Find ½ of KE of the BB:

$$\text{KE} = \tfrac{1}{2}mv^2$$

$$\tfrac{1}{2}\text{KE} = \tfrac{1}{2}(\tfrac{1}{2}mv^2)$$

$$\tfrac{1}{2}\text{KE}_{BB} = \tfrac{1}{2}(\tfrac{1}{2}) \cdot (0.0045 \text{ kg}) \cdot (46 \text{ m/s})^2$$

$$\tfrac{1}{2}\text{KE}_{BB} = 2.38 \text{ J}$$

The $\tfrac{1}{2}\text{KE}_{BB}$ is equal to energy taken to change temperature:

$$Q = \tfrac{1}{2}\text{KE}_{BB}$$
$$Q = mc\Delta\text{T}$$

$$mc\Delta\text{T} = \tfrac{1}{2}\text{KE}_{BB}$$

$$\Delta\text{T} = \tfrac{1}{2}\text{KE}_{BB} / mc$$

Calculate to find ΔT:

$$\Delta\text{T} = (2.38 \text{ J}) / (0.0045 \text{ kg}) \cdot (128 \text{ J/kg·K})$$

$$\Delta\text{T} = 4.1 \text{ K}$$

15. C is correct.

Vaporization is the process whereby a substance changes from a liquid to a gas. The process can be either boiling or evaporation.

Sublimation is the process whereby a substance changes from a solid to a gas.

16. A is correct.

Carnot efficiency:

η = work done / total energy

$\eta = W / Q_H$

$\eta = 5\text{ J} / 18\text{ J}$

$\eta = 0.28$

The engine's efficiency:

$\eta = (T_H - T_C) / T_H$

$0.28 = (233\text{ K} - T_C) / 233\text{ K}$

$(0.28) \cdot (233\text{ K}) = (233\text{ K} - T_C)$

$65.2\text{ K} = 233\text{ K} - T_C$

$T_C = 168\text{ K}$

17. D is correct.

Heat needed to change temperature of a mass:

$Q = mc\Delta T$

Calculate to find Q:

$Q = (0.92\text{ kg}) \cdot (113\text{ cal/kg} \cdot {}^\circ\text{C}) \cdot (96\ {}^\circ\text{C} - 18\ {}^\circ\text{C})$

$Q = 8{,}108.9\text{ cal}$

Convert to joules:

$Q = (8{,}108.9\text{ cal}) \cdot (4.186\text{ J/cal})$

$Q = 33{,}940\text{ J}$

18. B is correct.

During a change of state, the addition of heat does not change the temperature (i.e., a measure of the kinetic energy).

The heat energy added only adds to the potential energy of the substance until the substance completely changes state.

19. C is correct.

For a pressure vs. volume graph of the work done for a cyclic process carried out by a gas, it is equal to the area enclosed by the cyclic process.

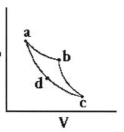

20. A is correct. Specific heat of A is larger than B:

$c_A > c_B$

Energy to raise the temperature:

$Q = mc\Delta T$

If m and ΔT are equal for A and B:

$Q_A = m_A c_A \Delta T_A$

$Q_B = m_B c_B \Delta T_B$

$Q_A > Q_B$

This is valid because all other factors are equal and the magnitude of Q only depends on c.

21. D is correct.

Find kinetic energy of meteor:

$KE = \frac{1}{2}mv^2$

$KE = \frac{1}{2}(0.0065 \text{ kg}) \cdot (300 \text{ m/s})^2$

$KE = 292.5 \text{ J}$

Find temperature rise:

$Q = KE$

$Q = mc\Delta T$

$mc\Delta T = KE$

$\Delta T = KE \,/\, mc$

Convert KE to calories:

$KE = (292.5 \text{ J}/1) \cdot (1 \text{ cal}/4.186 \text{ J})$

$KE = 69.9 \text{ cal}$

Calculate ΔT:

$\Delta T = (69.9 \text{ cal}) \,/\, [(0.0065 \text{ kg}) \cdot (120 \text{ cal/kg·°C})]$

$\Delta T = 89.6 \text{ °C} \approx 90 \text{ °C}$

22. A is correct.

When a liquid freezes it undergoes a phase change from liquid to solid.

For this to occur heat energy must be dissipated (removed).

During any phase change, the temperature remains constant.

23. B is correct. For an isothermal process:

$$\Delta U = 0$$

$$\Delta U = Q - W$$

$$Q = W$$

Work to expand an ideal gas in an isothermal process:

$$W = nRT \ln(V_f / V_i)$$

From the ideal gas law,

$$nRT = P_f V_f$$

giving:

$$W = P_f V_f \ln(V_f / V_i)$$

$$W = (130 \text{ kPa}) \cdot (0.2 \text{ m}^3) \ln[(0.2 \text{ m}^3) / (0.05 \text{ m}^3)]$$

$$W = 36 \text{ kJ}$$

$$Q = W$$

$$Q = 36 \text{ kJ}$$

Since the process is isothermal, there is no change in the internal energy.

Since the surroundings are doing negative work on the system:

$$\Delta E = 0 = Q + W = Q - 36 \text{ kJ}$$

Therefore:

$$Q = 36 \text{ kJ}.$$

24. D is correct.

Find the potential energy of 1 kg of water:

$$PE = mgh$$

$$PE = (1 \text{ kg}) \cdot (9.8 \text{ m/s}^2) \cdot (30 \text{ m})$$

$$PE = 294 \text{ J}$$

Assume all potential energy is converted to heat for maximum temperature increase:

$$PE = Q$$

$$Q = mc\Delta T$$

$$mc\Delta T = PE$$

$$\Delta T = PE / mc$$

$$\Delta T = (294 \text{ J}) / [(1 \text{ kg}) \cdot (4,186 \text{ J/kg/K})]$$

$$\Delta T = 0.07 \text{ °C}$$

For temperature differences it is not necessary to convert to Kelvin because a temperature change in Kelvin is equal to a temperature change in Celsius.

25. A is correct.

Find heat from phase change:

$$Q = mL_f$$

$$Q = (0.75 \text{ kg}) \cdot (33{,}400 \text{ J/kg})$$

$$Q = 25{,}050 \text{ J}$$

Because the water is freezing, Q should be negative due to heat being released.

$$Q = -25{,}050 \text{ J}$$

Find change in entropy:

$$\Delta S = Q / T$$

$$\Delta S = -25{,}050 \text{ J} / (0 \text{ °C} + 273 \text{ K})$$

$$\Delta S = -92 \text{ J / K}$$

A negative change in entropy indicates that the disorder of the isolated system has decreased.

When water freezes the entropy is negative because water is more disordered than ice. Thus, the disorder has decreased.

26. A is correct.

Copper has a larger coefficient of linear expansion than iron, so it expands more than iron during a given temperature change.

The bimetallic bar bends due to the difference in expansion between the copper and iron.

27. D is correct. Calculate heat needed to raise temperature:

$$Q = mc\Delta T$$

$$Q = (0.110 \text{ kg}) \cdot (4{,}186 \text{ J/kg·K}) \cdot (30 \text{ °C} - 20 \text{ °C})$$

$$Q = 4{,}605 \text{ J}$$

Calculate time needed to raise temperature with 60 W power source:

$$Q = P \times t$$

$$Q = (60 \text{ W})t$$

$$t = Q / (60 \text{ W})$$

$$t = (4{,}605 \text{ J}) / (60 \text{ W})$$

$$t = 77 \text{ s}$$

28. B is correct.

During a change of state, the addition of heat does not change the temperature (i.e., a measure of the kinetic energy). The heat energy added only adds to the potential energy of the substance until the substance completely changes state.

29. C is correct.

Convert to Kelvin:

$$T = -243\ ^\circ C + 273$$

$$T = 30\ K$$

Double temperature:

$$T_2 = (30\ K)\cdot(2)$$

$$T_2 = 60\ K$$

Convert back to Celsius:

$$T_2 = 60\ K - 273$$

$$T_2 = -213\ ^\circ C$$

30. D is correct.

If a researcher is attempting to determine how much the temperature of a particular piece of material would rise when a known amount of heat is added to it, knowing the specific heat would be most helpful.

31. B is correct. Convert units:

$$1.7 \times 10^5\ J/kg = 170\ kJ/kg$$

Change in internal energy = heat added (Q)

$$Q = mL_v$$

$$Q = (1\ kg)\cdot(170\ kJ/kg)$$

$$Q = 170\ kJ$$

32. D is correct. $Q = mc\Delta T$

If m and c are constant, the relationship is directly proportional.

To double Q, T must be doubled:

$$5\ C + 273 = 278\ K$$

$$278\ K \times 2 = 556\ K$$

$$556\ K - 273 = 283\ C$$

33. B is correct.

The mass of each material is required to determine the time the system takes to reach thermal equilibrium.

34. B is correct.

Body heat gives energy to the water molecules in the sweat. This energy is transferred via collisions until some molecules have enough energy to break the hydrogen bonds and escape the liquid (evaporation).

However, if a body stayed dry, the heat would not be given to the water, and the person would stay hot because the heat is not lost due to the evaporation of the water.

35. D is correct.

Calculate heat released when 0 °C water converts to 0 °C ice:

$$Q_1 = mL_f$$

$$Q_1 = (2{,}200 \text{ kg}) \cdot (334 \times 10^3 \text{ J/kg})$$

$$Q_1 = 734{,}800 \text{ kJ}$$

Calculate heat released for temperature drop ΔT

$$Q_2 = mc\Delta T$$

$$Q_2 = (2{,}200 \text{ kg}) \cdot (2{,}050 \text{ J/kg K}) \cdot [(0 \text{ °C} - (-30 \text{ °C})]$$

$\Delta K = \Delta °C$, so units cancel:

$$Q_2 = 135{,}300 \text{ kJ}$$

Add heat released to get Q_{net}:

$$Q_{net} = Q_1 + Q_2$$

$$Q_{net} = (734{,}800 \text{ kJ}) + (135{,}300 \text{ kJ})$$

$$Q_{net} = 870{,}100 \text{ kJ}$$

36. A is correct.

Object 1 has three times the specific heat capacity and four times the mass of Object 2:

$$c_1 = 3c_2; \ m_1 = 4m_2$$

A single-phase substance obeys the specific heat equation:

$$Q = mc\Delta T$$

In this case, the same amount of heat is added to each substance.

Therefore:

$$Q_1 = Q_2$$

$$m_1 c_1 \Delta T_1 = m_2 c_2 \Delta T_2$$

$$(4m_2)(3c_2)\Delta T_1 = m_2 c_2 \Delta T_2$$

$$12 m_2 c_2 \Delta T_1 = m_2 c_2 \Delta T_2$$

$$12 \ \Delta T_1 = \Delta T_2$$

37. C is correct.

Conduction is a form of heat transfer in which the collisions of the molecules of the material transfer energy through the material. Higher temperature of the material causes the molecules to collide with more energy which eventually is transferred throughout the material through subsequent collisions.

Radiation is a form of heat transfer in which electromagnetic waves carry energy from the emitting object and deposit the energy to the object that absorbs the radiation.

Convection is a form of heat transfer in which mass motion of a fluid (i.e., liquids and gases) transfers energy from the source of heat.

38. A is correct.

From the ideal gas law:

$$p_3 V_3 = nRT_3$$
$$T_3 = p_3 V_3 \, / \, nR$$
$$T_3 = 1.5 p_1 V_3 \, / \, nR$$
$$T_3 = 1.5 V_3 (p_1 \, / \, nR)$$

Also from the ideal gas law:

$$(p_1 \, / \, nR) = T_1 \, / \, V_1$$
$$(p_1 \, / \, nR) = (293.2 \text{ K}) \, / \, (100 \text{ cm}^3)$$
$$(p_1 \, / \, nR) = 2.932 \text{ K/cm}^3$$

Calculate T_3:

$$T_3 = 1.5 V_3 \, (2.932 \text{ K/cm}^3)$$
$$T_3 = 1.5 \, (50 \text{ cm}^3) \cdot (2.932 \text{ K/cm}^3)$$
$$T_3 = 219.9 \text{ K}$$
$$T_3 = -53.3 \text{ °C} \approx -53 \text{ °C}$$

Calculate T_4:

$$T_4 = 1.5 V_4 \, (2.932 \text{ K/cm}^3)$$
$$T_4 = 1.5 \, (150 \text{ cm}^3) \cdot (2.932 \text{ K/cm}^3)$$
$$T_4 = 659.6 \text{ K}$$
$$T_4 = 386.5 \text{ °C} \approx 387 \text{ °C}$$

39. B is correct.

Steel is a very conductive material that can transfer thermal energy very well.

The steel feels colder than the plastic because its higher thermal conductivity allows it to remove more heat and thus makes touching it feel colder.

40. B is correct.

An isobaric process involves constant pressure.

An isochoric (also isometric) process involves a closed system at constant volume.

An adiabatic process occurs without transfer of heat or matter between a system and its surroundings.

An isothermal process involves the change of a system in which the temperature remains constant.

41. D is correct.

Carnot coefficient of performance of a refrigeration cycle:

$C_P = T_C / (T_H - T_C)$

$C_P = Q_C / W$

$Q_C / W = T_C / (T_H - T_C)$

$W = (Q_C / T_C) \cdot (T_H - T_C)$

$W = (20 \times 10^3 \text{ J} / 293 \text{ K}) \cdot (307 \text{ K} - 293 \text{ K})$

$W = 955.6 \text{ J} = 0.956 \text{ kJ}$

Power = Work / time

$P = W / t$

$P = 0.956 \text{ kJ} / 1 \text{ s}$

$P = 0.956 \text{ kW} \approx 0.96 \text{ kW}$

42. C is correct.

Heat energy is measured in units of Joules and calories.

43. B is correct.

Convection is a form of heat transfer in which mass motion of a fluid (i.e., liquids and gases) transfers energy from the source of heat.

44. A is correct.

Radiation is the transmission of energy in the form of particles or waves through space or a material medium.

Examples include electromagnetic radiations such as X-rays, alpha particles, beta particles, radio waves, and visible light.

45. D is correct.

Convert P_3 to Pascals:

$P_3 = (2 \text{ atm} / 1) \cdot (101,325 \text{ Pa} / 1 \text{ atm})$

$P_3 = 202,650 \text{ Pa}$

Use the ideal gas law to find V_3:

$PV = nRT$

$V = (nRT) / P$

$V_3 = [(0.008 \text{ mol}) \cdot (8.314 \text{ J/mol·K}) \cdot (2,438 \text{ K})] / (202,650 \text{ Pa})$

$V_3 = 8 \times 10^{-4} \text{ m}^3$

Convert to cm^3:

$V_3 = (8 \times 10^{-4} \text{ m}^3 / 1) \cdot (100^3 \text{ cm}^3 / 1 \text{ m}^3)$

$V_3 = 800 \text{ cm}^3$

46. C is correct.

An adiabatic process involves no heat added or removed from the system.

From the First Law of Thermodynamics:

$\Delta U = Q + W$

If $Q = 0$, then:

$\Delta U = W$

Because work is being done to expand the gas, it is considered negative, and then the change in internal energy is negative (decreases).

$-\Delta U = -W$

47. B is correct.

Standing in a breeze while wet feels colder than when dry because of the evaporation of water off the skin.

Water requires heat to evaporate, so this is taken from the body making a person feel colder than if they were dry and the evaporation did not occur.

48. A is correct.

Conduction is a form of heat transfer in which the collisions of the molecules of the material transfer energy through the material.

Higher temperature of the material causes the molecules to collide with more energy which eventually is transferred throughout the material through subsequent collisions.

49. D is correct.

An isobaric process is a constant pressure process, so the resulting pressure is always the same.

50. B is correct.

This question is asking which type of surface has a higher emissivity than others and therefore can radiate more energy over a set period.

A blackbody is an idealized radiator and has the highest emissivity.

As such, a surface most similar to a blackbody (the black surface) is the best radiator of thermal energy.

A black surface is considered to be an ideal blackbody and therefore has an emissivity of 1 (perfect emissivity). The black surface will be the best radiator as compared to another surface which cannot be considered as blackbodies and have an emissivity of <1.

51. C is correct.

Calculate gap between the rods:

The gap in between the rods will be filled by both expanding, so total thermal expansion length is equal to 1.1 cm.

$$\Delta L = L_0 \alpha \Delta T$$

$$\Delta L_{tot} = \Delta L_B + \Delta L_A$$

$$\Delta L_{tot} = (\alpha_B L_B + \alpha_A L_A) \Delta T$$

Rearrange the equation for ΔT:

$$\Delta T = \Delta L_{tot} / (\alpha_B L_B + \alpha_A L_A)$$

$$\Delta T = 1.1 \text{ cm} / [(2 \times 10^{-5} \text{ K}^{-1}) \cdot (59.1 \text{ cm}) + (2.4 \times 10^{-5} \text{ K}^{-1}) \cdot (39.3 \text{ cm})]$$

$$\Delta T = 517.6 \text{ K} \approx 518 \text{ K}$$

Measuring difference in temperature in K is the same as in °C, so it is not required to convert:

$$\Delta T = 518 \text{ °C}$$

52. A is correct. Find seconds in a day:

$$t = (24 \text{ h} / 1 \text{ day}) \cdot (60 \text{ min} / 1 \text{ h}) \cdot (60 \text{ s} / 1 \text{ min})]$$

$$t = 86,400 \text{ s}$$

Find energy lost in a day:

$$E = \text{Power} \times \text{time}$$

$$E = (60 \text{ W})t$$

$$E = (60 \text{ W}) \cdot (86,400 \text{ s})$$

$$E = 5,184,000 \text{ J}$$

Convert to kcal:

$$E = (5,184,000 \text{ J}/1)\cdot(1 \text{ cal}/4.186 \text{ J})\cdot(1 \text{ kcal}/10^3 \text{ cal})$$

$$E = 1,240 \text{ kcal}$$

53. D is correct.

Conduction is a form of heat transfer in which the collisions of the molecules of the material transfer energy through the material.

Higher temperature of the material causes the molecules to collide with more energy which eventually is transferred throughout the material through subsequent collisions.

54. B is correct.

Heat given off by warmer water is equal to that absorbed by the frozen cube.

This heat is split into heat needed to melt the cube and bring the temperature to equilibrium.

$$Q_{H2O,1} + Q_{alcohol,Temp1} + Q_{alcohol,Phase1} = 0$$

$$(mc\Delta T)_{H2O,1} + (mc\Delta T)_{alcohol,Temp1} + (mL_f)_{alcohol} = 0$$

$$Q_{H2O,2} + Q_{alcohol,Temp2} + Q_{alcohol,Phase2} = 0$$

$$(mc\Delta T)_{H2O,2} + (mc\Delta T)_{alcohol,Temp2} + (mL_f)_{alcohol} = 0$$

Set equal to each other to cancel heat from phase change (since they are equal):

$$(mc\Delta T)_{H2O,1} + (mc\Delta T)_{alcohol,Temp1} = (mc\Delta T)_{H2O,2} + (mc\Delta T)_{alcohol,Temp2}$$

$$(m_{alcohol})(c_{alcohol})\cdot(\Delta T_{alcohol1} - \Delta T_{alcohol2}) = c_{H2O}(m\Delta T_{H2O,2} - m\Delta T_{H2O,1})$$

$$c_{alcohol} = (c_{H2O} / m_{alcohol})\cdot[(m\Delta T_{H2O,2} - m\Delta T_{H2O,1}) / (\Delta T_{alcohol1} - \Delta T_{alcohol2})]$$

Solving for $c_{alcohol}$:

$$c_{alc} = [(4,190 \text{ J/kg·K}) / (0.22 \text{ kg})]\cdot[(0.4 \text{ kg})\cdot(10 - 30 \text{ °C}) - (0.35 \text{ kg})\cdot(5 - 26 \text{ °C})]$$
$$/ [(5 \text{ °C} - (-10 \text{ °C}) - (10 \text{ °C} - (-10 \text{ °C})]$$

$$c_{alc} = (19,045 \text{ J/kg·K})\cdot[(-0.65 \text{ °C}) / (-5 \text{ °C})]$$

$$c_{alc} = 2,475 \text{ J/kg·K}$$

55. D is correct.

Using the calculated value for c_{alc} in the problem above:

$$Q_{H2O,1} + Q_{alcohol,Temp1} + Q_{alcohol,Phase1} = 0$$

$$(mc\Delta T)_{H2O,1} + (mc\Delta T)_{alcohol} + (mL_f)_{alcohol} = 0$$

$$L_{f\,alcohol} = [-(mc\Delta T)_{H2O,1} - (mc\Delta T)_{alcohol}] / m_{alcohol}$$

Solve:

$$L_{f\,alcohol} = -[(0.35 \text{ kg}) \cdot (4,190 \text{ J/kg·K}) \cdot (5 \text{ °C} - 26 \text{ °C})$$
$$- (0.22 \text{ kg}) \cdot (2,475 \text{ J/kg·K}) \cdot (5 \text{ °C} - (-10 \text{ °C})] / (0.22 \text{ kg})$$
$$L_{f\,alcohol} = (30{,}796.5 \text{ J} - 8{,}167.5 \text{ J}) / (0.22 \text{ kg})$$
$$L_{f\,alcohol} = 103 \times 10^3 \text{ J/kg} = 10.3 \times 10^4 \text{ J/kg}$$

56. C is correct.

The silver coating reflects thermal radiation into the bottle to reduce heat loss by radiation.

Radiation is a form of heat transfer in which electromagnetic waves carry energy from an emitting object and deposit the energy in an object absorbing the radiation.

57. B is correct.

Convert calories to Joules:

$$E = (16 \text{ kcal/1}) \cdot (10^3 \text{ cal/1 kcal}) \cdot (4.186 \text{ J/1 cal})$$
$$E = 66{,}976 \text{ J}$$

Convert hours to seconds:

$$t = (5 \text{ h}) \cdot (60 \text{ min/h}) \cdot (60 \text{ s/min})$$
$$t = 18{,}000 \text{ s}$$

Find power expended:

$$P = E / t$$
$$P = (66{,}976 \text{ J}) / (18{,}000 \text{ s})$$
$$P = 3.7 \text{ W}$$

58. A is correct.

$$\Delta Q = cm\Delta T$$
$$\Delta T = \Delta Q / cm$$
$$\Delta T = (50 \text{ kcal}) / [(1 \text{ kcal/kg·°C}) \cdot (5 \text{ kg})]$$
$$\Delta T = 10 \text{ °C}$$

59. C is correct.

For melting, use L_f:

$$Q = mL_f$$
$$Q = (30 \text{ kg}) \cdot (334 \text{ kJ/kg})$$
$$Q = 1 \times 10^4 \text{ kJ}$$

60. B is correct.

Find temperature change:

$$Q = mc\Delta T$$

$$\Delta T = Q \, / \, mc$$

$$\Delta T = (160 \times 10^3 \text{ J}) \, / \, [(6 \text{ kg}) \cdot (910 \text{ J/kg} \cdot \text{K})]$$

$$\Delta T = 29 \text{ °C}$$

Find final temperature:

$$\Delta T = T_f - T_i$$

$$T_f = T_i + \Delta T$$

$$T_f = 12 \text{ °C} + 29 \text{ °C}$$

$$T_f = 41 \text{ °C}$$

Atomic Nucleus and Electronic Structure – Explanations

1. A is correct.

Though alpha particles have low penetrating power and high ionizing power, they are not harmless.

All forms of radiation present risks and cannot be thought of as completely harmless.

2. C is correct.

A beta particle (β) is a high-energy, high-speed electron (β^-) or positron (β^+) emitted in the radioactive decay of an atomic nucleus.

Electron emission (β^- decay) occurs in an unstable atomic nucleus with an excess of neutrons, whereby a neutron is converted into a proton, an electron, and an electron antineutrino.

Positron emission (β^+ decay) occurs in an unstable atomic nucleus with an excess of protons, whereby a proton is converted into a neutron, a positron and an electron neutrino.

3. D is correct.

The de Broglie wavelength is given as:

$\lambda = h / p$

where h is Planck's constant and p is momentum

$p = mv$

$\lambda_1 = h / mv$

$\lambda_2 = h / m(2v)$

$\lambda_2 = \frac{1}{2}h / mv$

$\lambda_2 = \frac{1}{2} \lambda_1$

λ decreases by factor of 2

4. B is correct.

The Bohr model places electrons around the nucleus of the atom at discrete energy levels.

The Balmer series line spectra agreed with the Bohr model because the energy of the observed photons in each spectrum matched the transition energy of electrons within these discrete predicted states.

5. C is correct.

A radioactive element is an element that spontaneously emits radiation in the form of one or a combination of the following: alpha radiation, beta radiation, gamma radiation.

6. D is correct.

This is an example of an electron capture nuclear reaction.

When this happens, the atomic number decreases by one, but the mass number stays the same.

$$^{100}_{44}Ru + ^{0}_{-1}e^- \rightarrow ^{100}_{43}Tc$$

Ru: 100 = mass number (# protons + # neutrons)

Ru: 44 = atomic number (# protons)

From the periodic table, Tc is the element with 1 less proton than Ru.

7. B is correct.

A nucleon is a particle that makes up the nucleus of an atom.

The two known nucleons are protons and neutrons.

8. D is correct.

An alpha particle is composed of two neutrons and two protons and is identical to the nucleus of a ^{4}He atom.

Total mass of two alpha particles:

$2 \times$ (2 neutrons + 2 protons) = 8

Mass of a ^{9}Be atom:

5 neutrons + 4 protons = 9

Mass of a ^{9}Be atom > total mass of two alpha particles

The mass of a ^{9}Be atom is greater than the mass of two alpha particles, so its mass is also greater than twice the mass of a ^{4}He atom.

9. C is correct.

The superscript is the mass number (atomic weight), which is both neutrons and protons.

The subscript is the atomic number, which is the number of protons.

Therefore, the number of neutrons is equal to the superscript minus the subscript.

181 – 86 = 95, which is the greatest number of neutrons among the choices.

10. A is correct.

The number of neutrons and protons must be equal after the reaction.

Thus, the sum of the atomic number before and mass number before should be equal to after the reaction.

Mass number (superscript):

$$(1 + 235) - (131 + 3) = 102$$

Atomic number (subscript):

$$92 - (53) = 39$$

$^{102}_{39}Y$ properly balances the reaction.

11. B is correct.

Balmer equation is given by:

$$\lambda = B[(n^2) / (n^2 - 2^2)]$$
$$\lambda = (3.6 \times 10^{-7}) \cdot [(12^2) / (12^2 - 2^2)]$$
$$\lambda = 3.7 \times 10^{-7} \, m$$

Where c is the speed of light:

$$c = \lambda f$$

Convert wavelength to frequency:

$$f = c / \lambda$$
$$f = (3 \times 10^8 \, m/s) / (3.7 \times 10^{-7} \, m)$$
$$f = 8.1 \times 10^{14} \, s^{-1} = 8.1 \times 10^{14} \, Hz$$

12. D is correct.

Gamma rays are the most penetrating form of radiation because they are the highest energy and least ionizing. A gamma ray passes through a given amount of material without imparting as much of its energy into removing electrons from atoms and ionizing them like other forms of radiation do.

Gamma rays retain more of their energy passing through matter and can penetrate further.

13. A is correct. Use the Rydberg Formula:

$$E = hf$$
$$f = c / \lambda$$
$$E = (hc) \cdot (1 / \lambda)$$
$$1 / \lambda = R(1 / n_1^2 - 1 / n_2^2), \text{ where } n_1 = 1 \text{ and } n_2 = 2$$
$$E = hcR[(1 / n_1^2) - (1 / n_2^2)]$$
$$E = (4.14 \times 10^{-15} \, eV \cdot s) \cdot (3 \times 10^8 \, m/s) \cdot (1.097 \times 10^7 \, m^{-1}) \cdot [(1 / 1^2) - (1 / 2^2)]$$
$$E = 13.6[1 - (1 / 4)]$$
$$E = 10.2 \, eV$$

The positive energy indicates that a photon was absorbed and not emitted.

---

14. C is correct.

In β^- (beta minus) decay, the atomic number (subscript) increases by 1, but the atomic mass stays constant.

$$^{87}_{37}\text{Rb} \rightarrow\, ^{87}_{38}\text{Sr} +\, ^{0}_{-1}\text{e} +\, ^{0}_{0}v$$

Sr is the element with 1 more proton (subscript) than Rb.

$^{0}_{0}v$ represents an electron antineutrino.

15. C is correct.

The nucleus of an atom is bound together by the strong nuclear force from the nucleons within it. The strong nuclear force must overcome the Coulomb repulsion of the protons (due to their like charges).

Neutrons help stabilize and bind the nucleus together by contributing to the strong nuclear force so that it is greater than the Coulomb repulsion experienced by the protons.

16. A is correct.

Geiger-Muller counters operate using a Geiger-Muller tube, which consists of a high voltage shell and small rod in the center, filled with a low pressure inert gas (e.g., argon).

When exposed to radiation (specifically particle radiation), the radiation particles ionize atoms of the argon allowing for a brief charge to be conducted between the high voltage rod and outer shell.

The electric pulse is then displayed visually or via audio to indicate radioactivity.

17. B is correct.

The half-life calculation:

$$A = A_0(\tfrac{1}{2})^{t/h}$$

where A_0 = original amount, t = time elapse and h = half-life

If three half-life pass, $t = 3h$

$$A = (1) \cdot (\tfrac{1}{2})^{3h/h}$$
$$A = (1) \cdot (\tfrac{1}{2})^{3}$$
$$A = 0.125 = 12.5\%$$

18. D is correct.

In the Lyman series, electron transitions always go from $n \geq 2$ to $n = 1$.

19. B is correct.

Most of the volume of an atom is occupied by space.

20. A is correct. Alpha particles are positively charged due to their protons, while beta minus particles are negatively charged (i.e., electrons).

When exposed to a magnetic field, alpha particles and electrons deflect in opposite directions due to their opposite charges and thus experience opposite forces due to the magnetic field.

21. D is correct. Chemical reactions store and release energy in their chemical bonds, but do not convert mass into energy.

However, nuclear reactions convert a small amount of mass into energy, which can be measured and calculated via the equation:

$$E = \Delta mc^2$$

22. C is correct. The Curie is a non-SI unit of radioactivity equivalent to 3.7×10^{10} decays (disintegrations) per second. It is named after the early radioactivity researchers Marie and Pierre Curie.

23. B is correct.

The atomic numbers: $^{235}_{92}\text{U} \rightarrow \, ^{141}_{56}\text{Ba} + \, ^{92}_{36}\text{Kr}$

The subscripts on each side of the expression sum to 92, so adding a proton (^1_1H) to the right side would not balance.

The superscripts sum to 235 on the left and sum to 233 on the right.

Add two neutrons ($^1_0\text{n} + \, ^1_0\text{n}$) to the right side to balance both sides of the equation.

24. D is correct.

The atomic number is the subscript and represents the number of protons. The superscript is the mass number and is the sum of protons and neutrons.

The number of neutrons can be found by taking the difference between the mass number and atomic number.

In this example, there are 16 protons and 18 neutrons.

25. A is correct.

$$A = A_0(\tfrac{1}{2})^{t/h}$$

where A_0 = original amount, t = time elapse and h = half-life

Consider: (2 days)·(24 hours / 1 day) = 48 hours

$$A = (1) \cdot (\tfrac{1}{2})^{(48/12)}$$

$$A = 0.5^4$$

$$A = 0.0625 = 1/16$$

26. C is correct.

An alpha particle consists of two protons and two neutrons and is identical to a helium nucleus so that it can be written as ^4_2He

For a nuclear reaction to be written correctly, it must be balanced, and the sum of superscripts and subscripts must be equal on both sides of the reaction. The superscripts add to 238, and the subscripts add to 92 on both sides. Therefore, it is the only balanced answer.

27. D is correct.

The question is asking for the λ of the emitted photon so use the Rydberg Formula:

$$1 / \lambda = R(1 / n_1{}^2 - 1 / n_2{}^2)$$

$$\lambda = 1 / [R(1 / n_1{}^2 - 1 / n_2{}^2)]$$

Use $n_1 = 5$ and $n_2 = 20$ because we are solving for λ of an emitted (not absorbed) photon.

$$\lambda = 1 / [(1.097 \times 10^7 \, \text{m}^{-1}) \cdot (1 / 5^2 - 1 / 20^2)]$$

$$\lambda = 2.43 \, \mu\text{m}$$

28. D is correct.

When writing a nuclear reaction, the superscript represents the mass number, while the subscript represents the atomic number.

A correct nuclear reaction is balanced when the sum of superscripts (mass number) and subscripts (atomic number) is equal on both sides of the reaction.

29. C is correct.

A blackbody is an ideal system that absorbs 100% of all light incident upon it and reflects none. It also emits 100% of the radiation it generates; therefore it has perfect absorption and emissivity.

30. D is correct.

Carbon dating relies upon a steady creation of ^{14}C and knowledge of the rate of creation at various points in time to determine the approximate age of objects.

If a future archeologist is unaware of nuclear bomb testing and the higher levels of ^{14}C created, then the dates they calculate for an object would be too young.

This is because a higher amount of ^{14}C would be present in samples and make them seem as if they had not had time to decay and thus appear to be younger.

31. A is correct.

Gamma radiation is an electromagnetic wave and is not a particle. Thus, when gamma radiation is emitted, the atomic number and mass number remain the same.

32. C is correct.

In β^- decay a neutron is converted to a proton and an electron and electron antineutrino are emitted. In β^+ decay a proton is converted to a neutron, and a positron and an electron neutrino are emitted.

$$^{14}_{6}\text{C} \rightarrow {}^{14}_{7}\text{N} + e^- + \nu_e$$

33. D is correct.

In a nuclear equation, the number of nucleons must be conserved.

The sum of mass numbers and atomic numbers must be equal on both sides of the equation.

The product (i.e., daughter nuclei) should be on the right side of the equation.

34. B is correct.

The atomic number is the number of protons within the nucleus which characterizes the element's nuclear and chemical properties.

35. C is correct.

The Balmer series is the name of the emission spectrum of hydrogen when electrons transition from a higher state to the $n = 2$ state.

Within the Balmer series, there are four visible spectral lines with colors ranging from red to violet (i.e., ROY G BIV).

36. D is correct.

Electrons were discovered through early experiments with electricity, specifically in high voltage vacuum tubes (cathode ray tubes). Beams of electrons were observed traveling through these tubes when high voltage was applied between the anode and cathode, and the electrons struck fluorescent material at the back of the tube.

37. B is correct.

Beams a and c both deflect when an electric field is applied, indicating they have a net charge and therefore must be particles.

Beam b is undisturbed by the applied electric field, indicating it has no net charge and must be a high energy electromagnetic wave since all other forms of radioactivity (alpha and beta radiation) are charged particles.

38. C is correct.

Beam a is composed of negatively charged particles, while beam c is composed of positively charged particles; therefore, both beams are deflected by the electric field.

Beam b is also composed of particles; however, these particles are neutral because the electric field does not deflect them. An example of this kind of radiation would be a gamma ray, which consists of neutral photons.

39. C is correct. A helium nucleus is positively charged, so it is deflected away from the top plate and attracted toward the negative plate.

40. B is correct.

5.37 eV is the amount of energy required to excite the electron from the ground state to the zero energy state.

Calculate the wavelength of a photon with this energy:

$$E = hf$$

$$f = c / \lambda$$

$$E = hc / \lambda$$

$$\lambda = hc / E$$

$$\lambda = (4.14 \times 10^{-15}\ \text{eV·s}) \cdot (3 \times 10^{8}\ \text{m/s}) / (5.37\ \text{eV})$$

$$\lambda = 2.3 \times 10^{-7}\ \text{m}$$

41. D is correct.

Elements with atomic numbers of 84 and higher are radioactive because the strong nuclear force binding the nucleus together cannot overcome the Coulomb repulsion from the high number of protons within the atom. Thus, these nuclei are unstable and emit alpha radiation to decrease the number of protons within the nucleus.

42. D is correct.

Beta particles, like all forms of ionizing radiation, cannot be considered harmless.

43. D is correct.

$$A = A_0(\tfrac{1}{2})^{t/h}$$

where A_o = original amount, t = time elapse and h = half-life

$$0.03 = (1) \cdot (\tfrac{1}{2})^{(t / 20,000\ \text{years})}$$

$$\ln (0.03) = (t / 20,000\ \text{years}) \cdot \ln (\tfrac{1}{2})$$

$$t = 101,179\ \text{years}$$

44. B is correct.

Planck's constant quantizes the amount of energy that can be absorbed or emitted. Therefore, it sets a discrete lowest amount of energy for energy transfer.

45. D is correct.

The decay rate of any radioactive isotope or element is constant and independent of temperature, pressure, or surface area.

46. B is correct.

Larger nuclei (atomic number above 83) tend to decay because the attractive force of the nucleons (strong nuclear force) has a limited range and the nucleus is larger than this range. Therefore, these nuclei tend to emit alpha particles to decrease the size of the nucleus.

Smaller nuclei are not large enough to encounter this problem, but some isotopes have an irregular ratio of neutrons to protons and become unstable.

^{14}Carbon has 8 neutrons and 6 protons, and its neutron to proton ratio is too large. Therefore, it is unstable and radioactive.

47. C is correct.

Positron emission occurs during β^+ decay. In β^+ decay a proton converts to a neutron and emits a positron and electron neutrino.

The decay can be expressed as:

$$^{44}_{21}\text{Sc} \rightarrow\ ^{44}_{20}\text{Ca} + e^+ + v_e$$

48. C is correct.

A scintillation counter operates by detecting light flashes from the scintillator material.

When radiation strikes the scintillator crystal (often NaI), a light flash is emitted and detected by a photomultiplier tube, which then passes an electronic signal to audio or visual identification equipment.

49. B is correct.

When a Geiger counter clicks, it indicates that it has detected the radiation from one nucleus decaying. The click could be from an alpha, beta, or even gamma-ray source, but cannot be determined without other information.

50. A is correct.

The Pauli Exclusion Principle states that in an atom no two electrons can have the same set of quantum numbers.

Thus, every electron in an atom has a unique set of quantum numbers, and a particular set belongs to only one electron.

51. D is correct.

The atomic number indicates the number of protons within the nucleus of an atom.

52. C is correct.

Gamma rays are high-energy electromagnetic radiation rays and have no charge or mass.

Due to their high energy and speed, they have high penetrating power.

53. B is correct.

Calculate mass defect:

m_1 = (2 protons)·(1.0072764669 amu) + (2 neutrons)·(1.0086649156 amu)

m_1 = 4.031882765 amu

Δm = 4.031882765 amu – 4.002602 amu

Δm = 0.029280765 amu

Convert to kg:

Δm = (0.029280765 amu / 1)·(1.6606 × 10^{-27} kg / 1 amu)

Δm = 4.86236 × 10^{-29} kg

Find binding energy:

$E = \Delta mc^2$

E = (4.86236 × 10^{-29} kg)·(3 × 10^8 m/s)^2

E = 4.38 × 10^{-12} J ≈ 4.4 × 10^{-12} J

54. D is correct.

Boron has an atomic number of five and thus has five protons and five electrons.

Two electrons completely fill the 1s orbital, then the 2s orbital is filled with two electrons.

Only one electron remains, and it is in the 2p orbital, leaving it partially filled.

The electron configuration of boron: $1s^2 2s^2 2p$

55. C is correct.

$E = mc^2$

$m = E / c^2$

m = (3.85 × 10^{26} J) / (3 × 10^8 m/s)^2

m = 4.3 × 10^9 kg

56. D is correct.

When any form of ionizing radiation interacts with the body, the high energy particles or electromagnetic waves cause atoms within the tissue to ionize. This process creates unstable ions and free radicals that are damaging and pose serious health risks.

57. B is correct.

When a gamma ray is emitted the atom must lose energy due to the conservation of energy. Thus, the atom will have less energy than before.

58. A is correct.

The lower case symbol "n" signifies a neutron. An atomic number of zero indicates that there are no protons. A mass number of one indicates that it contains a neutron.

59. C is correct.

The uncertainty principle states that the position and momentum of a particle cannot be simultaneously measured over a set precision.

Additionally, the energy and time cannot be simultaneously known over a set precision.

Mathematically this is stated as:

$$\Delta x \Delta p > \hbar / 2$$

$$\Delta E \Delta t > \hbar / 2$$

where x = position, p = momentum, $\hbar$ = reduced Planck's constant, E = energy, t = time

To access online MCAT tests at a special pricing visit:
http://www.OnlineMCATprep.com/bookowner.htm

We want to hear from you

Your feedback is important to us because we strive to provide the highest quality prep materials. Email us if you have any questions, comments or suggestions, so we can incorporate your feedback into future editions.

Customer Satisfaction Guarantee

If you have any concerns about this book, including printing issues, contact us and we will resolve any issues to your satisfaction.

info@onlinemcatprep.com

We reply to all emails – please check your spam folder

Thank you for choosing our products to achieve your educational goals!

Made in the USA
Middletown, DE
08 January 2020